REV-ELATION

A Day-by-Day Devotional

For Christians and skeptics alike

By Herb Adams and Sidney Adams

INSTANT PUBLISHER

A Subsidiary of

FUNDCRAFT PUBLISHING COMPANY

All Scripture quotes from NRSV

Title: Rev-Elation

This title might sound a little strange for a daily Devotion, but let me explain. I have been in the ministry over 30 years, more than that if you count the time I worked with youth and taught Sunday school. My wife has always called me Rev rather than my real name, which is Herb. Everywhere I have been, church members have for the most part picked up on that and also called me "Rev". A member of the last church I served before I retired recommended calling our book "Rev-Elation" meaning "When the preacher is filled with the Joy of the Lord." Please take this in the manner in which it is intended: humble words coming from a humble servant of God.

I hope that you find spiritual enrichment reading this daily devotional. I have worked on it for several years. Since I have retired, with lots of help from my faithful wife Sid, it is finally completed. Throughout the years I have cherished the writings of C. S. Lewis, Oswald Chambers, Frederick Buechner, Henri Nouwen, and Deitrich Bonhoeffer and other great writers along with the spiritual guidance from the likes of Walter Wink and Steve Brown. Each one brought to my plate daily bread, like manna from heaven, God somehow speaking through their words into my ears and finally my heart. I do not presume to be "worthy to even untie the thongs of their sandals," let alone those of Jesus! May the words from these pages bring you somehow closer to our Lord. May you feel his presence as you meditate and spend time with him in solitude with his Holy Word. May it be His voice that you hear through these devotions.

2008 Herb Adams and Sidney Adams

Printed by Instantpublishers.com, a subsidiary of Fundcraft Publishing Company, publishing books for over 60 years.

ISBN 978 1 60458 202 4

Purpose of a devotional and how to meditate

Preface:

The purpose of this book is to give you a day-by-day devotional that will keep you in touch with God on a daily basis. Such a connection with God, our Father, takes practice and dedication. We would like to propose that you use this devotion as a gateway into meditation where you choose to listen and dwell in God's presence. By reading scripture and a devotion on that scripture and then a prayer, you can begin your process of meditation. Don't look at this as a chore or as something mysterious, it is simply talking to God and allowing him time to speak to you. Find a regular place to read your devotional each day, one that gives you a calm feeling and then spend just a few moments getting comfortable. Relax. Then read the devotional for the day. When you have finished the prayer close your eyes and allow God to breathe his words into your heart. If you practice this daily you will notice a difference - it will help relieve the stresses of your life and bring you hope and grace.

Stress has a way of keeping us from God. Worry and it's by product stress is a way of saying to God, "I am not sure I completely trust that you will take care of me." Meditation can bring us into closer contact with God and confirm to us that God does care and will be with us through every hardship we encounter. No, God wili not spare you of hardship for much of what causes us stress and worry cannot be spared unless the entire nature of this world is changed.

People are not perfect and sometimes even our closest friends can disappoint us and hurt us. All of these things cause worry and stress. In order to lessen that stress we need to learn to release those things to God and allow him to fill us with his love and grace. God is sufficient for all our needs and especially when we are in distress. Lift your problems to God in Meditation and let go. To say that Jesus is savior is to believe that He is God's Son who came to show us the way to God – to cover our sins and bring us His righteousness. To say that Jesus is Lord is to believe that He is the one we trust with all our being – the one who can take away our problems and worry. In Matthew 11:28 Jesus says to us, *"Come unto me all ye who labor and are heavy laden, and I will give you rest."*

I have followed the Christian calendar with devotionals on Advent, the four Sunday's before Christmas; Epiphany, the 12th day after Christmas (the first Sunday on or after January 6th); Easter and other Christian celebrations. As you read this devotional you will have to put those days on their specific dates as they change almost every year.

New Year's Resolutions — January 1 — Luke 2:19

"Mary treasured all these words and pondered them in her heart."

The beginning of the New Year is a time many decide on New Year's resolutions or it could be a time we decide not to make New Year's resolutions, which in itself is a New Year's resolution! So in this beginning of a brand spanking New Year, why don't we resolve to recommit ourselves to Jesus Christ? There will be many pitfalls a long the way. There will be hazards and risks with which to contend; it will take dedication to be faithful. It is daring, a risky thing to set out to conquer with love a world full of hate, a world full of pride not wanting to let go, a world full of gossip running wild attacking the fabric from which good folks are made.

Christians are called to change all of that and to replace the doubts of life with faith. We are even called to give up our own selfishness and meanness and self-centered ways. All of which is impossible until and unless we give ourselves fully to Jesus. In the second chapter of Luke Mary responds to the wonderful blessings of the impending birth of her child, Jesus, *"Mary treasured all these words and pondered them in her heart."* This new year, let us give ourselves fully to God and seek out what God wants of us. We have been blessed beyond our imaginations. Let us take in our blessedness. Let us sit down and *"ponder these things in our heart."*

Ask yourself, "Where am I headed?" "Where do I go from here?" "Is it worth the risk?" "Am I able and willing to be a child of God in a materialistic world?" Jesus does not want to hear an encyclopedia full of excuses; He does not want to hear that we don't have enough talents or gifts or money. He wants to hear that we are willing to take the risk. We either give ourselves to Jesus fully, time, talent, money, self, as we continue to seek our daily bread from Him or we belong to the flesh: pride, selfishness, greed, gossip, anger, jealously, envy, or a judgmental attitude. Gut check time is here. So what's it going to be?

Lord, as I go about living this New Year you have entrusted to me, open my heart to your will and your truth. Give me the grace to fulfill this pledge: to praise God more, to see God in all things, in all life's situations (the exhilarating moments and the tragedies) and in every face I see, even my own. In Jesus' name. Amen.

Do not Worry for Tomorrow **January 2 Matthew 6:34**

"Do not worry about tomorrow, for tomorrow will bring worries of it's own. Today's trouble is enough for today."

The New Year is here, ready or not, bringing with it all that it portends for our future; hope and sorrow, busyness and laziness, sadness and joy, crying and laughter. Chances are good that if you have lived long enough, you have already experienced your share of all of these things. Sometimes we think that we have already had our share of trials and tribulations and we want no more! You know the old saying, *"God will never put upon you more than you can handle."* (1 Cor.10:13) Sometimes we just wonder if God really knows us! Right?

When life gets that way, Jesus tells us to live one day at a time, live each moment as it comes to us, not thinking about what tomorrow may bring. Pretty good advice, isn't it? Besides, who can predict the future anyway? None of us knows what tomorrow will bring so why try to live in "tomorrow time"? I mean would you really want to know what is going to happen before it happens - good or bad? No? That's what I thought. So Jesus says, *"Do not worry about tomorrow, for tomorrow will bring worries of its own. Today's trouble is enough for today."*

Living in the past or in the future will only compound our problems. Consider prayerfully what you can do for today, do that, and leave tomorrow's troubles for its own day. Make it your goal in this New Year to live one day at a time, taking what life offers and brings, changing what you can for the better, and trusting in God for that which you cannot; and may He bring happiness and joy into your life.

Lord, this past year has brought with it many challenges; you know that; you were there with me. Help me to put them all behind me and celebrate this new day fully. Reliving the past is such a fruitless endeavor. I know that this New Year will bring many other surprises and struggles. Let me not cross that bridge until I get there. Let me celebrate each day that you have made for me as the singular gift it is. Give me your wisdom, your patience. I get ahead of myself. Let me never get ahead of you. In the name of your precious Son, Jesus. Amen.

"Jesus increased in wisdom and in years and grew in favor with God and man."

Jesus increased in wisdom and grew in favor with God and man. Now why and how was he able to do that? To answer let's examine his early life. Jesus knew that his parents loved him. He knew God loved him, not just because He was God's son, but because I am sure that Mary and Joseph told him that truth over and over. This is a story of a family devoted to one another and to their Heavenly Father. So no matter what kind of mischief Jesus may have gotten into as a child, and I'm sure he got into a little, he knew his parents loved him with an unconditional love.

I was a high school band and choral director before God called me into the ministry. I'll never forget what happened to one of my drum majors when we were performing at a marching band contest at a local college stadium. She had been selected for this leadership role in her junior year and this was the first time that she had ever been in a major band competition. When our band went out on the field, she strutted out into the middle of the field and I could see her parents sitting in the stands with tears coming down their cheeks. They experienced a joy that can only be felt by parents. I don't know, but I think it is the realization that this is a part of your life out there. God had given them a wonderful and special gift of a daughter and they loved her more than life itself.

When it was all over we gathered at the buses; I can remember her mother and father embracing her. Her father asked her how it felt being out there. She said, "Daddy, you just can't know; it's the greatest feeling in the world. I don't think that there's anything that can match the feeling that I had today." Her father looked at her and said, "Oh, yes there is. You'll discover that when you are sitting in the stands with thousands of people cheering and it's your daughter out on that field." Unconditional love can do wonders in developing our self-esteem to meet

Lord God, I have increased in years but not wisdom and surely not in your favor. Selfish, self-serving people have no room in their heart for God. Have mercy on me. Grant me the grace to see all children as yours and as mine. Together, Lord, we can be such a blessing and I can live out my destiny to love others as you have loved me, unconditionally and with great mercy, great joy! I pray in the name of Jesus. Amen.

Die and Be Reborn   January 4   Romans 6:8

"If we have died with Christ, we believe that we shall also live with Him."

There is a scripture found in Malachi, the last book in the Old Testament, which I have used during Advent, the Christian season in which we look forward to the coming birth of our Lord Jesus. We find in Chapter 3, verses 1-4 these words, *"Who can endure the day of His coming?"* For the Lord will *"purify the descendants of Levi - until they present right offerings to the Lord in righteousness."* In other words, there will be some who will dread the coming of the Lord. There will be some who will not be prepared in one way or another.

I guess the question we ought to ask ourselves today is, "Are we in that group?" Well are we? Are you? Paul says, *"In order to accept Christ and to be a part of the new kingdom, we must die to the old self."* (Romans 6) *"We must die to this life."* Be reborn before you die; there is no chance after that. What does that mean? Essentially, it means don't live this life as if Christ never came. Live in this world but don't live for this world and the things in it or we will surely die spiritually. When we live for Christ, we die to the things of this world and are reborn in Christ. Thus we die to fear and worry and anxiety, to wants and desires, and to anger. We die to the priority of self, of "What about me?" and are reborn in Christ where our hearts go out to others. It is in Christ alone that we are capable of really giving ourselves to others; that we are capable of love.

Therefore, we must go to Him through His Son, Jesus. It is in Christ alone that we can place the needs and desires of others above our own. It is in Christ alone that we can look past this thing called death, and truly have life eternally. So, if you wish to endure His coming again, go beyond believing in His name, give Him your life, die with Him, let Him have your will, your pain, your disappointments, and your grief. He will replace it with His Love, His Grace, His Joy. Was a better deal ever offered?

Lord God, I come before you with thanksgiving and regret. For you have loved me even as I rebelled against you; forgive me. Help me to die to the things of this world that keep me from you and be reborn to new life in Christ. You'll have to pry off my grasping fingers. For too long worldly rewards meant more to me than you. No more! In Christ, I can trust that He will see that I receive what I need most: a brand new me! Thank you Jesus, for this indescribable gift. How I love you so. Amen.

New Opportunities   January 5   Jeremiah 31:31

"Behold the days are coming, says the Lord, when I will make a new covenant."

The beginning of the New Year is here and with that comes the opportunity for change. I love the season of winter for several reasons. Winter means that we don't get outside as much as during the spring, summer, and fall. Time spent inside, as a family means doing more sedentary things together, like playing monopoly or working a puzzle or whatever it is you as a family enjoy. It also brings forth the time to just sit in front of the fireplace, read a book, or meditate. Building a fire in the fireplace and watching it burn seems to cleanse the soul some how.

Fire also can bring about a new beginning. I recall a terrific fire that burned down most of a city block in one town where I lived. At the time, it was devastating; my favorite restaurant was in that fire! Then the old buildings were torn down; new buildings sprung up; new life from the old. Scripture refers to a new beginning in different places. In Isaiah 65 God talks about creating a *"New Heaven and a New Earth."* In Jeremiah God speaks of creating a New Covenant with His people, *"Behold the days are coming, says the Lord, when I will make a new covenant with the house of Israel and Judah... I shall write my law upon their hearts."*

In Matthew we see the fulfillment of this New Covenant where Jesus says, *"This is my blood of the New Covenant which is poured out for many for the forgiveness of sins."* (26:28) Paul speaks of this New Covenant in 2 Corinthians 5:17f, *"If anyone is in Christ, they have become a New Being."* The old self has passed away and the new self is taking over. Now we see life through the eyes of Christ, not through our limited vision. Then the scripture makes a full circle in Revelation 14 where John says, *"And I saw a New Heaven and a New Earth."* A new season reminds us of new beginnings. It gives comfort to know that the God who foresaw all of this is the same God who is watching over us and giving us a New Beginning.

Lord God, as I begin this new year, help me to remember the New Covenant made with your people; a Covenant, which by the Holy Spirit, is written upon our hearts; a Covenant, come to life through the death of your beloved Son; a Covenant, which brings me your Grace and claims me as your adopted child. As I consider this New Year, let me begin it awash in your spirit, alive in the grasp of your glorious grace. We're Family now, Lord! And "family" is forever. In Jesus, I pray. Amen.

Epiphany   January 6   Matthew 2:11

"On entering the House, they saw the child with Mary His mother; they knelt down and worshiped Him offering gold, frankincense, and myrrh."

Epiphany is a very important event in the life of the church and every Christian. The church calendar begins with Advent, the four Sundays leading up to Christmas, when we look forward to the fulfillment of God's promise to send a Savior. On Christmas Eve we celebrate the actual birth. Following the birth of Christ, we have a span of twelve days called the "twelve days of Christmas" (Remember the song?) The twelfth day after Christmas is January 6th, "The Epiphany," which celebrates the joyful conclusion of the wise men's journey to the Christ child.

Symbolically, the twelve days represent a period of time between the birth of Christ and the coming of the Wise Men. Most scholars place that time around one year after Jesus' birth. This is based on scripture and logic. Matthew 2:1-2 says, *"Wise Men from the East came searching for the Child born, "King of the Jews."* The place was probably Mesopotamia. Now using logic, following a star meant traveling on clear nights. Such a trip would require a significant period of time. Matthew states, "Herod in trying to get rid of Jesus had all children in and around Bethlehem, 2 years and under, killed." So the Wise Men must have visited Jesus when he was around one or two. Also verse 11 tells us that Mary, Joseph and their child were now living in a house verses a stable as seen in Luke.

There are a lot of theories about the "Star" - perhaps a meteor or comet, however, the best way to consider this event is to ponder the magnificent wonder of it all. These wise men were astrologers, who would have been watching and would have noticed a new star shining in the night, but for them to interpret it the way they did and to follow with complete trust forsaking all else would take a miracle, don't you think?

Lord God, I too stand in awe of your omnipotence, humbled by the wonder of your infallible purpose working itself out in human lives, even my own. Thank you, Father, for the gift of the star that guided these Wise Men to the Child whom they sought and for their humbling story of utter determination and devotion to their holy mission. Is there a star to guide me in my humble search for my savior's touch? Is there grace enough that it may matter to me just as much? This is my gift. In His Precious Name. Amen.

Are we like Herod? *January 7* *Matthew 2:7-8*

"Herod secretly called for the wise men and learned from them the exact time the star had appeared. He sent them to Bethlehem, saying, "Go, search for the child; when you have found him, bring me word that I may also pay him homage."

Yesterday, we took a look at the story of the Wise Men. Today, let's focus on Herod. The Wise Men went to the King seeking information about this long awaited Messiah. Herod is troubled by this news. This child is seen as a threat to his power and must be destroyed. So Herod sends for the Wise Men and feigns devotion, *"Let me know when you find him so I too may worship him."* The Wise Men find the Christ they have sought but Herod's deceitful plan is thwarted. In verse 12 we find these words, *"being warned by God in a dream they shouldn't return to Herod, the Wise Men departed into their own country by another way."*

What if King Herod had caught the sense of this wonder? What if he had looked up to see the star, let go his fears, and listened to what was being said about the birth of this Messiah? He also might have seen the Messiah. Instead, he made an unwise decision. Let's not be too critical for we also make unwise decisions when it comes to Jesus. Our lives are broken; relationships strained; the last person we approach about all of this is Jesus. It's a matter of pride you see. We had rather see ourselves as right and perfect and use our time to look at the faults of others, to criticize, and to gossip. God forbid that we find ourselves to be sinful! Like Herod we want control - to follow our will rather than God's. Like Herod, we fear what finding the Christ Child will do to us or require of us.

As we prepare for this New Year and this new relationship to which God has called us, we too need to find the Bethlehem star shining and bringing us" *Good News of a great joy."* Once you truly believe in the Christ who gave His life for you, then you can trust Him with your life.

Lord, like Herod, I cling to my own dreams when your dreams for me are so much more. Like Herod, I fear what meeting the Christ Child will do to me, require of me. I fear giving up control of my life. What if your plans for me don't coincide with mine? Then what? Like Herod, I miss the wonder, the hope Jesus brought into this world. Oh, Father, grant me the courage, the wisdom to put my destiny into your hands. Confound my rebellious nature with the truth of your great Love. Let me live this life full of your joy, obedient to your will. In the name of the Christ Child. Amen.

"I tell you, on that night there will be two in one bed; one will be taken and the other left."

Christmas is over; New Year has passed; Epiphany too. Now maybe things will get back to "normal." At last! What is normal anyway? I suspect that if you look back over the past weeks, you will be amazed that you were able to pull everything off! Just make your own list: Christmas plays, Choir programs, visiting Santa, Christmas Eve service plus the normal services of Sunday morning. Add Christmas parties, caroling, open houses, holiday dances, New Year's Eve, and football bowl parties. Whew! It makes me tired just thinking about it! And let's not leave out traveling from town to town, state to state, to visit family and friends, cooking, eating, decorations - putting them up and taking them down - more eating, sending and receiving Christmas cards, visiting with friends and did I mention eating?

Now, it's the first of the New Year and we pray things will get back to normal, but what is normal anyway? Most would describe 'normal' as not doing all the things listed above, but if we do those things every year, isn't that normal? It may be that normal is filling our lives with such busyness that there is little time to think about what is most important, the reckoning that is the Second Coming of Christ. In Luke 17, Jesus reminded the disciples the way it was in the day of Noah when it was 'business as usual', they ate and drank and married and the flood came. *"So it will be when I come again. Two will be sleeping in one bed, one will be taken and one left...."*

Jesus says it will be 'business as usual'. So what is your 'business as usual', your normal day like? Will you be celebrating the joy of belonging to Jesus? Or will your 'normal' be condemning, criticizing, gossiping, judging, living a life of greed and selfishness? So how will you be spending that day for the rest of your life?

God of All our Days, I read this scripture about the fulfillment, your Kingdom come and I rejoice! No more sorrow, pain and toil, no more evil. Hallelujah! Lord, will there be no more of me? Will I be left? I have claimed Jesus; yet I have held on to my life. What a contradiction. Have mercy on me, a sinner. Overwhelm my will before another moment goes by! I don't want life without you in it. Come, Lord Jesus! Amen.

"God did not send his Son into the world to condemn the world, but in order that the world might be saved through Him."

One Christmas, I received a round wooden disc about the size of a quarter with one word printed on it –TOIT. It was a round TOIT. I wish everyone prone to procrastination would be lucky enough to get one! It seems like we all have the habit of putting things off don't we? When asked to take out the trash we respond, "I'll take care of it." Later when asked, "When?" We say, "I'll get a-round to-it." Our boss says, "Where is that report I asked for yesterday" we respond, "Don't worry, I'll get a-round to-it?" We keep putting things off until another day.

Here's the problem. Some things that we say we will eventually get to are of vital importance; salvation for example. John 3:17 states, *"God sent his Son into the world that the world might be saved through Him."* Jesus came to bring salvation. Has the salvation of Christ come to you? Has His saving work been completed in you? Your future, where you will spend eternity rests on how you will answer this question. We best not wait until it's too late! This is something we had better 'get around to'! If you want to show kindness, or if you plan to see someone who is ill, or write a letter to someone who needs to hear what you have to say, it's not wise to wait. You never know what tomorrow is going to bring.

If we are always waiting to "get a-round TOIT, we will miss the beauty of today. God sent His Son for our sake already. Salvation is ours now - so take it! Now is the time. If you have not accepted Jesus, do it. Fall on your knees and ask Jesus to come into your life. If you have accepted Jesus as your savior, then follow Him: if you are already saved by Christ then conduct yourself accordingly. You've given Him your life so quit being a rebel and turn your will over to Him and step out in faith.

Lord God, Great is your faithfulness, your saving grace to me in Jesus. Although I continually put things off, saying, "I will get around to it," you have already provided. Place in my heart the desire, the wisdom to accept what ever you have willed for my life. Procrastination is just the consequence of fear, fear of the future I'm forever putting off, fear of failing, fear even of you! Encase my trembling heart with the power of Perfect Love. Together we can do wonderful things. The future awaits us, Lord! In Jesus. Amen.

"In the beginning God created the heavens and the earth."

I am quite a sports fan. I have loved basketball and since my teens have followed the Kentucky Wildcats. I also enjoy football, golf, and tennis. My greatest love, however, was fulfilled when God called me into the ministry. Two great loves: God and sports. I realize that other colleges have had their fame and glory, but in the history of college basketball one team stands out in my mind, Kentucky – having won 7 national championships with four different coaches, an incredibly rich history.

We as Christians also have an incredibly rich history. Perhaps we should take a closer look at that history. This year why not take a "Journey Through the Bible." Start with the book of Genesis and make a journey all the way to Revelations. In order to do that you will not be able to study each book closely. But, as you read, look at your journey with God through those incredible books of the Bible and venture in far enough to try and grasp what it is God has revealed about Himself and you.

If you choose to make plans to journey through the Bible, don't get overwhelmed and turn it into a chore. Just set aside 20 minutes a day to read (more if you like) and don't be tempted to set a schedule of expected completion. Just finish whenever you finish. As you read the first few chapters of Genesis you will discover that they contain two different accounts of the Creation. As you read, see if you can discover why and their purpose. But the most important thing about these first chapters and all the rest is what they tell us about God, and not how they tell it. Remember that as you read and study. Also, remember that we see the Bible through the eyes of a Post Easter faith.

Lord, I come in prayer knowing that you have given me an incredible history. I have been unmoved; forgive me. There is so much of you, Lord, I am yet to uncover, yet to know. Let the Word so resonate in my heart that I may be transformed by the lives of your people. Open the eyes of my soul that I may more clearly hear and obey your will for us, your people. We have too long been walking together separately. Keep me in step, Father God; bring me peace and grace. I pray in the name of Jesus. Amen.

We are Predestined   *January 11*   *Romans 8:29*

"For those whom he foreknew he also predestined to be conformed to the image of his Son, in order that he might be the first-born among many brethren."

What can I say? It's in the Bible, God's Holy Word to us. I know that there are many who wish to dispute that they are predestined, but there are really only two ways to look at it. One: all circumstances of life are just that, circumstances where by you are left to deal with difficult obstacles and events in your life, many times wondering why God would allow such things to happen to you. Therefore going through life questioning every circumstance with which you do not agree and wishing life could be different; envying those whose circumstances are more in line with what you had in mind for yourself; temped to interpret life as one without joy.

Or a second way of looking at this life is that God is the God even of circumstances; that God has ordained and used all the circumstances of your life in order to direct you to the place He wants you. It is then God who has placed those people and events in your life so that He might *"mold you like clay"* into the vessel for which you were destined to become. When one becomes a child of God, accepting Jesus as Lord and personal savior, we must then realize that God has a plan for our life.

Can you imagine a God who created this wonderful universe, so vast and magnificent, yet without purpose or plan? If you cannot, then you also must imagine that the same God, who created the universe and life itself, has a plan for you, His creation. Accepting His plan will then destroy worry and stress and bring immense peace into our lives. *'Those whom he foreknew he predestined to be conformed to the image of his Son."* Why? To share in the resurrected life. Of course you have freedom of choice; you could choose not follow God's plan. But who would be crazy enough to not accept His Grace and forgiveness and love?

Lord, help me today to accept your plan for my life knowing that it is best for me and for all mankind, Giving up my plans voluntarily will be hard. Be my strength, Lord. Calm my anxious heart; bring me to the place you have created for me alone. My insistence on my own way ties me in knots and makes us both miserable. Oh Father, make me truly your child. Destroy all the worry, the stress, which try to consume me, robbing me of my joy, my faith. I'm worth the trouble. I could be so much more; I'm meant for so much more. I'm meant to be Yours. In the name of Jesus I pray. Amen.

Building God's Kingdom **January 12** *Matthew 16:18*

"You are Peter and upon this rock I will build my church."

Back in 1997, I ministered a church that purchased 15 acres of land in order to build a new building for God's Kingdom. By 2004, the church had raised over one million dollars and started this magnificent building. The following year, 2005, a new building was dedicated in service for God. That entire process had to be one of the highlights of my ministry. These Christians had met for better than 100 years in a building built in 1895. It was a beautiful sanctuary, but built for the young at heart. What I mean by this is you had to climb 15 to 20 steps to get anywhere.

I would be less than honest if I did not say that move brought about some ambiguous feelings. Many of those members had never been a part of any church except that beautiful old downtown building. It is difficult to give up something that has been a part of your life for so many years. The amazing thing was that one of the elders, a lady who had been baptized as a child in that church, was also the one who made the motion to build a new building for the ministry of God. She remarked, "The purpose and goal of the new church would remain as it had been for the past 100 years; the same as those pioneers who in 1895 left their beautiful old sanctuary to build a larger one 'on the outskirts of town.'"

It reminded me that we are all seeking to serve God and His Kingdom in the best way possible regardless of where we meet. The pioneers of the churches of today will set the stage for the next 100 years for God's churches. Jesus said to Peter in the 16th chapter of Matthew, *"On this rock I will build my church."* This is what my elder was saying, *"On our faith – God will build this church."* That is what it takes to go out on a limb and build a church, isn't it? Faith! In this New Year there will be many opportunities for all of us to step up and rededicate our time and commitment to God's Church and His Kingdom as we discover what He has in mind for us.

Lord, I thank you for the special place in which I worship; your Spirit is so very near. Strengthen my fragile faith that I may be dedicated to your worship, willing to take risks to bring others into your Kingdom. Give me the courage to use the talents that you have given me as you lead me. This is my prayer in the name of the one who sacrificed His life for my sake; Jesus the Christ. I owe you so much. Amen.

"A new commandment I give you, that you love one another; as I have loved you, that you also love one another."

Let's talk about love, Christian Love. Many people misunderstand. Christian love does not mean emotions. It is an act of the will, not feelings. Now certainly one can do both, what I mean is, you can love another person as an act of your will and with feelings. But if you only use feelings it can cause harm - like parents wanting their child to have all the things they never had and end up spoiling the child; teaching the child that they do not have to control their desire to want things - want it - get it. Or how about a husband loving his wife in such a way that he does not want her to do anything for herself - develop her talents. He becomes her will.

Of course there are those who say, "I don't love my spouse the way I used to or should." What they are talking about is "emotions and feelings." What they have not yet learned is that emotions and feelings must be controlled by the "will". If not, how will anyone be able to stay together or learn to accept one another and love in the truest sense? Jesus said, *"Love one another AS I have loved you."* Well are you perfect? No, yet Jesus loves you anyway. So we must love one another - with our will first, just as Jesus has loved us. If you deliberately work at loving and caring for the other person (power of the will) then you will grow to love them even more. If you concentrate on their shortcomings, you will "Not love your spouse the way you used to."

Paul says in 2 Corinthians 5:7, *"Walk by faith, not by sight."* In other words, live by our will; make the choice to believe in someone or in God; do not live by sight or through things we see that try to control our feelings and emotions; 'will' to love and to care for others. There is a spiritual law at work here: when we 'will' to love, our love will increase ten fold, because God will pour His love into us. It is important that we walk each day by faith controlled by our will, not our feelings and emotions.

Lord God, too often I allow my feelings to control me; unsound decisions follow. Strengthen me with your Holy Spirit that I may allow your will to take the lead; in that way I can walk in faith. Help me to concentrate on the goodness of others, not on their weaknesses, to see your Good working all around me. May I walk, act, think, and speak in faith by faith. And O Father, grant that I may LOVE! In the name of Jesus. Amen.

"According to the time, which he had ascertained from the Wise men."

My wife and I have always had candles in the windows of our home during Advent and Christmas. It has puzzled people over the years that we would not take them down until the second week of January. Some have asked me why we leave them up so long after Christmas. My answer, "We do not take them down until after January 6th (Epiphany) or the Sunday following, which would be Epiphany Sunday."

Most people grow up with the Christmas pageant - the shepherds and the wise men visiting the Baby Jesus at the stable and get the idea that these events occurred in the same time. If you recall what we discussed on January 6, Epiphany, you know that is not so! In Matthew the Wise Men visited Jesus in *a house* (2:11) not a stable. Also we noted that in verse 16 Herod ordered all male babies 2 years and under to be killed, *"according to the time which he had ascertained from the Wise men."* That sets the visit of the Wise Men at a year or so after the birth of Jesus. Also if you will recall the story in Luke 2:7 the Shepherds visited Jesus *"in a stable because there was no room in the Inn."* We celebrate the birth of Jesus on December 25th and then 12 days after his birth; January 6th we celebrate the Epiphany, the coming of the Wise Men.

The Shepherds represent the epiphany of Jesus to the Jews; the Wise Men represent the epiphany of Jesus to the rest of the world. As you meditate on these two stories, remember how great and awesome our God is even in revealing the birth of his son to the world. He leaves nothing to chance. You might want to leave your lights in your windows until the week after Epiphany so your neighbors will ask, "Why are your lights still up?" Like Advent, which helps us focus on the "Coming of our Lord"; and Lent (the 40 days before Easter) which helps us focus on Christ's death on the cross for our sake; the "12 days of Christmas" can help us focus on the wonder of a God who would go to such lengths to reveal Himself to us.

Lord, These stories are a wonderful revelation that Jesus came for all mankind, not just for some. I'd like to have fewer people to love, to forgive, to claim as kin. Forgive me for my prejudice, my hardness of heart. Help me to include all people everywhere in my prayers regardless of our differences. Grant that the light of Christ will forever burn in my life. Remind me it isn't a season, this Christmas time; it is a lifetime. In His name I pray. Amen.

"You are a chosen people, a royal priesthood, a holy nation, God's own people."

Each year in churches all over the world, Elders (called Deacons in some churches) are installed to serve their church for a specified term in office. The church of which I am a part is governed by Elders who are elected by the people to represent the people in making decisions for and about God's church very much like elected officials of our Congress. They follow God's will as best they can. It is an awesome responsibility. The office of Elder is never for privilege but for service.

We pattern our lives as Elders after Jesus who said, *"I came to serve and not be served and to give my life as a ransom for many."* Peter states in 1 Peter 2:9, *"You are a chosen people, a royal priesthood, a holy nation, God's own people."* Christians, as well as Elders, are elected to be God's own people in this world. We are to declare, *"The mighty acts of Him who called us out of darkness and into His marvelous light."* Elders or officers in the church are the ones to lead a church into that calling. Christians are a "connected" people. Hands have been laid upon our Elders down through history from the Apostles to today.

As we study our past and learn about our ancestors Peter and Paul from the New Testament times and other great leaders who followed up to the present, we must never forget who we are as God's elect. We can never put off our calling. As Elders we are called to serve God in a special way to lead His people as we search for direction in guiding His Church. And as Christians we can never put off our calling to be God's ministers and to follow His Commandments to *"Love one another as we have been loved."* In this New Year, let us all, whether we be an officer, or a church member, or just beginning to attend church, forge ahead to seek that which God is calling us to do. And remember, that He is the one guiding, strengthening, opening doors, helping us to take the leap of faith required to belong to Him.

Lord, I thank you for your calling to us as your people. Sometimes I balk at what you want of me and for my life. Forgive my rebellious nature. Strengthen me that I may be faithful to my calling. Keep me humble, Father. Keep me ever near. Remind me, lest I forget, that to serve your people is a privilege, undeserved. In the name of Jesus. Amen.

"I stand at the door and knock - If you hear my voice and open the door I will come to you."

My wife and I love paintings. We have a few originals; some by artists who are good friends; others by artists we have never met. All of these paintings mean a lot to us, but there are some paintings, which have real meaning in our life. I am sure that you also have your favorites. One of ours is Holman Hunt's "Latchless Door." It is a painting of Jesus standing at the door knocking. The door has no latch on His side. Other artists have painted this picture, but missed the point of scripture and included a latch on the door next to Jesus. "Latchless Door" is based on Rev. 3:20, *"I stand at the door and knock - If you hear my voice and open the door I will come to you."* It reminds us Christ is standing outside waiting to come into our lives, but we must open the door. Sometimes we don't open the door because we want to be in control of our life and we don't want to do what Jesus requires of us like "loving our neighbor as our self," and "loving our enemies", "doing kindness to those who hate us" and "praying for those who abuse us." What we would like to do is just the opposite; pay them back! Treat them the way they treated us!

Another religious favorite was given to us one Christmas by some dear friends: Mitchell Tolle's "Loaves and Fishes." It depicts the little boy who provided the food to Jesus that fed the 5,000. So what does art have to do with helping us live a Christian life? Simply this: it is another avenue through which the Holy Spirit can reach us. Looking at paintings, which depict great scripture scenes, can touch our lives and bring on the chance of transformation. Every time I go into a sanctuary to fulfill my calling, I realize what an awesome task it is to preach God's Word. Pictures like "Loaves and Fishes" and "Latchless Door" remind me to just open the door, offer willingly my meager supply and Christ will do the rest. Miracles happen. Christ Himself comes. People are helped. God is made known: In a painting: In real life.

Lord, I come to you in prayer realizing how much I fall short and how far I must come. Oh, Father, is this the whole point you're trying to make? To realize the impossibility of it all? But for you, Lord, nothing is impossible. Help me to realize that with your Holy Spirit in charge of my life I can do the impossible! But only if I open the door to Christ. My choice. My decision. In Jesus' name. Amen.

The Cure for Sin   January 17   Matthew 9:13

"I came not to call the righteous, but sinners."

What would you say is our calling from God?   Most will say that our call is to become religious people, to worship God and serve Him with our time, talents and tithes. You have probably heard that for most of your life. Now in doing all this we must be careful that the very thing we are called to do does not cause us to look too favorably upon ourselves. The problem which can occur is that we attend so many religious services that we begin to consider ourselves cured of sin and better than those outside the walls of the church. Nothing could be further from the truth. Paul says in Romans 3:10, *"We have all sinned and fallen short of the glory of God."*

Paul considered himself a wretched sinner in God's eyes. Jesus Himself said, *"I came not to call the righteous, but sinners."* (Matthew 9:13) In other words, Jesus is saying, "I come not to speak to those who think well of themselves, but to those who know they are sinners and wish to be saved from a wretched life to a wonderful, joyful life with God." Our call is not to just enjoy that life, but to live that life working to bring others to Christ that they too may have a wonderful and joyful life with Him.

Simply said, we must be witnesses. What do we have to witness? Only one thing: what God has done in our lives; how God has saved us and helped us through some very difficult moments. Actually, that is all we have to share, but it is very important. Share what God has done in your life and tell others He can also do the same in theirs. Too often what we actually do is receive the wonderful Gift of Grace God has given us and then busy ourselves with church activities. This kind of busyness causes us to become self-absorbed rather than being all about everybody else. This year let us find someone to tell our story to. Who knows, maybe that will be just what they are looking for, just what God had intended.

Lord God, I come asking for your forgiveness. You have called me to witness your power and grace in my life. I have turned the other way. Have mercy on me, Father. I was afraid of what others would think, afraid I'd say the wrong thing. I forgot, Lord, that witnessing is all about you and the people you place in my path. It was never about me. Never was it about me. Forgive me, Father. Lead me to a life of authentic witness through the things I do and say. For another chance to serve you I would forfeit the world and all its gain; I would. For another chance. In the name of Jesus, I pray. Amen.

We are Worthy!   January 18   Jeremiah 1:5

"Before I formed you in the womb, I knew you."

Today let's talk about being worthy. Are you worthy? Do you feel worthy? Do you feel worthy of a good job, worthy of a wonderful family, worthy of grace and salvation? Truth is many people do not feel worthy, I mean. From birth to adulthood is the most important time for developing our personality. There are many factors, which go into that development, none more important than the affirmation we receive or don't receive from our parents and those who love us. Everything that occurs later is a by-product of what we already believe about ourselves; the world.

As children growing up, if all we hear is "you are stupid, lazy, clumsy, too fat, too short, a nobody" then we are likely to become paralyzed by our negative feelings about our self worth. No one likes to be rejected and no one likes to have faults pointed out, especially if it's true! Can't we at least have *SOME* imperfection? But like it or not, many children grow into adults and find themselves crippled for a lifetime by the cruel things said to and about them while they were young. It's like a tape recorder inside our brain replaying those things over and over again.

So how, if possible, can we reverse those feelings? We would do well to listen to the advice God gave Jeremiah from Chapter 1, verses 4-5 & 17-19. *"Before I formed you in the womb, I knew you. I called you to be a prophet. So gird up your loins and be strong. Don't be afraid of what others say or do because, although they will try to tear you down, I am with you. It is I who will deliver you."* What wonderful and comforting news! What would it do for our self-worth if we truly embraced those words as our own and lived as if they were true for us? So what if others say we are stupid or clumsy, inadequate or incapable. God Himself has formed us; from the beginning He knew us and had a plan for our life. We matter. We are worth something!

Lord God, I come to you in prayer because I know, I trust that the God revealed in Scripture is real and is who He says He is. I know I am imperfect; I don't need others to point that out; I've lived that life already. What I need, Father, is for you to believe in me, for you to see, not just what I have been, but what I can be. Help me to overcome all the things others do to make them feel better or less imperfect than I am. Help me to remember that before I was anyone-else's, I was Yours. In the name of Jesus. Amen.

"Child, why have you treated us like this?" *"Did you not know that I would be in my Father's house?"*

Luke records the story of Jesus going to the temple at Jerusalem at the age of twelve with his parents. Rather than concentrating on the normal aspects of this story, let's concentrated how Mary and Joseph felt, they were upset with Jesus. Bet you never thought Jesus would upset his parents like your children upset you, right? Well, Mary and Joseph were upset with Jesus because he stayed behind and they could not find him. They talked over their situation. Mary expressed her disappointment, Jesus explained saying he must be about the business of his Father. They come to an understanding; Jesus returned with his parents and was *"obedient"*.

There is certainly a lesson here for us all. Here we see the foundation for a healthy family and for a healthy relationship with God or with anyone else. We all have disagreements from time to time in our relationship with our children, our spouse, our parents, and with others. We even have disagreements with God. We want what we want; He wants for us what He wants. It is a constant battle within our Spirit. Paul calls it the battle between "Spirit and flesh." What we must do is recognize that this conflict is not only common, but also healthy.

The conflict must move forward, however. We cannot stop with telling God what we want, desire or need. We must listen to Him, His wishes and desires for our lives. This is probably the weakest point for most of us. We don't want to spend time sitting, listening, meditating before God. Often people consider that a waste of time. They could not be further from the truth! Understanding leads to obedience. Once we understand what is expected and why, we can move to following the plans God has laid out for us. The story of Jesus and his parents can lead us to greater obedience with our Lord - in our own life - family, work and spiritual life. That will lead us to be healthier and happier, I promise.

Lord, as I consider this past year I can recall more blessings than I can count. Father, give me the gift of a serene and thankful heart. I can be so ungrateful at times. Forgive me my willfulness borne of fear and distrust. Help me to desire fully that your perfect will be accomplished in my life. Father, grant me your grace. Open my weary heart to seek each day your peace and love. In the name of Jesus I pray. Amen.

"Lord, give me "Living Water" that I might never thirst again." "Come and see the man who told me everything I have ever done. Cannot He be the Messiah?"

Evangelism is a word that makes many shiver, some not even knowing why. Many have the idea that evangelism means going door-to-door and asking people if they have been saved. Although there is nothing wrong with that, there is no record of Jesus doing this. In the fourth chapter of John when the woman at the well met Jesus he told her aspects of her life a stranger could not have known. He did so without condemning her. She was so excited when she realized who Jesus was that she returned to her neighborhood and told everyone, *"Come see this man who could see into my soul."* She proclaimed him to her neighbors.

Scripture calls us to also witness and evangelize. We do so by telling others of the "Good News" of God's Grace. When Jesus went around proclaiming the coming Kingdom and calling people to come follow, He did not do so by condemning them. Even the woman at the well who had lived a very questionable life style Jesus simply offered living water and called her to new life. Once people respond we are called to nurture them! Teach them! Accept then into the fellowship of the Body of Christ and help them discover the "Good News" of God's love and the lifestyle God wants them to live. To live in obedience to God, a life in close relationship with God and His Son Jesus - to love as God has loved us - to forgive as freely as He has forgiven us - to accept others as we have been accepted. To proclaim God to others is important.

People need to know God is real and loves them and wants them to be a part of His Kingdom. If however, we do not accept them in the church, warts and all, and if we do not demonstrate a Christ-like life to them and reach out to them in love and forgiveness, our efforts will be in vain. This year, let us make a pledge to ourselves and to God that we will become the best witnesses for His Kingdom we possibly can

Lord, I come giving thanks that you have loved me so. Knowing you has changed my life. Empower me to care so deeply about my fellow man that the thought of anyone living life without you, Father, is intolerable to me. I will have to become less self-centered, less self-absorbed, I know. Will you do this for me? Give me the wisdom and the power to live my life in radical obedience to your will. In Jesus' Name. Amen.

"But I say to you, love your enemies and do good to those that hate you."

How does an enemy affect us spiritually? Before we answer, let's define enemy. The enemy could be our child? They do have a way of pushing our buttons that cause us to act or react in ways we wish we hadn't, bringing out the worst in us. That's the real definition of an enemy, isn't it? Maybe your enemy is someone at work; even people for whom we secretly harbor ill feelings; someone who has hurt us and that hurt lingers and won't go away; someone we strongly disagree with and that disagreement has caused a barrier to come between us.

We need to who our enemies are before we proceed with how to deal with our enemies. Some retaliate! Newspapers are full of stories of people who have a grievance against someone else and try to settle that grievance with payback in kind. Retaliation is a form of spiritual death. It usually backfires and is hardly worth the cost. Others deal with their enemy by secretly harboring resentment toward that person. Deeply repressed anger is probably the most common spiritual problem among Christians. We are nice people. We wouldn't openly harm anyone, but boy can we carry a grudge! The problem with harboring negative feelings toward someone else is what those feelings do to us.

So how should we deal with our enemies? In answering that question we need to remember what Jesus said in Luke 6, *"Love your enemies and do good to those that hate you." "If you do good only to those who do good to you, what credit is that? Even mean, despicable people do good to their kind."* Forgiving our enemy is the first step toward loving our enemy. Now, you might say, "Well, what that person did to me was too terrible. I cannot forgive them." What if God were to take the same point of view and say, "What you have done to me, my child, is too terrible and I refuse to forgive you?" Answer this, "Who is your anger and resentment hurting the most?" Forgive and move on.

Lord God, I know that I am commanded to love my enemies, to forgive those who have wronged me, but it is hard. This I know first hand. To forgive I must first want to. To want to I must have Jesus in my heart. A heart full of resentment has no room for grace. Heal the part of me, Father, that feeds on the power of un-forgiveness. That part can never be a home for your perfect love, for you. In the name of Jesus, I pray. Amen.

Is Jesus who you Expected? January 22 Mark 3:22

"And the scribes who came down from Jerusalem said, "He has Beelzebul and by the ruler of the demons he casts out demons."

In 1996, my wife and I purchased a cabin near Pickwick Lake. To get there we had to go through Jackson, Tennessee; take 45 By-Pass, south. That trip always made me call up my patience. The traffic goes from 55 miles per hour to an almost dead stop on a railroad overpass. Then several streets converge before a stoplight in front of the federal building, an area referred to as "malfunction junction". Once you get past that, it's free sailing. The return trip is not much better. You had best just turn on the radio and put on your patience; you're going to need it. I've seen people cut in front of others, horns honk, fists shake - you name it. Even good Christian people; if you asked me to be honest, I would have to say I have been one of those who let their impatience get the best of them, more than once. That is why Jesus has had to work so hard with me. That is also why I understand others so well. I too have walked in the shoes of those who have lost their temper and done things of which I am not proud! I guess you could say, as a minister, I am not what people might expect. I do not claim to be perfect. I am a plain ordinary human just like everyone else. No better but hopefully no worse!

That was one of the problems some of the religious people had with Jesus. He was not who they expected! Some scribes even thought he was crazy – filled with the Devil himself!! Jesus did not fit the mold. He kept company with housewives and tax collectors. And although he was very popular, he walked his own path, playing up to no one. Some of His teachings contradicted Jewish tradition. He said, *"Don't judge." "Love your enemies." "Turn the other cheek." "Bless the poor." "Love as God loves you."* Unconditionally. What do you think? Was he out of his head? Many Christian's don't even follow these teachings. Can we be honest? Have you never judged? Do you always turn the other cheek? Maybe the question we ought to ask is, "Are we who Jesus expects us to be?"

Lord, I know that many in your day did not understand you. Perhaps, they did not want to for the changes knowing you would require. To know you, Father, is pure joy but following you is hard. Forgive me when I fall short of your expectations. Cover my sins with your righteousness and free me from the yoke of having failed you. Place me into your loving arms, Father God, for the world is ever around me and I am so alone. Amen

"Then He went home; and the crowd came together again, so that they could not even eat. When His family heard it, they went out to restrain Him, for people were saying, 'He has gone out of his mind.'"

Yesterday we looked at what some religious people expected of Jesus. Today, let us continue that thought as we consider how Jesus' own family viewed him. The scripture above vividly captures an encounter between Jesus and the people ending with these words, *"When His family heard it, they went out to restrain Him.'"* Even Jesus' own family did not understand him. They had heard some disturbing reports about his teachings and healing. It was all so radical that some thought he was *"out of His head."* So, when they heard Jesus was in their village, they set out in an attempt to bring him home.

If Jesus were here in flesh today, where might you find him? Which political party do you think Jesus might support? That I cannot tell you; I am not even sure I can tell you where Jesus would stand on some of the great issues of this day, and it would be presumptuous of me to try. I think Jesus was far too complex for us to pigeonhole. But I can tell you this: Jesus is for you and He is for me and He is for every man, woman and child on this planet.

While ministering in Kentucky, a lady in the church came to me distraught; her husband had left her. He was in a bar in a neighboring town and she asked if I would go talk to him. I did and he got on his knees asking for God's forgiveness and help. After that night their marriage experienced a rebirth. My guess is that's where we would find Jesus. I can see Him in bars, calling people to a new life; in corporate offices telling the CEO's that money is not the most important thing. He would be at little league ball games telling parents to not be so hard on their kids. He would be in homes - anyplace he could be, to comfort people because Jesus cares. A relationship of love with a risen Savior is the Christian faith.

Lord, too often I come wanting you to agree with my point of view. When faced with the tough issues of the world, I want to be able to tell others that you are on my side, not theirs. Such arrogance, Lord, betrays us both. Humble my heart that I may gladly follow your will for my life. Father, grant me the kind of courage that reaches beyond my mind into my heart, my will. Jesus, my brother, have mercy, forgive. In His name. Amen.

"My God, My God, why have you forsaken me? Oh my God, I cry by day but you do not answer and by night but find no rest."

Have you ever felt that you have tried as hard as possible but cannot seem to connect with God? You pray and pray but it seems that God is not listening? Any time I feel that way I turn to scripture. One verse that comforts me comes from Psalm 22, *"My God, My God, why have you forsaken me? Oh my God, I cry by day but you do not answer and by night but find no rest."* These words may not give me the answer I am looking for, but it does tell me I am in good company. It tells me that even God's favored one, David, felt the same feeling that I have felt.

By reading God's Holy Word to his people I am reminded that even when I do not feel God's presence, I know that he is there. I know that my ancestors before me trusted in God and were delivered. I remember also that following this great cry by David comes the greatest Psalm of them all, Psalm 23, *"The Lord is my shepherd I shall not want... he leads me by still waters, He restores my soul... even as I walk through the darkest valley (of my life), I will fear no evil for God is there and comforts me with His rod and His staff."*

As we go through those moments in our lives when we cry out and do not feel God's presence, turning to His Holy Word supplies answers for our broken hearts and quiets our souls. In His Living Word we can find the Mighty Acts of God where God has helped his people in the past and we can be reminded that even if we do not feel Him for the moment, God is Presence. He will come to us and rescue us, maybe not as we wish to be rescued, but He will bring comfort for our grief and strength for our broken hearts. As you seek God in those moments of feeling low, if you cannot feel His presence, go to His Holy and Living Word and read about His Mighty Acts with his people of the past. And may that bring you comfort as it has to generations before.

Lord God, At times I feel forsaken and alone; the weight of the world upon me and no one on my side; help me to know that I have you. For you, my shepherd, have helped me walk through the darkest valleys of my life and you will be with me even today. Grant me your presence, your strength. In the name of your precious Son, Jesus. Amen.

"Don't worry, but in everything by prayer and supplication with thanksgiving let your requests be made known to God. And the peace of God, which surpasses all understanding, will guard your hearts and your minds in Christ Jesus."

My wife and I have three cats and two children. One cat - "Baby Kitty" was an inside cat when we lived on Main Street in the house that belonged to the church we served. We "semi-retired" and moved to a cabin at Pickwick Lake, he now has the freedom to roam. A few months after retirement a stray cat decided to choose us as his family. It was a good move on his part because my wife had wanted a cat that loved her and would curl up in her lap. You see BK (Baby Kitty) liked only me. This new cat filled the bill and my wife named him Cashew, which matches his color. The next year along comes another! After Midnight, because after midnight there will be no more cats!!!

I have learned a valuable lesson from these animals; live your life without worry. Baby Kitty lies around most of the time curled up in a ball sleeping. My guess? Dreaming of hunting birds, which he loves to watch. The other cats love to hunt and to our dismay have brought us many surprises. These cats live each day knowing that we will give them love when they want it and food to eat. They have not one care in the world.

Now it dawned on me, if these dogs and cats, who are creatures of God, don't have a care in the world and trust us completely, imperfect as we are, why can't we, whom God has created and loves so much, trust God completely? God did not create us to be filled with worry and frustration, tension and stress. One reason most of us do not do better in life is because we don't live each day as a gift of Gods' grace. We often are looking into the future or back into the past causing us great worry and stress. God has blessed us tremendously. So, just do your best. Worry for today and do what you can, then trust in God to take care of yesterday and tomorrow.

Lord, I thank you for pets that bring me joy, and through whom you teach me of yourself. Mostly I give thanks that you have loved me, cared for me. Help me see the futile nature of worry. Give me faith to live each day as it comes, to leave yesterday and tomorrow in your capable, sturdy hands. In the name of Jesus I pray. Amen.

"Go from this place and I will make you a great nation and bless you."

Are you a dreamer? What do you dream? And where do your dreams come from anyway? I realize that our dreams of the night come to us in black and white, but God's dream for us is in full color. It is wonderful and glorious and magnificent. God said to Abraham in Genesis 12:1, *"Go from this place and I will make you a great nation and bless you."* Most people read the stories of our great patriarchs and while they do not question that God spoke to them, they refuse to accept that God actually speaks to us today.

The problem is that many either don't know how to listen to God or perhaps they find themselves too busy to listen. God gives you dreams for your life. He will either speak to you in your dreams of the night or through voices in your heart. Often we experience the dream but counter it with statements like, "That's just impossible. Or I cannot do that." We then go about our life accepting something less because of our unbelief. After God revealed the dream to Abraham in Genesis 12, Abraham followed up by obeying. Verse 4 *"So Abraham went as the Lord had told him."*

In all decisions of life we need to ask ourselves this question: "Is this what I want?" or, "Is this what God wants?" In other words, how would my response show my love for and trust in God? God has a dream for each of us, it may not be Abraham' dream to become the Father of a great nation, but God has a dream for you and for me. He reveals His dreams in many ways and it is up to us to listen and obey. To follow that dream does not guarantee that your life will be free of trouble and problems, Abraham encountered plenty, but it will guarantee that God will be with you to see you through and bless you and bring peace to your heart.

Lord, I hear your still small voice speaking to me in the night, but I dismiss it as a dream; forgive me. I hear your voice speaking to me inside my very soul, but I dismiss it as my own desires; forgive me. I hear your voice speaking to me through others, but I dismiss it; forgive me. Grant the gift of discernment in my heart and soul that I may truly listen and hear your voice. Then, Lord, give me the courage to follow the dream you have planned for me since before my earthly life began. In the name of Jesus I pray. Amen.

"Let us make humankind in our image and according to our likeness, and let them have dominion over everything that I have created."

There is a special relationship that was established in Creation between God and mankind. Genesis 1:26 tells of that relationship. And then in the 2nd chapter, God gives a warning to not eat of the fruit of *"tree of the knowledge of good and evil."* Of course, there seems to be built within our nature a red flag that goes up when someone says, "You cannot do that." Satan took advantage of that nature within us when he said in Genesis 3:4-5, *"You will not die; for God knows that when you eat of it, your eyes will be opened, and you will BE LIKE GOD."*

Isn't that really the greatest temptation within each of us? We want to control our own destiny, do things our way, and have life go the way we want it to go. Satan's temptation, of course, was a trick; there is no way we can have everything go the way we want it. Truthfully, we certainly don't want others controlling us, so what makes us think they want us controlling them? Satan used this lie to separate us from God then and is still doing so today!

In John 15:4, Jesus gives us a glimpse of the way back, *"Abide in me as I abide in you. Just as a branch cannot bear fruit by itself unless it is attached to the vine, neither can you unless you abide in me; apart from me, you can do nothing."* Jesus lets us know that he is the true vine, and we are the branches. Metaphorically, it is like going back to the *"tree of the knowledge of good and evil."* That tree separated us from God; the vine, Jesus, will bring us back to that special relationship with God. Just remember, with Jesus, it is all or nothing. "Abide in me" Jesus said. Our cost is to give up our will to Christ and to receive what we need from him: the vine feeding the branch to produce fruit.

Lord God, I know there is distance between us, but I want to place the blame anywhere than at my own feet. Forgive me for giving Satan in that decision a victory. Give me the wisdom to recognize evil when temptation comes, the strength to resist its destructive power. Remind me that for a Christian, all battles are spiritual; that Satan is the Great Liar; the Truth comes only from you. Give me faith to abide in Jesus that I may bear your peace, love, and joy to the world. My life I entrust to you. In Jesus. Amen.

"None is righteous - no, not one."

Who are we spiritually? And where is our weakness? These are important questions to consider because Satan has a favored way of entering into our lives to trick us: that door is through our weaknesses. If you know yourself and know your weaknesses, then you will also know from whence Satan will come knocking. We must start our journey to self-knowledge by first admitting "who we are - sinners in need of forgiveness." In the sixth chapter of Isaiah, verse 5, Isaiah, son of Amoz said, *"Woe is me, for I am a man of unclean lips."* In Luke 5:4f, Peter stated, *"Depart from me for I am a sinner."* And in Romans 7:15f, Paul stated, *"I do not do what I want, but I do the very thing I hate - wretched man that I am."*

The Bible teaches us that we are, "corrupt at our very center - our heart." We are all infected in every part of our being and we cannot come to God or please God except by His grace. Paul points this out in Romans 3:10, *"None is righteous - no, not one."* So our beginning point is discovering "who we are" and where our weaknesses lie: to confess that we are not righteous, but sinners, and then our eyes can be opened to our specific weaknesses.

If your weakness is lust, be careful that Satan does not use that to tempt you and destroy your marriage and family. If you don't believe it will happen, just look around you. If your weakness is food, don't let a craving for food replace your craving for God. If your weakness is alcohol, over work, or perfectionism, acknowledge it and ask for God's strength to withstand the temptations, which Satan will surely send. If it is gossip or being judgmental, then remember that you too are sinful and in need of forgiveness. Then pray that God will touch your heart and change it so that you can become a powerful witness of the love and grace of Jesus who gave His life for you and us all.

Holy Lord, why I am here? What is my purpose? Will you tell me? How can an imperfect, irredeemable sinner be of any use to you, to anyone? Convict my fearful heart that you, Lord, are not like the world, critical, unforgiving. Remind me that no one is too flawed to be saved; show me my weaknesses that I may live in peace with others, with you; forgive my sin; embrace my soul with your everlasting love. Do this for Jesus. Amen.

"God destined us to be His children through Jesus Christ, according to the purpose of His will."

The New Year is here and chances are it has already made its mark on your life bringing some good with it and some bad. Now we need to move forward into to this New Year with all of its new adventures and challenges. As we do, I think it is important to sit back and evaluate what we are doing with this life God willed for us. During Advent and Christmas, we look to the promises God made through His Son, Jesus. Advent means "looking forward to the coming of God's Son into the world." Christmas is the fulfillment of that promise. As Christians, we need to focus on the affect that the coming of Christ – Emmanuel, God with us - has had on our lives. Paul says in Ephesians 1:5, *"God destined us to be His children."* We must ask ourselves, "Do I truly believe that?"

Paul says, *"We are destined to be God's."* Do you believe that you were put on this earth for a purpose? Do you believe that written into your DNA is a life script put there by God? If you believe you have a purpose, have you found it? People who believe that God has a plan for their lives and accept that plan are more joyous and content than those who don't. What can account for that result? Simply said, if you believe that God is in control, you can finally give up your attempt at running the universe yourself. Even your attempt to control the lives of those around you: your spouse or your children or even your own, that burden, you can lay down too. Once you do that, you can just relax and live the life God has planned out for you. Isn't that what faith is all about? Isn't it realizing that someone "up there" is watching over you and if you will trust and let him, God will see to it that you have the life he meant for you, joy filled and love inspired? We are destined to be God's children through Jesus.

Father, I come wanting to discover what it means to be yours. First, I must give up my desire to run my life. I cannot alone. I am much too controlling, manipulative, weak. Such arrogance and pride! Together they disguise a lot of fear and anxiety. I know. This is not the life you died to give me, is it? Lord, turn my life over to you. Destined to be yours, let me live my life believing and trusting that enormous act of enduring love and abiding grace. Fill me with your joy and peace and love. For Jesus, Father, Amen.

"Then the woman left her water jar and went back to the city. She said to the people, "Come and see a man who told me everything I have ever done! He cannot be the Messiah, can he?" They left the city and went to him."

One important aspect of the Christian faith is "Telling Your Story." Remember the old gospel song, *"I love to Tell the Story"* of Jesus and his love? We all have stories to tell. Stories of how God has touched our lives in extraordinary ways; sometimes through dreams or visions - sometimes through the miraculous healing of diseases; sometimes through a quiet presence letting you know that he is there, watching over you, keeping you safe. The entire Bible is God's Story. In the Bible are many extraordinary stories of how God touched, called or influenced the lives of those people recorded in the Scriptures: Like the Centurion's servant in Matthew 8 and the story of Paul's conversion in Acts 9. This is what makes Christianity different from other religions. Most religions require a rigid following and obedience of the Law.

The Jews follow and obey the Ten Commandments and rules they established trying to interpret God's Word and will. Jesus poked holes in their understanding by saying things like, *"You understand the law as such 'You shall not kill.' But I tell you, anyone who has hate or anger for his brother/sister has already killed them in their heart."* He tried to help people understand that the faith to which they are being called is not a faith in impersonal laws but in a living God; that laws were given to protect us and help us live a better life, not for us to worship. Our calling is to be faithful in our relationship with Jesus, not blind obedience to a set of rules. Therefore the stories of our personal relationship with this living God are vital for our faith and understanding of who this God is. If you have never done so, write down all the personal contacts you have had with Jesus. Write down the moments, which were told to you by your parents or others. Keep them close and share them with others. God is a living God, a personal God and you should cherish your experiences with Him.

Lord God, you have blessed me in so many ways - in my times of need I have called upon you and you were there. Impress those moments firmly into my heart that I may never forget. Help me to call upon them during times of despair and hopelessness. May my encounter with you lift me and strengthen me for this life and open my heart and mind to the life to come. In the name of Jesus I pray. Amen.

"Be quick to listen, slow to speak - slow to anger."

The Bible is full of great advice like this one from the letter of James, "Be quick to listen, slow to speak - slow to anger." Later in his letter James says, "Those who do not bridle their tongues deceive their hearts." Can it be stated any clearer? I mean, is this great wisdom or what? Can we be honest? What usually happens when someone hurts you and "makes" you angry? Many people do just the opposite don't they? They are "quick to speak, slow to listen and quick to anger!" They do not "bridle" their tongues and therefore deceive their hearts.

I think the major reason for our poor listening skills, our rampant desire to have a corner on truth, and our quickness to righteous anger is that we forget the first lesson we should learn when we become a Christian: "We are *all* sinners!" We all fall short of God's glory; we all miss the mark - all-of-us. Now if we can grasp that first rule of Christianity, we can then realize that others sin also; other people fall short; other people are slow to listen, quick to speak, and quick to anger. We all own the weaknesses. Fact is, in order for us to become a Christian we must realize and accept that we are sinners deserving condemnation. If we cannot fall on our knees and confess that we have tried to run our lives and have failed miserably, we will not be able to accept that Jesus is Lord of our life.

It is when we realize the hopelessness of the road we have taken that we are able to allow Jesus to take control of our lives. Only then will we be able to "Be quick to listen, slow to speak – slow to anger." For when we begin to allow Jesus to run our lives, we then drop all pretence. We don't have to protect ourselves, for He protects us. We don't have to get angry for He is in control of our lives and our future; Jesus owns our hearts. Who would want it any other way?

Father God, I am far from being able to live this command. I am quick to speak, quicker to anger, slow to listen. I have a good reason! Slow to speakers don't get to share their bountiful knowledge! And temper can often sway debate quicker than reason! Must I give this up to be truly yours? I know that as a Christian, I am expected to be different. Oh Father, I have a problem with letting go. I do so love the sound of my own voice; the control of people and situations that often results. Help me, Lord, to let go of me, to take hold of you. In Jesus' name. Amen.

"Do not judge, and you will not be judged; do not condemn and you will not be condemned; forgive and you will be forgiven."

Are you kicking yourself and enjoying it less? Well, join the crowd. It seems that there are more and more people punishing themselves for making mistakes these days. If they aren't busy doing that, they are busy bashing other people for their mistakes. Just listen to the news, any station. Sinfulness runs rampant. The assignment of blame is a verbal contact sport. We have forgotten the lesson from the scripture, *"Love the Lord with all your heart, mind and soul and love your neighbor AS you love yourself."* (Luke 10:27) We are commanded to love our neighbors and ourselves – warts and all.

But there is also a warning in Luke 6:37, *"Judged not and you will not be judged! Forgive and you will be forgiven."* That also goes for forgiving yourself. It is helpful to consider the life of the disciple Peter. Early in his relationship with our Lord, Jesus revealed to him that he would be *"crucified"*. Peter denied this, saying that such a thing should never happen to his Master. Jesus called on the devil to then *"sift Peter"*. In the Upper Room, Peter refused to let Jesus wash his feet. Then came the "biggest" mistake of his life. When Jesus was arrested, Peter denied being one of his followers - not once, but three times before the cock crowed at daylight just as Jesus had predicted.

Could there be a positive outcome to such a failure? Yes. We can now admit that we are all sinners - falling short just like Peter. We know that just as Peter was forgiven so will we. Jesus named him *"Rock"* just after Peter's confession that Jesus is "the Messiah." Jesus named him so, not because Peter was so solid that he could make no mistakes or so virtuous he could do no wrong, but because even in his failure Peter still confessed that Jesus was the Son of God, the Christ. Being a Christian is a process of growth. Next year we can become more forgiving and loving and less judgmental all because of Jesus. Falling short? Confess Jesus!

Lord, I come asking for your forgiveness. Like Peter, I have failed you. I never meant to in my heart but I did. I am beholden for your steadfast love even as I have disappointed you time and time again. Abide with me today that I may become in each encounter more accepting, more loving, more forgiving. Enable me, precious Jesus, to see everything through your eyes. Amen.

"Put on the whole armor of God, so that you may stand against the devil."

This last lesson in Ephesians is one we all need to hear and take hold. The apostle Paul advises the Christians in Ephesus not to go to battle without God's help. *"Put on God's armor."* The adversary they face is the devil in whatever disguise he has chosen. Paul highlights the challenge of getting along with others in chapter six. The problem is a familiar one. When trouble comes our way, we resort to fighting with the use of our armor. That protection consists of arguing, put downs, name calling, half-truths, whole lies, and ostracism. Our armor cannot protect us from the general need to be affirmed by the things of this world; nor does it protect us from making too important what people say about us.

Using our armor creates two problems. First, the Bible is clear, "No one is good but God" and second, whatever good we do, we cannot take the credit. It was either God's Holy Spirit working in us, or it was for selfish gain. The wiles of the devil are most effective if our focus can be kept on ourselves, away from God. Paul says instead of using *your* armor, put on God's armor. Why do we need this armor? Paul says, *"So the devil will not be able to trick you with a lie."* Evil tries to trick us into believing our battle is with one another, with flesh and blood, it is not. It is with the *"spiritual forces of evil in the heavenly places"* (the devil and his angels).

Does that mean if we put on the armor of God, we will now agree on everything as Christians? Does it mean we will now be perfect? Does it mean we will not hurt another's feelings or get hurt ourselves? No, it means God's armor will deflect evil's lies and tricks and protect us from harm. Only God can fight our spiritual battles. We are great sinners in need of divine forgiveness; we cannot achieve or deserve only request. When we let God fight our battles, God rejoices and the devil slinks dejectedly away - for now.

Lord, I know that I am deeply flawed, living life in search of worldly affirmation. I have accepted undeserved praise, rather than giving you the glory. In these ways I have given the devil his day. Forgive my weakness; crush my malignant pride. Strap your armor on me that I might be an advancer of your Kingdom. Remind me that evil lies close at hand to tempt, trick, confound. Should I foolishly try to go it alone, whisper gently, "Is there something you forgot to take with you, child of mine?" In Jesus' name. Amen.

"We must show love toward enemies, do good to those who hate us, bless those who curse us, and PRAY for those who abuse us."

What a "Life of Prayer" is like, why we need it, and how might we accomplish it? The expectations of Jesus for the authentic Christian life as outlined in today's scripture are overwhelming. Reread it and ask yourself, "How is that possible?" The answer is only through a life of prayer! If left to our own devices, what we would really like to do is to take revenge on those who hurt, condemn or abuse us. If you are honest, I have a feeling you would agree. How do we circumvent that powerful desire to strike back at those who harm us? Prayer: prayer strikes at the heart of faith.

A stumbling block for many is the belief that our prayers must follow a certain formula to be heard. Some pray for God to correct others. You know, pointing out the *"splinter in another's eye while ignoring the log in their own."* (Matthew 7:4) Others pray to God all the time, which is not in anyway bad unless one is trying to completely escape this world so they will not have to be involved in helping God and His church. Others take courses in the "proper technique" of prayer thinking that if they do it wrong God will not listen. Truth is if one studies and listens closely they will discover how sinful they are and how forgiving God is.

Jesus tells us that we must not try to correct everyone else, but we must "show love" even toward our enemies — "do good" to those who have harmed us — "bless" those who curse us — and "Pray" for those who abuse us. In short we are called to be instruments of God's love and peace: kindness and forgiveness in this fallen world. It is not easy — really impossible on our own. A life of prayer is the only answer — to fall on our knees and beg God for His forgiveness for all our sins and then to give us the strength and wisdom to obey His command. Maybe then we can pray for others, including our enemies, instead of attempting to remove splinters from their eye.

Lord God, I find it hard to love those who love me; let alone those who hate me. By your grace alone would I be able to pray for my enemies. Open my eyes to my own sinfulness. Let me see that the log in my own eye is remarkably similar to the splinter in my neighbor's. Lord, help me to claim the righteousness, the love of Jesus. Sour-faced old hypocrites never did anyone any good. Save me from myself. In Jesus, I pray. Amen.

"Jesus took with him Peter and John and James, and they went up on the mountain to pray." "A voice came from the cloud, "This is my Son, my Chosen; listen to him!"

In the 9th chapter of Luke is a remarkable story known as "The Transfiguration." The dictionary defines this word as *"to change the form or appearance of."* Three disciples, Peter, James and John, went with Jesus up on the mountain to pray; this is the setting. While there, Jesus prayed and *"the appearance of his face changed and his clothes became dazzling white"* and suddenly, Moses and Elijah appeared with Him. The disciples themselves were caught up in a cloud and a voice came from the cloud saying, *"This is my Son, my Chosen; listen to him."*

We too need to remember and to heed – Jesus is God's Son, God's "Chosen One" - listen to Him. We seem to listen to everyone else, don't we? We listen to the news, which tells us that we live in a world that is falling apart, yet Scripture tells us, God is in control! We listen to the Internet; even trust the facts we find there when there is no proof of authenticity. We listen to our friends who tell us what we want to hear, we even listen to our enemies who try to tear us down and tell us we are not worth much. If that were true, would God have sent His only Son, *"His chosen One"*, to come to this fallen world to die for worthless people? Jesus said, *"I am the truth, the way and the life."*

Now there are other so-called "truths" out there and many fall for those empty philosophies. But no one can reach absolute reality or truth without Jesus. If you wish to save your life, give it away to Jesus. Jesus is the answer to life. He is the one who can feed our hunger and thirst. He is the one who forgives our sins and covers our unrighteousness with His perfect love. Once we give our all to Him, God breaks through to state what we have all longed to hear, "You are my Beloved."

Lord God, I stand in awe of you. Like a loving parent who easily differentiates a hurt cry from a cry of hunger, you know the catalyst behind our every response, the cry of fear versus the cry of doubt. How wonderful you are! Help me to trust you completely. I hear the voices of this world, people not led by you, who do not know you, or trust your truth. Forgive me, Father, for I am weak; overwhelm me by your Spirit, then will I listen exclusively to the voice of Jesus, the only answer to life. It is in his name, Amen.

"Why are you afraid? Have you still no faith?"

Jesus asked the disciples "Why are you afraid? Have you still no faith?" as they were huddled in a small fishing boat in the middle of a large lake. The boat was being tossed to and fro during a storm. Jesus was asleep; trying to get some much needed rest. The disciples were, shall we say, "Scared out of their wits!" So they came to Jesus in a state of panic and awakened him, saying, *"Teacher, do you not care that we are perishing?"* Jesus got right to the heart of the matter. He identified their problem and its underlying source. The disciples had been with Jesus for some time now; they had witnessed many miracles. Yet, when a storm arises, the disciples, dominated by doubt, forget all they've seen and heard at Jesus' side. So Jesus asked, *"Why are you afraid? Have you STILL no faith?"*

Why is that the truth for them, for us? Is it because we give in to the fears of life? Is it because we place more importance on the life we live rather than the life to come? When most of us get a little depressed or upset, it is usually because we wanted something to go our way and it didn't. Or maybe we wanted something of material value and could not afford it. This is the way evil tricks us. If you really think about it, once you get your way or once you get what you wanted in material things, are you as happy or content as you thought you would be?

Real happiness does not come that way. Rather as we have faith and trust in God, who provides us with all good things, joy fills our life. Happiness is an inner grace and its only source is God. When we are afraid, we must open our eyes to an essential truth, we have failed to trust in God. Remember, He is the source of all good things; He is the source of all security; He is the source of true happiness and joy.

Lord, forgive me when I claim to be a Christian yet live my life full of worry and fear. I rationalize and justify my feelings by saying anyone would feel the same. But I'm not anyone; I'm yours. Yet, my fear exists because I do not place my complete trust in you. Forgive me, Father, and strengthen me that I can look to Jesus, the true source of my happiness and my security. May he be my all in all. In His Name, I pray. Amen.

Why Worship?   February 6   Romans 10:13f

"All who calls upon the name of the Lord shall be saved - BUT how can they call on one they don't know and how can they know and believe in one of whom they have never heard and how are they to hear without someone to tell them."

Do you worship God? Do you have a specific place, a specific church, a group of Christians with whom you gather to worship and praise God? Or not? Does worshipping God really matter? Today's scripture provides a few reasons why: to seek salvation and to know him when he comes. How do you know you are following or listening to God if you have no idea how God operates or in what manner God reveals Himself? We learn these vital truths through prayer, Bible Study, and listening to the Word preached. But, to *understand* God's word takes faith and faith, as Paul states in Ephesians 2:8, " *is not your own doing, it is a gift of God"*.

The grace of faith comes and is put into our hearts in two ways: the preaching and hearing of the Word and in the administration and partaking of the Sacraments (Baptism and the Lord's Supper). Both of these encounters with the Living God increase and strengthen our faith, which sustains us day by day. Without a regular diet of these two, our faith is in danger of weakening. Now if you like, you can decide whether or not you agree with Paul's flawless argument, but this is not something Paul or any other pastor made up. It was God who created this world we live in and it was God who sent his Son as our savior and it was God who decided that this is how it would be. Faith is spread thorough hearing the Word preached, through God's Sacraments and through God's Holy Word. If you look elsewhere for a glimpse of God, you may find something, it just may not be what you seek or even want from God!

Lord God, forgive me when I think I know better than you what I need. Such arrogance on my part astounds even me! Either you must have enormous patience or enormous love! What's that, Father? If I read the Bible more, prayed more, worshipped more I would know? You're right; you're so right. Forgive me, Lord, for thinking I can receive your Salvation and Faith apart from the community of believers. Impress upon me the need for your Holy Word preached and for your Sacraments to bind us, Father, heart and soul, mind and spirit. This is the prayer of a grateful, humble child in the name of Jesus, my Lord and my Savior Amen.

Worship 2   February 7   1 Corinthians 10:31

"Whatever you do, do everything for the glory of God."

Yesterday we looked at two reasons we should worship: to know God through hearing the Word preached or Bible study and through receiving the Sacraments. Today lets look at other reasons we worship. The primary reason we worship is to praise and give God thanks. It is not enough to just get to know God or to receive Him through His Word and Sacraments, we must respond in gratitude for all he has done for us, a bunch of undeserving sinners.

It is clear that God has chosen how he will spread faith in Himself through His Son, Jesus. The scripture tells us that Jesus came that we *"might have life and have it abundantly." (John 10:10)* The scripture also is clear in telling us that our main purpose is to worship and glorify God. The Ten Commandments tell us that God says to *"Have no other god's before me"* and to *"Remember the Sabbath and keep it Holy."* (Exodus 20; Deuteronomy 5) How can we do that better than in the context of worship in a place, the church, designed specifically for worship?

Here is another thought. God has given us all of those intangible things that make life worth living, our talents, our vocations, our spiritual gifts, our children, their children, our extended families, loved ones, friends we've met and are yet to meet, our health, our joy, eternity. Once we truly see how blessed we are, we should want to come and give God thanks - to worship and praise him as a family of believers so abundantly blessed. So, if you have not already, make a commitment to Worship regularly; fill yourself with Thanksgiving and ready yourself to receive God's Word and Sacraments. Let us fill our lives with prayer and thanks; Let us indeed glorify God and enjoy him forever!

Lord God, I come giving thanks for the many blessings of this life, so abundant, so undeserved, and yet, by your great grace, mine. I ask for one thing more, Lord. Calm my rebellious nature with all its restlessness and striving, give me a heart for you, Lord. For you and you alone deserve my praise, my worship, my very life. Fill me with your Presence and your Peace. Do this for Jesus' sake and for mine. In His name. Amen.

"Since no idol exists, there is nothing wrong with eating meat offered to one. However, if it causes even one convert to stumble, I will not eat it."

Do we as Christians have a responsibility to those who are weaker? Paul addresses this in our scripture today. As an example, he uses eating the discarded meat of animals offered as sacrifice to pagan idols. There were new converts to the Christian faith who were concerned about fellow Christians eating food which had been sacrificed to idols. Paul's basic answer was that since no idol is real, it is not wrong to eat the meat offered to one. Then he addresses the matter from a practical viewpoint, *"However, if it causes one convert to stumble, I will not eat it."*

Paul was talking about our responsibility to others, especially believers who are weaker in the faith. He was talking about making a sacrifice to give up something for another's sake. This gesture of sacrifice seems to be a foreign concept in the 21st Century! Today's attitude seems more like the one like I heard a movie star say when questioned about his life style: "If my lifestyle offends you, get used to it!" Most problems today exist because we have forgotten the basic principle Jesus taught about loving God completely and our neighbor as ourselves. Can you think of opportunities where you might sacrifice in order to help another person?

Health constraints abound for most of us: Low fat, no fat, less sugar, no sugar, some meat, no meat, to smoke or not to smoke, to exercise or to plan to, to caffeinate or decaf our lives and on and on; So many ways to sacrifice for others; So many ways to respect and assist others in their struggles; So many ways to love, really. For you I decline that free dessert or that second helping. For you I decline to smoke, although I've yet to make that decision for myself: For you. We cannot have a vital faith or good relationships without sacrifice. Christ willingly sacrificed himself on a cross for our sins. Can't we sacrifice even in a small way for another? In his Holy Name: for his glorious sake.

Lord God, I know that I need to help those who are weaker, but sometimes I just want to say, "What about me?" So concerned am I about my own feelings, my own needs, that I forget that to sacrifice for another is a privilege and a blessing from You; Forgive me. Renew me with your Holy Spirit day by day lest I fail in this opportunity to love someone else more than myself. In the name of Jesus, I pray. Amen.

"God Himself will provide."

In the 22nd Chapter of Genesis we find one of the most difficult passages of the Bible. It is the story of Abraham taking his son to a mountain as God had directed him and offering his son, Isaac, as a sacrifice to God. The whole request sounds archaic, outrageous, and unthinkable. Would God actually make such a request? Would God actually expect such a request to be followed? The amazing thing about this story is that Abraham does not question God, but acts in complete faith and trust in the God he knew and loved. I do not believe for a second that God intended for this sacrifice to take place. Rather, it was a way of testing his servant, Abraham. It is also a testing that most of us have trouble dealing with or explaining. We just cannot quite take this story in.

But this story is about obedience to God and God's faithfulness to us even in times when we do not understand. God's ways are not our ways. But we have to also approach this story from another point of view. Remember that God had promised Abraham a son who would carry his name and had promised that, *"His descendants would be as numerous as the stars."* That son was Isaac. So right off the bat, we question whether this will take place. Abraham acted out of an abiding faith and trust; he knew somehow that God would provide. Even as he and his son are making their way up the side of the mountain, Isaac turns to him and says, *"We have fire and wood, father, but where is the lamb for the offering?"* Abraham responds, *"God Himself will provide."* And of course, as the story concludes, God does; a ram caught in a nearby thicket serves as the sacrifice. Afterward, Abraham names the place, *'The Lord Will Provide"* because that is exactly what took place. This remarkable story is truly about faith lived and faith affirmed by life. Abraham acted out of faith, even as he understood not. Faith knows that even though you are troubled you trust that the Lord will provide at the right time and for the best benefit of all concerned.

Lord God, often I am troubled forgetting that you are truly sovereign; forgive my thoughtless presumption. Often I go through life foolishly trusting in myself; forgive my ignorance and unbelief. In times of testing, remind me that you always have my best interests at heart. Abraham knew and trusted the life of his beloved son in that faith. Give me the wisdom that in all times and in all places, I too may believe that You will provide. In Jesus' name, I pray. Amen.

Choose your Faith   February 10   John 15:5

"I am the vine and you are the branches. Those who abide in me and I in them bear much fruit, because apart from me you can do nothing."

We must "Choose carefully the faith we live by" for it can determine the outcome of our life. Faith can be viewed in several ways. You can think of faith as intellectual assent to certain creeds and doctrines. While we need creeds and doctrines to help spell out our faith, we cannot make them our faith. Faith can only be understood as a way of shaping our reality by seeing through the eyes of our God – it is a gift from our Creator. Expressing our faith using Creeds and doctrines can be helpful, yet without personal experience, faith is frozen or dead.

Now certainly our experiences vary greatly, but they should all lead us in the same direction: *To seek the one who sent the experience in the first place.* We begin by placing ourselves into the hands of the one who created us - God. There is where our assurance and confidence should lie. Faith is trusting that the reality we receive from God is real and trustworthy and that all will be finally right with those who trust it. We must throw ourselves completely into the arms of God and let Him form our reality. In that way faith is powerful. What we trust or see as real determines how we live our life. If we have faith that God is removed from us, our faith may cause us to live in despair. If, however, we believe that God is active in our lives and throw ourselves completely into His arms - that kind of faith enables us to live obediently, thankfully, and joyfully. Lets say that your father or mother loses their temper and hit you and you believe that they hate you; your life would be one of despair. But what if they hit you and your reality is tempered from above, seen through the eyes of God, realizing that most all people from time to time lose their temper; then you would live a life of hope. The same is true with God. If we have faith that God loves us and is trying to bring to us the very best for our lives, we can stop worrying, let Him be in charge and say, "O.K. Lord, I'm ready for what ever you have in mind for my life today."

Lord God, I come this day with a weary heart. I have looked at this world and those around me through my own eyes. Disappointment followed; harm was done. Help me to choose the faith found in Christ Jesus; to abide there at peace with you and myself. Help me to see this world, even myself, through the Savior's eyes. Apart from you, Lord, I can do nothing. This I know only too well. In the name of Jesus, I pray. Amen.

Grace and the Sacraments   February 11   1 Peter 1:3

"By His great mercy he has given us a new birth into a living hope through the resurrection of Jesus Christ from the dead."

Our acceptance in God's sight is His living Word in us: His Son Jesus living in our soul by the power of the Holy Spirit. That is the root of true love, all virtues of life, and it is the Seed of Eternal Life. 1st Peter tells us that we have been given a new birth "into a living hope" because Jesus rose from the dead. It goes on to say that we should rejoice even if for a while we "suffer various trials" in order for our faith to be tested because the outcome will be "salvation of our souls." Peter opens with this great hymn of praise regarding this life of grace freely given through Christ. That grace leads to our salvation if we are faithful to the love of God.

The Christian religion is somewhat mystical; it is also sacramental. To be honest, the sacraments are mysteries within themselves in which God's Spirit and our spirit work together under the power of His divine love. The sacraments are the "visible signs of an invisible Grace"; an external testimony to God's spiritual work in our soul. They are the outward signs that grace is ours. The sign is necessary for us; it is not necessary for God. It is something that awakens our hearts and our minds to respond to this grace that God has already given. We need these holy signs to continue to remind us what God has done and is doing. I know that some people will argue, "Why does it have to be this way?"

It is not for us to decide how God will communicate with us; He will be the one to determine the way in which He communicates and shares life. God begins by addressing us with His word. When we hear, receive His Word and respond, then we are moved to be baptized; cleansed by the waters of repentance; the first Sacrament. The second, the Eucharist, or the Lord's Supper nourishes us with the spiritual food represented by the wine and the bread that our Lord has given through His body and blood saying, "Do this in remembrance of me."

Lord God, I thank you that by your great mercy you have given me, a forgiven sinner, new life; that by the sacrifice of Jesus, I am given life for eternity. Forgive me when I forget these great truths or give them less weight in my decision-making than they deserve. Strengthen me day by day to receive this life as you intended. Help me to see you in all the ordinary things of life and in every face. In Jesus, I pray. Amen.

Grace and Sacraments 2   February 12   John 6:57f

"He who eats my flesh and drinks my blood abides in me and I in Him. The Father has sent me; I live because of the Father, you shall live because of me."

The scripture is clear, Jesus wants us to come to Him not just by faith, but through the sacraments, just take a good look at the scripture verses above. Now don't get too hung up on what seems to be but is not a literal interpretation. This passage is talking about those who "feed" on Jesus; those who seek their life from Him; those who look to Jesus for the answers of life; those who call Him Lord and Savior. To them Jesus says, "This is my body". It is a spiritual act fulfilled in a tangible way. When you partake of the sacrament, you eat the bread but you receive Christ.

There is a story in the Old Testament where Moses prayed in the wilderness for food and God sent them "manna", bread from heaven. This bread sustained them temporarily; this bread of Christ is forever, giving us eternal life! It is through faith and the sacraments of faith that we partake of the life of Jesus. We become one with Him in *"spirit and in truth."* We first become members of Christ by the sacrament of baptism; our souls are cleansed of sin and selfish desires. Now don't get the idea that now you no longer sin, your sins are covered by the righteousness of Jesus. Paul says in Ephesians 2, *"It is by Grace that we have been saved through faith; this is not our own doing, it is a gift of God."*

Through Baptism we accept this Christian life, leading us to give ourselves to Christ, renounce our sins, and dedicate ourselves to a life of love. The sacrament of "The Lord's Supper" reminds us of God's gift of His Son and our pledge to Him. Through the sacrament of the Lord's Supper we are continually renewed and made holy by the grace of Jesus. Faith and grace are gifts from God given to us as daily bread, manna from heaven. As you partake, remember God and His Son Jesus and all that He has done in your life. Then give thanks!

Lord, I ask for your forgiveness, your patience. For I know the life you have called me to live, yet I continue to live the life I want. You have called me into union with you through Jesus, and yet I refuse; have mercy. Give me strength and wisdom. Through the Sacraments, make me one with Christ. I am yours this day, Father. Tomorrow, we begin again. I pray in the name of the one whom you gave, Jesus, the Christ. Amen.

Grace through Faith   **February 13**   *Romans 1:17*

"For the Righteousness of God is revealed through faith for faith; as it is written,
"The one who is righteous will live by faith."

Most Christians should be familiar with the term, "Salvation by grace - through faith." In case you aren't, this is an important Biblical principal, the cornerstone of the Reformation Movement, beginning in the 16th century by Martin Luther. Luther was a monk and theologian during the time that the church was issuing "indulgences" (in essence, giving money or land to the church so the church would grant you salvation). Luther in his studies of the scripture found himself at odds with the church on indulgences; he was not the first, Wycliffe did so in the 14th century.

In studying scripture, Luther ran across Paul's letter to the Romans where he discovered an answer to a problem that had hounded him for years: "The Righteousness of God". That discovery lead Luther to understand we do not earn salvation or have a right to purchase it by means of money, land, or good deeds, but that salvation comes by grace through faith. Paul says in chapter 3:28, *"We hold that a person is justified by faith apart from works of law."* Salvation by grace through faith means we cannot earn or purchase God's favor. It is a free gift (that's what grace means!).

Grace is God's hand outstretched to us in love through Christ; Faith means stretching out our hands to accept God's grace, trusting in God's forgiveness and love rather than our own "righteousness" or "good works." If your salvation depends in any way on your good works or ability to do good works on your own, then what was the purpose of Jesus giving His life on the cross? Good works are merely a reflection of Jesus living inside us. The Bible is clear about this: Romans 3:10, *"There is none righteous, no not one"*; and 3:22, *"All sin and have fallen short of the glory of God."* Grace is God's gift to all who would receive, even faith is His gift; without it we could not turn from trusting ourselves to trusting Him.

Lord God, I bow before you this day giving thanks for the grace I have received through Jesus .In past times, I have relied on my own so-called goodness to find favor with you; I have even thought that I am not that hard to love, all things considered. In this way I have failed you; forgive me. Open my eyes to see my true sinfulness: but just a glimpse. The full truth, as you know, would crush me. For a fresh start I would give my life. This is my prayer for Jesus, and for me. Amen.

Play Christians   *February 14*   *Luke 14:20*

"If you want to be my disciple, you must sit down and count the cost."

Are you a "Play Christian"? That theme came to me via a friend who goes to another church. Her family has belonged to a denomination different than mine for generations. And if the truth be known, I think she would love to be a part of my denomination. Anyway, since I cannot be her real pastor, she calls me her "Play Pastor." The truth of that description hit me. That's the way many people approach Christianity. Jesus said so in the text for today. Dietrich Bonhoeffer pointed out what discipleship entails in a book he wrote called, "The Cost of Discipleship." Certainly following Jesus, giving your life to Him, will bring with it a *"peace that passes all understanding,"* but also there is a tremendous cost.

There are a lot of people today who not only don't want to count the cost; they believe they can be a Christian without obeying our Lord. They are at best just "Play Christians," pretending that God's not interested in our life, our ways. Some folks feel, "Well, I can be a Christian without going to church." Or, "I can be a Christian without ever giving of my time and talents and tithes to God's Kingdom." Some feel they can be a Christian without giving Jesus their hearts, or wishes, or sins.

So my advice to anyone who believes any of these things is: at least be honest with yourself! Call Him Jesus if you must. Call Him the Son of God if you want. But let's make no pretenses - He is not your Lord. Jesus said there is a price tag for being His disciple and it comes through service. Matthew 20:26f, *"If you wish to be great; you must be a servant, if you wish to be first, you must be a slave. For the Son of man came not to be served, but to serve and give His life as a ransom for many."* So let us count the cost of our commitment to Jesus. I guess what I am saying is this, "Do we want to be a Play Christian or a Real One?"

Lord, open my heart that I may look truthfully at the way I choose to live my life as a Christian. This step won't be easy for either of us, Father; real discipleship never is. Help me to be honest with myself and you. Silence the rationalizations for my failures that will surely come. No excuse is good enough, never was, never will be. I ask for Jesus to be not only my Savior but also my Lord. Grant me this wish For Jesus, for me. Amen.

Deny Yourself   *February 15*   *Mark 8:34*

"If anyone would come after me, let them deny themselves, take up their cross and follow me."

There is a scripture in Mark 8, also found in Matthew 16:24 and Luke 9:23, that tells us we must "deny ourselves" if we would become a follower of Jesus. At first glance we may suppose it means to become a martyr. But this little scripture does not mean we must deny getting some of the things we want, like that piece of chocolate, or your favorite ice cream cone, or even the opportunity to play golf on a beautiful afternoon. It means to "Renounce the Self." Let go of control and give it over to Christ. Let Christ be your Lord rather than yourself or money or other things of this world and *"Take up your cross."*

Many take that to mean that we will have hardships to bear. I'm not saying that we will not have to endure whatever life brings, we will and some of these things will severely test our faith. I am saying this is not what Jesus meant. We will face trials whether we follow Jesus or not! To take up our cross means to willingly give up our right to our self and to take on the life of Jesus. It is to stand firm for the faith and for God and the Gospel and for what Christ would do in the same circumstance.

On one hand, this is humanly impossible; on the other hand we must remember that Jesus himself is within us, picking us up when we fall, forgiving us when we make mistakes; strengthening us to carry our cross. Then this scripture says, *"Follow me."* That is not a passive statement like sheep following the shepherd around, but an active statement of living as Jesus would if he were here in the flesh; it is the call to walk in His shoes; to live out the love He lived, forgive as He forgives, to accept as He accepts, to comfort others, to forget about yourself and to realize that Jesus is sufficient for all your needs. Wow, what a Savior! What a life to be lived!

Lord God, life is hard and people can be so difficult. Give me the will to take up the cross of every situation and to carry that cross willingly, gratefully, knowing, that it is you I'm following, you my actions reveal. I'm not that person now. I refuse to deny myself, thinking only of my needs, my all ready over-burdened life. For all the times I've failed you, forgive me, O Gracious Father. Help me to be the kind of Christian you have called me to be, to minister to others as Christ has ministered to me. O God of second chances, may I have another? This is my prayer in the name of Jesus. Amen.

The Narrow Door February 16 Luke 13:24

"Strive to enter through the narrow door; for many, I tell you, will try to enter and will not be able."

I was a teacher before answering the call to become a minister. There are two methods of teaching: the deductive method where you guide students to reason from the general to the specific; the inductive method where you guide them to reason from the specific to the general. If we compare that to life, the deductive method would be one where, in the beginning, anything goes; a do as you please, whenever you please, to whomever you please. Don't like school? Quit - drop out! Want to run around acting like a kid all your life? Go ahead - it's your life. Now at first, the deductive method seems great! You get to live and do as you please, but as time passes, everything begins to fall apart. Due to a lack of education, good jobs pass you by; because you are unfaithful, your spouse leaves you, and so on. Life goes from wide to narrow.

Then the inductive method is one where you narrow your options. You think about others first, you do things you like, but not at the expense of others. You stay in school even if you don't like it; you come to church even though you had rather stay in bed; you stay away from drugs even though you would like to experience them; you are faithful to your spouse even though you are tempted to stray. In the beginning, the inductive method seems confining but then good jobs come your way because you stuck with your studies; your marriage gets better and better because you give of yourself out of love; life gets freer, until you experience real freedom. In one way, the door to come into the Kingdom is "wide open", who you are and what you have done matters not. Also the door is "narrow"; meaning you must be willing to give up something. That something is your will, your right to your self. You must leave behind your will and accept God's will for your life; let him mold you and guide you.

Lord God, I come today giving thanks that you have called me to enter through the narrow door. But why must giving up my will, my right to own my life, be so hard? Not to mention all the other lives I want to run! I would like to do as I want when I want, but I know that way of living has consequences. I know, Father, you want only my good. Lead me down the narrow way, Lord, that each day I might grow in grace and love. Lord, I do so want to be free. In Jesus' name, I pray. Amen.

Resist Temptation   *February 17*   *1 Corinthians 10:1f*

"I do not want you to be ignorant of the fact that our forefathers were all under the cloud and all passed through the sea .... nevertheless, God was displeased with them because they were engaging in sin."

Today let's talk about "Resisting Temptation." It is a topic that we all need to know more about, because old Satan is very good at luring us into sin! To tell the truth, most of the time, he does not have to work too hard, does he? It just seems that we have a difficult time learning from our many mistakes. Not only do we keep committing the same sins over and over, we are committing the same sins that have been committed for generations! There is truly nothing new under the sun!

In 1ˢᵗ Corinthians Paul gives a warning to the people of Corinth, citing Israel's History. He says don't be ignorant of the fact that our forefathers were under the cloud and passed through the sea. All ate the same spiritual food and drank the same spiritual drink; nevertheless, *"God was displeased with them."* Then Paul points out the reason -*"Because they were engaging in idolatry and sin."* Now the truth of the matter is, we all sin. All of us, even those we consider to be saints! Paul points this out in Romans 3:23, *"All have sinned and fall short of the glory of God."*

We are all sinners, but God is calling us to repent of our sins, and to turn to him. He tells us that he will not lay any burdens upon us too great for us to handle. He also tells us that he will provide for us a way out so that we may be able to endure. Most of us have fallen to temptation because we went looking for it. You know what I mean don't you? We allow our minds to wander and wish and before you know it temptation has consumed us! The cure? Give your will to God!

Lord God, I give thanks for this wonderful new day in my life. I'm going to need you today I can already tell. I'm feeling overwhelmed. Will you walk with me especially close? Keep me focused on you, Father, for the world is ever near and I'm not as strong as I think. Thank you for Jesus who gave me your grace. Thank you for your Holy Spirit, which brings me your strength and wisdom. Every day evil works to bombard me with lies and half-lies so tempting to believe. Save me from myself and the Evil One. Cover me with your most gracious wings. Here I go, Lord, walking in His footsteps, walking in the footsteps of Jesus! In His name. Amen.

"Then the Lord God formed man from the dust of the ground, and breathed into his nostrils the bread of life; and he became a living being."

Let me ask you, "What do you want more than anything in life?" I know that question opens up a can of worms. There is no telling how some would answer! What I believe every person, church or un-churched, would eventually say is, "I want to live forever without stress or pain. I want to be resurrected into eternal life." These wishes do not go together; being immortal and being resurrected are very different. By definition, immortality is "life - not subject to death." There is one certainty of life and that is we shall all die. Never the less, we want our soul to live on.

Why is that so important? We believe that somehow we had something to do with developing our soul even though scripture makes it clear that we did not. God created both our body and our soul and when we die, all of us dies. And if you somehow believe that you had something to do with building your soul, then you may be a part of the world Jesus came to save, but not one who belongs to him. For Jesus' words are addressed to sinners, not "the righteous." Until we realize that we are sinful, totally depraved, having no motive that is not at least tainted with sin, and realize that Jesus died for our sins then salvation is just a dream. By definition, resurrection means, "being brought back to life again."

For the believer, Christ lived for us, died for us, and rose again to a resurrected life for us. Now, repent and give your life to Jesus. Some make that a one-time thing. I repent. Jesus changes me so that I sin no more; I don't make any more stupid mistakes. Not so. We must die to our old self every day, be forgiven and receive new life; relying upon God is not a one time thing. Once we die for good, we shall be raised to eternal life. But for now, we need to go to the Father for our "daily bread."

Lord God, forgive me your child for I continue to desire that which cannot be mine. I want to live forever; I cannot - at least not on this earth in this body. I continue to try and save myself by my "goodness", thinking I am somehow better than others because of the way I live my life; I am not. I am sin, I know this; I've always known this since I've known you. Will you forgive? Restore me to your side, Father, that I may again feel you breathe your Life into me, giving me a living soul, built for eternity, and for all my todays until then. In the name of Jesus I pray. Amen.

"Arise, shine; for your light has come, and the glory of the Lord has risen upon you."

If I were to ask you to name what you consider to be ingredients of a great year in your life or the life of your church, how would you answer? I am sure that some of you would say, "If my salary were to double this year that would constitute a great year." No disappointments; no loss, a life without stress; a life full of peace; that would constitute a great year. If you were to consider your church, you might say, "To have 20 new members (in a small church) or a 100 new members (in a large church) would translate into a great year." And in many ways you would be correct, and yet you may have missed the point.

Let us look at this wonderful verse from Isaiah, *"Arise and shine; for your light has come, and the glory of the Lord has risen upon you."* Certainly if you consider the things we have mentioned above, then *"the glory of the Lord HAS risen upon you!"* But what about the first part? Yes, *"the glory of the Lord has risen upon you"*, so now *"Arise and Shine."* This could be your best year yet! Not in numbers or in salary, for that would be missing the point. Success cannot always be measured in accumulations and accomplishments. If we grow in our faith, if we grow closer to those we love, if we become more committed; then it will be a great year.

One of the secrets to success is to know who you are and where you are going. Life can be a burden if you go it alone; it can be a joy if you know that Christ is with you every step of the way, carrying you over the rough roads, thru the swamps, and over the mountains. Success does not happen because we are great, it happens because we are faithful. *"Glory has come upon us"* because *"the Lord has risen upon us."* If that has happened, it does not matter that our life is still full of disappointments and stress for God has blessed us and Jesus will carry us every step of the way. Now, remember your calling to "arise and shine".

It's a new day, Lord, but life is hard and I am tired. Could I just sit this one out? Forgive me when I try and go it alone, for I know that my strength is in you. Help me to grow in faith that I may see blessings in all of life's circumstances. Coax me to let go of my worldly ways; that is the real blessing of life: to feel and experience your presence and respond: to arise and shine! The new day awaits and I must be about my Father's work; your love is my destiny and my privilege. In the name of Jesus, I pray. Amen.

*"Because no prophecy ever came by human will, but men and women
moved by the Holy Spirit spoke from God."*

Peter says that "men and women" were under the control of
God's Holy Spirit and the message they spoke came from God through
the power of God's spirit. This scripture is talking about "inner life." There is
external life in which we live our life through what we see with our eyes
and hear, feel and taste. When we live our life in that way, we rely on
gossip and what we see to tell us who people are. We become critical
and judgmental and think that we are right and others are wrong. Paul
calls this "living in the Flesh", or living by the way of this world.

Then there is life inside us by which we live believing and trusting in
Jesus, truly accepting Him with our heart and our heart is changed. Our
life is no longer our own, but belongs to Jesus. Jesus is our master. We
allow Jesus to take over our being and we see this world and others
through His eyes; through the eyes of compassion and acceptance and
forgiveness because we know that we are as great a sinner as those we
would like to be critical of and we know that God forgave us. Therefore
we want to forgive others and help bring them closer to God.

When we live that way everything looks different because we
realize that our eyes deceive us and trick us. God is in control. He is in
control of our hearts, our souls, our minds, our fears, our doubts, and when
that happens, "everything has become new." We then realize that it is by
God's grace that people are transformed and it is by His grace that we
have life inside us as well as outside us. Jesus then becomes the most vital
element in our life. He is our reason for being. He is our joy; He is our
purpose; He is our everything. Our whole life changes from worry to one
of joy and thanksgiving because we know that God so loved us that He
placed His son on this earth to undergo the unimaginable just for us.

*Lord God, it is so tempting for me to live my life in an external way,
forgetting that you are the one who made me, forgetting that I am yours; forgive
me. Transform my selfish spirit; it dishonors us both; it grieves the Holy Spirit.
Indeed, by your grace, it grieves me. Yet, I remain human and flawed. The
external life looks so right until I look at life through the eyes of your Son, Jesus.
Give me grace to see this world and those around me as you see them. Take away
my fears; replace them with your joy and hope. In Jesus' name. Amen*

Giving Thanks   February 21   2 Thessalonians 1:3f

"We give thanks to God for you, brothers and sisters, as is right, because your faith grows abundantly, and your love for one another is increasing."

Paul says, "We give thanks to God for you... as is right." I am sure that if you sit down and spend a few minutes thinking about your life you can find many things for which to be thankful. Certainly the most important being God's Grace. God reached his hand out to us in love through Christ. To receive that love takes faith, stretching out our hand to accept God's Grace. To do so is to trust in God's loving forgiveness rather than our own righteousness and good works. If we are truly thankful and love the Lord, "our life would surely show it" as the little song goes.

The great Christian writer, Bonhoeffer, who was killed in prison by the Nazi's, was opposed to what he called "cheap grace". This is probably the downfall of many Christians. Cheap grace "believes that God gives us pardon for our sins without demanding repentance and obedience." Yes, God freely gives us his pardon, if not grace is not free. But we must not forget that grace cost Jesus his life and it must cost us something also. Let me make this perfectly clear. We are justified apart from our works, but we are sanctified through works of love.

Look at it like this. Once faith has had its birth in us, once we belong wholly to Jesus, we will bear fruit; we will show love, understanding and forgiveness to others because Christ lives in us. And although the grace we received must lead to discipleship, we must also remember that the one bringing forth obedience and works is the Holy Spirit dwelling within. We do not do this so that we can receive salvation; we do this because we love the in dwelling Lord. There is a cost to belonging to the Lord. That cost is not "we MUST do good works", but that we give control of our heart to Jesus willingly and for all time. Jesus is either Lord of our life or he is not - period! The fruit of the Spirit is merely proof that Jesus possesses our heart at the moment the good deed takes place.

Lord God, I gripe and complain about what I don't have rather than giving thanks for what I do, forgive me. You deserve better. You have blessed me so in Jesus, yet I take all that you have done for me for granted, forgive me. Let me wholly give my heart to you that your Holy Spirit may dwell within me. Give me a grace afire in love and praise that I may be grateful in all that I do; for all that comes undeservedly my way. In Jesus name; my joy; my Lord. Amen.

"In Christ we have obtained an inheritance… So that we may have hope in Christ and live in Him."

God chooses us; ever thought about that? Paul says in Ephesians 1:4, *"Just as God chose us in Christ before the foundation of the world. He predestined us to be His children through Jesus."* Why? So God could bestow upon us His wonderful grace. In Christ *"we become children of God."* In God's world there are no illegitimate children. Each of us is a child of God *"in Christ."* We are chosen. We are his children in Jesus Christ. Jesus set us free. Jesus was born into this world to let us know that we are chosen and forgiven by God, now live your life fresh and new each day, don't be trapped by the sins and mistakes of yesterday.

In Ephesians Paul tells us that we have obtained an inheritance through Christ, *"So now we have hope and live in Him."* I'm sure that if you examine your life closely, you will admit you have done a few things that were pretty tough to swallow. This past year some have made a lot of money, some have lost their job; some experienced divorce, illness; some lost loved ones near and dear to them. Those things have caused much stress and strain on these tired old bodies of ours. To you, Paul says, *"If you are in Christ, you have been set free."*

But remember, our freedom came with a price; Jesus gave His very life for our freedom and forgiveness. In Christ we have been set free, but just as our freedom is a gift of Grace, it requires a response. Do you say the Lord's Prayer? Believe in it? *"Forgive us our sins as we forgive those who sin against us."* You see God offers us forgiveness, but to be set free from our sins we must forgive one another. To refuse to let go of the offences of another is to refuse the mercy of God. So although we have been set free "in Christ" - to be "in Christ" we must set others free. That is what God said and I for one believe He means what He says.

Lord God, I come today with a new desire to be "in Christ". I have chosen to live otherwise. Will you forgive, Father, and cleanse my self-centered self? So willing am I to ask for forgiveness but unwilling to offer it, have mercy, Father. I have used the mind you've given me to rationalize my failures and transfer my guilt to others. I am enslaved in my sin, refusing to acknowledge it. Set me free with your grace that I may be "in Christ". In His name. Amen.

"Pray always and do not lose heart"

In the 18th chapter of Luke, we find Jesus telling the parable of the "Unjust Judge" to his disciples. The story is told as an example of prayer. Jesus tells them to *"pray always so you will not lose heart."* Then, He follows with this parable as an example so they will never forget. *"In a certain city is a judge who does not respect God nor people."* A widow comes to him for justice. It was a judge's duty in that day to see to it that widows were taken care of, but evidently this judge had taken a "kick back" from the landowner and would not hear her case.

The widow, however, was not about to let the judge off the hook easily. She went to his house and pestered him night and day until he finally gave her justice - not because of his compassion; not because it was the right thing to do, but *"I will grant her justice so that she may not wear me out by continuing to bother me."* Now Jesus compared God to that unjust judge. If this unjust judge will hear the widow's case, how much more will our heavenly Father who loves us and knows us listen? Jesus is reminding the disciples (and us) that when we go in prayer to God, we are not appearing before an unjust judge - but a loving Father.

We need to trust that God will listen to us. He may not give what we want, but He will provide all we need. And since faith is a gift from God through His Holy Spirit, prayer is the most important way of seeking it. We must resort to prayer constantly all through our life of faith because through prayer we receive help and guidance for our daily living. Go to God every day and ask for faith and what ever is needed for the moment, God will provide. God will hand out the necessary faith to answer our need for that moment. So pray and *"Do not loose heart".*

Lord, I come gratefully knowing that you will listen for you are my Heavenly Father. You sent your son that I may better know and understand who you are and how much you love and care for me. Thank you, thank you! Come and comfort me so that I may not lose heart. Give me faith to believe and to withstand the temptations which will come my way. Compel my heart to whisper your Name: Jesus! Jesus! a constant prayer. For I know that whatever I need for this day you will provide. How could you, the God of all Grace, overlook even one glance of love? In the name of Jesus, I humbly pray. Amen.

All things are Possible February 24 Matthew 19:26

"For mortals it is impossible, but for God all things are possible.'"

As you move forward in your faith and devotion to Jesus Christ, there are several things of which you need to be mindful. None as important as remembering who you are, your relationship to God as one of His people; your calling to be His Light in a world filled with darkness. As you do that, let us recall this scripture from Matthew. The disciples have just heard Jesus telling a rich man he must *"sell all that he has, give it to the poor, and then come and follow him."* The man walks away because, *"He had many possessions".* He just could not let go. He was too attached.

Jesus turns to the disciples and says, *"How difficult it will be for a rich man to enter the Kingdom of Heaven."* The disciples are in shock and ask, *"Then who can be saved?"* Jesus said, *"For mortals it is impossible, but for God all things are possible."* This scripture was talking specifically about our salvation, but it also refers to everything in our life. We mortals worry, doubt, fear; have insecurities about our future. But when it comes to God, *"All things are possible."* I concur! I have been in the ministry over 30 years, 10 more counting the time I spent working with youth and music before being ordained and I have witnessed that truth over and over.

First, to think that God would call a sinner like me into the ministry and convince me to give my life in service to Him is a miracle within itself, knowing how I so want to control my own life! Also in all seven churches I have served I have witnessed that truth. Several churches dreamed big dreams without knowing how it could possibly come true. God made it come to pass. A new building; a rise out of the ashes of death from 38 people attending to over 300; lives changed; people converted - big dreams come from God. We may dare to doubt God's dreams; we may even question His wisdom, but deep down in our hearts we know that, *"all things are possible,"* with God.

Lord God, I know you have called us to be your light in this dark world, but I am weak and I fail you so often. Forgive me. I feel overwhelmed. Doubt seeps in and tells me "that is not possible". Strengthen me for the calling you have in mind for me. Let me dream your dreams and walk the path you set before me knowing, trusting, and believing that with you, Lord, "all things are possible". This is my earnest prayer in the name of Jesus. Amen.

Don't lose Focus **February 25** *1 Corinthians 1:10f*

"I appeal to you, brothers and sisters, by the name of our Lord Jesus Christ,
that all of you be in agreement and that there be no divisions among you,
but that you be united in the same mind and the same purpose."

When we as Christians lose our focus, we are in, can I say, "grave danger." Often what is destructive are not major issues but people disagreeing about the color of the new rug or the new preacher verses the old one. It's so easy to lose focus. Someone hurts you and you want to hurt back. Your spouse leaves you for another and you want to make sure they pay and pay dearly! Something goes wrong at work, it's not our fault, but we get the blame and we lash out at the one who pointed the finger at us. All of these things can cause us to lose our focus on Christ.

Paul was very sensitive to this possibility. Paul, you see, wanted the Corinthians to focus once again on Jesus, their Savior. He wanted them to understand that everyone has a purpose and something to contribute to God's work. After Paul left Corinth, Apollos arrived and began work there. It is believed that Apollos was a traveling merchant from Alexandria who was a deeply committed Christian. He was very persuasive and some were so taken with him that they began to form clicks saying, *"I belong to Apollos."* Others said, *"I belong to Paul."* Problems arose.

Paul responded, *"Has Christ been divided?"* The answer, "of course not." They were not followers of Paul or Apollos but of Christ. They no longer focused on Christ but the messengers of Christ and that was the problem. Throughout the history of the church, God has been able to use people with different gifts. Just because some focus on the emotions of faith and others on the facts of faith does not mean that we have two churches or that Christ should be divided. There is only one church, one God, one Lord in whom we trust. If Christians can't get along with each other, then what kind of example do we leave for others to see?

Lord God, it is so easy for me to be led astray. I know you know this. Life can be difficult and people can be difficult and all of us can feel betrayed and disappointed by hurtful words said in anger to enrage or to divide. Have mercy on us and help us to see that the world is watching how we treat one another, watching to see if we truly believe in your hope and love enough to live it in our everyday life. Keep my focus on you, Jesus. Guard my heart and my ways. It is in your name, Lord, I pray. Amen.

Baptism: Give our heart   February 26   Matthew 3:15

"After John told Jesus, "I need to be baptized by you!" Jesus said, "Let it be so (you baptize me); for it is proper for us in this way to fulfill all righteousness."

Here in Matthew we find the Baptism of Jesus. There are some puzzling aspects to this scripture. Why would Jesus need to be baptized? He is God's Son! Since He had no sins to be forgiven why would he need this sign to show that he belongs to God? But in order for God to identify with us, Jesus had to do this. Many ask, "Can God identify with what I am going through? Can God understand my suffering, fear of dying or the weight that my mistakes have placed on my heart? How can God understand me if he in fact has never experienced what I experience?"

On the banks of the Jordan, Jesus shows us how. He identified with us. Jesus came to suffer and die and carry the weight of the sins of the world so that God would know what it is like to be a man. Here God shows us that He became like us in order to enable us to become like him. Our baptism helps us to identify with Jesus. Through our baptism, we become sons and daughters of God, filled with God's love and goodness. We receive the righteousness of God by being baptized with Jesus.

Now this does not mean we are now good, for our goodness is in direct relationship to the degree in which we allow God to control our hearts. We cannot be understanding or loving or compassionate or caring of others if we control our hearts. Baptism is the act of giving our hearts to God. Thus begins the life-long battle of our will, as we try to take back control, verses leaving our will in God's capable hands. We like to think we can make "good" decisions apart from consulting Jesus. But if we can, how do we belong to Him? Why would he need to come save us, if we can do that for ourselves? If we are to be truly loving and caring and full of God's righteousness, then God must own our hearts.

Lord God, I give thanks that you have been here in the flesh. For through that act, I know that you understand what I face each and every day. Often I try and carry the weight of my sins, facing all obstacles alone, behaving for all to see as the spiritually orphaned child I'm not by God's grace. Can you forgive me? Gracious God, give me the wisdom to turn my will over to you and leave it there, trusting your plan and direction for my life. Guide my steps, O Lord of my life. Guide my will. In Jesus I pray. Amen.

"Do not talk evil of another, but speak to build others up – so that it may impart the grace of God upon them."

There is an illness in our country and it seems to have drifted over into our media. Heaven knows, I am not advocating that we give our stamp of approval on immoral actions or sexual misconduct. And while I believe it to be fine for the press to expose the "goings-on" of those in political office, it seems that the media has been on a rampage to "dig up" every misconduct they can. Never mind how long ago it happened. Never mind that they may have been sorry for their actions and repented of them. Never mind they learned the truth of what gives real pleasure in life, serving our Lord Jesus. They sinned and the public MUST know!

The real harm comes when we as Christians participate by speaking evil of them, pointing out their mistakes and sins, as if we are perfect! What is wrong, it seems to me anyway, is we are so busy searching for wrong and being critical of those who are imperfect, that we miss the truth. We are all imperfect beings. People do wrong - allow their old nature to take over with its greed and lusts - but when we try to correct them by using our "old nature" (speaking evil of them, running them down, criticizing them) what does that say about us?

The solution comes to us via the Apostle Paul, "Let your words be a blessing to others." My mother used to say to me, "Son, if you cannot find something nice to say about someone, don't say anything." Christians are called to remind others of their higher calling to build others up. To tell of the goodness that can be a part of them if they allow God's Holy Spirit to guide them and not be caught up in their "old nature". So whenever you are tempted to attack the character of another, just remember that we are all imperfect - choose to find something good to say - lift them up - let your words be a blessing to them.

Lord God, it is so easy to be critical, to find fault in others. What better way to take the spotlight off ourselves! Forgive me; make me worthy of the sacrifice you made for my salvation. Remind me that I too am a sinner in need of your great Grace. Give me a sprit of gratitude that I may be a blessing to others and through the things I say, may your Grace be imparted to them through the Holy Spirit. In the name of Jesus. Amen.

Climb the Tree   February 28   Luke 19:5

"When Jesus was passing through Jericho, he saw a man in a sycamore tree. He looked up and said to him, "Zacchaeus, hurry and come down; for I must stay at your house today."

Today lets deal with the story of Zacchaeus. It is a powerful story, which can help as we go through this season of Lent - the 40 days before Holy Week when we search our hearts and remember what Jesus did for us on Maundy Thursday, Good Friday and Easter. Zacchaeus was a tax collector and it had made him wealthy. When he encountered Jesus in this story, his whole life changed and he promised to give to the poor and repay anyone he defrauded by returning 4 fold! Because of this, Jesus told him, *"Salvation has come to this house today."*

Now one important point we must not overlook is found in verse 3, *"He was trying to see Jesus."* Somehow Zacchaeus knew his life was not right and he was trying to see this Rabbi who everyone was talking about, the one who could forgive sins and make life new. We are much like Zacchaeus in many ways. We look for life in worldly things: money, wealth, power, in busyness. We will spend time with God in prayer and meditation if there is any time left over in our busy day! We go to church and bible study if time permits or if we are not worn out from our busy life! "There are so many important things out there we must attend to", we say to ourselves.

And who is the loser? We are. We try to satisfy ourselves with worldly possessions rather than spiritual ones. Like Zacchaeus, we need to come to the point in our life where we seek after Jesus: climb a tree if you must, walk a mile, just let the man from Galilee come in. Let Jesus be your shepherd, let him lead you beside still waters, give you rest in green pastures, restore your soul. Then and only then can we be the persons God created us to be and witnesses of his love and grace.

Lord God, I come today in prayer asking for your forgiveness. I need it more than I deserve it, for I continue to seek after the things of this world and neglect the more important things of the Spirit. More honestly said, I neglect you, Father. Help me to see and do what ever is necessary to find my peace in you. In the name of Jesus. Amen.

Be Careful how you Live March 1 Ephesians 5:15f

"Be careful how you live, not as unwise people...."

It would be good to take stock once in a while on how we use our time. Paul says, "Be careful how you live, not as unwise people, but as wise, making the most of time, because the days are evil. Don't be foolish; understand the will of the Lord." The story of most healthy Christians goes like this: we begin our Christian conversion at the age of 12 or thereabouts. Most of the time during those early years we would be considered unwise. As we listen and try and understand the will of the Lord, we begin to move more toward wisdom. Make no mistake. In this lifetime we will never fully gain wisdom, for we are imperfect beings.

Paul goes on to tell us how to find the will of the Lord. He says be filled with the Spirit; cultivate a positive attitude; "Address one another in psalms, hymns, - make melody to the Lord with all your heart." The unwise use of time causes us to focus on the negative. Ask yourself honestly, "Am I selfish? Do I gossip? Am I prone to anger, hate, violence? Do I hide in alcohol or drugs, or sensual pleasures?" If so, evil has tricked you into discounting the search for the Lord's will. In order to use time wisely, we must focus on the positive. Go to God in prayer, lift up those negative, God will unburden your heart. Let God be a part of ALL of your life.

You see many tell of all the wrong that has occurred in their life and how they have been mistreated. That occupies their mind with the negative. Instead we are to tell people of the significant things God has done. How He has touched us and helped us through difficult moments; how worship has inspired us; how worship, music, the Bible, and the faith of fellow Christians have had a positive impact. Let those significant moments occupy your time and your mind. When the negative consumes our mind, we are controlled by doubt, anxiety, and hopelessness. When we turn it over to Christ, we discover that "all things are possible with God" and Christ will fill us with hope.

Lord, I only see the glass half-empty. The 24-hour news cycle provides a smorgasbord of tragedy perpetrated by mankind; proof that evil is unleashed, unchecked as feared. Is it that I can't see you at work, Father, or that I don't want to see? Is winning the negative argument more important to me than sensing the presence of God? Dissect my heart, Lord; tell me what you see; then fix me. Do this for Jesus, for me. Amen.

Relationships: Be Subject *March 2* Ephesians 5:21

"Be subject to one another out of reverence for Christ."

This is a topic that has always drawn a little debate. What does the Bible say about relationships within the household or family? Many Christians can quote Ephesians 5:22, *"Wives, be subject to your husbands."* Some might even remember 5:25, *"Husbands, love your wives, just as Christ loved the church and gave himself up for her."* But most really don't have a clue as to what Paul means. Paul is spelling out a healthy relationship between husbands and wives, which applies to everyone.

Men in Paul's time ruled their homes according to the law of the day. Women and children and slaves were property, just like horses and tables. The man held the power of life and death over them all. Paul does not challenge that authority just the exercise of it. Paul says that husbands are to love their wives so much they are willing to forfeit their own life for them, as Christ did for the church (Verse 25). The wife is to voluntarily subject herself to her husband and he puts it this way. *'The law says your husband owns you, I say you can demonstrate your obedience to Christ by being subject to your husband."*

If you look at the text that introduces these verses to us (5:21), you can see the radical nature of Paul and Christian relationships, *"Be subject to one another out of reverence for Christ."* Paul did say husbands are to be the head of the house, meaning they are to take full responsibility for seeing to it that the family is cared for, not so they may somehow abuse those within their family. In 6:4, he says to fathers, *"Do not provoke your children to anger, but bring them up in the Lord."* This is all a unique and revolutionary relationship between husbands and wives, parents and children. If you decide that you want to be Christian, Paul reminds his readers, it requires a mutual subjection. Subject yourselves to each other and to Christ.

Lord, it is hard to have good relationships especially in the family. We are all so self-centered, controlling, manipulative, and so alike! Such behavior goes back generations in my family! Grudges so hard to lay down, guilt so addictive. How wise of you, Lord, to ask us to sacrifice our will out of reverence for you. We would do anything for you; even cede power when we hold the best hand. With practice, Lord, we can even do it for each other. Out of reverence, Lord, for you. Out of love. In Jesus' name. Amen.

"Jesus asked them, "Do you think that because these Galileans suffered in this way they were worse sinners than all other Galileans? No, I tell you; but unless you repent you will perish just as they did."

We find in scripture several places where people come to Jesus asking if tragedy had befallen a person or persons because they were great sinners. In the "Sermon on the Mount" (Matthew 4:45) Jesus had this to say, *"God makes the sun rise on the evil and the good alike."* Then in a story from Luke 13, where Pilate had slaughtered many Galileans, people asked, *"Were they greater sinners than other Galileans?"* Jesus answered, *"No, I tell you! But unless you repent you will perish just as they did."* As much as we would like to think so, God does not always reward us for our good or punish us for our bad - not at least in this world.

Here is what we are left to live with, "If we want real justice - immediately - all the time – it won't happen - we will have to wait until judgment day." Another truth is that sometimes, bad things happen to good, decent people just because they were in the wrong place at the wrong time, or because of the consequences of the physical laws that govern our universe. Many a book has been written and many a thought contemplated on the subject of the sovereignty of God. Our problem is we want control over those things that affect our life. It will never happen.

We may carry a rabbit's foot, check our horoscope, even call the psychic hot line in order to know and control our fate, but the truth is it doesn't work. It is just wishful thinking. "Luck" finally runs out. We have only our faith to depend on. By faith, we must willingly surrender control of our lives to God and blindly accept his perfect will. Until we do, we are living on cheap grace; claiming the right to be a part of God's kingdom, without any responsibility to God. Jesus gave himself for us on the cross and if we do not give our life to him then we are living by wishful thinking.

Lord God, I have tried to live by wishful thinking. I want everything to go the way I want. I am inconsiderate of others. This universe belongs to you, yet I try to control fate. Are these the ways of someone who knows you, trusts you, loves you? Have mercy. Forgive. Restore a right relationship with you, Father, then with others. Give me humility. In Jesus' name. Amen.

Children of the Light　　March 4　　John 12:36

"While you have the light, believe in the light, so you may become children of light."

This is a wonderful verse from John's gospel. Jesus says, *"While you have the light, believe in the light, so you may become children of light."* I believe this scripture can be interpreted in several different ways, so let's take a look at it. I really believe that Jesus gives us two thoughts to ponder in this one little verse. One - *"While you have the light - believe in the light."* The Holy Spirit will open our hearts to the light, which is Jesus Christ. And while our hearts are opened, the opportunity to believe is available for us. Once you are given a glimpse of what God was willing to do and how far God was willing to go to allow His Son to be placed on a cross, to endure the pain and suffering, just for our sake, then believe in the light, accept Jesus as your Lord, one who controls your life, and as your Savior, the one who brings you grace and salvation.

The second thought to ponder in this verse is, *"Once you believe in the light, become children of the light."* Become Jesus' disciple by sharing his light to the world. Pattern your life and your choices after his. Go about doing what He would be doing if he were here - Jesus went about spreading the "Good News", so should we. Jesus went about spreading God's love and joy and peace to those around him, so should we. Jesus forgave those who harmed Him, so should we. Jesus even went to the point of saying a prayer for those who hung him on the cross, *"Father, forgive them, for they know not what they do."*

There are many people out there walking in darkness. They are missing that wonderful love and forgiveness offered by God through Jesus Christ. They need for us to tell them what they are missing. They need people who are full of God's love sharing that love with them. Won't you do that? Won't you become children of the light?

Lord God, you gave a precious gift through your son Jesus and I love you; thank you for saving me from myself, for saving me for you. Called to become "children of the light": to participate in the very plans of God! I have wanted to do even your things my way. Give me the courage to be wrong; the grace to let you be right. Walk with me, Jesus, so I may live in light until I shine, dimly, but someday bright! In His name. Amen.

"All who receive Him (Jesus), who believe in His name, He gave power to become children of God."

In order for us to really put our life on track, we must learn to fully accept Jesus Christ. Today's scripture tells us how. During the baptism of our Lord, Mark 1:9f, John pours water over Jesus' head and suddenly the Holy Spirit descends upon him like a dove and a voice from heaven says, *"You are my beloved Son, on you my favor rests."* Wouldn't it be wonderful if somehow we too could hear those words truly said of us? To those who accept Christ, who believe in his name, becoming adopted children of God, to you, God says, *"You are my beloved - on you my favor rests."*

The conflicts and criticisms of the world often prevent us from experiencing this scriptural and spiritual truth. Evil strikes at our confidence in Jesus through hurtful words from loved ones and enemies which say, "You are no good, you are worthless, you are wrong, you are a poor mother or father, you are a poor excuse for a wife or husband, you are a nobody!" All these words bind us with the bands of self-rejection, self-hate. If we all focus on the opinion and evaluations of others to find who we are, we will be trapped in a "small" world telling us that we are small, unimportant people.

But there is an inner voice calling and saying, "I have known you from the beginning of time. I have called you from all eternity. You are mine, I am yours, and we are one." We are God's adopted children, but at the same time we must fight off all the destructive voices of the world to hear and become His beloved children. Once we discover and truly believe that *"we are the beloved"*, nothing can destroy our joy. We will feel very special and when we feel very special, we can make others around us feel special. Receive Jesus, Believe Jesus. And the power to become children of God is yours.

Lord, the world erodes my confidence, stifles my joy; even ones I love see I am worthless. Worthless says regretful words; does cruel things. Come to me, for when I feel you near, I feel cherished. Then I can say loving, healing words, God-words. Help me to seek my worthiness in you, Lord. May the name of Jesus grace my heart in hurtful times to forgive and forget. It's a tall order, Father, except for God. In Jesus I pray, Amen.

Making things New   *March 6*   *John 6:10*

"Make the people sit down."

The passage from John speaks of the feeding of the 5,000. This text refers to the goodness of God and the blessings he showers upon us. It also gives us a good look at how we receive God's blessings. In verse 10, Jesus says, *"Make the people sit down."* We experience God's blessings when we take time to "sit down." In other words, take time to slow down from this busy world and make time for Jesus. We fill our days and nights with so much busyness that we can hardly hear God speak to us. Our busyness squeezes out little by little the amount of time we set aside for God. This scripture states that we can hear God best when we take time.

Verses 10 and 11 state that Jesus *"took the loaves and fish and gave thanks and distributed them and everyone had as much as they wanted."* The outcome of sitting down, listening, and spending time with Jesus is the miraculous provision of all our needs. Our problem is that we are so on the go that we don't take the time to slow down and listen. We don't think we have time. When we do, we are always making demands upon God. "Well, I'm here God, listening, I've only got a few minutes." But it takes time for good things to happen. Don't just sit down, wait patiently for God and receive what he has to offer.

When we do sit and wait, we realize that God not only provides our needs, he gives abundantly! In verses 12-13, Jesus told the disciples to *"gather up the leftovers - it filled 12 baskets!"* God not only puts food on our tables, he gives abundantly. Psalms 23 says that God, *"Sets us a table before our enemy - fills our cup to overflowing."* Most of our worries would disappear if we would rest upon the blessings of God. Faith and worry are incompatible. God is a generous God. He cares about us and will see to our needs. He also cares about His church, the spiritual body of Christ. My suggestion? Make yourself sit down, wait patiently and in expectation for his Presence, and receive the wonderful, abundant gifts of God.

Lord God, how great are your blessings to me! Yet I make excuses for my absence. I have forgotten how important gratitude expressed is for my spirit. Have mercy, Lord. Make me slow down and listen for your voice. Keep me grounded in reality. Help me prioritize correctly, for my intentions are good. It's just that I'm so.... Are you pushing out that chair for me, Jesus? Is this a good time? Here I am! Here we are! Amen.

" In this you rejoice, even if now for a little while you have had to suffer various trials, so that the genuineness of your faith - being more precious than gold, though perishable, is tested by fire - may be found to result in praise and glory and honor when Jesus Christ is revealed."

Why is it we always have to learn the hard way? Why can't we just listen to the wisdom of others and learn from that? My guess? It is in our nature to learn through experience. After all, we start that experiential learning at a very young age! As parents, we tell our two-year-old, "Don't touch - that's hot!" Of course, they have no earthly idea what hot means; that is until they touch and experience hot! We tell our teenagers, "Don't smoke, that's bad for you." They have no concept of the harm that will come in 40 years. They get with other teens and puff away. Then comes the hack and cough and the possibility of lung cancer or emphysema.

The dilemma is that seldom will we learn from the advice or wisdom of others. We can pick up the works of some great Christian writers like C. S. Lewis or Thomas Merton, but we end up ignoring their advice, setting out to find answers to life in some other way. We just don't want to forfeit control of our lives or our right to make our own decisions, do we? We don't even want Jesus to have full control! We don't want to give him our all. Maybe we don't fully trust him, what do you think?

What if God's will for me and my will don't coincide? Then what? The genuineness of my faith is tested by fire. We just don't want to face the truth that we cannot do without God. God is right and I'm not. This is a tough pill to swallow, believe me. In 1st Peter informs us that when we suffer trials, our faith is tested and we turn and give praise and glory and honor to Jesus. Through trials, through our learning on our own so to speak, we begin to see the depths of our sinfulness and the full measure of God's great love. So ignore the wisdom of others if you must, but don't ignore to the truth revealed to you by God as you attempt to go it on your own.

Lord God, I give thanks that my eyes have been opened to the depths of my sins. I know how low you had to stoop to take my hand to save me. My gratitude is boundless. I owe you my very life. Forgive me when I forget this truth and act like a fool, thinking I know better than you do, forgetting the cost you bore. May I be thankful even in suffering and trials. May I honor you all my days, Beloved Jesus, Precious Lord. Amen.

*"The Spirit drove Jesus into the wilderness and He was there
for forty days, tempted by Satan and He was with the wild
beasts; and the angels waited on Him."*

This story of Jesus in the wilderness occurs just after his baptism. This is a story about temptation on a monumental scale. The players are Satan, evil personified, and Jesus, the incarnate Son of God, fully human yet fully divine. The portrait that Hollywood paints of Satan is one of "a wild beast!" But I'm afraid that our encounters with Satan are much more subtle. Temptation is a simple reality of life, something we cannot avoid, but we can choose to resist.

There is a Biblical principle here: "The more we give in to temptation, the easier it gets and the weaker we become. The more we resist temptation, the stronger we become." Our problem is usually "getting started". It's like going on a diet. Through the winter, we have a tendency to put on a few extra pounds. You know eating those wonderful sweets through the holidays plus less exercise because it's too cold! But, the longer we put it off, the harder it is to start. Conversely, the quicker we decide, the easier it becomes. We don't stand alone in this. The disciples had their days of temptation. They argued over who was the greatest and who should sit at Jesus' right and left in glory. Just like us, they fell for that wanting to be recognized and honored trick. Satan loves that one, always works. Jesus reminded them greatness is humbleness, being a servant.

The temptation in the wilderness should remind us that if we wish to stay on the path with Jesus, we are going to have to learn, as did those first disciples, how to resist temptation. For the more we resist the devil, the stronger we become and the less influence he has us. You cannot defeat Satan alone! He knew your weaknesses before you were born, so don't underestimate his power or his deceit, but never underestimate the power of God. You have a proven advocate in Jesus Christ, the Righteous.

Lord God, I am dependent on you in all things, for all things. Give me the grace to see that when I am weak you are strong. That is the way of faith and discipleship .Too often my pride causes me to rely on my own cleverness to overcome temptation; that too is my weakness. Let me not be deceived, Father. Give me your wisdom; give me your strength that I may resist temptation and live my life as a witness to Jesus. It is in his name I pray. Amen.

"I have learned in whatever state I am in, to be content."

Where do we find contentment? (Not to be confused with happiness, though it often is.) The Apostle Paul said, " I rejoice in the Lord greatly that now at last you have revived your concern for me." Then to make it clear that he is not in need, "for I have learned to be content with whatever I have." Paul states that he knows what it is to have little or to have a lot and has learned the secret of life concerning having plenty and being in need, "I can do all things through him who strengthens me. For I have learned in whatever state I am in, to be content."

Now he does not say he is happy all the time. Christians who smile through every single problem and crisis of life are phonies, or, at the very least misguided! Even Jesus cried! So, let's talk about it. You can put your faith in the wrong things and you will find neither happiness nor contentment. Money will buy what you want but banks can fail. Governments can provide certain protection but governments cannot be everywhere. You can depend on your own intelligence, but as you grow older memory fades. Paul's statement of abiding faith was based on the promises of God, which never fail. The world has a way of demanding more and more, no matter how much we have given. Discontentment runs rampant and unabated by human effort.

So how do we satisfy the basic longing of the human heart to know contentment? Go to the source of that peace. Paul makes it clear that he can do all things *"through him who strengthens me."* He is speaking of Jesus, the one who can satisfy our hunger, our longing. The peace Jesus brings is unlike any other, unlike the peace received from owning an acre of land, unlike cherishing something purchased with hard earned cash. The peace of God is a direct result of our relationship with Christ and His with us. Enjoying the peace or contentment of Christ depends upon our recognizing that truth.

Lord, I long for the peace that only comes from you, yet I seek it everywhere else, much to my dismay and your hurt. Forgive me, Father, for my willfulness. Why can't I accept the truth? I have sought contentment in money, influence, power. There may have been some satisfaction in those things for a while, just a while. But they do not last, nor satisfy. Show me the way; grant me your peace. Do this thing for me, Jesus. Amen.

"The tempter said, "If you are the Son of God, command these stones to become loaves of bread." But he answered, "It is written, 'One does not live by bread alone, but by every word that comes from the mouth of God.'"

The Scripture for today has to do with temptation and each of us has to deal with temptation more than we can recall. Jesus was tempted also but knew who was doing the tempting. When we're tempted, it's important to realize the source. Quite often we don't even recognize we are being tempted. God is not the one tempting us to do wrong, Jesus is not enticing us to sin, and the Spirit is not guiding us into temptation. It has to do with a tricky little devil! So know who is behind your temptation.

The first temptation was to turn stones into bread. The devil knew Jesus was hungry after fasting for 40 days so he tempts him to turn stones into bread. Do you think Jesus could have done so? In response to this temptation, Jesus quotes scripture, *"One does not live by bread alone, but by every word that comes from the mouth of God."* (Deuteronomy 8:3) Jesus is saying that there is more to life than having a full stomach - one of the great temptations to always have just a little more. Happiness is just around the corner if we have a few more things, a little more wealth, more of the finer things in life. This message bombards us constantly.

Our daughter once had a job that paid her handsomely. Only problem was she was in an airplane every week spending most of her time in a motel. She made great money, but was it worth it? She did not think so and opted for a job two blocks from where she lives. But what a dilemma, what a temptation! That is what happens much of the time isn't it? Not that we are tempted to do great evil things, but we are tempted to accept the lesser good. Busyness can deprive us of spending time with our children, our family or even a relationship with Jesus. We give bread when what is needed is God's Word. That's the way temptation works, isn't it? It's not easy to make choices or to even see them as temptation.

Lord God, how can a people for whom the world was made be dissatisfied? Yet we are; forgive us; forgive me. Keep me close to your heart, Father, for I am so easily swayed by the world's temptations. In placing my priorities in the wrong places, I fail us all, even you. Open the eyes of my heart to choose wisely and well. Help me to love you more; trust you fully in all my doings. In the name of Jesus I pray. Amen.

"The devil placed him on the pinnacle of the temple, "If you are the Son of God, throw yourself down; for it is written, 'He will command his angels and they will bear you up, so that you will not dash your foot against a stone.'" Jesus said, "Again it is written, 'Do not put the Lord your God to the test.'"

This is the second temptation Jesus encountered from the devil. When Jesus refused the first, the devil immediately tempted again; this time taking Jesus to the pinnacle of the temple and daring him to jump. To make the temptation more appealing, the devil then quotes Psalm 91, "God will command His angels concerning you and on their hands, they will bear you up, so that you will not dash your foot against a stone."

Jesus once again countered the devil's temptation by quoting scripture back to Him, "Do not put the Lord your God to the test." (Deuteronomy 6:16) Truthfully, Jesus could have jumped and angels would have rescued him securing for him an instant following. It would have been sensational to watch someone jump off tall buildings and have angels appear and catch them. But then you know how people are; soon they would tire of it and would want Jesus to jump from higher places. Jesus resisted. He knew that faith could rest on sensationalism. We soon get accustomed to the sensational and it becomes ordinary.

Look at the space program: I remember vividly the first trip into space. Everyone was mesmerized; could not leave the TV set. Then came launch two and three and four, suddenly people were no longer watching. Space flight takes an enormous amount of planning, calculating everything down to the minuet detail. Yet people still see it as commonplace, until something goes wrong. That's the way sensationalism works. It gets our attention at first and then we loose interest. Jesus knew people would put their faith in the event rather than in God. Don't let the need for spectacular events replace a true relationship with Jesus. Don't do it, if only to confound the Devil. It was his idea first.

Lord God, my heart has rejoiced at your wonderful works: your beautiful world, a newborn child, a tender moment between friends, your sheer Presence in prayers. I can sometimes miss the little things you do. Forgive me, my Father. Create in me a heart that longs for you, that longs to be challenged, discipled, not entertained. You do know how I can be! In Jesus' name Amen.

"Again, the devil took Jesus to a high mountain and showed him the kingdoms of the world and their splendor; and he said, "All these I will give you, if you will fall down and worship me." Jesus said, "Away with you, Satan! For it is written, 'Worship the Lord your God, and serve only him.'"

Jesus resisted the first and second temptations then the devil hits him with a third. Let's take a look at that one today. The devil showed Jesus all the kingdoms of the world and promised that he would deliver them to him if he, Jesus, would just fall down and worship him, the devil. Look closely at his words. Read between the lines. The devil is asking Jesus to compromise both his ministry and mission. He was handing Jesus the entire world if Jesus would only worship him.

None of this was the devil's to give in the first place; it all belongs to God. If Jesus had given in to this temptation, he could win believers and possibly bypass his suffering and death on a cross. It would be a shortcut. But Jesus refuses to compromise, telling Satan to get away saying, "We are to worship the Lord our God, and serve only Him." (Deuteronomy 6:13) This question comes to mind: why would the devil need to tempt anyone to worship him anyway?

Some fall to his temptation because they simply don't believe the devil exists. Others I believe have an unhealthy interest in the devil. Either way they (and we if we follow in their footsteps) are in trouble! To avoid him, there can be no compromise! We must belong to Jesus and him alone; we must resist evil in all its forms; and we must claim the power of Jesus to prevail over evil. These three temptations sum up the most enticing temptations we will all face in life: to use our gifts for self gain; to be able to do something sensational; or to accumulate as much of the material things in life as possible. I'm not saying those things are bad in themselves, just that we are always tempted to want and have more and more replacing the ultimate good with something mediocre.

Lord God, it is so tempting to have what Jesus turned down, the world and all its comforts, the prestige of wealth and acclaim, the adoration. Bring me to a place where I am content with the blessings you have provided, seeing them as the abundance they truly are. Give me strength to resist evil, courage to stay the path you have chosen, and wisdom to see that the last thing evil wants is for me to be happy and to be yours! In Jesus. Amen.

Foot Washing　　　**March 13**　　　*John 13: 1f*

"Jesus began to wash the disciples' feet and wipe them with the towel that was tied around him. He came to Simon Peter, who said, "Lord, you will never wash my feet." Jesus answered, "Unless I wash you, you have no share with me."

We find in the gospel of John this story of Jesus washing the feet of the disciples. Just to give you a bit of history, foot washing was very common during Jesus' day. Part of a servant's job was to wash the feet of everyone entering the house. It was an act of hospitality. Jesus used this common act of service to illustrate a significant theological principle and he did it in actions not just in words. Jesus took His robe off, wrapped a towel about Him, poured water in a basin, and washed the disciples' feet. He came to Peter, who responded, *"Lord, you are not to wash my feet."*

What do you think was behind Peter's refusal? Maybe a sense of unworthiness? He thought it beneath Jesus, the Son of God, and the long-awaited Messiah, to perform a task relegated to household servants. Jesus made it clear that he came to serve, not be served, and those who follow him are called to do the same. At one point, Jesus said, *"If you want to be mine, you MUST be a servant of all."* Here is what Jesus says in response to Peter (Verse 8), *"If I do not wash your feet, then you have no share with me - we will have nothing in common."* In other words, "receive from me or you will have nothing to do with me."

Now that's quite a twist from what we are used to. What most say is, "Well, if you really care about me - if you really love me - if we are really friends - if you are truly a good Christian, child, parent, then you will do this or that to help me – you will give to me." Jesus zeroes in on the opposite side, *"Peter, if you cannot accept FROM me - you will cut yourself off from me."* If the truth be known, Peter had nothing to offer until he received from Jesus Christ and neither do we; until and unless we allow Jesus to come and wash us clean, we have nothing good to offer anyone.

Lord, I see the truth of this event to Jesus, to those who would follow him. I too discount my worth; magnify my faults; decline to have you stoop to serve me. Without the gift of your son, his mercy, humility and grace toward me, his willful child, I would have nothing to offer you, Father, nor anyone else. Apart from your grace, I am nothing, my efforts less than nothing. Have mercy on me, Father God, and forgive me my stubbornness, my pride. I pray in the name of my Lord, Jesus. Amen.

"If he found any belonging to the Way, he might arrest them and bring them back to Jerusalem to stand trial -"Saul, Saul, why do you persecute me?"

Some people are confused about conversion. Many who call themselves Christians are only halfway converted. They like to straddle the fence, to halfway commit. Many may have no trouble at all accepting that Jesus is the Son of God and our Savior but have trouble making him Lord. They believe, but fail to trust. Remember the famous story of St. Paul's conversion? Paul, a Jew and a Pharisee, had been living a life fueled by self-righteous hate, hunting Christians down and stoning them to death.

In the 9th chapter of Acts Paul went to the high priest and asked him if he might send a letter to the synagogues at Damascus so that if he discovered any persons belonging to "The Way" (early name for Christian), then he would arrest them and bring them to "justice". He received permission to go. As Paul was approaching Damascus, he was struck blind. A voice comes out of nowhere and confronts Paul, *"Why are you persecuting me?"* That voice identified itself as the resurrected Jesus. Paul was dumfounded! Through that encounter with the risen Christ, Paul, the self-proclaimed enemy of the faith, was converted to "The Way."

This conversion of Paul's was complete! He decided to totally trust his life, future, and ministry to the Lord Jesus. Often we live miserable lives because we have not made that decision. "Yes, Jesus is the Son of God", we say, "but what does that have to do with my tomorrow?" We live a life of worry. Will our money run out before we do? Am I raising my children right? Will the church meet its budget? Will I survive the next downsizing at work? The worry goes on and on. Just as being self-righteousness and saying we trust in the righteousness of Jesus cannot co-exist, neither can worry and trust. So make your conversion complete!

Lord God, I come confessing a truth you know more fully than I. Halfheartedly, I given my life to you. I say I trust in you, I continue to worry. I say you are Lord of my life; I have hate in my heart. I have refused to forgive those who have hurt me; I have ignored your urging to forgive those I've harmed. I have enjoyed feeling powerful and superior and right. I need a "Damascus Road" experience! Conversion from self-serving righteousness to love and grace. I once was blind, but now I see, now… I see. In the name of Jesus. Amen.

Lay down your Life   March 15   John 10:11f

"I am the good shepherd. The good shepherd lays down his life for the sheep. The hired hand sees the wolf coming and leaves the sheep and runs away. The hired hand runs away because he does not care for the sheep."

In many ways this is a hard, cruel world we live in. All you have to do is pick up the newspaper to read about some part of the world where people are being tortured and killed. From Afghanistan to Bosnia to Iraq to Vietnam to the Holocaust, all the way back to the Kings of Israel, human beings have been killed in the pursuit of peace. If the truth be known, none of us is totally innocent. However, there was one man in history who was totally innocent of all charges made against him. He "laid down his life for his sheep", the truly guilty. His name? Jesus.

How does the hired hand respond to the wolf threatening the sheep in his care? *"The hired hand runs away because the hired hand does not care for the sheep."* It is all about preserving his life. Again, you can pick up the paper on any given day and read where children kill their parents for the money, or a mother drowns her children for a new life with her "new' boyfriend, or a live-in boyfriend shakes a six month old until it is brain dead because "the baby was bothering him by crying." Jesus calls them, "the hirelings," for they do not care about the lives of others. They always place themselves first. Jesus leaves us a different example.

The Lord of Lords laid down his life for such as you and me. I don't know about you, but I know that I am not worthy of such a sacrifice. But I am truly grateful that Jesus thought I was. He gave his life, even though we don't deserve it. And, he calls us to be in his flock, sons and daughters of God, brothers and sisters of Jesus. He has cancelled our past and future debts, nailed all our sins to his cross and given us the right to be adopted children of Almighty God. But be careful. For often we want to see ourselves as good people, loving and giving and thoughtful and righteous. Christ did not come to save perfect people, but sinners.

Lord God, often I am unwilling to make the slightest sacrifice for your Kingdom. It's the truth; we both know it is. Oh, Father, so fill me with your Spirit that I may face life without allowing it to overwhelm me. At those times I see only myself. I become the hireling you described to my shame and your dismay. May your Spirit guide me in all that I do; may I be willing to lay down my life for anyone else. In Jesus, I pray. Amen.

Thorn in the Flesh   March 16   2 Corinthians 12:7

"Therefore, to keep me from being too elated, a thorn was given me in the flesh, a messenger of Satan to torment me. Three times I appealed to the Lord about this, that it would leave me, but he said to me, "My grace is sufficient for you, for power is made perfect in weakness."

Much has been written about Paul's "Thorn in the Flesh." Some speculations are outrageous, some even funny. Some mysteries serve mankind better unsolved so let us just concentrate on how Paul used his "Thorn" to glorify God. Three times Paul asks unsuccessfully for God to remove it but finally realizes that the Lord's grace is sufficient for his need. He then says, *"I boast in my weakness so that the power of Christ may dwell in me."* So be thankful for your thorn in the flesh.

We all have those thorns in the flesh, but most people see them as a curse, rather than a blessing. Why is that? I believe it is because most have this false notion that life is supposed to be easy, with few bumps in the road, and none too great to handle. This is not the way it is, or was, even for the apostle Paul. We all have thorns in our flesh, don't we? So, it's important to understand that these thorns are not sent to punish us, but are common occurrences or infirmities meant to convince us that we need to be totally dependant upon God and his mercy.

That is the "power made perfect", as Paul says, "in weakness." When Paul received his, thorn in the flesh, he prayed God would deliver him. Instead God responded that His Grace is sufficient and will be made perfect in weakness. In other words, God was calling upon Paul to trust in him. God will work through us even if we have a weakness; the weakness will open our eyes to our need for God. If life is always smooth, we may begin to rely too heavily on our abilities rather than on God's grace and that could spell disaster! Just think of it this way, if your thorn in the flesh causes you to rely upon God for your strength and wisdom to survive, it is a blessing beyond words.

Lord, I come giving thanks knowing all I have comes from you. Yet I do not live gratefully. I want life to be perfect. Then something happens to spoil my dreams; I get so angry! Then I can't come to you, Lord, out of spite or hurt. Yet you are the answer to the challenges of my life! By your power, enable me to know that your grace is sufficient! May I live my whole life as a sacred gesture of thanksgiving. Forgive me, Lord, love, even me. In Jesus name, I pray. Amen.

"From now on we are to regard no one from a human point of view."

How do we grow as Christians? Let me give you two passages which may be of help: Romans 7:21, *"I find it to be a law that when I want to do what is right, evil lies close at hand"*, and 2 Corinthians 5:7, *"Walk by faith and not by sight."* These are wonderful, truthful words, but simply stated advice is not always simply done. How do we "walk by faith" especially when "evil lies close at hand", raising doubts and encouraging us to see things from the "human point of view"?

One of the most difficult things for human beings to do well is to communicate with each other. It is so easy to misunderstand what is being said whether our conversation is between husband and wife, parent and child, or friend to friend. If we live by sight, then we take things as we see them and, being imperfect, our feelings can affect our interpretation. Even baggage from past relationships colors our response. Living by sight, we assume what people say is what they actually meant and what we heard is not tainted by our emotions or pride or insecurities. Then we can become hurt or angry assuming they mean to hurt us.

Living by sight allows our feelings to control us. Instead, we as Christians are called to see life through the eyes of Jesus. Living by faith means that everything we hear coming from another must undergo the test of faith. Remember we are all sinners and make mistakes; remember who that person is to you; remember that they love you and would never mean to hurt you. So gather the facts. And then remember God's commandment to, *"Forgive one another as you have been forgiven by God in Christ Jesus."* That command goes even for those who intend to hurt us. They especially need our forgiveness. So whether the other person deserves it or not, forgive them. When you learn to live by faith, you will discover the power to see others through the eyes of Jesus, not your own.

Lord God, it is so hard to grow as a Christian, many obstacles are in the way: none as great as my depraved vision, my own willfulness. Often I look at others through the eyes of my feelings. I do not see them as they are to you, Father, but not today! Today, I will be truly yours! Today, with your help, I will regard no one from a human point of view! I've never "seen" the world from your perspective, Lord. Keep me on track! For evil lies close at hand and he's always had my number. In Jesus' name. Amen.

"But know this: if the owner of the house had known at what hour the thief was coming, he would not have let his house be broken into. You also must be ready, for the Son of Man is coming at an unexpected hour."

In the twelfth chapter of Luke, Jesus had been talking to a large crowd. Then he turns to his disciples and gives instructions to them to "be prepared" for his coming. He puts it in terms of a man protecting his house from the unexpected break-in by a thief. As Christians we must "be prepared" and be ready. How do we do it? If you want to be successful at anything in life, you must work hard and prepare. To be a good golfer you must work on your swing, develop your short shots, learn to read the slope of the greens, and keep your drive in the fairway.

The same is true of any sport be it golf or basketball or tennis, you have to practice over and over - work at being prepared. Jesus reminds us that people who are prepared are better equipped to experience the blessings and benefits that faith has to offer. Too many depend on their conscience for guidance. If our conscience had the power to resist, would there be injustice in this world? Probably not but that is not the case, is it? It takes more than our conscience to resist evil and follow the path of "good". It takes being prepared.

It is God's Holy Word that helps us to discern right from wrong and it is his presence in our lives, which gives us the strength to choose to do what is right. If we are prepared, if we have read and studied God's Holy Word, if we know the difference between right and wrong, if we pray and meditate to build our relationship with God, then we can be prepared for those unexpected moments and the right action will just come naturally. When the storm clouds of life arise, those difficult moments, which tear at our soul and challenge our faith, we will not collapse spiritually. Rather we will turn to the one who can carry us, who has carried us all along.

Lord God, I have prepared for everything else but for you. I have saved; I have stocked my pantry; I have insured my possessions; I have even insured my life. But have I secured my soul? All the worldly trappings of responsibility and security have made their home with me. But have I left for last the most important thing? O Lord, I heed your words, let it not be too late... for Jesus' sake, I pray. Amen.

"Seek first God's Kingdom and His righteousness and all these things shall be yours as well."

I saw a movie years ago that made an impression on me. It concerned the things we think we really need in life. The movie was called "Needful Things." It really drives home the point I want to make. Often we become overloaded with the things of life to the point of breaking down. People are under pressure today because we desire too many "needful things". There's pressure at work, pressure within our marriages, pressure with raising our children.

Our world offers so much and we want to make sure that our children don't miss out. The source of much of our stress and theirs is the treadmill-type life we have chosen. This is not to say that sports or music lessons, and so on, are bad or wrong, they just are not the highest good. In the movie, "Needful Things," the star, Max, owned a shop with unusual gifts, things that people desired to have. Just like the things for our children, they were not necessarily bad; they were "needful things." These items were offered to people without any monetary cost to them, but Max is really the devil and he makes a deal with them. They can have the needful thing if they will do something for him in return. That something is always wrong and harmful to someone else. But, because of their desire to have the object they want, the people will do anything.

The problem is the same in real life; there is a price one has to pay for the needful things of life. Our focus becomes the desire to have what we want, rather than to place God first and to seek His kingdom and His righteousness above all else. If the Lord is not your highest priority, then the things of life will be out of balance causing you great stress. But the closer we are to Jesus, the better able we are to turn our cares and worries over to him, asking for His guidance and direction, following His will for our lives.

Lord God, forgive me when I seek after needful things, placing them above you and your will for my life. At times, I become obsessed with wanting, with keeping up with what everybody else thinks is essential, only to discover they never seem to provide satisfaction. Help me to place you first that I may discover true peace and joy in my life. Let this be the thing I desire, the "needful thing" I offer to all. In his name, I pray. Amen.

Build your life Wisely   March 20   Matthew 7:24f

"Do not build your house on sand where it will be washed away,
but build it on rock."

The teachings of Jesus Christ stress upon us the importance of learning to live wisely. The scriptures are full of stories where Jesus stresses this point. In Matthew 6:14 Jesus warns us about placing our trust in the treasures of this earth saying that "moths" can consume important items, "rust" can destroy, and "thieves" can steal. But, Jesus says, *"store up treasures in heaven."* In Matthew 6:34 Jesus tells us to quit worrying about tomorrow. Besides, we don't yet know what tomorrow will bring anyway! He says, *"Let today's trouble be enough for today."* And in the gospel of Luke - 14:28, *"Who would build a tower without first estimating the cost?"*

You see it is not enough for us to go about living our life; we are called to live wisely. To achieve wisdom we must first recognize and acknowledge the source. Wisdom comes to us thru God's Holy Spirit. It begins when we ask Jesus to come into our life, there to rule our hearts and influence our decisions. To do so is to build our house on the rock of faith in God and commitment to God's kingdom. First, we need consider what giving our life to Jesus means. Is a verbal commitment enough? Is joining a church enough? Or are there broader requirements?

Well let me ask, "Do you spend much of your time worrying about tomorrow, what it will bring?" If so, your god has become worry. "Do you fret over money? Does it occupy a large portion of your time?" Then your god has become money. "Do you spend most of your time storing up treasures here on earth, fearful of losing them?" Then your god has become your possessions. Living wisely begins with a total commitment to Jesus Christ. He must be the one you turn to in every need, in every joy, in every thanksgiving. He demands to be your only Lord, your only Savior. He brooks no rivals. He does this for your sake. Turn to Him first and let your life flow from there. A spiritual house built on sand cannot stand.

Lord God, Guardian of my Life, Keeper of my Soul, this devotion causes me to pause and consider a truth about my life I would rather not know but cannot deny. I have lived on sandy soil too long, trusting in myself, rejoicing in accumulated things, but not in you. I come before you guilty. Lord, I can change. I will need your wisdom, your strength, your presence. Forgive me, Lord, renew my spirit. For Jesus' sake and ...for mine. Amen.

That you may have Life　**March 21**　*John 20:3Of*

"Jesus did many other signs… which are not written in this book. But these are written so that you may come to believe that Jesus is the Messiah, the Son of God and through believing you may have life."

We all want to have "life" in Jesus' name– eternal life, here and now, and in the hereafter. But many are confused about how to obtain it. We misunderstand God's word. We want security in this life on our own terms. In order to get it, we end up putting ourselves "in prison", robbing us of our freedom in Christ. Such behavior builds a counterfeit faith where others think for us, where we live by rules and laws in order to become safe. When this applies to our spiritual life, we are on dangerous ground.

Let me explain. John says through *"believing"* you have life in the name of Jesus. And we want to say, "Ok, I'll accept that, but in order to remain saved, I must do something, like follow the 10 Commandments, go to church twice a week, teach Sunday School, pray without ceasing - look, act and think like a Christian." When we say that, we are saying that our salvation depends on us, not Christ alone. I realize there's a thin line here. Should we keep God's Commandments? Absolutely! Is the law important? Yes! But you see the Law was written to help us, to protect us from ourselves, not save us. It's a matter of focus on Jesus, or on us.

Saving grace comes through Jesus. It happened on a Cross at Calvary and you, great sinner, were given a passing grade, an A+, and you can do nothing to earn it. This is the plan of the Almighty God, as a redemptive act of sheer love and grace. The Holy Spirit fills our hearts and mind with grace and what we call "good works" actually is Christ shinning through! All this we do out of love, as a response to the love we received; otherwise we water down Christ's saving power and actually say we are accepted through our righteousness and good deeds.

Lord, I come asking your forgiveness. Though I have given you my life, trusting you for salvation (I really do!) I continue to think that I have to do something to remain in your grace. It's the worldly way, Father, so hard to unlearn. If I do well at work, I'm rewarded, if not, I'm not. If I behave as society expects, I'm accepted, if not, I'm not. If this way of living is not of you, then who? Convict us all that it is through believing that we have life in the name of Jesus. That it comes just because you love us so and sent your Son to save us. Grace: unmerited, undeserved, and unearned. What a Savior! Amen.

Doubt   # March 22   *John 20:24f*

"The other disciples said, "We have seen the Lord." But Thomas said to them, "Unless I see the mark of the nails in his hands, and put my finger in the mark of the nails and my hand in his side, I will not believe."

The story about Doubting Thomas remains instructive today. It was Sunday evening after the crucifixion of Jesus on Friday. The disciples were in a locked room, holed up as if criminals, fearing for their lives from the threat of the Jews and the Romans. Here they are gathered together with fear and doubt being the common denominator between them. Suddenly, Jesus comes among them, appearing as if out of thin air, saying, "Peace be with you." It must have been quite an entrance, enough to change their lives forever!

Thomas, however, was absent. Perhaps, he was with his own family, maybe he had tried to make it but was detained by the authorities, or maybe he was the type who liked to be alone in his grief. When the disciples tell him what happened, he responds, "I'll believe it when I see it." He finally got his wish as we are told in John Chapter 20. Jesus appears to the group as before. To Thomas, who had to see the proof of the wounds to believe, Jesus invites him to satisfy his doubt. Then, Jesus said to Thomas, *"Do not doubt but believe!"* Thomas did. Jesus responds, *"Have you done so because you have seen me? Blessed are those who have not seen and yet have come to believe."*

After this event, Thomas not only believed, but his heart burned deep for the Kingdom until the authorities finally took his life just like they did the other disciples. This story ought to be a good example for us. When we gather in God's presence, no matter where that is, gather expecting to meet the living Lord in the Spirit. There in His presence we are given the faith and courage to continue on, not just to meet life's challenges, but also to let our hearts burn with fire for the Kingdom.

Lord, I come as your child, more like Thomas than I care to admit, even to myself. Once again I see you respond to doubt with gentleness and proof, saying, See! Touch! In remorse, I come as one who has seen proof of your presence in this world, yet, have not believed completely, unreservedly. I come as a sinner in need of your grace. Free me from the bondage of doubt, to embrace belief even when I cannot see. Grant me the blessings of faith and forgiveness. In the name of Jesus, Beloved Savior. Amen.

To Serve - not to be served March 23 Matthew 20:26

"Whoever wishes to be great among you must be your servant, and whoever wishes to be first among you must be your slave; just as the Son of Man came not to be served but to serve, and to give his life a ransom for many."

What is the major quality that Christians should display? Many a Christian has had some unchristian ideas about the church. Some believe the church exists to serve them. They want the church to reach out to teach them, work with their children, provide entertainment and a place to socialize, to somehow answer all of their problems of life, and provide comfort for every need they have or ever will have. Well I have some startling news. The church doesn't exist for you; it exists for Christ.

Now, having said that let me say that the church does and is supposed to help with the needs of the family. But, our true help comes not from the church but through the church. Jesus Christ is our Savior, not the church. The church is Jesus, made up in the sense of Christians who together, carry his spirit and call upon his spirit. If we are those who only wish to be served, we do not carry the Spirit of our Lord. We carry the spirit of pride, selfishness, and preoccupation with ourselves. If we notice others at all, it is only in terms of whether or not they are useful to us, whether or not they have anything of value to offer.

The true church is a group of Christians who meet, fellowship, study, worship, and serve together. Christians are those who know they are blessed because they know Christ will not judge them, but will show them mercy. A church filled with people like that will be a blessing to their community, and to others, for they will be concerned not with being served, but with serving. They will be concerned about those who have not found Christ. They will give of themselves to strengthen God's household of faith. If you are wondering what God has in store for you this year, pray about it; when you feel the call to answer that prayer in some way through service in His church, do it. You will be greatly blessed!

Lord God, often I seek to be served in this world; forgive me. I often place my needs above everyone else's; forgive me. I even seek a church, which will give to me and my family rather than seeking a body of Christ where I can serve, where I can be family. Open my heart, Lord. Lead me to serve that others may benefit, that my life may amount to something for somebody... even for you. Do this Lord, for me. In the name of Jesus. Amen.

Helping those in Need **March 24** *Matthew 10:40*

"Whoever welcomes you welcomes me, and whoever welcomes me welcomes the one who sent me; and whoever gives even a cup of cold water to one of these little ones in the name of a disciple – truly I tell you, none of these will lose their reward."

In the 10th chapter of Matthew, Jesus tells us that if we care, we will offer water to one who is thirsty. At the heart of the Christian faith is giving - now don't reach back and hold onto your pocketbook, because giving goes far beyond that: Far beyond. Giving has more to do with faith and compassion than it does money. It means giving of the whole self, being less self-centered: giving love and compassion to others.

Giving, you see, has less to do with your pocketbook and more to do with your heart. All one has to do is survey the gospels and take a look at the life of Jesus. There was nothing self-serving in what He did. His heart truly went out to those in need and He calls us to do the same. Remember His words from Matthew 6:21 *"For where your treasure lies, there your heart will be also."* Wherever your 'pocketbook' lies, there lies your heart! The very heart of faith is a "spirit of giving" - giving of our money, giving of self.

Giving has to do with doing for others, giving of ourselves to others, and helping by participating. In other words, we are called as the Apostle Paul said in 1 Corinthians 12, to be the "arms and legs and hands and feet and eyes of Christ." We are the body of Christ and we need to work together. It is our responsibility to reach out and minister to those in need, those who hurt, and those who are sick. By helping them, we help the one who sends us. Giving has to do with the "work of God." So our giving should also include the local church, which is responsible for making disciples. Disciples are the ones who carry on both aspects of the ministry of Jesus for the future; making new disciples and taking care of the needy. Are you doing your part?

Lord God, I saw you on the street the other day. I was too busy to stop. I was running late for a meeting; church people talk about you if you're tardy. Otherwise, I would have stopped; will you give me another chance? Send me to give water to one who thirsts; to feed one who hungers; to warm one who is cold; anything for you. Letting other people down does not compare to letting you down, Lord. I would give my life for a second chance! This time I'll get it right. Oh, Lord, have mercy on me! For Jesus. Amen.

Jesus said to him, "I am the way, and the truth, and the life. No one comes to the Father except through me. If you know me, you will know my Father also. From now on you do know him and have seen him."

Going to church and living the Christian life is as much a habit as anything else. Do you have it? Look at it like a Fitness Center. Why do they exist in the first place? Because most of us cannot keep fit without them! They encourage us and make it easier by providing the proper equipment and training. The church is also a body; the spiritual body of Christ: it keeps us fit for the life for which we are called. Just as exercise is essential for a healthy body, exercising yourself spiritually through worship, study, and prayer are essential for renewal and, in the end, salvation.

I recall one young adult I was trying to get into my church say, "I read the Bible every once in a while and I pray sometimes. I don't believe that you have to go to church to believe in God." I had asked him if he believed in God and he had said he did. Then I asked him how he could believe in Christ and reject his body, the church? That is when he gave me that answer. When asked where he got that theology, he said he didn't know. Scary, isn't it? We have a generation designing theology to suit themselves. While the young man is correct in one sense, "You do not have to go to church to believe in God", Scripture clearly states that one worships what one believes in.

To believe "in" God is to follow, obey and worship Him. To worship God means to serve Him. You can believe there is a God and yet not trust your life to him, you can believe Jesus is your savior without making him your Lord – devoting your life to him and letting him tell you guide you. Do you think Jesus would say, "You don't need to go to church? Church is not important to Christians." Jesus did said, *"I am the way."* He did not say that some other way is the way, or that you can do it on your own, he said "I am the way."

Lord God, I sometimes think I know it all; that I do not need you or your church to instruct me or guide me along the way. Has a bigger fool ever been born? Forgive me, Jesus; open my heart to your truth. Let me believe in you, trust you. Take away those things, which compete with you for my time, Lord. May I find comfort in your presence. Someday I'll have quite a story about turnarounds to tell. In Jesus' name, I pray. Amen.

Rock Man　　**March 26**　　*Matthew 16:18*

"You are Peter, and on this rock I will build my church, and the gates of Hades will not prevail against it."

Today let's talk about the "Rock Man". This title refers of course to Peter and the scripture, which has to do with Peter being called the rock. Jesus said to Peter that he would build his church *"On this rock."* And that he would give him the keys to the kingdom and told him that, *"whatever you bind or loose on earth will be bound or loosed in heaven."* In other words, whatever you make important on earth or whatever you make unimportant to you on earth, God will know and hold you accountable. Therefore, it should prove to be of importance to us that we are aware of which things we bind and which things we let go of.

Don't misunderstand. This is not a testimony of our faith in Christ or a statement about being saved or not saved. We are saved by faith in the Grace of Jesus, not by what we do or don't do. These words only reflect our resolve to follow and obey Him. Too often the busyness of life gets in the way. Life is demanding and our focus becomes our kids, our home, our job, our work, or our spouse; all are important, but get the message, *"Whatever you bind on earth will be bound in heaven."* Jesus is the Son of God and Jesus is the savior, is He yours? Trust in Him or trust in yourself, but make no mistake, you cannot do both. You cannot place Him first as well as yourself or this world. You've got to do one or the other.

So make up your mind; get off the fence; show some resolve. To follow and obey God I must get to know Him by participating in His body, the church. Then I will offer and share the talents He has given me; then I will reach out to draw others to Him, spread his "Good News"; then I will give so that others may be helped. I do this because I have done the first; I have gotten to know him. By doing these things we become the modern day "Rock Man".

Lord God, I praise you for your love and Grace for even while we were sinners, Christ died for us. Such an act of sheer mercy and love must change the choices I make, not for my sake, but for my love of you. May I bind those things, which do you credit: love, holiness, forgiveness, obedience. May I loose those things, which dishonor you: selfishness, un-forgiveness, arrogance, pride. Give me the faith to stand against evil, the will to follow in Jesus' steps. It is in his name that I pray. Amen.

Dress up the Inside   *March 27*   *Romans 12:1f*

"I appeal to you therefore, brothers and sisters, by the mercies of God, to present your bodies as a living sacrifice, holy and acceptable to God, which is your spiritual worship. Do not be conformed to this world, but be transformed by the renewing of your minds, so that you may discern the will of God."

Have you ever noticed how some of us try to dress up the outside of our person in order to somehow show others we are better? Many do this to impress others and to be accepted by them, but when we do that we fall for the standards of this world. Look at it like this: you can dress up your dog – he is still a dog. Paul said in Romans 12:2 *"Do not be conformed to this world."* The standards of this world, no matter how good they may seem, are not the standards of God.

What the world tries to do is trick us into thinking we are better than we are. So we become afraid that people will somehow uncover the outer core of our being and see the real selfish, self-centered self, which lies behind. When we do that we become more concerned about the outward appearances others may see than the inner real self. Haven't you noticed how difficult it is for politicians and movie stars, really for most everyone to admit fault? People will go out of their way trying to explain why they did what they did to avoid saying, "I'm sorry. I made a mistake. Forgive me."

Paul was warning us against that. *"Present your bodies as a living sacrifice - do not think yourself more highly than you ought to."* Do not conform to the ways of this world, but give yourself fully to the one who can set you free because he sees you as you are, a sinner in need of salvation. You will find that he forgives without question and to your amazement; you will discover that people will also, those who acknowledge their utter dependence on Jesus and place their faith in his righteousness not their own. To them you are a fellow sinner. And if they don't see that, they are not worth your time and energy.

Lord God, I come asking forgiveness and mercy. I have deceived myself and others. Garbed in a cloak of unmerited righteousness, I have been a paragon of false virtue: unwarranted piety. In short, I've been a fraud and a hypocrite. In honoring myself I have dishonored you; harmed you and your church. Forgive me - I don't deserve forgiveness; never did. But for Jesus, I could be given a new start; I could be a new person, committed, humble, saved. In his name. Amen.

"The people who walked in darkness have seen a great light; those who lived in a land of deep darkness - on them light has shined."

To tell you the truth, we don't really know complete darkness. And it's hard to grasp the idea that light has shined, unless we do. Until recently, most of the world lived in true darkness at night and the hearers of the words of Isaiah knew exactly what he meant. In 1994 I lived in an area of the country that was hit with a tremendous ice storm. It caused power outages all over town. Some areas did not get their electricity back on for weeks. But even then we had light in many places.

Just before that storm there was a complete outage of power caused by a malfunction of a power grid; the sky was overcast so the whole city was pitch black. It was eerie - frightening in a way because you could not see two feet on either side of you. My wife and I got in our car and drove around town. There were hundreds of cars out. So, the city still was not truly dark with all the car lights. But it was darker than I have ever seen! True darkness is without light.

Our ancestors who lived in the days of Isaiah knew the meaning of darkness. When the Biblical writer claimed that *"the people who walked in the darkness have seen a great light"* - they were speaking of something dramatic, something vivid, something hopeful. When John spoke of Christ as the light of the world stating, *'The light shines in the darkness and the darkness did not overcome it"*, he was placing on Jesus the ability to transform this world from one of darkness and despair to one of hope and joy. Jesus was the great light of whom Isaiah referred. Jesus shows us in His own life what God is all about. You cannot capture God or put Him into a capsule or even explain Him adequately in a book. We only know things about him, but, in Jesus, we see God as he is; he is the light that shines in our darkness.

Lord God, I come, a person in deep darkness. The world's artificial light tries to dispel the darkness, but it is there still to hide my sins, to cover my need for redemption, to deceive my soul. Let the light of Jesus shine in my life that I may be witness to your joy and hope. Father God, illumine me, my heart, my soul, my all. Darkness was meant for evil, not for love, nor truth, nor me. In the name of Jesus, I pray. Amen.

Light of the World part 2   **March 29**   *Isaiah 9:3f*

"You have multiplied the nation, you have increased its joy; they rejoice before you as with joy at the harvest, as people exult when dividing plunder. For the yoke of their burden, you have broken as on the day of Midian."

Yesterday we talked about living in complete darkness and what that might be like. To that Isaiah said, "a light was coming into this world." That light was and is Jesus. What did that light bring and what is our responsibility to that light? There are many lights surrounding us: some real, some artificial. There is the light from the sun (real) and light from the moon (artificial). They both supply us with light when needed. The gospel calls us to go out as light into the dark world. Now don't fool yourself into thinking that you could ever be 'the' real light. We are artificial light. The real light reflects on us just as the sun reflects on the moon.

What this scripture is telling us is that there is a loving God out there who cares a great deal for us; so much so that he "multiplied the nation – increased its joy – removed their burden." Remember the story from Luke about the "Parable of the lost sheep"? It's a story of a shepherd who leaves 99 sheep in the wilderness and goes in search for the one that's lost. Or recall the story following - the "Parable of the Lost Coin"? There the woman has 10 coins and looses one. She lights a lamp and sweeps the house until she finds that one lost coin. Each time Jesus tells us that there will be "Rejoicing in Heaven when "one" which is lost is found."

These stories point out as Isaiah did that we have a loving God who is watching over us at all times and rejoices when we find him. The light of which Isaiah was speaking is Jesus. Our responsibility is to be the ones who bear that light. Now we are not responsible to create the light, just allow it to reflect off us and onto those around us. Although the moon has no light of its own, it still stands out in the night bright enough for us to find our way in the dark. And although we have no light of our own, if we allow the light of Jesus to shine on us, it will be more than enough for others to find their way in this dark world.

Lord God, I come today seeking forgiveness. I have seen your holiest light and benefited from that light, yet have not shared it as you have called me to do. Strengthen me with your Holy Spirit that my heart may be open to receive your light that it may reflect upon those around me. Such a privilege you offer to such a sinner! Surely you must be God! In the name of Jesus, I pray. Amen.

Obeying without Question **March 30** **Mark 11:2f**

"Go into the next city and find a colt. Untie it and bring it to me. And if someone should ask why, you are simply to say, "The Lord needs it."

Jesus and the disciples began their journey from Jericho coming southwest to Jerusalem. As they pass by Bethany and Bethphage and the Mt of Olives, they would have a great view of this beautiful city of Jerusalem, which could be seen for miles in any direction. The city looked peaceful from this distance. As they approached the city, Jesus tells his followers, "The hour has come." He instructs two disciples to go to a nearby village where they will find a colt. He tells them to untie the colt and bring it, "And if someone should ask - you are simply to say, "The Lord needs it."

With that assurance, the two disciples set out in search. Imagine their surprise and joy when they find the colt just as Jesus said. And sure enough, as they were taking it away, somebody asked them why they were untying the colt; the disciples reply, "The Lord needs it" and the person allowed them to continue without any further questions. The disciples returned to the shouting of a huge crowd. There was excitement in the air! Some were spreading their cloaks on the road; others palm branches. There was singing and shouting. The people were ready for a change. They wanted someone to lead them into a better life. They had high hopes that Jesus was going to be that someone.

How about you? Are you ready for a change, ready for a better life? Do you seek hope? Do you want the Lord to come marching in to take over your burdens and worries and leave you with a little peace and joy? Remember this demonstration all started with the disciples doing as Jesus instructed: finding the task to be as he had described. The colt was found; Jesus sat upon it to enter Jerusalem. A life of peace starts by trusting Jesus, by remembering that he did not come to make us perfect but to expose and forgive our sins. I mean - do you expect to find peace in the one who came to bring peace if you don't trust him completely?

Lord God, Is there something you' have need of' in me? Is there a task you want of me, my Savior? You have called me to give up my will, to believe in you completely. Yet I continue to follow my own way: Lord, forgive. I do want peace. I want a better life: no burdens, no worries. I want hope. I want joy. Is there a question you want to ask me, Lord? "Do I trust you with my life?" ....Oh, Lord, I have no words,… no words. Amen.

Palm Sunday   March 31   John 12:13

"They took branches of palm trees and went out to meet him, shouting, "Hosanna! Blessed is the one who comes in the name of the Lord – the King!"

This Sunday we celebrate Christ's victory, riding into Jerusalem with shouts of "Hosanna!" from the people. We also celebrate His passion, His crucifixion and death on the cross. Now we don't really celebrate the death and suffering of Jesus, but his atonement. Christ has made it possible for us to be "at one" with God. He has torn down the walls that separate us from God and built a bridge for us to cross into eternal life.

How is that accomplished you say? Jesus submitted his will to the will of God. In Mark 14 Jesus says, *"Father, if it is possible, take this cup from me."* Jesus wanted the cup removed, but in the end he knew what he must do, so later in that agonizing night of prayer, he says, *"Not my will, but thy will be done."* Jesus submitted, gave himself to the cross; spilling his blood for us. Through all this Jesus built a bridge; riding a donkey he made it possible for us to receive a free ride into the Kingdom by his blood. The human race was dying a spiritual death; God's heart was broken (still is) from the loss of so many of His children. Christ changed all of that.

The blood of Christ is a sign and symbol of the atonement Christ' death created between God and us. Look at it like this: God used the cross, a symbol of suffering and shame to bring us salvation. Paul called the cross, *"A stumbling block to the Jews and folly to the Gentiles."* (1 Corinthians 1:23) A crucified person was understood "to be cursed" by God - not sent by God to redeem us! Yet God used this curse of the cross for our benefit. The willingness of Jesus to experience humiliation and give His blood became a means for the divine and human to be reconciled. And Jesus placed this into motion on Palm Sunday as he rode into Jerusalem; A humble God/Man riding a humble animal to give his life that we may become a part of God's wonderful family. Let us never forget!

Lord God, I owe you so much: my life, my complete allegiance, my trust. I was dying a spiritual death, living my life in pursuit of my wants, my plans. Then I met Jesus, and sacrifice, surrender, wholeness, and joy. I met them too. In many ways, I have failed you; I surely will again. But in the righteousness of Christ, you can offer the forgiveness I need to receive, and you, Father, need to give. Atonement: what a wonderful way to love. In the name of Jesus, I come in thankful prayer. Amen.

Monday of Holy Week   **April 1**   *Matthew 16:21*

"From that time on, Jesus began to show his disciples that he must go to Jerusalem and undergo great suffering at the hands of the elders and chief priests and scribes, and be killed, and on the third day be raised."

Somewhere around the end of March or the first of April each year is the beginning of Holy Week, a time when Christians recall Christ's Passion concluding with Easter Sunday. It is a time for us to re-examine our commitment to our Lord. Jesus rode a donkey into Jerusalem on Palm Sunday; the disciples thought He was going there to take power like a King. He had told them over and over that they were mistaken. I guess it was just too much to take in – to be told that your master, the one whom you had followed and adored for the better part of three years would undergo suffering and be killed. Peter even said, *"God forbid it, Lord. This must never happen to you."* But the time had come and it would.

The time has come also for us. At times we live pretending that people don't disappoint us and we don't disappoint them. We live making decisions as if God never existed or if He does, his suffering and the cross was not for us. Jesus had the habit of being very human and very honest with God. If you don't believe it, just look at his prayer in the Garden of Gethsemane. Jesus would always lift every decision up to God before He made any move. My guess is He did it this way because He knew the Father well and knew that this is the way God wanted it.

Might be the way God wants it for us also. What do you think? There is one thing about God that we sometimes refuse to accept and that is He is around us all of the time wanting us to give every burden, every thought, every decision to Him. That way we will spend all day, every day with Him and that presence will make a big difference in the way we act, react, or even the priorities we set. To live this way would be to trust Him totally and that's the way He wants it, always was.

Lord God, as Holy Week begins, impress upon me what you endured on my account. You'll have to get my attention. Sometimes "Christian" is just another word in the vast lexicon of my life and not even the most important. I know you gave your life for me, but my living does not recall. Open my heart to what is required of me. Help me to release every burden to you, to go to you in every need and in every joy that I may find your peace. I'm not worthy, never was. But for Jesus. Amen.

A Little Bit of Heaven   April 2   Matthew 26:72
"I do not know this man"

Have you ever had those moments in your life that you felt were just "A little bit of Heaven?" Well, I have had my share. Let me tell you a few. Usually, they have to do with a special service occurring in the Christian calendar. One example was our last Christmas Eve Service at a church we served for fourteen years. We had a packed house for our candle light service of Scripture and Carols. Afterward my wife and I held our usual open house for those who attended the service and others. We enjoyed reliving the special moments of the service and of the year. We stood around our piano and sang Christmas Carols through out the night. What a wondrous event! It was like a "little piece of Heaven".

Another occurred during Holy Week. We started the week out with services at different churches in town. At midday we would have a 30-minute service with a 30-minute luncheon. On Good Friday we had a "Cross Walk" down Main Street stopping each time we read the "Seven Stages of the Cross". Each walker had the opportunity to help carry the life-sized cross. No one could carry it alone for it was much too heavy. At the end of the walk, several Elders and I gave each participant a horseshoe nail as these words of Simon Peter were spoken, "I do not know him, I do not know this man." Such a personal denial even by proxy brought many to tears. It was a "little piece of Heaven". Kind of the way one would depict heaven to be like.

I am sure you have had your moments of feeling God's presence in such a way as to not forget! Keep them in your memory for God supplies those to help us in moments when we will feel down and out. Those "Little Pieces of Heaven" in your life will remind you that there is something even greater in store for those who, like Peter, have disowned Christ for a moment, but who have been transformed never-the-less by the experiences He has provided.

Lord God, thank you for those "Little pieces of Heaven" through which I feel your great grace. Times such as these strengthen my faith and reassure me of your presence. Forgive me when I fail you as did Simon Peter. Transform my life that I may truly be your disciple. Give me the grace to be joyously obedient and faithfully yours. This is my prayer in the name of Jesus who loves me and gave Himself for me. Amen.

The means of Grace   April 3   1 Corinthians 2: 1f

"I speak to you not in words of wisdom, but with the power of the Spirit, so that your faith may not rest on human wisdom but on the wisdom of God."

I grew up with one "fault" that has hounded me! Everything has to make sense; must be logical. Let me give you an example. When I was young I never missed Superman on T.V., remember that old show? I tried to watch the show later, after I had grown older. It just was not the same. Everything had to be logical! You see, in most every show the "bad guys" would empty their guns on Superman and the bullets would bounce off his chest. Then they would throw the gun at him and he would duck! Does that make sense to you? Paul says in our scripture today that God's wisdom is different than worldly wisdom. The world questions anything that is not logical, but if you follow worldly logic, would you have faith?

Before the time for Jesus to enter Jerusalem he told his disciples once again what was to come. The disciples were in turmoil and tried to convince him that this cannot happen to him. After all, worldly wisdom would tell you that if you die, you die. They wanted to somehow change God's plan, but of course they had no idea what they were asking. They too would be the loser if this plan were not played out. The cross became the means by which God bestowed upon us his grace through his son.

Once Jesus was in Jerusalem some asked, *"Who is this man?"* Others said, *"This is the prophet Jesus from Nazareth in Galilee."* They did not fully understand why Jesus had come. But neither did the disciples, and if you want to know the truth? Neither do we! Oh, we think we do. But the older I get the more I realize how much I have never understood this wonderful gift of Grace given through Jesus; it is not logical. We say that we would never forsake Jesus given the privilege to stand for him. But is that true? Or would we be just like Peter and run for our lives? It was not until later that the disciples got it - the truth about the cross. But when they did, they turned the world upside down. So can we. So.. can.. we!

Lord God, I want discipleship to be easy: grace to be free. I don't want my life to radically change. Yes, I want to be like Jesus, but to lay down my life, to forgive ones who have harmed me in various, deliberate ways is not easy. No one knows that better than you, Lord. No one can show me the path of grace like the one who has made the trip a thousand times. Lock arms with me, my Jesus, together I can follow. In His Name. Amen.

Maundy Thursday   *April 4*   *Matthew 26:20*

"When it was evening, Jesus took his place with the twelve; and while they were eating, He said 'Truly I tell you, one of you will betray me.'"

Today is Maundy Thursday, the time when Jesus was denied, betrayed, tried before the High Priest and beaten. The cross of Calvary is a cross of pain, and love, and hope. It all started with the disciples eating together in the upper room. While there Jesus says, *'Truly I tell you, one of you will betray me."* Then they partook of the Lord's Supper. Jesus told the disciples that they would all deny him before the night was over. Peter said, *"Even if I must die with you, I will never deny you."* Jesus told him that before the cock crowed Peter would deny him 3 times. And he did.

At the Garden of Gethsemane, Jesus prayed that the cup be taken from him, but ended, "Yet not what I want but what You want - Your will be done." And it was. Judas was the one appointed to do the deed. He arrived at the garden with an armed mob sent from the Chief Priest and Elders. They arrested Jesus and took him before the council who questioned him and beat him. During this Peter denied Jesus not once, not twice, but three times. The last time he was asked, Peter replied, *"I do not know the man"* and the cock crowed and Peter remembered what Jesus had said and he wept bitterly. Peter also went on to become one of Jesus' greatest disciples. He turned his back, yet he was still chosen.

That gives us all hope for we know our sin is as great. We too must remember that God forgives. Jesus did not endure what he endured for us to be perfect, but for us to be saved. We sin. We break God's Laws. More significantly, by our sin we break the very heart of God. Maundy Thursday reminds us of the price paid for our salvation. So examine your life. Repent of your sins. Rededicate your life to follow in the footsteps of the one on the night He was betrayed, broke bread and shared it with His disciples, all of them. Every one: even Judas.

Lord God, when I relive this night of all your nights, I am humbled. I know there is a Judas that lives in me just as capable of betrayal. We have met many times, he and I. Peter lives in me too, desiring your best, yet waiting to break your heart again. Oh, Lord, is there a look of forgiveness for me? Forgiven, I can forgive. Unworthy though I am, if loved, Lord, I could love. I could love the betrayers. It would be my gift to you, if only you forgive. Do this for Jesus. Amen.

Good Friday   April 5   John 19:30

"When Jesus had received the wine, he said, "It is finished." Then he bowed his head and gave up his spirit."

Today is a day of vital importance for the Christian church. This is the day our Lord Jesus was crucified on the cross for our sins, crucified to bring salvation. However, if we had been there that day, we may have seen a different sight. Instead of shouts of jubilee, we would have seen solemn faces. Even though Jesus had tried to prepare everyone, they were not ready. Are we ever prepared? Do we ever really listen? Truthfully, we would have been just like Jesus' followers; we would have been afraid when they came to arrest him.

If we had been there, we may have seen the horror on the face of Judas as he realized what he had done. We would have witnessed the denial of Peter, exactly as predicted, just before the cock crowed at the rising of the sun. We would have seen the mocking; the beatings Jesus endured on our behalf; the tears in his mother's eyes and heard as he asked his beloved disciple to take care of her after his death. We would have witnessed the shaking of the earth as He died and the confession from a most unlikely source, the centurion watching over the crucifixion, *"Truly this man was God's Son."* We would have heard Jesus say, *"Lord, forgive them for they know not what they do."* And *"It is finished."*

But we were not there. So today let's remember Good Friday as best we can through the eyes of faith. Let us remember this is not the end of God's plan through Jesus but the fulfillment. When Jesus said, *"It is finished."* He did not mean, "I am finished." Rather God's earthly plan for him was finished. Now he will be at his Father's side in glory. And although we were not there to see his face, touch his garment or experience his presence, because of Good Friday we can experience Jesus anytime - anywhere. Just remember in your time of great need, Jesus is not finished, he is just beginning to bring you God's grace and love, to bring to you to himself.

Lord, I don't like "Good Friday". It's too hard on me. Father, must I endure the remembering every year? Pardon? Oh, yes, I'm grateful. Yes, I embrace your Presence. No, I don't miss the weight of the world on my shoulders or the burden of my sins. Father, how you enlighten me. Jesus paid it all. All to Him I owe. I remember and I'm glad. In His name I pray. Amen.

God's night night light   April 6   Mark 15:34

"At three o'clock Jesus cried out with a loud voice, "Eloi, Eloi, lema sabachthani?" which means, "My God, my God, why have you forsaken me?"

Do good things happen to bad people? You bet! Do bad things happen to good people? You bet! But the story does not end there. We could say life is hard to deal with at times and that we want to cry out just as Jesus did, "My Lord, My Lord, why have you forsaken me?" Wasn't it an innocent Jesus whom the chief priest and elders took to Pilate to be put to death? So the question should never be, "Do bad things happen to good people?", but, "When bad things happen, what do you do?"

There are times in life when it seems nothing good has come: the death of someone you love dearly, job loss, divorce, or the serious illness of a child. There seems to be a dark and gloomy cloud over life, competing with our hopes, our dreams. But remember, when Pilate asked the people what they wanted to do with Jesus, they cried out, "Crucify Him." Someone must pay for our misery. We've all been there, desolate, at wits end, abandoned, bereft. Jesus understands. Jesus knows. Jesus lived life perfectly, was the Son of God, God in the flesh, one with the Father. What did the world do to Him? But that wasn't the end of the story. Storms can look very mean as they come on the horizon but soon they pass, the sun comes out, and the day is bright and beautiful.

When my son was four years old, we were coming from a church I was serving while in Seminary. The sun was going down and the moon was coming up. He asked me what the moon was. I told him. He asked what it was for. I said, "To provide light at night after the sun goes down." He replied, "Oh, it's God's night-night light." From the mouths of babes we see the power and majesty of God. The Lord watches over us during the day and during the night illuminating our way, our life. God did not forsake Jesus on the cross and He will never forsake us. Bad things will happen. But those who turn to Him receive eternal life and His presence in our need.

Lord God, I come to you remembering. On this day, your people lived under a dark cloud. Jesus was dead. Even forewarned, they were aggrieved and afraid. I too am afraid, afraid of losing hope, afraid of making poor choices, afraid of being alone. Thank you, Father, for the greatest sign you have ever sent - the life lived, the death borne, and the resurrection power of Jesus. Fear be gone! Today. Always. I pray. Amen.

Easter: God is Great! April 7 Luke 24:5

"Why do you look for the living among the dead?"

These words confronted Mary Magdalene, Joanna, Mary the mother of James, and the other women when they approached to tomb that first Easter morning. These words confront us today. I have a relative who asked me, "Why don't you go to the cemetery more to visit your mother and dad?" My response to her was, "They are not there." Later this verse from Luke popped into my head. I remember wishing it had done so at the time. But then I would have used it to put her in her place rather than using it for the right purpose; to remind me, "You don't have to go to the cemetery to search for the living - they are not there!"

That is what Easter is all about, isn't it? You and I don't have to search for the living among the dead because *our redeemer lives.* Easter is an important event in the life of a Christian because the empty grave brings us the proof of Jesus' victory over death, the proof that God is in all things, the proof that evil and sin will finally be defeated. Early on the first day of the week, the women had come to the tomb bringing spices and found the stone rolled away and Jesus missing. That is when the men in dazzling white spoke. They ran to Simon Peter and John saying that someone had taken the Lord and they did not know where. Imagine their feelings that Easter morning when Mary Magdalene told them the tomb was empty; they had been numbed by the crucifixion and now this!

It is great to have these accounts to read, but you and I also know that the resurrection is real because we have experienced the risen Christ at work in our lives. Because Christ lives, we shall live. Because Christ lives, those we love are now with Him. Those who have passed from this earthly life into eternal life live also and life is wonderful because of His resurrection. Now don't misunderstand, I know that life is hard, but I also have experienced that God is great. He can help us to overcome any obstacle, which stands in the way of our faith, even death.

Lord, I come on this Easter grateful for blessings. Where to begin? I thank you for Jesus, for His sacrifice for me and for His resurrection, which bought me eternity. Forgive me when I fail; forgive me when I take lightly what was done for my sake. Be with me today to remind me that in good and bad, you are with me and because you are with me, life may be hard but God is great. In the name of Jesus, Beloved Lord. Amen.

"Do not be afraid, but go tell my brothers to go to Galilee and there they will see me."

Yesterday, we celebrated Easter. Today I want to talk about the stone, which sealed the entrance to Jesus' tomb. The scripture tells us that the women went to the tomb with one reality; left with another. Let's use this as an example of how truth and reality work. Often our reality is not truth. Certainly when the women went to the tomb to put spices on the body of their Lord, their reality was that Jesus was still in the grave. However, the truth is he was alive. When they saw the stone rolled away and then met him face to face, they, *"Took hold of His feet and worshiped Him."* (v. 9) He told them, *"Do not be afraid, but go tell my brothers to go to Galilee and there they will see Me."* (v. 10).

That encounter totally changed their reality. Now truth and their reality were the same. That can happen to us. Once you were controlled by anger, the angel of the Lord came down, rolled the stone away, and released you from your tomb. Once you were obsessed with alcohol and drugs: you had no control over them, rather they had you. The angel of the Lord came down, rolled away the stone, and released you from that tomb. Once you felt insecure, so to disguise this reality, you took it out on others by being critical and judgmental, a diversionary tactic to conceal how insecure and sinful you were. The angel of the Lord came down, rolled away the stone, now you feel the gladness of a forgiven sinner, humble enough to forgive, your reality has changed. God has filled you with love and forgiveness; you are no longer in that tomb. How shall we respond to this grace of God who can change our reality and bring us out of our dark tomb into His marvelous light?

Lord God, often I see reality through my own eyes; forgive me. I operate out of insecurity; I am critical, judgmental, so hard of heart; forgive me. Rescue me from the dark tomb that is my reality; bring me into the realty of your truth. Jesus was not raised for my sake so that I could remain dead to grace, dead to life. Will you send me help too? This stone is too heavy to roll away on my own. In His Name. Amen.

Shadow of the Cross   *April 9*   *Matthew 28:6*

"Do not be afraid, I know that you are looking for Jesus who was crucified. He is not here, for He has been raised as He said."

Easter may have has passed but the Season of Easter has not. We live in the Post-Easter times. We celebrate Lent and Holy Week as a way of reminding ourselves once again what our Lord went through on our behalf. And today we live not just in the shadow of the Cross, but also in the reality of the resurrection.

In the Gospel of Matthew, we have the first account of the Resurrection told. Mary Magdalene and the other Mary had gone to the tomb. There was an earthquake and an Angel of the Lord descended from heaven and rolled the stone from the Sepulcher. The Angel then said to the women, "Do not be afraid, I know that you are looking for Jesus who was crucified. He is not here, for He has been raised as He said." Mary Magdalene ran to tell the disciples - and once they discovered the truth, they ran to tell everyone else. They had just discovered the greatest news the world had ever heard. This news not only changed their life that day, it has changed the world as we know it forever - we cannot possibly imagine the impact it has had on this world for thousands of years and even on our lives.

Today we live in the Shadow of the Cross. And although we all must go through adjustments in our marriage, through the difficulty of raising children, or if you are single possibly the difficulty you face because of living alone. Our jobs can be stressful; people can be hard to deal with. We all have fears and worries in life. But the Good News is Christ is risen and we live in the Shadow of the Cross. Yes, life may be difficult, but do not be afraid for Jesus is watching over us. God brought His son into the world; He died for us, was raised for us, and now awaits us in heaven.

Lord, life can be so difficult. Conflict and turmoil undo me! I hold on to issues I should let go of; I let go of things for which I should stand strong. Forgive me when I try to deal with life without realizing that you are with me; your spirit guides and comforts me. Jesus gave his life that I might find rest and peace in you. So when things look dark, help me to remember that I live in the shadow of the cross. In Jesus' name, I pray. Amen.

Road to Emmaus　　*April 10*　　*Luke 24:15f*

"While they were talking and discussing, Jesus himself came near and went with them, but their eyes were kept from recognizing him."

On the same day after Jesus rose from the grave, two men were going to the village of Emmaus, some seven miles from Jerusalem. They were recounting events that had happened; each adding some small detail unnoticed by the other. How Jesus had been handed over to the chief priest who in turn handed him over to the Roman emperor for trial, the cruel death, and the reports of his resurrection. These two were in a daze. They were depressed, down hearted: unaware of a stranger who joined them inquiring about their concerns.

That happens to us also, doesn't it? There are times someone hurts us deeply, and in our hurt or despair, our self-pity, we are so blinded that we would not see Jesus or recognize Him if we stumbled over Him. Am I right? We were too hung up on the bad things that happened to us like these disciples. Like them, there are times when we just know that the crucifixion means, "This is the end." There are times we just know that things will never change – hatred among races, random acts of violence, people loving money more than each other, and themselves more than God. We know our sorrow, we know our sinfulness, we know we will never be forgiven, never become even remotely like Jesus - WE JUST KNOW!

But if there is a humbling point that comes ringing through post Easter, it is WE DON'T KNOW. You don't know and I don't know. We get so caught up in our pessimism that we forget the meaning of the Gospel. We forget that God's grace is sufficient; there are avenues of healing, sources of meaning, reasons for joy that are beyond this world. To receive these blessings, we need have faith, to trust even when we don't have the answers, and to realize the risen Christ is bringing new ways for us to be reborn and resurrected as new persons. When your heart is ready to hear, your eyes will see the One who has always been there.

Lord, I come to you in prayer asking your forgiveness. I too have closed my eyes to your resurrection power. Oh, the facts I have, it's the truth I missed. You know this already. You've suffered through my doubt, my despair. I too have allowed my "why, Lord" moments blind me to your truth, your hope, your grace. Forgive me. Open my eyes that I may do great things in your name. With you beside me, Jesus, we could rock the world! Amen.

*"Sin pays off with death. But God's gift is eternal life given by
Jesus Christ our Lord."*

I remember a great song we sang in choir called, "Jesus Paid It All." We have just celebrated the second most important time in the life of our Lord, the most important being of course, his birth! Palm Sunday is the beginning of Holy Week and the end of Lent. Lent is the 40 days leading up to Holy Week in which we fast and remember what Christ endured in His march to Jerusalem on Palm Sunday, His cleansing of the temple, challenging the Jewish leaders because of their misuse of the Law of Moses to construct their own "human laws." In the Garden of Gethsemane He prays over His personal struggle with the upcoming cross - while Judas, His own disciple, is plotting against Him to turn Him over to the authorities.

We saw Him endure Peter's denial - the disciples running to hide, while He faced the music with the Jewish leaders and the High Priest; His trial before Pilate in which He could have defended Himself. Remember Pilate realized that the Jews were doing this out of jealousy and offered Jesus a chance to defend their trumped-up charges - He refused, for He knew the path He must take. Then, of course, His death on a cross between two criminals who were guilty as charged. This He did to bring us salvation: to bring us grace and hope and eternal life.

He endured great suffering and humiliation in order to carry the weight of our sins. He walked the path, out to Golgotha dragging a heavy cross, weighed down with the sins of the world! That is what the cross represented. Jesus foresaw that and knew it. He came into Jerusalem riding a donkey knowing that He would walk out carrying a heavy cross, weighed down with the sins of the world, your sins and mine. Jesus made great sacrifices for us. Lent and Holy Week and Easter are a reminder to us, lest we forget and become self-absorbed in our own selfish desires to have things our way, that Jesus gave His all for us.

Lord God, I am humbled as I remember the sacrifices made for me, sinner as I am. Words are insufficient to express my great gratitude. You endured immense suffering that I might have new life. How can I ever repay you? "Take up your cross, child, and follow". Oh, Lord, not I!!! I offer so little. I've no discernable talent, no great gift. I can't even….."Can you love?" Well, yes. Yes, I can! " "Come." In Jesus, I pray. Amen.

It's A Matter of Trust　　*April 12*　　*Mark 8:4*

"How can we feed these people with bread here in the desert?"

If I had to guess, I would say that besides pride, the one thing that plagues most Christians is a lack of trust. The scripture contains story after story of about the disciples' lack of trust. In a story in the 8th chapter of Mark we find that the disciples lack the trust that Jesus can provide food for 4,000 people with seven loaves and a few small fish. The disciples say to Jesus, *"How can we feed these people with bread here in the desert?"*, as if Jesus had not noticed the obvious difficulties in fulfilling his request.

My guess is Jesus also knew they lacked trust. He had spent the better part of three years of his life with these disciples already. Later in the 8th chapter of Mark, Jesus says to the disciples, "Do you still not understand – still not get it?" As we all know, any relationship must begin with "trust." Without trust you are left with lies and suspicion. When I was a young, one of my favorite singers was Billy Joel. He wrote a song called, "It's a Matter of Trust." The song is all about love. Some of the words go like this:

> *Some love is just a lie of your mind.*
> *You make believe 'til it's a matter of time.*
> *You might be able to adjust,*
> *But it was NEVER a matter of trust.....*
> *But that can't happen to us*
> *Because it's **always** been a matter of trust.*

Relationships with one another must be based on trust or you will drive the other person away with your jealousy and suspicions. The same can be said of God. Without trust, what do you have? A God you cannot trust or you refuse to rust - a relationship that goes only so far because you do not believe God can or will do as He says. Examine yourself. Where does your relationship stand with Jesus Christ? If you do not trust in Him, maybe you need to take a look at why? It's a matter of trust, you see.

Father God, this matter of trust is the most difficult aspect of faith and belief. I feel as if I am always trying to do the impossible with too little time, too few supplies, too little preparation, too little energy. Is there a lesson in this for me? Teach me, Lord, to seek your will, your power, your strength. May my overwhelming moments be an opportunity to trust you, Jesus, in you all things are possible. In His name. Amen.

Born Again   April 13   John 3:3

"No one can see the Kingdom of God without being born again."

In John, we find the story of the Pharisee Nicodemus going to Jesus in the dark of night to avoid his colleagues seeing his actions. He wanted to find answers for his life. He had studiously followed the Law. Yet something was missing spiritually. He confesses to Jesus that he knows he is a teacher from God, *"For no one can do these sings that you do apart from the presence of God."* Jesus responds, *"No one can see God's Kingdom without being born again."* Nicodemus did not understand, so Jesus explained to him that he came into this world born of flesh and blood and now he must be born of *"water and spirit"* for what is born of flesh is flesh and what is born of Spirit is spirit. Nicodemus still doesn't get it.

We all have those moments, don't we? Moments were where we just have trouble getting it? The ways of God are not our ways. Logic cannot take us where God wants us to go, only faith can, and only through the power of the Holy Spirit. No wonder we look to God and say, "How can these things be?" At those moments when confusion hits us, the Bible says, "Look to the Cross." Jesus was wounded for our sins and by His stripped flesh we are healed. No logic, only faith. The Cross is our hope.

There is power in the Cross and the only thing that will take that power away is our refusal to let go of control of our life - be born again. Jesus wants to transform us from a life of law to a life of love – from a life controlled by self to a life controlled by God. Jesus tells us that God's devotion for his children is beyond measure. It is love without condition. Jesus gave His life so that we might all become sons and daughters of God. Some day all that the Father has will be ours as His heirs, His children. He does this for the greatest sinners ever born and ever to be born. No logic, only faith. Only Love abundant and free, just for you, just for the asking, for the taking.

Lord God, forgive my manifold sins. Nary a day goes by that I don't set back the cause of Christianity by my words, my deeds. Sin is ever true about me, but it is not the greatest truth about me. The greatest truth is I am a sinner for whom Christ died. In that truth is this: I have experienced through God's grace the rebirth of my soul. I think about myself still. I seek to fulfill my desires still but not so much. I seek a life of the Spirit where I live for Christ alone, a new life, a new birth. In the name of Jesus, I pray. Amen.

Jesus Alone   *April 14*   *Jeremiah 31:31ff*

"The days are surely coming, says the Lord, when I will make a new covenant with the house of Israel and the house of Judah. I will put my law within them, and I will write it on their hearts; and I will be their God, and they shall be my people - for I will forgive their iniquity, and remember their sin no more."

A few years ago a new Christian song hit the scene. I especially love the words, "Jesus alone can wash away my sins." I think it is human nature to feel that we are good, decent, law-abiding people. As a matter of fact, I have met more people who think they are O. K. but everyone else is wrong! Let's just say that the number one problem in most relationships is finding fault in others and assigning blame everywhere but in our self. We are very slow to give out compliments or to see our own sinfulness. Apologies are rarely offered. Forgiveness is just a byword to end the standoff. We must quit focusing on mistakes (ours and others) and take an honest look at who we are: sinners saved by the blood of Jesus.

Why do we question ourselves and criticize others in the first place? I believe it is because of the guilt of sins past and present. We are unable to let them go, hanging on as if our life depended upon it. But does that reflect our view of the nature of God or of ourselves? In the 31st Chapter of Jeremiah the Lord says, *"I will forgive your sins and remember them no more."* Does God mean what He says? I for one believe that He does as incredible as that seems.

It is through faith that God achieves His will in our lives. We are saved, not because of our worthiness, but because of the worthiness of Jesus. Faith is not the assurance of a state of holiness or an ability to be sinless. It is confidence in the saving power of God through our Lord Jesus Christ. We have faith - not in faith - but in the God who offers us love and forgiveness and salvation. "Jesus alone can wash away our sins." So let's remember that although we are sinners, God has forgiven our sins and forgotten them. Maybe that will give us cause to do the same.

Lord, will you wash my sins away? I have long made a habit of focusing on the faults of others, criticizing, judging, choosing to have no dealings with known sinners. You alone, Father, are capable of judgment. Transform my mind and heart that I may see my sinfulness and seek forgiveness where it may be found. Have mercy on me, Jesus. May I honor you in all I do from this day forward. In Jesus' name. Amen.

"Teacher, when will this be, and what will be the sign?" Jesus said, "Beware that you are not led astray - you hear of wars and insurrections - for these things must take place first, but the end will not follow immediately. Nation will rise against nation, and kingdom against kingdom - they will arrest you and persecute you – This will give you an opportunity to testify"

Today we look at the world in which we live and we see violence, crime, and racial tension, hatred expressed among whites, blacks, Hispanics, Arabs; among Christians, Muslims, Jews. We read about child abuse, spouse abuse, drug abuse. Television stations everywhere are broadcasting schools in lockdown to prevent children from killing children, disturbed people are carrying guns into businesses killing fellow workers; madmen are strapping on explosives and blowing up innocent people. And we say, "Things have never been so bad."

This state of affairs should come as no surprise to us if we know history and scripture. Jesus said in the 21st chapter of Luke that before the "end of time" comes, *"nation will rise against nation; there will be great earthquakes, famines and plagues, dreadful portents . . . etc."* Jesus was saying that when the world is coming to an end you see these things; not when you see these things the world is coming to an end. Jesus was emphasizing that these things will occur repeatedly until the end of time. He also warned, "Beware that you are not led astray; for many will come in my name and say, 'I am He.' 'The time is near.' "Do not follow them."

Jesus also said in Matthew 24:36 that no one knows the day or time, "not the angels, not the Son, only God. The time will come when God wills it and God is in control. We need not concern ourselves with end times or attempting to pinpoint when it may occur. Our focus is to be with advancing His Kingdom. We are to trust in the power of God in our lives to give us what is needed when the moment comes. God reigns. We have a lot of work to do: loving work, encouraging work, bringing people to Christ; Yes, bad things do happen around us, always have, always will.

Lord, I ask for your assurance. I do not know where to turn or what to do. I see a world around me that is full of evil violence; I do not always see you. Grant me your wisdom and grace. Enable me to speak your truth, to witness your gospel, to confirm that you are truly God. Empower me to trust that the answers to all problems flow through your son Jesus. In His Name. Amen.

Bear the Cross!　　April 16　　Luke 9:23

"If any want to become my followers, let them deny themselves and take up their cross daily and follow me."

Holy Week has come and gone as we celebrated Maundy Thursday, Good Friday, and Easter Sunday. During Holy Week we talked about the cross, spoke of Jesus' suffering, looked at the events leading up to the crucifixion, and talked about the importance of the cross in the life of the Christian. Now the question I think all of us need to ask ourselves is this: Just how important is the cross to me - to us? Do we just wear a cross around our neck on a chain? Is that how deep it goes? Or do we bear the cross with all our heart? Jesus said in the ninth chapter of Luke, *"If anyone comes after me, let them deny themselves - take up their cross and follow me."*

We have a choice to make dependant upon our individual walk with Jesus. Where ever we stand Jesus wants more for us and of us. Maybe you have never truly given yourself to Jesus; maybe you have half-heartedly given yourself, but don't want to take the next step and give Christ your will; maybe you continue to subscribe to the thinking that if you try hard enough you can solve most every challenge that comes your way. But Jesus' message is clear, *"You want to come after me? Give it up!"*

We wear a cross for any number of reasons, but to bear the cross has to do with a total commitment of all that we are and all we hope to be in the service of the One who created us and sent His Son to die in our stead. So, do you really want to follow the Master? Do you really want Him to make a difference in your life? Then get off the fence and turn your life AND your will over to the man from Galilee. Then trust that only he can lead you down the right path. Tell him, "Lord, I trust you and what ever your plan is for me today I know it will serve the common good."

Lord, you sent your Son to give his life for my sake; yet I see commitment as a duty to be checked off some list. You deserve so much more, so much more. You have asked me to deny myself; I ask "How long?" I do so need a Savior. Have mercy on me. I'm going to take a lot of work. If I could just grasp your hand, garner your strength, I can learn to bear my cross with purpose, with joy! In Jesus I pray. Amen.

Seek from Above   April 17   Colossians 3: 1f

"If you have been raised with Christ, seek the things that are above, where Christ is, seated at the right hand of God, not on things that are on earth, for you have died, and your life is hidden with Christ in God. Put to death, therefore, whatever in you is earthly (which is idolatry)."

Did you climb trees as a kid; build tree houses? Why did we do that? I think partly because it enabled us to see things below with more clarity, and gave us an advantage over those below. When you look out the window of an airplane the land below looks very different, like pieces of a puzzle fitting perfectly together. You can see how this town connects to that one, how this stream flows into that river. It all makes sense. Yet, it reveals a humbling truth. I am so very small and this enormous world does not revolve around me. It is this new perspective that the apostle Paul referenced in the 3rd chapter of Colossians. We need to get our view of this life and this earth from above. We need to follow Jesus up into heaven and see the world from God's perspective. From now on let us pledge to see everything in the light of eternity. Paul says if we have been raised with Christ, we ought to set our mind on things from above and not on earthly ones. You see, from heaven everything looks different.

The world and its values are no longer important. Now you see the world in a different light. You live for eternity and the world's ways no longer settle comfortably on your heart. You are different. You are God's. Just because I have no earthly idea how a computer stores all that memory in its ram, it does not mean that it will not give the information back if I ask the right question. In like manner, even though God's ways are a mystery to us - when we read the headlines or see some awful happening on the Network News it does not mean God is not there or has somehow lost control. Jesus is Lord of the universe: He is seated at the right hand of God the Father. He is there for us. So live your life as if that were so. This life leaves us with a slanted, narrow view of truth: God gives us truth through His son Jesus. The choice is yours; choose wisely.

Lord God, I need a new perspective, my outlook is all out of kilter. Those who know me, but still love me they can confirm this unhappy truth. I have lost my way as a person of faith. Oh, I believe! I just have trouble with trust. The ways of this world have entrapped me and I cannot free myself. Father God, could I have a glimpse of heaven? Then I will see clearly what you have in mind for me. In Jesus I pray Amen.

"For by grace you have been saved through faith, and this is not your own doing; it is the gift of God — not the result of works, so that no one may boast."

A few years ago I served a church in Tennessee, which decided to build a new church. The old church had been constructed in 1885 just after the Civil War. There was no way to expand the sanctuary and the three-story education building was built in the 1920's with the first story about halfway in the ground. That presented another problem. You had to climb stairs, and a lot of them, everywhere you went. It was difficult for the older members and even for some of us getting older.

My point has nothing to do with why we chose to build a new church, but when the old buildings were built. Did you catch the dates? Just after the Civil War and in the 1920's — remember the worse Stock Market crash ever? How did they do it? The south was very poor at that time. The only answer can be "they built on faith" - faith that was put into their hearts by God's Holy Spirit. They trusted they were doing the work of Christ and so He would see to it they succeeded. When we voted on moving, the longest standing member of our congregation, an elder who was baptized in that church as an infant, reminded the congregation of what I have just said. They voted unanimously to move on faith!

Luke 13 states, *"Strive to enter through the narrow door, for many I tell you will try to enter (in other ways) and will not be able to."* Why? Because they will try to enter on "good works" - on deeds done for God - but that's the wrong door! The Reformation took place when Martin Luther stated we are, "saved by grace through faith in our Lord Jesus" - period! Nothing else will do. That's the narrow door Jesus is speaking of. We are saved by grace, *"For by grace you have been saved through faith - and this is not your own doing."* Even our faith is a result of God's work in our lives; it is a gift from above. To live by faith we must take the leap. It is easy to say, "I have faith", but to live by faith – that is daring!

Lord God, I come before you today as your imperfect child, asking for your mercy. Forgive me, Lord, not just because I have fallen short, but because I have refused to believe that I cannot save myself. I have trusted in my goodness rather than your saving Grace in Jesus. I did so out of ignorance and unbelief. Grant me the gift of faith; then trust will follow in its path. Do this, I pray, not for my sake, but for Jesus. Amen.

"I have learned to be content with whatever I have. I know what it is to have little, and I know what it is to have plenty. In any and all circumstances I have learned the secret - I can do all things through him who strengthens me."

There are several well-known phrases immediately recognizable when quoted. "I have a dream!"- Martin Luther King. "It's not so much what your country can do for you, but what you can do for your country!" – John Kennedy. There are some who say, "Pray and place your hand on the T.V. and all your worries will be cured" like penicillin cures an infection. Others declare they alone have the answer to all wants and wishes. Catch phrases and half-truths abound. "You want wealth, trust God. He will deliver." "You want good health? - God will make it so."

Although there is an element of truth in each of these statements, we all know that just saying, "It's what you can do for your country."- Does not make it so. It's just not that simple. Reality confirms otherwise. Then there are those outside the faith who are using our legal system to root out any semblance of religion from our government, public schools, and work places. Wear a cross around your neck or anywhere visible on your body and it becomes "religious harassment". To them "I have a dream," means a life without God's interference, not the fulfillment of His heart's desire.

When anti-religious positions get the blood pressure to a boiling point, remember: Jesus lived in a society much like ours. Jesus knew that Christians would face the same failures, the same quick-fix charlatans, and the same disappointments in life as everyone else, maybe more. We go to God to seek answers; sometimes He makes clear the path He wants us to take but that is not what He promises us. Jesus tells us that God does not give all the answers to all our questions, but gives Himself. He **IS** the answer. In your darkest moments of life, call on God and He will give Himself – his love, his hope, and his peace. Then you will learn the truth of Paul's words, *"I have learned, in whatever state I am, to be content."*

Lord God, I come before your presence a novice in the faith despite my years. I seek your truth in a world filled with pat phrases for complex issues. Everywhere I turn someone tells me they have the answer. It's amazing what you can take as gospel. Set my feet on the path of true faith. May I be content in all areas of my life, no matter what happens, no matter where you lead me. Lord of my life, I love you so. In Jesus. Amen.

"And I saw a new heaven and a new earth – and the one seated on the throne said, "See I am making all things new."

When my son was young he loved "Winnie the Pooh" books. I would read to him for hours at a time. He knew the books so well that if I changed one word, he would correct me! He never tired of hearing them over and over. In one of the books, there is a scene where Eeyore is in the river. He and Pooh are having a casual conversation when all of a sudden Eeyore begins to sink. He calls out, "If it's not too much trouble, would you mind rescuing me, Pooh?"

The Church of Jesus Christ is in the rescue business. We are called to proclaim the good news that in Jesus we are forgiven and accepted by God and that all who turn to Jesus, allow Him to be their Lord and Savior are made right by the Cross of Calvary. We all want to know when this great time is coming when we will see a "New Heaven and a New Earth", when all will be well and there will be no more evil, no more grief, no more stress. And although much has been made about the Second Coming, Jesus was clear in that it is not for us to know. It is for us to concentrate on being His witnesses.

Some day there will be a New Heaven and a New Earth, but for now we are God's instruments on earth to carry out His will. We will never be adequate for the task and the only way we will be able to even do the task is to throw ourselves on His mercy every day and rely upon Him completely and without hesitation. Jesus is our source of power. Every generation must be rescued all over again. One is not born a spiritual birth at their physical birth they must be led to Jesus. Every generation must be told of the love and grace of Jesus. If not, Christianity will fade away. Call upon God and He will give you the power to spread His love, hope, peace, and the irresistible grace of Jesus.

Lord God, I come before you a sinner with but one request, "If it's not too much trouble, would you mind rescuing me, Jesus?" I have felt your gentle urgings calling me to speak the words of Life. In disobedience, I have held back. Give me confidence to speak of my faith. Remind me that the outcome is up to you, not me. Fill me to the utmost that I may share with others who, like me, need a rescue. In Jesus I pray. Amen.

Stability   *April 21*   *Hebrews 13:8*

"Jesus Christ is the same yesterday, today, and forever."

In a world where so many things change, it's good to know there's someone who never changes. I'm not really a stargazer, but I do know a bit about stars. I was a boy scout and they taught me among other things about the North Star. It is a permanent fixture in the sky; something we can count on as always being where we think it will be. The North Star is located at the end of the little dipper and all of the constellations rotate around it like the hands of a clock. The other stars move, but the North Star basically remains stable. It does rise and lower at the horizon between summer and winter, but nonetheless remains a constant. Sailors have long plotted their course on the vast ocean using it as guide and compass.

In a world where nothing seems constant or fixed, it is comforting to hear these words from Hebrews, *"Jesus is the same yesterday, today, and forever."* Would that were so in our lives. Neighbors come and go, friendships run hot and cold, religious affiliations change over the least disagreement, no one has a job for life or would want one if offered. There is a true story of a young man with seemingly everything going for him; good career, great marriage, wonderful family but an overwhelming deep conviction that something important was missing from his perfect life. I suggested it might be a spiritual wasteland he was in, that maybe Jesus wanted him for his own. He said he would think about it. Sometime later, I ran in to him. I asked how he was. He had taken up the banjo he said. And your life; how is it? About the same, he replied, about the same.

It is Christ who offers us purpose and stability in an every changing world. It is Christ on whom you can rely in a world full of shallow people who disappoint and discard. It is Christ who provides a guiding light, a permanent fixture of hope and strength. For those who are imprisoned by doubt and worry, anxiety and insecurity, Jesus gives us a fixed light to follow. He offers a presence that will never forsake us, a comfort in all times of need, for Jesus is the same yesterday and today and forever.

Lord, I come today as your beloved child beaten down by life. I come as a sinner guilty of the same behavior I condemn in others. I too have disappointed those I love, even you, Lord; forgive me. Help me to place my trust in you, Jesus, knowing you will never disappoint nor abandon me. Empower me to depend on your promises all the days of my life. For I pray in His name. Amen.

"Everyone who drinks of this water will thirst again, but those who drink of the water I give will never be thirsty - this water will be in them a spring of water gushing up to eternal life." The woman said, "Sir, give me this water so that I may never thirst again."

I purchased a small cabin in the woods in 1996 in order to have a place for retirement. It was one of those fixer-uppers and I'm something of a handy man. I blessedly have a lot of handyman friends. After I retired we had to transform it from a weekend "hideaway" to a place of residence. We built a new entrance, walk in closet/storage room, painted the ceiling, stained the wood walls, and put down a new floor. There were other smaller projects and one was to put in a spotlight to shine down from the ceiling onto the mantle over our fireplace. It took a little doing!

First time I got it installed, the light was too far back and did not shine the way my wife had envisioned. That meant redoing the ceiling around the light to move it forward and make it look like I did not move it forward! At first, I was resistant. "It looks fine to me!", I said, opting for the easy way. But I realized it would always look like a botched job. Even if no one else noticed, I would. At this same time, I had been working on the story of the Woman at the Well for a sermon. I thought, now this is really appropriate. We all like quick fixes much like this woman at the well so we won't be inconvenienced by drawing water again.

But, quick fixes often look just like they sound. We can cover up our sins, but we cannot remove them. We always know they are there. Somehow they will show through just as this woman's did under the penetrating gaze of Christ. We opt for easy solutions, a quick glass of water to quench our thirst; Jesus offers us living water that will quench our thirst forever. There is a catch. To accept you must change. Living water is yours to drink but you must go to Jesus. Once you do, you cannot help but keep going. The waters of eternal life welling up in the human heart; just imagine! Just for the asking: the taking.

Lord God, I always take the easy road in my faith walk; forgive me, Father. Will you give me the "living water" of which Jesus spoke? I realize I cannot remain as I am. I know truth radically changes people. I'm ready, not unafraid, but ready. Fill my heart your love and grace. With all that selfishness gone, there will be plenty of room for you, Lord, plenty of room- just for you. I pray this prayer for Jesus' sake. Amen.

"Call your husband." - "I have no husband." - "You are right in saying, 'I have no husband'; for you have had five, and the one you are living with is not your husband. The woman, "Sir, I see that you are a prophet."

Jesus confronts the woman at the well with the truth about herself. He had told her about the "living water" and she was intrigued. Now, he lets her know that he can see everything about her! That is a frightening thought, isn't it? Whatever we have done, Jesus knows. When Jesus told her to go get her husband, he knew she had none and was living with a man with whom she was not married. The woman responds, "I have no husband." To her partial truth Jesus adds the full truth.

Can you imagine what it must have felt like? You go to draw water from the well. A stranger speaks, asking for a drink. After engaging in a theological discourse on water vs. living water, He jumps in with both feet telling you who you are; not the beautiful, perfect person that you hope everyone sees, the image you portray for the benefit of others. Jesus sees the real you: the critical, imperfect "you" who is quick to judge, slow to praise: the "you" who looks for faults to complain. The "you" who thinks you know what is right for everyone else; the "you" who thinks you are better because you have never committed the sins others have.

How could a perfect stranger know all of this! The woman calls him a prophet. Well, yes and much more. And when the woman told Jesus that she knew the Messiah was coming, he tells her, "I am He." That should come as no surprise, for He has already revealed the inner secrets of her life and still spent his time saving her sinful soul. He'll do the same for you. If you must live falsely, pretending to be perfect, strong and pure, go ahead. Just don't try and go to Jesus that way. He will see straight through you. He knows the real you. Jesus came to confront you with the truth about yourself for a purpose - to set you free from the unacknowledged sins that condemn you and separate you from a righteous God.

Lord God, I have tried to live my life hiding all my sin, even from you. I have pointed out the sins of others so that I don't have to acknowledge my own; forgive me. Open my eyes that I may see the real me! You'll have to hold me, Lord; such utter truth will kill my fragile self. But it must be done, otherwise how will I ever know the content of divine love and the depth of divine forgiveness. In Jesus, I pray. Amen.

"Then the woman went back to the city and said, 'Come and see a man who told me everything I've ever done. Cannot He be the Messiah?'" "Many Samaritans from that city believed in Him because of the woman's testimony."

The last two days we have taken a look at the story of the Samaritan woman. The woman wanted the "living water" Jesus was offering; then to her amazement Jesus tells her who she is, warts and all, but He does not reject her. The woman's response to her encounter: she tells others about Jesus. When Jesus confronts us with the truth about ourselves, we too can go tell others, but not before. Once we face the truth about ourselves, then we can be changed and set free. What a story then we will have to tell others!

Jesus confronted the woman at the well with her sinful past and offered her the gift of a new life. She was overwhelmed. I think all Christians need to go to an AA meeting, if for no other reason, than to hear them introduce themselves. They do it like this, "Hi, I'm Herb and I'm an alcoholic." They respond, "Hi, Herb." They don't say, "I'm a *cured* alcoholic." They tell the truth: I am what I am. How would that work with Christians? "Hi, I'm Herb and I'm a sinner", not a cured sinner but a sinner through and through. The good news is that Christ died for our sins and God will not hold any sins against those who belong to Jesus.

When the townspeople heard about Jesus through this unlikely witness of the woman at the well, John tells us, that they wanted to hear him for themselves! No longer just because she had told them, but because they too had now heard and believed that he is truly the Savior of the world. If Jesus can use such an unlikely candidate as this woman to bring others to Him, He can certainly use sinners like you and me. But only if we're willing to face the truth about ourselves and share that truth. For that is our story: the story of how Jesus has taken us away from the slavery that is sin and given us the living water that is salvation.

Lord, I thank you for this story; in it I can see my story. It is a story of searching, of going down path after path until I am finally confronted with Jesus and his salvation. I know that I have sinned greatly. I pray for your forgiveness. I now recognize the healing aspect of true confession and the repentant heart that makes confession possible. "Hi, Lord, it's me. I'm a sinner." "Hi, you." I pray in the name of Jesus. Amen.

"Paul spoke to Felix concerning faith in Jesus. And as he discussed justice, self-control, and the coming judgment, Felix became frightened saying, 'Go away for the present; when I have an opportunity, I will send for you.'"

Felix had heard Paul speak about faith in Jesus Christ, about "justice, self-control, and the coming judgment." Concerning Justice, there are some who contend that the world is morally corrupt. I suppose they mean more so than in years past. Based on history, I'm not so sure. The story of Sodom and Gomorrah bears consideration. Actually, we don't have to go that far back. The past history of the United States should convince us that things are actually better, not worse. In the scripture today, Paul has been placed under arrest; brought before Felix and his wife, Drusilla, a Jew and daughter of Herod Agrippa. They wanted to hear more about Christianity but only on a superficial level. As the scripture says, *"Felix had a rather accurate knowledge of The Way."*

Felix was a cruel man and his wife was no prize. As a matter of fact, Felix was her third husband. For a period of over two years, Felix heard Paul's defense of the Gospel, but would not release him because he hoped to get some money from him. Paul defends himself before the governor and his wife. What he has to say caused them to shake in their boots. He spoke of justice. Justice deals with doing that which is morally right, fair, and honest. It is built upon individuals who see what's right and make a commitment to do what is right before God.

The problem is we want to make choices without suffering the consequences. We mistakenly think that we can be perfect and pure without the presence of Jesus in our hearts. Soon we discover that is not possible. So before we are too hard on Felix and Drusilla or anyone else for that matter, we might want to remember that we are all sinners, unacceptable to God in that state. But thank God, in his mercy He has made it possible for us to be put right with Him through His Son, Jesus.

Lord God, I come acknowledging that I am a sinner in need of your grace. Could you keep that terrible truth between us? Some people expect perfection, shunning known sinners, crushing the soul. I have tried to remake myself. Is it worse to have tried and failed than never to have tried at all? Cover me with the righteousness of Jesus. Open my heart to forgive as freely as you have forgiven me. I pray in the name of Jesus. Amen.

"Paul discussed justice, self-control, and the coming judgment, Felix became frightened and said, 'Go away!'"

Yesterday we looked at this scripture from Acts and discussed what frightened Felix, the governor. One was Paul's talk about "justice" another was his discussion of self-control. We who live in the United States enjoy some of the greatest freedoms the world has ever known, sometimes even to our own detriment. Some worry so about political correctness that they overlook the wrong they allow to go on. In order to be politically correct, they believe that they cannot point out wrong or evil. We certainly don't want to embarrass anyone, even if to point out the realities of life as an act of mercy and compassion. Paul would have trouble in our society!

Although Paul knew his audience well (he knew that Felix was Drusilla's third husband and his lack of morals was notorious) he still pointed out their faults. He spoke the truth with power. Now remember, Paul is in prison at the mercy of this governor and still he has the courage to say what is right and just. He informed the governor and his wife they must have self-control if they are to be a part of the kingdom. Remember what Paul says in Phil. 4:13, *"I can do all things through Christ, who strengthens me."* Paul is saying we can have "self-control" through Christ, who strengthens us.

Our political correctness has blinded us to the problem. We attack symptoms rather than the real problem. We do that in medicine. Instead of focusing our resources on cure, we focus on treatment. People have high blood pressure; they prefer to take a pill instead of changing their diet, exercising and practicing meditation. We can remove the temptation, but that does not take away the real problem, a lack of self-control! There is power released through living with Christ. And that power helps us exercise self-control, helps us resist temptations that have the potential to bring us down and result in tragic consequences.

God of Grace, I see my lack of self-control and I cringe at the damage I do to myself, to others, and even to you; forgive me. Remind me in everything I do to seek your strength and power. You alone can save me from myself; save me for Jesus. In His name I pray. Amen.

"As Paul discussed justice, self-control, and the coming judgment, Felix became frightened and said, 'Go away for the present; I will send for you.'"

We have examined these scriptures for the past two days. Today let's look at the third subject that Paul mentions to the governor and his wife, "the coming judgment." Just as Paul stood before the judgment seat of Felix, Felix would one day stand before the judgment seat of God. There is going to be a reckoning! Felix and all the rest of us will some day have an accounting for our lives. Felix was so shaken, as was his wife, Drusilla, that he sent Paul away to be recalled when he had "opportunity". It wasn't long after that Felix was swept from power.

One thing I wish to point out is this: judgment goes both ways. Recall the parable of the sheep and goats from Matthew 25. The "son of man" judged that the sheep be placed on his right hand and to inherit the kingdom prepared for them by God from the beginning of time; the goats were judged to be placed to his left and were to receive eternal punishment. The naked truth of life is this, we cannot hide anything from God, our sins will find us out; we reap what we sow. Truthfully, we also reap what others sow because the consequences of sin have a way of spilling out into the lives of those around it. What we do matters; sin does not just harm our lives; it harms the lives of everyone it touches.

We are acceptable to God through faith in Jesus Christ. To receive God's hope and salvation, we must receive Jesus through faith, come to repentance, and give Him control of our life. In His skillful hands, He will remold us and re-make us and help us to live the life that God ordained us to live from the very beginning of time. It is the only true way to peace and joy in our life. When we surrender to Jesus completely, we need not worry about judgment for God will judge us as sheep and we will inherit the Kingdom.

Oh Lord, when I consider my sins I am overwhelmed with fear and regret. Have mercy on me for I have danced to my own drummer, willful in my disobedience. Is there room in your great heart to forgive me? To spend eternity without you would be a hell of my own making, fit consequences for one so headstrong. Help me to live the life you planned for me this day and forever. Do this, Father, for me and Jesus. Amen.

Light in the Darkness   April 28   John 1:5

"The light shines in the darkness and the darkness did not overcome it."

When John spoke of Christ as the light of the world, he was placing on Jesus the ability to transform this world from one of darkness and despair to one of hope and joy. Remember the song, "This Little Light of Mine"? And the point of the song is? "I'm going to let it Shine." It talks about hiding your light away or letting Satan blow it out and the response to each option in the song is "No! I'm going to let it shine." You see Jesus did not touch our hearts and call us to become His followers, to be a part of his body - the church, just so we can be saved ourselves or experience a spiritual awaking, or to grow spiritually. There is so much more!

There's a biblical principle at work here and that is, spiritual growth is impossible if you do not share your light with others. Now, before you start with all the excuses, let me ask you this. How many years have you been a Christian? Surely by being a Christian or being around Christians all these years something has rubbed off. When I was a young man, I grew a vegetable garden. I raised potatoes and would save some of the better potatoes back and place them in a very dark dry area under my house for the winter. In the spring, I'd bring them out, cut them up and plant them. One spring, I brought them out from under the house and discovered my potatoes had sprouted. How did this happen? Light! The sun evidently shined through the air vents, hitting a tin pan under the house. It was just enough reflection of light to make the potatoes sprout.

Now, you may not consider yourself to be a great light, but you see whatever small light of His shines through us will be enough, because it will be coming from Jesus. Jesus is the Light of this world and He calls upon us to carry that light to others. So whatever light Jesus gives you, don't hide it or let it be extinguished by doubt, or fear, or indifference to the plight of others. Your spiritual growth will be to the measure of how much you share. Or not! Your choice.

Lord God, you came into my dreary life with your marvelous light bringing hope, bringing grace, bringing joy! It would be so easy just to gather gladness and hide it away in a closet, kept until needed. This is not your way. You are to be shared! Give me the courage to tell how you have made a difference in my life. I will need great love to do this well. Will you send me an extra dose of Jesus? I can never have too much. I pray. Amen.

Plowed Ground   *April 29*   *Matthew 5:45f*

"Your Father in heaven makes his sun rise on the evil and on the good,
and sends rain on the righteous and on the unrighteous. For if you love
those who love you, what reward do you have?"

Farming is a lot like faith. It takes a lot of courage. Rain is needed to keep things growing. If you are a farmer, you depend on it for your livelihood and it is always a gamble. You never know what to expect. You plow the land, get it ready, plant the seeds in the ground, and cover them up. Then you wait. You wait for the rain and the sun to take over and cause the seed to germinate and grow. That is God's part.

But besides faith, farming also takes doing on your part. As a matter of fact, if you don't "do", don't plant the seed in the first place, there will be no crop to grow. The same is true about our spiritual growth. Without spiritual feeding we lose our strength to fight the good fight. This battle is not, as the Apostle Paul says, "With flesh and blood" or with "each other." This is a spiritual battle and without spiritual food we will fail Jesus. God supplies all that is needed for us to grow spiritually. He gave his son, Jesus to bring us grace and to cover our sins with his righteousness. He sent the Holy Spirit to give guidance and to open our hearts to receive his grace and his commandments.

But we still fight God. We don't want to plow the land inside our souls to receive the seed. And if we do not plow, the seed won't get deep enough to catch hold. But we need more than feed from God's Word. Just as in farming, it takes some doing to cultivate God's fertile fields so His Kingdom will grow and prosper. We do that so others can also learn of His love and receive His spiritual food. If we don't "do", the fields will not be prepared for God's good rain and sunshine. Then there will be no spiritual food for tomorrow, for our children, and our children's children. Just ask Jesus, "What can I do to help?" Then, listen and start planting!

Oh God, Creator of sun and rain and fields to plow and seeds to plant,
you have blessed humankind with needed work for your Kingdom. I thank you
for that trust. Help me to see my particular "field" to plant. Give me through
your grace the faith to try. Plow deep my hardened heart. Remind me of all the
wonderful things you have done for me, sinner though I am. I want so much to
serve you well. Make good my meager efforts. I do so love you, my precious Lord
and my God. Amen.

New Beginnings   *April 30*   *Luke 9:62*

"No one who puts a hand to the plow and looks back is fit for the Kingdom of God."

What do you suppose Jesus meant when he said those words to the gentleman along the road to Jerusalem? At first glance, it appears he is saying that looking back is wrong. He seems to condemn the natural response that New Beginnings bring. I believe what Jesus was really saying is that we should not let the past hamper us to the point where we are not free to live the present or work toward the future. Some people have heart attacks and worry about death all the time. They are not free. Some are consumed with going on into the next life. They are not free! Some make a mistake in life that haunts them forever! They are not free!

It is OK to recall those things of the past that are good; to recall and reflect on them as we face a new beginning. Such reflection gives us strength and security. But we want to reject those things that are bad, which cause us to become trapped in the past. We need to concentrate on the present and not on the past. As you begin any new beginning just place yourself into God's hands and trust that he will take care of you.

We affirm our faith in different ways, but mostly in the form of a story. A story of how we believe God delivered the house of Israel out of bondage in Egypt and into a new beginning; a story of God delivering the Christians out of the bondage of sin and death thru the atoning power of His son, Jesus Christ; a story of how God continues to deliver us out of separation from Him and into new beginnings. *"Once you start to plow, don't turn back - if you do, you are of not use to the kingdom of God."*

Now that does not mean that we cannot reminisce about the Past - think about it, bringing back fond memories to cause us to laugh again and help as we start a new beginning. But, we cannot let it hamper us - we cannot yearn for the past wishing things were the way they used to be. For then *"We are of no use to the Kingdom of God."*

Sovereign God, you know my life. You know all there is to know about me, my propensity to dwell on the past. When I do so I punish others and myself all over again. In so doing, I lose my present and my future with all its possibilities. Save me from my harmful ways. Hold my hand to the plow and my face to your future. Be gracious to me, a sinner. Set me free once more. In Jesus' name. Amen.

"In this is Love. Not that we have loved God, but that He has loved us and gave His Son to be the expiation for our sins."

If you ask anyone to quote a piece of scripture, invariably they will quote John 3:16, *"God so loved the world that He gave His only begotten Son. That whosoever believes in Him should not perish, but may have everlasting life."* Can you think of anything the world needs more than love? To realize that the nature of God is Love and that is what He offers you and me is almost beyond our comprehension. 1st John 4:10 states, *"In this is Love. Not that we have loved God, but that He has loved us and gave His Son to be the expiation for our sins."*

This is a biblical principle: You have neither the power to love God nor anyone else if you have not first been loved. You see faith is not a response to the fear of God. Faith is not a response to an intellectual knowledge of God. Faith is our response to God's love. That is why the Cross of Calvary is so important to the Christian faith. It is on the Cross that we see the love of God most clearly. Will in the end we find only love and no judgment? In the 3rd chapter of John, verse 19, Jesus says the judgment is that light, He, has come into this world and because people were so enamored with evil, they loved darkness more! We are all liable to judgment because we all sin and we all fall short of God's standards.

The true question is not, "Will there be judgment?", for there most certainly will, but rather, "Will we open our eyes to the Light?" - to Jesus Christ? In the verse following in John 3, Jesus says that the ones who believe in Him, who live the truth, will have life everlasting. What is true is this; we are sinners in need of forgiveness. We must open our eyes and acknowledge that Jesus is the only one who can forgive us of those sins. His righteousness covers all sins - past, present, and future. He came to bring us light, to open our eyes to that truth. So open your eyes, for the Light has come into the world and that Light is calling us out of darkness.

Lord, I come to you in prayer acknowledging that without your divine love, I would be lost. Without your divine love, Father, I would not know how to love, nor would I have love to give. Fill me to the utmost! Grant me the faith needed to open my eyes to your light and your truth. Do this, Father, for Jesus and for me. Amen.

"Will not God grant justice to His chosen who call on Him day and night?"

How do we obtain peace in a world of doubt, confusion, and distrust? There is a wonderful little parable in the 18th chapter of Like about the unjust judge and the widow. She goes to him time and again to get justice and the judge refuses. Finally he gives in making the statement that although he does not fear (respect) God nor man, he will give the widow justice because he is warn out by her continual pestering.

To that Jesus goes on to say, *"You notice what the unjust judge says? Now, would not God see justice done to His chosen ones who cry to Him day and night!"* The real reason we do not have peace of mind has to do with doubt. We go through life saying, on one hand, we believe in God, but on the other hand we doubt that He will fulfill His promises to us. Frederick Buechner says, "Doubts are the ants in the pants of faith." What is meant by that is doubt is O.K. if we see it for what it is; a stumbling block put into our path by the evil one. So don't misunderstand, although doubt is a natural part of faith, we are not meant to give in! That would be like giving in to your fears.

Let's say that God has given you a beautiful singing voice but you fear singing in front of a crowd. If you give into that fear no one will ever hear your beautiful voice. Satan is the author of fear and doubt; don't let him fool you. To obtain peace in this world, you must believe these words of Jesus, *"Will not God vindicate His elect who pray to Him day and night?"* To hang on to doubt or to give in to doubt is to confess that your image of God is this: a weak God who does not make good on His promises. You don't really believe that, do you?

Lord God, I confess I have allowed doubt to rule my life. I say with my words that you are Lord of All, but my actions tell a different tale. My actions say you are weak, unworthy of my trust. It isn't you I have described, Father, is it? Forgive me that sin and the harm it has done. Help me see that doubt, born of fear, is not the end, but the catalyst that opens my eyes to your love, grace, and truth. In Jesus I offer this prayer. Amen.

The Pharisee **May 3** *Luke 18:11*

"Thank God that I am not like other people... I fast and give my tithe."

This passage from Luke may be very familiar. So many Christians think just like this Pharisee who gives thanks to God that *"he is not like other people."* Most Christians will agree that we are sinners in need of forgiveness; that we must go to God in order to satisfy that "need for forgiveness". But many fall into a trap in choosing the next step. We like to think that because we are Christians, we are somehow better than those who do not go to church! This passage should set the record straight.

Jesus gives the illustration of a Pharisee, a church-going-religious person, going up to the temple to pray. In his prayer he says, *"I thank God that I am such a Good person.... I am not like other people - I give of my tithe faithfully... I fast and pray... aren't I great!"* Is there anything bolder or more foolish? At the beginning of this parable the scripture says that Jesus tells this parable to *"some who trusted in themselves that they were righteous"*. We all want to somehow take credit for our "goodness" on our own and without help from anyone including God. Otherwise, why would we presume we are somehow better than someone who does not go to church?

This is what the Pharisee was doing. He was faithful in attending the temple; he was faithful in giving of his tithe; he was faithful in praying to God, but why mention aloud these things already known to God? The Pharisee is telling God that he is better than those around him because he is doing "good". He is forgetting that God is the one who made us all. God is the one who put His goodness in us. We can take no credit. So if we are to give thanks to God, let us give thanks because He cares so much for us that He gave His unconditional love to us even while we were still sinners. That is what grace means.

Father God, there is such empowering smugness in judging another's sin. Hypocrites! How do you bear us? I would have long ago given up on the whole sorry lot if I were you. I'm not; thank God, I'm not. Open my eyes that I may see myself as a sinner in need of your forgiveness, for until I do it will be impossible to find my way into your grace. Help me to place all my pride at the feet of Jesus. For it is in His name that I dare to offer this prayer. Amen.

The Tax Collector   May 4   Luke 18:13

"God be merciful to me a sinner!"

Yesterday we focused on the Pharisee - today the Tax Collector. He was a man despised by all. The Jews hated him because he worked for the occupying Roman government collecting taxes from his own people. The religious leaders considered him a "sinner". The Romans thought him a Godless mercenary. In this parable, Jesus places in comparison a highly regarded religious person, the Pharisee, with a highly despised sinner, the Tax Collector. Jesus had been talking to the Pharisees and to his disciples in the passages before this, so we can presume that when the scripture says Jesus told this parable to *"some who trusted in themselves that they were righteous,"* he meant the Pharisees.

I can just see their faces getting red and their anger rising! They were made to look bad while the self-proclaimed sinner was made to look good! While the Pharisee in the parable bragged about *"being such a good person"*, the Tax Collector saw himself as just the opposite. He would not would not even look up to heaven, but beat his chest saying, *"God forgive me a sinner"*. If you remember, Jesus tells us that the devout Pharisee went home un-forgiven while the sinful tax collector went home right with God. How can this be? It is preposterous for anyone to go before a Holy, Perfect and Almighty God and pretend that they are also perfect and holy!

If you were to list your sins for just one day or one week they would fill a book! How many books would it take for a lifetime of sin? So before we make complete fools of ourselves and still insist that we are better or more righteous than those outside the church, let this parable burn deeply into our hardened hearts. Hypocrisy harms all it touches. Forgiveness thought unneeded goes un-requested. Forgiveness un-requested remains unclaimed. Forgiveness unclaimed lies fallow in the field of sin. If we were honest with ourselves we would have to follow humbly the Tax Collector and fall to our knees praying, "Lord forgive me a sinner!"

Lord, as I look at my life, my sins are too numerous to count, too many to recall. While you have forgiven me and accepted me, sin and all, I have held the sins committed against me in my heart refusing to let go. Bring me to true repentance, Father. Enable me to give mercy in the same healing way that I have received mercy, undeserved, from you. I have lived as a hypocrite all my life; please don't allow me to die as one. In the name of Jesus; precious Savior. Amen.

"When the Holy Spirit comes, He will prove the world wrong about sin and righteousness and judgment."

We are all free to believe and trust in something; it would be best if we trust that which is true, that which is sacred, that which is of God. Some trust in money, only to find it does not bring the happiness, peace, or even security they thought it would. Some trust philosophers, in great thinkers, only to discover somewhere down the road another great thinker proves them wrong, if not in all things, at least in some. Some people trust in principles. If you work to be good, you can; treat others with kindness, they will treat you with kindness only to find that untrue. They cannot be as good as they thought and no matter how nice you treat some people, they remain unmoved, unchanged, jerks through and through.

Instead use God's living Word. See if it works in your life. Does it work to believe your body is the temple of the living God and you need to take care of it? Does it pay to be faithful to your spouse? Does it pay to love and honor your parents and your children? Does it pay to follow the 10 Commandments? Does it help to love the Lord with all your heart, mind, and strength, and your neighbor as yourself? What do you think? Do the principles of religion work? Certainly, it goes beyond human effort because Christianity is not following rules; it is a relationship with a living Lord, Jesus Christ. It is an openness to listen and follow the Holy Spirit.

Too often we think that our job is to point out the sins of others and then judge them. But John reminds us here that is the job of the Holy Spirit. Now I don't know about you, but that takes a load off my mind! Here I thought for years that my job was to get people into the Kingdom, to tell them what is wrong and right, and to decide if they are worthy to be a part of the family of God. Today's passage states unequivocally, that's the business of the Holy Spirit. The Holy Spirit will do the convicting, we are to do the witnessing, and that's it. This should free us from the bonds of judgment - to now look at the sins of others in the same way as our own.

Lord, I come confessing my great need for a Savior, giving thanks for your Holy Spirit as advocate and guide. Truly I am lost without you, Father. Help me live my life daily in faithfulness; assist me in every decision I face. Free me from the burden of judging others; free me to leave God's work to God. Open my heart to see You, Jesus, in all those around me. Let me live for you, Father, and you alone. Amen.

Act Shrewdly   May 6   Luke 16: 1f

"There was a rich man who had a manager; charges were brought to him that this man was squandering his property. He summoned him and said to him, 'What is this that I hear about you? Give me an accounting of your management, because you can no longer be my manager.'" V.8 "The wealthy landowner commended the dishonest manager because he acted shrewdly."

Jesus tells a parable about a wealthy landowner and his clever steward. Word got back to the landowner the steward was embezzling money. So the master says, "Get your books in order and then you are fired." The shrewd steward decided to work out a scheme with all the master's creditors. He lowered their bill to put him in their favor; he thought that by doing so the creditors would feel obligated and the steward would have someplace to go after he was fired. But instead this ended up making the steward look ingenious in the eyes of the rich landowner. He commended the clever steward, "because he acted shrewdly."

There are qualities in the steward that Jesus wants us to have. Through this story, Jesus reminds us that material things are "dishonest wealth." We have these things because God has gifted us and given us the talents to obtain them but they do not actually belong to us, they belong to Him. God has a purpose in mind for them. Of course, the steward actually was a thief and acted illegally in lowering the bills of the creditors. Jesus does not want us to have those qualities! But He does want us to be as shrewd in our attempt to gain goodness as this steward was in obtaining money and security. To use "dishonest wealth" wisely for the kingdom in order to obtain the true wealth which is in heaven.

The servant, or slave, in this story had no time that was his own. All his time, every ounce of his energy belonged to his master. He lived in the master's house, ate the master's food. In the same way, serving God cannot be a part-time job. Once we choose to serve God, every moment of our time, every atom of our energy belongs to God and His kingdom must come before everything else.

Lord, I have dealt dishonestly with your wealth and your kingdom. I have considered everything I own as mine; worked for and deserve. How easy to forget everything I have and everything I am I owe to you, Lord; forgive me. Help me to live wisely and to act shrewdly when it comes to building your kingdom. Free me to serve you with energy, gratitude, and unrestrained joy! In the name of Jesus I pray. Amen.

"Sing psalms and hymns making melody to the Lord in your hearts;
Giving thanks to the Father at all times and for everything in the
name of our Lord Jesus Christ."

One May years ago, we had some especially bad storms roll through our neck of the woods. A favorite member of my flock said to me, "Rev, why don't you preach a sermon entitled, "Storm clouds bring out your true color." So I did. It just so happened that another good friend died not long after that and I preached his funeral. His name was Emmett but we all called him Buddy. He had a heart of gold and an unforgettable sense of humor.

Some storm clouds that come into our life cause us to grieve; certainly the loss of someone you love is one of them. But, also the way you handle the loss can be very important. After Buddy's funeral, we all went over to his house and sat around swapping stories about our dear departed friend. There was much laughter because Buddy was not only a great storyteller; he created some real life stories that were priceless. Stories are a way we get to know one another. If I don't know your life story, I really don't know you.

Sharing those real life stories helps us to get past the sorrow we feel. Sharing our stories is what love is all about. It helps us to remember; helps put a smile on our face, and helps us get past the moment. When life itself gets you down and you are caught out unprepared in storm clouds, ask God to take away your fear and replace doubt with faith and trust. Gratitude is the gift of finding God's grace in all things. Ask for it. Paul tells us to give thanks to God all the time and for everything! That attitude change can truly change our life!

Lord God, I complain about everything. No one can make a mountain out of a molehill quicker. 24hour News keeps me enthralled. How can a person of faith dwell on catastrophe? Is it some morbid proof that you can't be trusted, Lord? If I say it before it's my fate, will it hurt less when it is? The storm clouds of my life reveal the faithless, negative thinking, persecuted wretch I truly am. Living in my strength tells, so does living in God's. Remake me in your image; I don't want to be this me any longer; I dishonor us both. In Jesus; Amen.

"So if anyone is in Christ, there is a new creation: everything old has passed away; see, everything has become new! All this is from God, who reconciled us to himself through Christ, and has given us the ministry of reconciliation; 21 For our sake he made him to be sin who knew no sin, so that in him we might become the righteousness of God."

Paul's words allow us to draw some parallels between God's love and a mother's love. In some respects, each one offers a kind of love resembling the other. Our mothers know us, all of us, our shortcomings, faults, weaknesses, strengths, our dreams. She knows us warts and all and loves us anyway! God also knows us. We are personal to God. Our sins are fully known, fully grieved by God. Desiring us well, in Christ God makes us into a "new being" because He knows no other way will suffice.

So much of this world projects an artificial love; people seeking for others or for some worldly standard to give meaning to life. We continue to look in all the wrong places, bringing much grief into our lives. But, with God, we are at home. His love is personal and generous, like a mother's love. God gave us the means of reconciliation through the atonement of his sinless Son. No greater value can be assessed to mankind. Everything you have, everything you have ever had, everything you will ever have comes from God as an act of love and grace.

We have given so little in comparison to what God has given us but He keeps on giving. That is His nature. He is a giving God. Just as a mother keeps on giving, no matter what we do, so does God. God cares about us and does not give up on us. We are His precious children. To my mother, I was her precious son. Even though I did wrong, in another sense, I could do no wrong in her eyes. Besides, she did not love me because of my accomplishments, or the deeds I had done, or honors I received. My mother loved me because I was hers. That's the kind of love God has for us. When we sin, which is often, He waits for us to come to Him and confess. Then He does not say, "I told you never to do that again" rather, God says, "My child, you are forgiven."

Lord God, I stand in awe of your great grace, your abiding love. I can never repay your gift of Jesus through whom I am reconciled for all time to you. Thank you for mothers who watched as we made mistakes in life and loved us anyway. For some that was a first glimpse of God's love. You, Lord, have watched us, forgiven us, loved us. Give me this day your love and peace. Grant me your grace. In Jesus' name. Amen.

Hearing God's Voice · May 9 · 1 Samuel 3: 1f

"Now the boy, Samuel, was ministering to the Lord under Eli. The word of the Lord was rare in those days; at that time Eli, whose eyesight had begun to grow dim so that he could not see was lying down in his room; the lamp of God had not yet gone out and Samuel was lying down in the temple of the Lord where the ark of God was. Then the Lord called, 'Samuel, Samuel.'"

Have you heard God's voice? Before you answer, let me tell you there are many voices trying to occupy the spaces of our minds. There have been people who heard voices and shot presidents; others heard voices and shot famous musicians; committed violent murders. Some have heard voices and sold everything they had and joined groups on mountaintops awaiting the second coming. These voices certainly could not have been the voice of God. So how can we tell if it is God?

First we have to believe that God does speak to us. In Samuel it says the word of the Lord was "rare", not that God no longer spoke, but that it was rare. I believe that one reason many do not hear God anymore is that they don't listen. They do not expect to hear God. Also there is Pride. Willful disobedience. We resist going to church. We resist turning our life over to God. We resist answering his call to do whatever it is he wants because our pride gets in the way. We know how we should live. We know to treat others, as we want to be treated. We know that in order to receive we must give. So why do we resist? Pride.

Pride is the chief cause of problems in relationships today. If we get into an argument it is because we think we know best and the other person is wrong. Pride. How can we hear God speak if we already have all the answers? God would just be wasting his time. So first we need to repent of our pride. Set-aside time to be still and listen and then we may hear God speak. And when he speaks, you will know. He will not ask you to harm another or to harm yourself. He cannot contradict Himself. He will call you to fulfill the destiny He planned especially for you before the world began. Sit in His presence, wait, and listen.

Lord God, I do believe that you speak to your children. Is there a word of truth and love for me? Set aside my pride so that I may hear and follow your voice and accept your will for my life. This will be a reversal for me, willful and unyielding as I am. Give me the gift of discernment, O Lord, and save me from the voices of the evil one. Shelter me, Lord and, if it be your will, come to me, speak my name. In Jesus' name. Amen.

"And the Lord called, 'Samuel, Samuel,' and he said, 'Here I am.' And he ran to Eli and said, 'Here I am, for you called me.' But Eli said, 'I did not call you, go back to bed.' So the Lord calls to Samuel a second time, 'Samuel, Samuel.' Now a third time, the Lord said, 'Samuel, Samuel,' and again Samuel ran to Eli and said, 'Here I am, for you have called me.' And then Eli perceived that the Lord was calling him."

Yesterday we spoke of how we might hear God's voice. An important tool in discerning God's voice is by comparing it to Scripture. Like Samuel, we run in the wrong direction; to the wrong sources. TV has become one authority, at least for some. Some believe that whatever the reporter says is the Gospel truth. For others it is the Internet. Whatever they find there is Gospel truth. I had a relative who once said that we are reliving what happened a million years ago. I asked him why he said that? He responded that he read on the Internet about a large jet that was uncovered which was almost a million years old. Can we say gullible? We read books written by Christian leaders, and I'm not saying that in itself any of these are bad but none is the real thing.

The Bible contains the truth. Don't substitute it with something of lesser value and don't let some other book tell you how you should interpret the Bible without going directly to the Bible and checking it out. Alternative answers just toy with our emotions and feelings. If you don't have your head on straight, they can trick you. I knew a young man in Kentucky who had been confused by a professor in college. He came home distressed one summer because this professor had told him that God did not exist. I told him to just go read the Bible. Start with the Gospels and Paul's letters and then come back and we would talk.

After reading the scripture, he realized that the professor wasn't as smart as he thought he was. Reading God's word helped this young man discover God's true voice and brought him back to the faith. Many have listened to other people and been led astray. The Bible contains a record of God's words and deeds. It helps us to see and understand God's nature and how He operates. If you truly wish to know God, make reading the Bible a daily habit.

Oh Lord, how extraordinary to think that you would speak to someone like me! Yet this is a truth my heart longs to hear, to believe. Guide me and strengthen me as I seek you through your Holy Word and, seeking, find. This is my prayer this day and every day. Oh, Lord of my Life, I await your Presence. Come, Lord Jesus, come. Amen.

"The Lord called Samuel again a third time. He got up and went to Eli and said, 'Here I am, for you called me.' Eli perceived that the Lord was calling and said to Samuel, "Go lie down and if he calls you again you say, 'Speak Lord, for your servant is listening.' So Samuel did and the Lord came calling as before, "Samuel! Samuel!" And Samuel said, "Speak for your servant is listening."

The last two days we have spoken of how we might prepare to hear God's voice. Today, let's explore the witness of the Body of Jesus, the church. Samuel continued to run to Eli when he heard the voice calling thinking it was Eli. Eli was a man of God. He represents the church in our scripture story. He knew the scripture. Eli understood how God speaks and operates and he advised young Samuel to go back and lie down. And this time, when the voice comes say, *"Speak, for your servant is listening."*

Now why should God show himself to one and not to another? Samuel was just a young boy. Why him? I cannot really answer as to why God chooses one and not another. I can only say that there are truths that open the door to hear God speak. Samuel had a pure heart. He was at the temple because he wanted to be involved in God's work. He was there while other little boys were out playing games and enjoying being little boys. Once you come to know God and listen to him you realize the incentive always lies on His side. If he does not speak to you, there is not much you can do about it. Just give yourself as fully to God as possible and place yourself in a position to hear. Let God do the rest.

The community of Christians – the church – is the only institution adequate for learning about God. But beware because some institutions call themselves the church, but are really false prophets leading you down the wrong path. Trying to sooth your ego and make you feel good and right rather than tell you what God requires. C. S. Lewis said, "Christ did not come to torment your natural self, he came to kill it." No half measures will do. So if you are looking for God to come and give some word in agreement with you to make you feel right and important, think again. He will come and demand to have all of you as he did Samuel.

Dear God, Sovereign Lord, I chose you over all the other authorities who seek to control me by telling me what I want to hear. Strengthen my resolve. I can be so easily misled! Keep calling me by name as you did with young Samuel. Open the ears of my heart to hear and obey. Speak, for your servant listens. In Jesus' Name, I pray. Amen.

"For I am convinced that neither death, nor life, nor angels, nor rulers, nor things present, nor things to come, nor powers, nor height, nor depth, nor anything else in all creation, will be able to separate us from the love of God in Christ Jesus our Lord."

It is important to understand how you view God, for our view of God shapes who we are and who we will become. I believe in a "sovereign God." In Exodus 3:14 *"God said to Moses, "I AM WHO I AM."* Our plan of salvation and our security as believers comes from our view of God. The dictionary describes Sovereign as "one who has a supreme power and authority." It is a term that refers to God's unlimited power. God has "sovereign" control over the affairs of nature and people.

Do you see God that way? Although I may not always see God's actions or even the results of His actions, I believe He acts and that He is in control. If you believe in a weak God, you will be surrounded by fear and uncertainties and anxiety. If you believe in a strong God, you may still be attacked by fear, uncertainties and anxiety but you will be moved to courage and action. The Bible tells us that God is working out His plan of salvation and that nothing will stand in the way. Paul affirms that in the 8th chapter of Romans, *"For I am convinced that nothing will be able to separate us from the love of God in Christ Jesus our Lord."*

The entire Bible is God's story of redemption. From Genesis to Revelation God lays out how he loves the world and the creatures he created. For us humans, God gave a special status and set us over all that he has created. When we truly see the awesomeness of God, it makes us conscious of our own weaknesses and sin, and our need for Him. God holds the destiny of the whole universe and us in His hands. If you believe that, you will be inspired to overcome evil and will be capable of accomplishing great things with this life God gave you. You will be filled with His joy and love.

Lord God, may I always see you, as you are my Sovereign Lord. When I consider your great love for me made complete in Jesus' sacrifice, I am moved to offer you all I am: my life, my thoughts, my actions, my will. Help me to have this mindset always. Be my strength and my guide always and forever. In Jesus' Name. Amen.

*"For the Son of Man came not to be served but to serve, and to
give his life a ransom for many."*

Many believers do not feel any evidence of "the deliverance of God" because they want the easy road. People don't want to become disciples; don't want to make commitments; don't want to have to turn everything over to God.   Today, people have adopted a "consumer mentality"; they want to receive rather than give. Yet, wasn't it Jesus who said, "*I come not to be served, but to serve.*"

The problem stems from our society. People are on the go. They want life paced with instant gratification. If one fast food restaurant does not satisfy them well, there are always two or three others just around the corner. If one department store does not cater to their immediate needs, there is always another just one block away. If this spouse does not meet his or her needs, there is always someone else. If this church does not offer what they want, well there is always another church. As a result of this "consumer mentality" many have became consumers even in the church rather than disciples. Jesus wants disciples and there is no shortcut.

The church is not a commodity for one to consume. The church is the body of our Lord and Savior Jesus Christ; it is a place to come and offer thanks and praise; to worship and to share your talents to build God's Kingdom. The church is family, a family of God's children who share responsibilities, who work together and help one another. If the church answers your entire consumer needs, yet fails to make you a disciple, you may have what you think you want, but God will not have what He wants. The life of discipleship may not be easy, but our Lord never said it would be. The best lesson we can teach to our children is for them to learn to serve, not become consumers. I do promise you this: if you will give yourself up to become a disciple, you will experience God's presence in your life and His deliverance as you never have before.

God of Grace, this passage hits home. I am indeed a "consumer" in so many parts of my life, that I am a consumer in my relationship with you fills me with shame. Have mercy, Lord, forgive me and change me. Make me alive with the desire to serve you and your church. Let me begin right now. Guide me in your servant ways; grace me with a servant's heart. In Jesus' name. Amen.

"A lawyer tested Jesus. "Teacher, what must I do to inherit eternal life?" Jesus said, "What is written in the law?" He answered, "You shall love the Lord your God with all your heart, soul, strength, and mind; and your neighbor as yourself." Jesus said, "You have answered right; do this, and you will live." But wanting to justify himself the lawyer asked, "And who is my neighbor?"

This is the story of the Good Samaritan. It begins with a lawyer asking Jesus how one could "inherit eternal life." Jesus throws the question back asking what the law requires. The lawyer responds, "Love the Lord your God with all your heart, soul, strength and mind; and your neighbor as yourself." But the lawyer was not satisfied even with the law so he asks Jesus, "Who is my neighbor?" Jesus responds telling the story of the Good Samaritan to illustrate to us the answer to that question.

In examining the story, let's not be too quick to condemn the priest or the Levite, who each ignore the man lying robbed and beaten beside the roadway, especially until we look closely into a mirror. We experience people in need every day. We either reach out or we walk by on the other side: empathetic, moved into action or judgmental deciding whether a person deserves help before offering. In other words, we don't go to God and ask, we don't look into the person's heart to see their need, we simply become judge and jury, deciding if help is deserved or not, that determines whether we will become involved. Priest and Levite?

What Jesus is trying to get across to us is, "We are neighbors of each other", not just of the person next door or our close friends, but we are neighbors to every person in need. We must see their pain and hurt as our own; then we will become motivated to help. That help can come in many ways. It may come as a visit. It may come as a note or card telling the other person we miss them or we are thinking about them. It may come as a comforting embrace. It may come in the form of our money or our time. How will you respond, my neighbor?

Dear God of Mercy, I too am like the lawyer, asking questions of you only to justify myself, proving I have the right answer but not the right heart. Oh, God, for the sake of mankind and my soul, create in me compassionate heart, one of courage and love. I cannot know fully what I am agreeing to, but I know this. There will be no peace or joy in my life until there is peace and joy in yours, even if I barely know you, even if we never met. In Jesus' Holy name. Amen

Obedient Slaves   *May 15*   *Romans 6:16*

"Do you not know that if you present yourselves to anyone as obedient slaves, you are slaves of the one whom you obey, either of sin, which leads to death, or of obedience, which leads to righteousness?"

In the third chapter of Romans Paul mentions that a person is justified by faith apart from works. My fear is that too many people today continue to build their faith on "good works" rather than "saving faith." When anyone says things like, "I try to live a good Christian life. I study the Bible. I try to keep the commandments, to do what is right, to live by the Golden Rule. I try to do good works" then what are they saying except, "I hope all that I am doing will be good enough to get me into heaven."

There is the danger. Don't misunderstand. All of the above effort is expected of Christians. Even "necessary!" However, the emphasis is what is important. Do we say, "I try to live right" so others can see I am a Christian? Or do we say, "I thank God that His spirit is alive in me and causing me to do His work." Saving Faith is trusting in Christ alone by grace alone. Now, this does not mean we receive salvation by believing a certain way or by doing things a certain way. Rather, it means we receive salvation by resting our life on the merits of Christ before God instead of our own merits, trusting in what Christ has done rather than what I am doing.

This does not exempt us from going to church, studying the Bible, giving our tithe, or doing good works. Paul pointed out in Romans chapter six that we are "slaves of the one whom we obey." If you present yourself as obedient to God in Jesus Christ, you will also want to do that which will please him: worship him, praise him, and submit your life to him. We will not be doing any of this so we can gain anything, we already have everything in Christ, but we will be doing all of this because we love the Lord who first loved us and gave his life for us.

Gracious God, as I read and consider the above passage I see myself all too clearly. I am tried and convicted, guilty of doing "good deeds" for self-serving reasons, out of indebtedness, perhaps even guilt. I have obeyed to gain favor even misguidedly to coerce you, Father, to accept me out of obligation. Merciful God, forgive me and restore me to your care that I may love as you have loved me. In Jesus' name. Amen.

"Brothers and sisters, join in imitating me, and observe those who live according to the example you have in us. For many live as enemies of the cross of Christ. Their end is destruction; their god is the belly; and their glory is in their shame; their minds are set on earthly things. But our citizenship is in heaven!"

Where do you have your eyes fixed? On earthly things? Or on Heaven? I once knew a family that kept an incredibly cluttered house. It was so messy that when you came in the front door there was a narrow passageway about two feet wide in which to walk. On either side were piles of "things"; books, magazines, clothes, toys, and the like blocked your path. My guess is this family did not even notice the clutter any more. Their eyes were so fixed on something else, the house looked, I guess, "straightened up" to them.

Paul reminds us that it is very important to keep our eyes fixed on heaven rather than on earthly things. He is not really writing about people who keep a messy house or a messy office but people who keep messy lives. Their lives are cluttered because they've never made a basic choice about whom they will worship. Not having made a choice is actually a choice made. St. Paul writes about *those whose "god is their belly"*, not those who eat too much but people who live only for today and for the pleasures of life with no thought about tomorrow or how that might affect them in eternity. He's talking about the cult of instant gratification.

In a way Paul is talking about people not that different from you and me. Don't we sometimes settle for the easy road? In our culture it seems pretty clear that many prefer comfort to commitment, self-indulgence to self-sacrifice, and possessions to people. The sad thing? Many don't even realize they are doing so because they have not fixed their eyes on that which is truly important - Heaven! Those who keep their eyes fixed on things above see that their "citizenship is in heaven" and follow a higher order, a divine order. So where do you have your eyes fixed? That is a choice you and only you can make.

Most Holy Lord, help me to see the truth about my choices. Have I focused on the things of earth when your prayer for me is that I focus on you? Forgive my pride and my self-indulgence. Grant me an uncluttered heart so that I may live with eyes fixed on Heaven alone. Be my master and my guide. In Jesus' most precious name. Amen.

"See that none of you repays evil for evil, but always seek to do good to one another and to all. Rejoice always, pray without ceasing, give thanks in all circumstances; for this is the will of God in Christ Jesus for you."

Paul's letter to the church at Thessalonica charges us to be responsible for one another. As a minister I am acutely aware of this calling. People have come to me with the most heart-breaking stories you have ever heard. They reach out in their anguish and desperately want me to soothe their pain and make them feel all right. Years ago there was a Sit-Com on TV called "Cheers". I loved the song in that series. The words in the song talked about going to this bar where "Everybody knows your name."

There is something special about everybody knowing your name, isn't it? We all love to be recognized for who we are or what we do, but mostly we just want to be accepted and have people really know us, especially the "good" us. We all cry our in our pains of life and we hope there is someone who hears us and understands us. The irony is that we are tempted to do just the opposite of what we want done to us. Paul says for us to not repay evil for evil, but boy do we want to! When we hurt someone else we just hope they will overlook that and forgive us.

But when we attempt to know everybody's name, it becomes harder to hurt them and easier to "do good to them" as Paul states. We must realize that God has blessed us to be the bearers of His Good News of Jesus to this world – to reach out and get to know everybody's name so that we can see that all are our neighbors, not just the ones who think like us and like to do what we like to do, but all of God's people are our neighbors. We must reach out to all with the love and forgiveness – the grace of Jesus. You want everybody to know your name, right?

Lord of all grace and compassion, I see the needs of this world and I want to run away. Aren't my problems enough for me? What about my need, my pain, who helped me? Convict my heart with the truth that Jesus has helped me. He can and will help others through me. Give me the words, the love I need to speak His truth. Give me the grace to care more about someone else than I do about myself. Give me a heart for Jesus. In His most worthy name. Amen.

"When you give a banquet, do not invite your friends or your brothers or your relatives or rich neighbors, in case they invite you in return, and you would be repaid. But invite the poor, the crippled, the lame, and the blind."

Jesus is going to dine at the house of a Pharisee. Excited to have a guest of such notoriety as Jesus, he has undoubtedly invited his friends, his relatives and his rich neighbors. The religious leaders are trying to trap him, so Jesus asked them, *"Is it lawful to cure people on the Sabbath, or not?"* They were silent. They knew the answer but somehow it felt incorrect to say 'No'. Then Jesus presents this problem, *"If your child falls into a well will you not immediately pull that child out even on the Sabbath?"* Again they stood silent uncomfortable, unsure of themselves.

That is when Jesus teaches them about the Great Banquet telling them to not invite friends or relatives or rich neighbors for they can repay. Instead invite those who cannot repay, those they never considered inviting. Now they are really uncomfortable and ready to hear Jesus. There's a subtle theme present throughout the Gospel about a God who throws parties; the story of the woman who finds the lost coin and throws a party; the prodigal son who comes home and his father throws the party; the story of Jesus at the wedding making the best wine ever tasted. Jesus was a man filled with life and joy, a spirit of celebration. Joy is an essential part of the Christian life; celebrations are joy shared.

Jesus tells us that God will be throwing a feast and we are invited. All we have to do to accept the invitation is acknowledge Jesus as Lord and Savior. Don't worry about being good enough to be invited, the only ones worthy of this invitation are those who don't deserve to go and can do nothing to repay the host! Salvation comes through what God does. There is not one work of righteousness we can do to be saved. We are saved by the righteousness of God - God's mercy - His grace: undeserved, unmerited favor to someone who is totally unworthy. So come with joy to the party. Jesus has personally called you. Personally paid for your ticket.

Oh Lord, rescue me from my incessant need to be accepted by the in-crowd, to be admired for my good deeds, to be dining with the best people. I can be such a show-off at times that I miss your truth, your invitation to the Great Banquet whose ticket you bought for me. What greater affirmation is there? Grant me humility. Grant me joy! In Jesus' name. Amen.

"If you forgive others their sins against you, your Heavenly Father will forgive you; but if you do not forgive others, neither will the Father forgive you."

The subject of forgiveness is more important than most think. Those who have a closed heart, who are unwilling to forgive, are blocking a relationship with Christ. I will go further and state that Jesus cannot always break through the barriers in our hearts unless we open our hearts to him. "Un-forgiveness" blocks the paths of our Spirit from receiving God's Spirit. Now I base this conclusion on several observations. God wants us to hold nothing back from Him. If we refuse to forgive others, or even ourselves, we are holding back a part of us from his healing presence.

The Scripture today states that if we are willing to forgive those who have sinned against us, our Heavenly Father will forgive us. But if we are unwilling to forgive others their sins against us, then our Heavenly Father will not forgive us. Truth is we cannot truly forgive. In other words, forgiveness is a power we do not possess. In Luke 5:21 we find these words, *"Who can forgive but God alone?"* This passage was directed at Jesus from a Pharisee, but the gist of it is correct. Only God has the power of forgiveness and that power comes to us through His Son, Jesus, and is pumped into our spiritual veins by the Holy Spirit.

On the one side, until we forgive, our hearts are hardened with the poison of un-forgiveness. On the other side, we do not have the power to forgive apart from Jesus. That is where prayer comes in. Prayer is essential in clearing out the bitterness caused by disappointments and heartache. We must lift to God the pain caused by life and others and ask Him to replace that burden with His forgiveness and love. That request will open up our hearts and allow the pain we feel to flow from us to Him; He can then take it away. Then and only then will we have the power to forgive. It is a gift from our Heavenly Father through His Holy Spirit.

Oh God, I long to be a forgiving person but I have lived so long with deep resentments, I cannot imagine myself without them. To savor the power of forgiveness withheld, to relish the control of giving pain for pain, hurt for hurt, tit for tat – who can let that go? Can soul-death be so irresistible? Only in the power of the Holy Spirit, can such evil wickedness die in me so that soul-life can live. Have mercy on me, dear Lord, make me yours alone. This is my only prayer. In Jesus' Name. Amen.

The Pioneer of our Faith   May 20   Hebrews 11:1f

"Faith is the assurance of things hoped for, the conviction of things not seen."
"By faith Abraham obeyed when he was called to set out for a place that he was
to receive as an inheritance; and he set out, not knowing where he was going."

Years ago I ministered a church that decided to move from their historic site built in 1895 to a new place that God would show them. It was not an easy thing to do. In making a move as a Christian we must focus on two things: faith and the witness of those who went on ahead of us. The writer of Hebrews explains faith as the assurance of things hoped for and the conviction even when we cannot see. By faith Abraham obeyed when called to set out to a place not knowing where he would be going.

Faith is not faith when we know where we are going, know exactly how we will get there, know exactly what it will cost along the way, and know exactly where that money is coming from. Faith is the, *"conviction of things not seen."* That does not mean we as Christians follow "blindly". It is important to test the spirits to make sure we are following God but ultimately, we must step out in faith not knowing what tomorrow will bring. Remember the witness of those who went before us. The church I was serving had a rich history dating back to 1825. In 1895, seventy-five members stepped out in faith and built a new church on what was then the outskirts of town.

The writer of Hebrews reminds us of our spiritual ancestors. It is important to see and embrace those who went before us. He lists examples of Abel, Enoch, and Noah, Abraham and Moses. He charges that we are surrounded by a great cloud of witnesses, therefore let us *"run with perseverance the race set before us – looking to Jesus who is the pioneer and perfecter of our faith."* Those who went before us molded our present with their faith in the future. We are called to do the same. As God's chosen people, we are called to step out in faith and answer His call to do His work whatever that is. It is not easy, impossible without His help. Those who went before us can give us the courage to follow.

Dear God, I thank you for the witness of your Holy Word that compels me to trust in you with confidence and for the presence of this great cloud of faithful witnesses whose stories inspire me to act on that trust. May I too honor your Holy Name with acts of faith too great for me but not to great for Us. May your Holy Name be praised now and forever. This is my prayer in the name of Jesus. Amen.

"I am the living bread that came down from Heaven. If you eat of this bread, you will live forever." "Those who eat my flesh and drink my blood abide in me and I in them. Just as the living Father sent me and I live because of the Father, so whoever partakes of me will live because of me."

Communion is a time when we come together to share in the glory of God. We share in the body of our Lord Jesus, but we share more than that. Jesus says in John 6:51, *"I am the living bread that came down from Heaven. If you eat of this bread, you will live forever."* We partake and share in each other's joys and burdens. Our differences are put aside and forgotten when we kneel together to receive the bread and the cup that God offers us through Jesus Christ. When we open our hearts in prayer to God; when we come before His presence; our sins are revealed and we see only our need to confess and repent and seek forgiveness.

We realize as we come in His presence that we are no better than anyone around us. We realize that we are one and that the eternal food that we receive is something only Jesus can give. Jesus tells us that when we eat of his flesh and drink of his blood we abide in him and he in us. For just as the Father sent Jesus and He lives because of his Father, whoever partake of Jesus will live because of Him. There is no substitute for Jesus; turn your eyes upon Him. The true food and the true drink is Jesus Christ.

There is only one way to participate in the Eternal life offered by God and that is through Jesus Christ. When we come to the table of His presence, we come hoping and seeking to be forgiven for our sinfulness: our gossiping, and lies, our covetousness, and our selfishness. We come hoping to be transformed by the bread and the cup. There we realize that Jesus does for us what we cannot do for ourselves. We cannot work our way into heaven; we cannot enter on someone else's faith; we cannot be good enough. When we stand or kneel before the Table of our Lord, there we fall upon His mercy and there we receive it.

Lord, I thank you that you sent your Son Jesus to save and to sustain my thirsting soul, as food and drink nourishing my spiritual body. Thank you for anticipating my need for sacramental life, to celebrate together as a community of forgiven sinners the bread and the cup. May your presence continue to transform my life each and every day. Abide with me, my Beloved Jesus. Abide in me. In Jesus' name, I pray. Amen.

It's Beyond Our Control   May 22   Romans 8:26f

"We are weak; we do not know how to pray as we ought, but the Spirit intercedes with sighs too deep for words. - We know that all things work together for good for those who love God, who are called according to His purpose."

I saw a wonderful movie years ago. The two main characters challenged each other in games of love. The game backfired when the male character actually fell in love with an innocent woman who was the object of the game. She, being unaware of the game, professed her love seeking a like commitment. With these words, he had won the game. It was only left for him to respond with, "It is beyond my control." He was thus victorious. We all like to win, to take credit for our accomplishments; be rewarded for the sacrifices that we make in our hard work, even for the Lord! It is difficult to admit that there are some things in life beyond our control. One of the basic principles of Christian living is accepting the fact that many things are beyond our control.

We cannot choose our parents. We cannot choose the color of our skin or the country in which we are born. We cannot choose the care we receive as infants or the quality of our education. Even though we cannot control these things, remember the Spirit will intercede for us. Not that the Spirit will get us what we want, but will pray for us when we do not know what is best. We have a tremendous desire to control and what we wish can actually put us in opposition to the will of God. The Spirit can and will sort those things out.

Realize that the will of God is beyond our control and be glad! Instead of fighting to gain control yourself, fall back upon the Spirit and rely upon His wisdom. Pray and then leave it up to the Spirit. Let go and rely upon faith in a Wise and Loving God! Many things are beyond our control. We simply can never hope to have enough knowledge or wisdom to perfectly determine the path of our lives, let alone our children, or anyone else's. But nothing is beyond God's control. He is able to make "all things" work for good for those who love Him and trust Him to work out.

Oh, Merciful and Gracious God, forgive me for I am weak, wanting what I want when I want it. Give me a bearable glimpse of the truth about myself: my selfishness, my arrogance, my pride. Come, Holy Spirit, and intercede for me with sighs too deep for words. For I long to live according to your perfect will but I will be stubbornly, weakly human until the day I die. Have mercy. In the name of Jesus. Amen.

Repent: Open your Eyes May 23 Jonah 3: 1f

"The word of the Lord came to Jonah, saying, 'Get up, go to Nineveh, that great city, and proclaim to it the message that I tell you.' So Jonah set out and went to Nineveh, according to the word of the Lord and going a day's walk into the city he cried out, 'Forty days more, and Nineveh shall be overthrown!'"

A lot of people feel sorry for their sins; the ones they see that is! Many sins go un-repented because our eyes are never opened. Even with the sins we do see, our lives are filled with guilt and regret, but seldom change. Let's see what God says about repentance in the third chapter of Jonah. Nineveh was a large city "three days across" and there must have been a great deal of sin for God to decide to destroy the city. But before the people could repent, they had to be told of the need to do so.

If you were asked to identify anyone who needed to repent who would you pick? Your neighbor or yourself? Most of us would pick our neighbor. Most would think that their own "sins" are not nearly as bad as the "sins" of others. The Apostle Paul, the greatest single writer of the New Testament had this to say about himself, *"Wretched man that I am."* In 1 Timothy 1:15, Paul says, *"Christ came into the world to save sinners - of which I am the greatest one."* Take a close look at yourself. Do you criticize and make judgments about others? Do you decide that they are not as loving as they should be or that they make "poor choices" in their life vs. the "good choices" you have made? Do you gossip? Do you talk about others behind their back in a way that harms them?

Do you lust? Now some might say that there is nothing wrong with admiring a beautiful body, but then there is a fine line between admiring and desiring, isn't there? Do you envy? Do you have pride? I can go on and on. No one knows how bad he or she is until they try very hard to be good! And to be good one needs to know what to avoid. And to know what to avoid someone has to tell you. Jonah was the one God sent to Nineveh to open their eyes and let them know what to avoid. Who does that for you? Church - friends – scripture? Or no one; No one at all.

Holy Lord, open my eyes today that I may see my sinfulness. It is so easy to focus on the sins of others and overlook my own. So much easier to condemn than to face the truth I long to avoid. Show me my faults, Lord, and give me the words of remorse that I may speak from my heart to your heart. Lead me to true repentance that I might be close to you, a forgiven sinner, in the embrace of a Merciful and Loving God. In the name of Jesus I pray. Amen.

Repent 2: Confess Wrong   May 24   Jonah 3:5

"And the people of Nineveh believed God; they proclaimed a fast, and everyone, great and small, put on sackcloth."

Repentance first requires that our eyes be opened to our need to repent. After we see the need to repent we then must confess. When Jonah preached as the Lord had instructed, the scripture tells us that the people of Nineveh believed God, proclaimed a fast, and put on sackcloth. Putting on sackcloth is not something we do today. Many don't understand what it means. It was an outward sign of an inward repentance. Everyone who saw a person in sackcloth knew this person had done something very bad and was repenting of that badness.

Repentance might mean getting rid of a bad habit. Certainly it would be in our best interests to do so because most bad habits are very unhealthy. Most of us have at least a few bad habits we could be rid of. Some I mentioned yesterday: gossiping, lusting, envy, judging others, or just plain ol' meanness. A change of lifestyle or habit may mean we quit doing nothing and we get involved in doing something; like giving of our time to those less fortunate or quit doing nothing and to become more loyal to the church. It may mean a willingness to talk to others about your faith, the things that really matter to you in life, to commitment to make your life count for those things that are lasting and spiritual.

But before you do all that, confess. Confession, they say, is "good for the soul." Confession is a way that the soul repairs itself. Being a Christian does not mean we never go wrong, never sin. It means we are now able to repent, confess, pick ourselves up after each stumble, and repair the wound it caused. Just remember, that it is the Christ life inside of us that enables us to do so and without him, nothing is done; we remain unchanged. He died a voluntary death on the cross to repair our soul of its sin. Our confession in a small way fulfills one purpose of His sacrifice, to give us grace and restore our relationship with God. Only you can say whether his sacrifice for you was in vain.

Merciful God, I have overlooked my own sins while proclaiming those of my neighbors. I am the loser. That's not all of it. You, Lord, are the loser too. You lost the possibility of me. Open my heart that your Holy Spirit may repair my damaged soul. Enable me to confess fully; knowing that nothing I tell you is a surprise, knowing that confession is a gift that brings me ever closer to you. In the name of Jesus I pray. Amen.

Repent 3: Change Directions May 25 Jonah 3:10

"When God saw what they did, how they turned from their evil ways, God changed his mind about the calamity that he had said he would bring upon them; and he did not do it."

We talked about opening our eyes and confessing in order to repent. Now let's talk about the need to change directions. Today's scripture tells that when God saw they had repented, he changed his mind! Now did you get that? "God changed his mind." Some translations say "God repented" Do you think that God sins or is in need of repentance? Of course not! So what does it mean that God repented? Here repentance means a change of direction. God was going to destroy the city and he decided not to. When he saw how they turned from their evil ways, God was willing to forgive them.

Our motivation for change comes from God through His Holy Spirit. Repentance makes us realize that the repair of our soul can only be done by Christ himself; we cannot do it. We are told that Jesus died for us, that his death has washed away our sins, that if you believe in him and accept him as your "Lord and Savior", you will have eternal life. Paul tells us that Jesus has "killed the old self" in us and offers us new life. Repentance makes it possible for us to accept all of that and turn and move our life toward Christ. God was going to destroy Nineveh and their repentance changed his mind.

Are you willing to humble yourself, open your eyes, confess and be forgiven? Now, don't think you must do this in order to be saved. You are saved by your belief in Jesus as Lord and Savior. Think of it like this, if you cannot see the need to repent and confess; if you can only see that other people sin, do you really believe in the Jesus whose sacrifice you don't need? Who gave his life for the sins you deny having? Forsake your willful blindness. With seeing eyes, confess sin then repent because you feel so grateful for what Jesus has done undeservedly for you. Thus forgiven you can then turn and walk toward Jesus with an honest heart.

Lord, I have pretended to repent many times. I have even felt remorse, but I have not changed my mind or my heart or my direction. Can a person such as this really belong to Jesus? You waited patiently for the truth I would not speak, for the forgiveness, I would not request. Forgive me. Humble me that I may see my sin and repenting, turn my eyes toward you. Let my old self be gone and the new self, created by your Holy Spirit, now live! For Jesus. Amen.

"So the slave who owed ten thousand talents fell on his knees before the king, saying, 'Have patience with me, and I will pay you everything.' And out of pity for him, the lord of that slave released him and forgave him the debt."

Grace is a subject most Christians do not grasp. My guess is it is too wonderful for most to believe. Many have the belief that in order to "get" grace they must be "Good Enough!" I have heard people declare at funerals, "I know she will go to heaven because she was such a good person." Somehow they have accepted a false belief that grace comes to those who have lived the perfect life of discipline and obedience to God. Well, they have it backward. Grace comes because God *"So loved the world that he sent his only begotten son."* Grace is ours for the asking. Just believe and trust in Jesus and it is yours. That's the Gospel! That is why it is called "good news". You do not have to earn it to receive it.

There is also another side. Once sinners have received grace, they become obedient to God, not to hold on to Grace, but with Grace in their hearts, they want to be obedient. Otherwise, we Christians would be none other than the "New Pharisees", depending on our righteousness rather than being covered with the Righteousness of Jesus.

In the scripture above the King forgives his servant a great debt, the servant did not deserve it! The parable is an illustration of grace. Grace is there defined as granting forgiveness to one who could not possibly pay the debt owed. The servant's debt was ten thousand talents. Let me put it into perspective. One talent was worth 15 years wages. In other words, it would take the Servant 150 thousand years to pay the debt! It could never be done! His plea for patience to pay it all was just the desperation of a guilty man playing his last card. So it is for us. It is impossible for us to repay the debt we owe God, yet as with the king, God has pity on us and forgives us. Grace - that is why it is so wonderful! We receive grace and gain forgiveness, not on our goodness, but because of the goodness and righteousness of Jesus. Grace! Pass it on.

God of All, forgive my need to earn my way into your heart, to impress you and others with my goodness. In these ways I dishonor us both. Convict my self-righteous heart of the truth that in Christ I am forgiven and restored to you. Remind me I owe a debt impossible to repay. But Jesus paid it all. Enable my gratitude to result in loving deeds of mercy and grace. Great Sin forgiven manifests itself in Great Grace shared. May it ever be so in me. In Jesus, Amen.

"Discipline yourselves. Keep alert for your adversary the devil prowls around like a roaring lion seeking someone to devour."

The next few days we will discuss Grace, it certainly deserves more than a few days discussion! The scripture references and much of what I know of grace has come to me through seminars with the great preacher and teacher, Steve Brown and his books "When Being Good is not Good Enough" and "IF Jesus has Come". This scripture tells us there are enemies of Grace so keep alert! One enemy of is actually our desire to save ourselves by good works. But what is behind that desire? Peter says, "The devil!" Some people don't really believe there is a devil while others form their image of the devil from Hollywood: a sleek, devious character, sometimes with horns, sometimes red in appearance, but when challenged, turning into another worldly creature. So identifying the devil may take some doing. What we do know is where he will attack. Paul says in Romans 7:21, "I find it to be a law, when I wish to do good, evil lies around the corner trying to trip me."

That is an accurate description of where you will find him. Every time you try to do what is right, there he is. The devil can be found every time we try to help someone who is down and out by bringing them in their unkempt appearance, into the hollowed walls of our beautiful sanctuary. Just try that and catch the judgmental stares of those around you. Sure there will be a few who will be accepting – but the devil will be lurching! He will appear out of nowhere as soon as we attempt to do what is right and good; you wait and see! There is a spiritual battle going on and the devil is looking for someone to devour. Beware!

Don't think that this battle can be won by your wisdom and wit. That has been the downfall of many. This is a spiritual battle and the only one who can win over evil, the devil, is God through his son Jesus. Take the battle to Him. He is your strength. He is your wisdom. He is your wit. God has already defeated the devil through his son Jesus. Give the battle to Him. This is one adversary you were never equipped to best.

Oh, God, save me from the devil and myself. I am vulnerable at every turn. If I think too much of myself, he wins. If I think too little of myself, he wins. Only you, Lord, can save me and turn temptation to your purpose. Will you tell him, as he slinks defeated, that I sent you? That forever and always, you, Lord, speak for me? By your grace, I cannot succumb to evil's power. Together, Lord, we never lose. In Jesus' name. Amen.

"Humble yourselves under the mighty hand of God so that He may exalt you in due time. For God opposes the proud but gives grace to the humble."

Grace is the foundation of the New Testament message. Without it we would fall back under the law, and who wants that? Working to be saved; working to be good enough; where is the good news in that I ask you? Grace is something we do not deserve and can never obtain through work hard. Besides, if we worked for grace wouldn't it be given as payment due? In the verse above, Peter tells us that Grace comes when we humble ourselves before God. There lies the catch and the dilemma. Most people may know that they need grace but have a hard time becoming humble in order to receive. We had rather God give us Grace and then acknowledge in front of all our friends and enemies how wonderful and great and deserving we are.

Isn't that the truth? We do not like to see ourselves as inferior and being humble says we are inferior. Being humble is somehow associated with weakness. So we continue to pretend that we don't need grace. Peter says, *"Humble yourself and in due time God shall exalt you."* If you feel you do not need to humble yourself so be it, grace is not yours; after all, you don't need it, right? Why would you need Jesus and his grace if you somehow think you have already by your goodness saved yourself?

So for those who don't want to become humble, fine, don't. But for those who wish to be recipients of God's grace, for those who have come to the realization that they have tried everything else and their efforts have not been good enough and that they need God, grace is yours. For grace comes to the ones who know they need it and know they cannot earn it. So when your life is falling apart and you have nowhere to turn except Jesus that is when you experience God's grace. Now isn't that better than pretending that you are great and deserving?

Father, in my stubbornness and pride, I set myself in opposition to you and the gift of Grace you intend to offer. Lord, have mercy on me, a sinner. Convict my heart so that I may humble myself; fall to my knees before you. Have mercy, have mercy. Grant me your Grace, your undeserved favor, out of your righteousness and mercy. I have nothing to offer you, Father, but my failure and my need. In Jesus' name. Amen.

"Cast your anxiety upon God for he cares about you.... And may the God of all grace who has called you to His Eternal Glory restore you."

Most of the time we live with our anxiety rather than casting it upon the Lord. I'm unsure why. Perhaps, it is because we fear that God really does not want our burden and does not care that much about us. After all, we are such small creatures in his enormous universe filled with thousands upon thousands of galaxies and million upon million of stars. Truth is, people have had this trouble since the beginning of time even when they did not realize the tremendous scope of our vast universe with all of its solar systems. Maybe, just maybe, it is because we still operate under the belief that we must qualify for God's attention and therefore hold on to the lie that God cares only for the good, the righteous.

No wonder we are anxious! When you think about it, what is anxiety anyway? The encyclopedia describes that word as "distress or uneasiness caused by fear of danger or misfortune." "To torment oneself or suffer from disturbing thoughts." An antonym would be "assurance" or "confidence". Peter is trying to provide us with that assurance and confidence that *"God cares about us"* therefore we need not be afraid to "cast our anxiety upon Him." We have all tried to satisfy our desires and needs with worldly things and human companionship, but those things will never do. Only God can satisfy my deep hunger because he is the one who made me and I was made for another world, not for this one.

God has called us to this other world and has given us a way to get there. In the 14th chapter of the Gospel of John Jesus is telling his disciples what is to come. He tells them that he is going to go to His father's house and to prepare a place for them. Thomas, the one who was always doubting and questioning said, *"Lord we do not know where you are going so how do we know the way?"* Jesus says, *"I am the way, the truth and the life. I am going away but I will return and show you the way."* The God of Grace not only sent his Son to bring us grace, he also will send his Son to show us the way home because he *"cares about us"*.

Sovereign and Merciful God, when I consider that you care for me so much that you ask to take on my burdens in my place to put an end to my anxiety, that you desire to restore me, these truths about you are so great I am humbled and I am grateful. Help me to never question your devotion or run from your presence. In Jesus' name. Amen.

Grace 5: Be Still   *May 30*   *1 Peter 5:10*

"And after you have suffered a while, the God of all grace, who has called you to His eternal glory in Christ, will Himself restore you - support you - strengthen you and establish you."

This scripture above gives us the result of grace in our daily lives. The ultimate result of grace is seen in the middle of this text, *"who has called you to His eternal glory in Christ."* In other words, grace will lead us home to be with God in Christ in heaven. Most would just like to know how grace will benefit them now in this life on this earth. The last part of this text deals with that: God Himself will *"Restore us, support us, strengthen us, and establish us."* But all of this is for naught if we do not go to Him. If we decide that we can do this on our own and do not ask him to take it away, how can he?

Many people do not know how God operates. They want their freedom of choice but somehow think that God should not allow bad things to happen to them. If that were so, there would be no freedom of choice! God has given us "free will" and allows us to make choices even if it means we don't choose Him! But if we want God to come into our life and to "restore us, support us, strengthen us" then we must go to Him and ask. There is no other way. Grace is ours for the asking.

There is a real difficulty today to hear God because of all the busyness going on in our life. How can we hear God if we are constantly listening to the racket of this world? It used to be you had peace and quiet when you drove your car from one place to another. Now a-days just look out your car window and you see most everyone on cell phones talking with the music as a background. You want peace? You want God to come in and place you solid ground? Then talk to him! Get on your knees if necessary. Find a quiet spot if you will, but go there and talk to him. He is the one who supplies you with grace both now and in the times to come. So be still and let him come and calm you. Let him come and give you his grace now.

Sovereign Lord, Merciful Savior, I have known suffering. Now I am ready to call on your name to accept your Grace; ready to be still in your presence; ready to cease all my futile efforts; ready to trust fully in your mercy. Come and restore me, your wayward child. I need your support, your strength. Settle me securely in the place your will chooses for me. I am ready to let go. Come, for the sake of Jesus. Come. Amen.

"Then one of the elders addressed me, saying, "Who are these, robed in white, where have they come from?" They have come out of the great ordeal and have washed their robes and made them white in the blood of the lamb... who will be their shepherd, and he will guide them to springs of the water of life, and God will wipe away every tear from their eyes."

Memorial Day can be traced to the spring of 1866 just after the Civil War. A group of citizens marched through their desecrated town to the cemetery and decorated the graves of their soldiers who had died. Memorial Day is a day when we try to remember. What is it we need to remember and why? We can start with those who have given their lives in countless wars to gain and defend our freedom, to protect it and preserve it. Freedom is often taken for granted.

If you don't go to the cemetery on Memorial Day, at least pause and remember and say a prayer for those who fought to gain and preserve your freedom. To honor those who fought in war is not to say that you condone war. It would truly be a blessing to live in a world where everyone respected one another and lived by the Golden Rule – "Do unto others as you would have them do unto you", but the last time I checked that world does not exist here on earth, yet!

We also should remember those who gave their lives but never wore a uniform - those great Spiritual forefathers who through the years have given their lives to preserve the faith we live by. The verses from Revelations 7 makes reference to those who *"Have come out of the great ordeal, they have washed their robes and made them white in the blood of the lamb."* These are those who have given their lives in service to God. They chose to die rather than denounce faith in Jesus as their Lord. Remember them. But most of all remember Christ who gave his life that we might be justified before God.

Almighty God, Creator of all my yesterdays and my tomorrows, Lover of my soul, in your divine wisdom you made the human heart long to be free: free from want and need, free from oppression and degrading circumstances, free from guilt without a chance of repentance, free from sin without redemption, free to be and become all that the mind and heart of a loving, and generous God willed I could. Grant me, Oh Father, the strength to be truly free and truly yours. In your most precious name I pray. Amen.

"Make disciples of all nations, baptizing them in the name of the Father, Son and Holy Spirit. And teach them what it means to obey God's commands."

I hope the following will help us all gain a better understanding of the church and of our role as Christians. The first question I ask is one which has been asked of me many times, "If I give myself to Jesus, does that mean I have to go to church to be saved?" The answer is "NO"; but I must speak further. The church in NOT the building although it has a building in which to gather; the church is NOT a denomination although it usually belongs to one which helps it to utilize its resources with other churches and keeps it from straying too far from scripture and the truth. The church is NOT the minister however often Jesus shines through a word or deed.

The church is a group of people who are joined together by the Spirit of God. They have a common belief about their purpose to advance the Kingdom in obedience to God not their own wishes and desires. Their sole purpose for being is stated by Jesus Himself in our scripture today known as The Great Commission. As a church, we are called into a unique relationship with God through faith to make disciples.

We belong to Christ through faith and in belonging to Him we are a part of His earthly, Spiritual body, the church. My father-in-law had this expression when I would ask him how he felt, "I may not feel great, but the alternative is worse!" So does one have to go to church? My answer is still "No", but the alternative is worse; you either belong to Christ and His Body or you belong to something else. Now if you belong to Christ, then you will want to go to church and participate in His Kingdom, His Body. In reality, a person cannot be a Christian and reject the church. For what you will be saying is, "I don't believe in Him who calls me into relationship with Himself - nor do I wish to serve Him through His body - the church."

Lord God, it is so easy for me to fall for wishes and desires which serve only me. I am only human. I would like to have it both ways:: salvation and freedom to do whatever my heart desires. Teach me that the purpose of church is to bring me closer to you and to equip me to bring others closer to you. Make me your disciple. Strengthen me in the work you have for me. I don't want to die having lived only for myself. In the name of Jesus, Amen.

"How can one know God without the preaching of the Word."

Yesterday we talked about the church as the Body of Christ and our role to make disciples. Today, let's discuss two other important functions: Word and Sacrament. Paul says in Romans 10:15, *"How can one know God without preaching?"* When preachers preach they take God's Holy Word and by the Spirit's power relate it to life situations. The Holy Spirit enters listeners' hearts and minds and speaks to their particular situations. The Word then becomes alive to them. When the Spirit speaks through the Word, we sinners experience hope, healing, and the power to lived changed lives.

We also receive God's presence through the sacraments: Baptism and the Lord's Supper. When we baptize an infant or an adult, we baptize them into the Household of God. We acknowledge that person belongs to God. God's spirit dwells in them. And vice versa, because God's spirit dwells in them they belong to God. In Acts 1:4f Jesus says, *"John baptized with water, but you shall be baptized with the Holy Spirit."* In other words, God's spirit comes into our hearts and stakes a claim. In I Corinthians 11:23f Paul gives instructions on the Lord's Supper, *"This is my body which is for you - do this in remembrance of me."* It is in the church that we receive the presence of God through Baptism and the Lord's Supper.

Without these Sacraments, without God's Holy Word, there is no church. The water is symbolic of the presence of the Holy Spirit in the person's soul. When we eat the bread and drink the cup at the Lord's Supper, the Holy Spirit comes and confirms the promises of God's Word. In these human actions, we take hold of God's Word. Through them, God cleanses us of our sins and renews us into life. Without them, we do not feel the presence of the Holy Spirit as we are meant to by God. This is what the church is all about. Your life is empty without it. Your spirit is hungry and unsatisfied.

Lord God, I can't be a Christian on my own. I need your Spirit to connect us and make me complete, your Word to nurture me with your Wisdom, and Sacraments to remind me of what you have done for me in Jesus. Open my heart to your Word that I might be transformed into the person you created me to be. In Jesus' name I pray. Amen.

"Worship the lord your God and serve only Him."

In order to call ourselves the church we must have the Word being preached and the Sacraments of Baptism and the Lord's Supper being performed. Earlier we said the church is the Body of Christ, not a building, but a people gathered together. Christ said, *"Whenever two or more are gathered in my name, I will be there."* Still we as Christians must meet somewhere to worship. Christians generally call the "Place" where they worship "the church". That should not be confused with how many people gather, or who the preacher is, or what he says, or with raising money.

Worship is simply this: Our response to God who calls. In worship, God calls us, speaks His Holy Word through the words of the preacher made perfect for our ears by God's Holy Spirit. God commissions us to live Christ- like lives, and then sends us out to spread the Good News. Worship is like a re-enactment of the Gospel. In Christ, God came and walked among us on His own, we did nothing to cause Him to enter our lives; God moved to us first. Christ calls his followers to come to Him for comfort, rest, peace, strength. Through the Word we are taught the meaning of our life here on earth and we are called to make new decisions about our lives. We receive the Holy Spirit and then are sent out into the world to witness the transforming power of God.

Do you see the significance of Worship? No Christian should go without it - it must be very important to us, because in each service, we reenact the coming of God in Christ, the Call of God, we are confronted by the truth of God through his Word, and we are commissioned to share His works - ALL OF US! To the Christian, God must be the source and aim and strength of our lives. When we approach worship in this manner, with pure hearts and minds, God answers the deepest questions of our hearts and satisfies the hunger deep within us. Each time we spend that time in worship, our lives will be renewed through God' Holy Spirit.

God, my Father, I know how I have failed you; forgive me my sins. At times I have not made worship important; other times I have been there in body but not really listening or participating. Such a lackadaisical response is so undeserving to the One who loves me so. Empower me to worship you fully and with joy. You are the source and strength of my life. By your great grace, let me ever remember. In the name of Jesus I pray. Amen.

Church Part 4　　　**June 4**　　　*Acts 2:42*

"They devoted themselves to the apostles' teaching and fellowship, too the breaking of bread and to prayers."

As disciples, we are called to use our talents to advance God's Kingdom. The scripture, which serves as a guide on this subject comes form Acts 2:41f, *"Those who heard the Word from Peter and welcomed his message were baptized.... They devoted themselves to the apostles' teaching and fellowship, to the breaking of bread and to prayers."* This scripture tells us what the early Christians did. I suggest you take a moment and read the second chapter of Acts. As Christians, we are called to PRAY, an essential part of the Christian life, to STUDY, the habit of reading the Bible daily, pondering its truth alone or in a group, and to FELLOWSHIP with one another.

The first two are clearly important, but just as important, is fellowship. When we come together as Christians, we get to know one another so that we may uphold each other and comfort each other as the physical presence of Christ. Worship is vital to building our relationship with God. We cannot say that God means anything to us and be serious about it, unless we participate in worship. Those who are God's disciples are eager to hear His Word. A witness in the courtroom is "one who has first-hand experience of the case being tried tells what they have seen and heard." Likewise, as Christian witnesses we need to tell of first-hand experiences of God's power, which has touched us and profoundly changed our lives; tell how His amazing Grace has saved a wrenched undeserving sinner like me.

But until and unless we discover the gifts, which have been given us and then use them for Christ, we have yet to open our "Real" lives to Jesus. In essence God gave you all that you have. You are a steward of those gifts and God expects you to use all of them for the advancement of His Kingdom. You see it is impossible to accept Jesus Christ into your life and leave out all of His commands. For Him to be your Lord, you must be committed to Him, His church, His Kingdom: to praying, studying, fellowshipping, worshipping, witnessing, giving.

Lord God, help me to truly understand what it means to be your disciple. No, that is not correct. Help me to want to be! As I consider these disciplines laid out for me, I see it is all of my life you require, all of me you claim. Forgive me my hesitation born of fear. By your great power, may I live in such a way as to bear witness to those around me of your great vision, your unqualified Love. In the name of Jesus, Amen.

Church: The Body of Christ June 5 Ephesians 4:12

"To equip Christians for ministry and to build up the Body of Christ."

Paul presents the Christian with this theme: *"Christian life is lived in relationship to the church - the body of Christ."* He builds his case by saying that Christ gave certain gifts to certain people to be "Apostles, Prophets, Evangelists, Pastors, and Teachers." The purpose was to "equip Christians for ministry and to build up the Body of Christ" until such time that those being taught might attain the "Unity of Faith and the Knowledge of Christ to be mature." Paul further builds his case saying that without the guidance of those appointed by Christ, the "lone Christian" would be like a child tossed to and fro by cunning and deceitful people.

Without the benefit of the guidance of those appointed, one can easily be carried by the ways of this world and fooled by every earthly doctrine along the way. To illustrate this point, I mention the German people who turned their backs on three great ministers: Bonhoffer, Barth, and Brunner who gave them the word from God with the Barman Declaration. It should have opened their eyes to Hitler. Instead, they listened to the words of a lesser god and some six million innocent men, women, and children died a horrible death in the gas chamber; others died on the battlefields. Clearly Divine Guidance ignored is disastrous.

So can one be a Christian and not be a part of the church? I doubt it! For one - they would be divesting themselves of the guidance of God's appointed ones. They also would be rejecting Christ's body on earth - the church. Apart from the church one is left to draw conclusions from oneself and left alone with the cunning of Satan, one is easily fooled into becoming a fool. True, there is much diversity of opinion in the church. Paul recognized that and called for everyone to *"speak the truth in love - and to work together for harmony - unity."* The church is to bring people to Christ and through their appointed ones, teach them until they in turn attain unity and maturity. Then Christ will appoint those who have discovered the secrets of unity and maturity to the next generation of Apostles (ambassadors), Prophets (guides), Pastors (shepherds), and Teachers (those who instruct).

Lord, thank you for the anchor which is the church. Father, I am naïve in the faith and therefore easily swayed by words purporting to be your truth but are not, words which speak to my emotions and my biases, but not to my soul. Protect me from myself and the harm I can cause. I have so much to learn. Open my heart to accept your will for my life. Grant me the humility and grace to follow. I do so easily wander astray. In the name of Jesus I pray. Amen.

"When you thus sin against members of your family, you sin against Christ."

The scripture today discusses eating meat given to idols. I'm sure you're probably thinking what do the problems with the congregation back then eating meat sacrificed to idols have to do with me? I mean, what's the big deal? Well, here's the big deal; the church is a family. As Christians we care about one another, about each other's welfare, about each other's feelings. We're not just members of a club or a social organization, we are family. Paul says that when we sin against one another we sin against Christ.

In a family, there is caring even sacrificing for one another. However, there are some people in every church who feel threatened if other people do well. There are Christians who are jealous when another Christian receives recognition believing that they ought to be praised and congratulated more than anyone else. Fortunately, most Christians understand that they're just a part of a big family, that we're all alike. We're all the same in Christ Jesus. No one is more important than anyone else. Besides, why should one deserve recognition for doing what is expected? In Luke 11:42 Jesus admonishes the Pharisees for bragging that they give their tithes telling them they should have done that, but he says, *"You have neglected justice and the love of God for your neighbor."*

The church at Corinth had some folks who did not really care about the weaker members of the congregation. Let's just state it like it is. They considered themselves spiritually enlightened and above others. In their opinion, they did no wrong in eating food that was offered to idols. So why waste a good steak? The problem was their refusal to have any regard for the feelings of new members of the faith who had once been idol worshipers and were highly offended. Paul wants both groups to think like a family and to encourage and support one another. This scripture reminds us that we also are a family, the family of God in Christ. And we are to consider the feelings of our family in all that we do.

Lord God, I cannot look up. I cannot face you. I know now what I knew not before; when I harm a member of your church, I harm you. I have done just as those early Christians. I have considered myself spiritually better (than Jesus). I have not considered feelings nor made any sacrifices (for Jesus). I have neither cared nor loved someone (Jesus) more than myself. Oh, Lord, condemn me not for the sake of Jesus, who none the less loves me still and forever. Amen.

"Do not provoke your children, but bring them up in the discipline and instruction of the Lord."

Why is home important? Sounds like a silly question at first glance, but many people don't quite grasp it until something shakes their foundation. Home where we grow up, protected and fed by our parents, nurtured and taught the important things of life. Home is also where we are born spiritually and grow in grace, where we are protected and fed by the Spirit, nurtured and taught the really important things of life. The second home is the most important: the first can enhance or hinder it.

Our earthly home is where we should learn values and character. Certainly the important values of life come from God but they should be learned from our parents at home. The church can and should teach your children all about God. But, if you, the parent, do not place God or values high on your list, neither will your child. One of the modern day problems with child rearing is that many parents want to be "good friends" with their children. That may be fine when your children grow up and become adults, but while they are children, they need for you to be parents. Set the rules. Set the boundaries. Don't expect kids to act like adults; expect them to be who they are! You be the parent. Realize that children are *supposed to misbehave* and the parent is *supposed to correct*. That's our role.

Psychology has proven that children appreciate knowing there are boundaries that protects them and makes them feel safe. Children who grow up with discipline and rules have higher self-esteem than those who grow up with very permissive parents. Children actually appreciate and respect parents who set boundaries, especially later in life. Undisciplined children actually have no respect for their permissive parents. In Ephesians, Paul tells us to not provoke our children, instead treat them with kindness and patience and *"bring them up in the discipline and instruction of the Lord."* Be firm, yet kind. Your children will learn values and character from someone! It is your choice to make.

Lord God, I come to you giving thanks for children you have placed in my life; whether by flesh and blood or as spiritual children under my care. Give me your wisdom and grace as I work with and raise these precious children of yours. Forgive me when I fail you and them. Teach me, O Lord, to love, just to love... as you in Christ have loved me. In the name of Jesus I pray. Amen.

"Since we are justified by faith, we have peace with God through our Lord, Jesus Christ, through whom we have obtained access to this grace in which we stand."

Many people are confused as to how we obtain salvation. Some are adamant that we depend only on faith; others say that once we receive Christ, we now have to depend on good works. So let's talk. The scripture is clear on this matter: we have been made right through Faith. This scripture from Romans is a perfect example of that. Now, if you're looking for that one essential element - so that you will be acceptable to God and inherit salvation - this is it. Faith - faith in the promises of God.

Now, why is this so? Why does it work this way instead of say, through our good works? The answer to that is very simple; that's the way God set it up. God sets the rules and guidelines when it comes to religion and He has said that we obtain salvation through faith in our Lord, Jesus. So that is that; case closed. Now, if you want to try it some other way, go right ahead, but don't blame God when you find yourself in the pit of hell. He has told us how we are to be justified. If you believe another way - fine - just don't call yourself a Christian. Christians are those who have faith that Jesus alone is their Savior not their good works. Good works are a reflection of Christ inside the body and spirit of the believer.

Many live, not in faith, but in fear, dreading tomorrow, expecting the worst. We become like frightened passengers in a car driven by God but who are continually grabbing hold of the controls because we don't like the direction in which the car is headed. We damage our health with worry; we deny dreams because we fear the leap of faith; we dampen enthusiasm and joy with anxiety. We need to stop, turn our lives over to God and trust in His promises. There is no truth more important for the Christian life than this one. We are made right with God by faith in His promises that Jesus died for our sins, that Jesus makes us right with God not ourselves, and that Jesus is both our Lord and our Savior.

Lord God, I come today giving thanks that you have provided a way for me to be saved from my sins. Jesus! Foolishly I have tried to save myself through trying to be good enough, forgive me my pride and my conceit. Help us to accept your way and to give you control of our life. Take away my fears and worries. Grant your peace. Come live in this day with me; give me my daily bread. In the name of Jesus. Amen.

"All of the disciples were with one accord, devoted to prayer, along with several certain women, including Mary the mother of Jesus, as well as his brothers."

We are called to worship the Lord our God and to keep the Sabbath holy. Christians worship on Sunday, the first day of the week to honor the day that Jesus rose from the grave. Others worship on the Sabbath, which is Saturday. Church is very important in the life of the Christian. There are to elements that are essential for a vital church. Luke mentions them in our text today: fellowship and prayer. We are called to devote ourselves to prayer and to be in one accord. In order to be in one accord, we must care about one another. To care about others we need to fellowship with them, right?

The way you get to know the other person is through those moments of gathering together and sharing life experiences. Fellowship is the key to growing close to others, without it we would only be a people who serve a common Lord, but who know nothing of the aches and pains, the sorrows and joys of one another. To care for one another is a great calling of the church. We belong to Christ and therefore we belong to one another, we are family. If we are a happy, growing, loving, caring family, it will be a powerful witness to others; fellowship is the key.

We also must pray. Through every difficulty of His ministry, Jesus went to be alone and pray. Jesus trained disciples and sent them out two by two to tell of His coming. They came back giving glowing reports (Luke 10) - Jesus then prayed and gave God thanks. Albert Schweitzer prayed for God to make his presence known to the suffering of Africa - God sent him to do His work. Prayer has to do with engaging oneself in the very ministry and vision of God. Therefore we must realize that prayer always involves the one who is offering the prayer in the very work one prays for. That may very well be one reason many people are afraid to pray! They are afraid God will say, "I'm sending YOU!" But the church gets its power through prayer. Fellowship and prayer are the works of the church of Jesus Christ - a church of joy, of power, of faith.

Lord God, I come today confessing a truth I'm not proud of; it's all about me. I use people; I even use you. When life is kind I go my way, but when things get tough then I turn to you, Lord. Then, I need you. How can I have true fellowship with others if I don't have fellowship with you? Is that your Word for me? Forgive me. Lead me in a life of prayer and fellowship with you, my Jesus, that manifests itself into a life lived for others. In your name, I pray. Amen.

"Come aside by yourselves to a deserted place and rest a while." "So they departed to a deserted place by boat. But the multitude saw them and ran on foot and arrived before them to the place they were going."

Do you need a time off? We all need vacations. Time off from the routine things we have to deal with every day can help us to put things into perspective and to not take our jobs or our selves too seriously. Time off also builds memories, which help make those difficult moments go down a bit easier. I still have some fond memories of vacations when I was a child. One thing that seems to stand out most in my mind was the squabbling over who was going to sit where! We had a large family and if you got stuck in the middle of the back seat, you could not see much of the scenery. It also was difficult to play those, "I see something that you don't see" games. Remember those? That's the way we children passed the time riding in cars before the invention of ipods and game boys.

In Mark, the disciples had just returned from their first solo mission; they were excited and wanted to tell Jesus all about it. But Jesus could tell they were tired and exhausted and needed rest - a vacation. So He suggested they sail down the lake to a remote spot to be alone, maybe do a little fishing and relax. However, the people on shore saw where they were headed and rushed ahead. This was one of those vacations that just was not going to be. I am sure that the disciples were annoyed and tired and wanted to send the crowd away, but here they would learn a valuable lesson about their Master, Jesus. Jesus saw the physical and spiritual hunger in those gathered and refused to turn them away; instead He ministered to them and taught them. Jesus sees the hunger deep down inside our hearts and He longs to heal us. Remember that when you are down and out and need a listening ear. Remember that when you are tired and exhausted and in need of a little rest. Jesus is there to minister to our need. He will be there for us whenever we need Him.

Lord God, I come to you in prayer asking your forgiveness, your mercy. You often get pushed down the list of importance. Work is too important in my life. Sometimes I have no control over work; it controls me. At times all the things I must deal with in everyday life take a toll: children to raise, spouses to satisfy, aging parents to care for. I became exhausted, worn out, and in need of a break. Give me your peace and rest from my everyday routine so I may have the patience, the fortitude to deal with those things as you would have me to do. Help me make time daily for you. In the name of Jesus I pray. Amen.

New Phariseeism　　　　*June 11*　　　*John 14:5f*

Thomas said, "Lord, we do not know where you are going. How can we know the way?" Jesus said, "I am the way, and the truth and the life."

Religion can so easily be distorted. My wife and I attended several seminars at Kentucky Lake with the great Steve Brown. My friend Steve preaches the best sermons on grace I have ever heard. He summed up this problem something like this, "There is a new Phariseeism lurking in our churches." He was referring to the attempt by some to put the emphasis of salvation on things "we" are doing rather than the one thing God has done. The problem with that is it shifts the emphasis of our salvation from something that comes from God to an act of humanism.

In our text today Jesus is tells the disciples he is leaving them in order to go prepare a place for them. Thomas states the obvious, "*Lord, we do not know where you are going. How can we know the way?*" Jesus said to him, "*I am the way, and the truth and the life.*" Some confuse this by saying we must follow Jesus' example if we wish to be saved and end up writing a bunch of laws to follow making themselves the "New Pharisees." But Jesus did not say, "Be perfect like me. Obey the law. Make no mistakes." He said, "*I am the way.*" We need not worry so much about doing the right thing as giving our heart to Jesus. For truth is, once we give our heart to Jesus, we will have difficulty doing the wrong thing.

However, we have trouble following directions, don't we? You stop to ask for directions and end up more confused than ever. The best direction I ever received came from a lady who said to me, "Stay where you are, I will come get you." I had called her on my cell phone. That is what Jesus was trying to tell His disciples. Even though He would have to leave them physically, He would not let them get lost but would come again and take them with him. Can it be any clearer than that? Just keep your eyes on Jesus and when the time comes, you can follow Him back. And yes, try to live a good life, not because it will save you, but because your heart belongs to Jesus and you want to.

Lord God, I come to you in prayer knowing that I am not perfect. I come knowing that I have failed you in so many ways, forgive me. Sometimes it is hard to discern what so many are saying. I want to follow you; I want to do what is right; I want to live eternity with you. Direct me in the way you want me to go. I know that you have said that you are the way, help me to follow you, to give my life and will to you. For you are the way, the truth and the life. I give myself to you today. Take me and lead me home. In the name of Jesus. . Amen.

"Blind Bartimaeus calls out to Jesus, "Son of David, have mercy on me!" Jesus stood still saying, "Call him here." And they called the blind man, saying to him, "Take heart; get up, he is calling you."

There are many families today lacking the leadership of a father. Tragically, divorce is on the rise and children are growing up without a stable family life of mom and dad. But the issue goes even deeper. Many families have both mom and dad in the home, but still don't have stable leadership. Psalm 121:1 says, "Unless the Lord builds the house (family), those who build, labor in vain." Never has a statement resonated so true as this one. Often today's parents allow children to make decisions they are not mature enough to make.

I remember asking one parent about their 13-year-old who had quit accompanying her to church. Her response? "He doesn't want to come and I let him make his own decisions, he's old enough." We learn from the decisions our parents make, I am who I am today because of the things my dad taught me (and my mom, of course). We as parents are called to follow in the footsteps of Jesus and to let him build our house.

Today we read the story about a blind man named Bartimaeus. From that story, we can draw this conclusion. Jesus is accessible; the Lord of the entire universe makes Himself accessible to all of us. Jesus and the disciples have been in Jericho. As they are leaving, a crowd gathers by the side of the road. Blind Bartimaeus calls out, "Jesus, son of David, have mercy on me!" The crowd tries to quiet him; they did not want this beggar to bother this man they considered a holy man of God. But he calls out even louder! And Jesus not only stops, He listens. As Jesus listens to the blind man, He listens to us, He cares, He asks; He is concerned. Jesus is Lord of all things, even the little things of life.

If you want to have a good influence on your children, this is the example we have. Be there for them, listen to them, and follow through, do whatever you say you will do. However, first and foremost, we must let the Lord build the house. Give your children the gift of grace through your unconditional love and forgiveness of them. Give them Jesus

Lord God, children are a precious gift. I thank you for them. Help me to see the importance of "bringing them up in the Lord." I know how I have failed. No matter how hard I try; being a good parent is difficult, impossible at times. Give me your wisdom and grace, your patience. Instill in our family a thirst to know you and to love you. Let it begin with me. In the name of Jesus. Amen.

Fathers in Christ   **June 13**   *Matthew 5:18f*

"Jarius, a leader of the synagogue came to Jesus saying, "My daughter has just died; but come and lay your hand on her, and she will live."

When a baby is born a father is born also. Often we discount the importance fathers play in our lives. I had an exceptional father, he was not perfect, and at one time allowed the taste of alcohol to gain importance in his life. He was not rich in a worldly sense, but very wealthy in other ways. He taught me the really important things of life. He would give you the shirt off his back and often did just that. He worked hard and gave his children an example of good work ethics. We grew up learning to work hard for what you get. In the long run, that principle will make you feel good about yourself and your accomplishments. But we must never forget that it was God who gave us our talents in the first place.

I will never forget something my father said to me later in life. He was reminiscing about what could have been. He said, "Son, I could have been a millionaire. I've made enough money to be one, if I had not had so many children spending it all." (There were 5 of us.) Then he added, "But I would not trade any one of you for a million." I understand what he meant on both accounts, because I too am a father. Children are of unparalleled value. My father taught me all that, but the most important lesson was his love. He demonstrated his love by providing for us, through disciplining us; he showed it through his affection and acceptance of us. What more could a father be?

Jaruis, the leader of the synagogue, was that kind of man. For him to even approach Jesus placed his life in danger. The Pharisee's did not accept Jesus, yet he sought out Jesus to heal his daughter. Jairus was a caring man, a humble man, a tolerant man, and a man of genuine and deep faith. That's who my dad was. That's the kind of men and fathers we need today. I challenge you to set your goals high to have your children speak of you in this way when they are grown. By God's grace, they can. They will.

Lord God, I come knowing how I have failed you and my children; I am unworthy of your love. Help us all to reach out to children, our own children and those that are ours in Christ, and give them the love and instruction they need and deserve. Oh, Lord, give me Jarius' kind of faith that believes and trusts fully in you. Let me live that faith aloud as I deal with the complex problems that arise in raising children. I pray this in the name of Jesus. Amen.

Vacation Time   June 14   Mark 14:32

"Jesus took with him Peter and James and John to a place called Gethsemane. And he said, "I am deeply grieved, even too death; remain here and keep awake." And going a little farther, he threw himself on the ground and prayed."

Well, summer is here and it's the time when we usually take our vacations. Vacations are a very necessary thing. A break from the routine is good for the soul and mind. For one, it helps us to better appreciate what we have when we get away from our job, our family, even our extended family. A break in routine is like cleaning out your closet. Every once in a while, you have to pull all of those things out of your closet and just take stock. Take stock of those things you threw in when you had company coming over and you wanted to get clutter out of the way in a hurry. Clean it out every once in a while and you might be able to find your coat or hat. You also realize how much you already have, how great have been your material blessings.

Similarly, a vacation has a way of cleaning out the closets of our mind, getting the clutter out of the way so your mind can function, as it was intended to function. The Old Testament prophets and the New Testaments disciples, even Jesus, spent time in solitude to get their minds clear so they could hear God's Word to them. We all need that. It is difficult for God to get His Word through to us when our mind is cluttered with so many things. There are many accounts of Jesus withdrawing to be alone in order to pray or to seek rest. This is a difficult world that we live in. We are all learning how to get along and get by and trying to understand what God has planned for us. It is going to take uncluttered minds for us to be open to hear God's message. So take your vacations. Clear your minds. God has a word for you. Relax and listen. Really listen.

Lord God, I come in prayer today with a divided heart and a cluttered mind. You alone, Lord, can help me. Give me courage to risk the world running without my say so. Give me rest from this need to control that I may prepare my mind to listen for your Word and to respond. Forgive my habit of filling my days with busyness as if that will somehow be satisfying - it isn't. Open my heart to your love and grace and give me rest in the name of Jesus. Amen.

My Plans for you   *June 15*   *Jeremiah 29: 10f*

"For thus says the LORD: I will fulfill to you my promise. For surely I know the plans I have for you, plans for your welfare not for harm, to give you a future with hope. When you call upon me and come and pray to me, I will hear you. When you search for me, you will find me; if you seek me with all your heart, I will let you find me, says the LORD."

This scripture is one of my wife's favorites. Once you read it you can see why. To think that God has made promises to us and will fulfill his promises is an awesome thing! God's promise is to watch over us. He has plans for our welfare; a concern for our well-being. Not only that, God knows the plans He has for you. That truth is just more than one can fathom. The God of all-the-universe has taken the time to form plans for my life. Not that He has singled out me of all people, but He has plans for all of His children. The biggest problem most of us have is trying to discover His plans for us, am I right? Don't you wonder every day or at least from time to time what plans God may have for your life?

When I wore a younger man's clothes I am not sure I worried all that much about what God had in mind for me. I was more concerned about what I wanted for my self. If you are honest with yourself you will say the same. Somewhere along the road of life, God made Himself known to me and called me to be a minister. I was about 17 at the time and interested in being a Rock and Roll star. I played in a band lead by my good friend, Alex Harvey, who wrote "Delta Dawn" and "Ruben James", among other hits. I resisted God's call and ended up in college majoring in music. It took 17 more years to answer that call

How did I know? The key to knowing is found in these verses above, "When you search for Me you will find Me; if you Seek me with all your heart I will let you find Me." When the time is right for you; when you become desperate enough; when your desire to know overwhelms you, get down on your knees and search for God – seek Him with all your heart and you will find Him and His plans for your life. He has promised!

Sovereign Lord, Almighty God, like other followers, I expected belief to shelter me from wrong turns and catastrophic mistakes. It did not. Like other followers, I wanted belief to spare me the pitfalls of poor choices and prideful errors. That is not your way. I know this now. Now, I come free of my epic willfulness, wanting only what you have always wanted for me – your best for my life. I have at last sought you with an undivided heart and seeking, I have found! Thanks be to thee, my Jesus, for all you are to me. I pray. Amen.

"Jesus said, "Why are you frightened? Why do doubts arise in your hearts? See my hands and my feet; it is I. Touch me and see; for a ghost does not have flesh and bones as I have." And see, I am sending upon you what my Father promised; stay here in the city until you have been clothed with power from on high."

How many of you are troubled? How many are worried and unhappy? How many of you worry about the future or the past or even the here and now? In the Sermon on the Mount we find the most famous scripture about worry Where Jesus tells us to place his Kingdom first and everything else will be taken care of. Having said that, I know it does not stop the worries. People loose their jobs; small businesses go bankrupt; retirees are unsure that social security or the pensions they depend on for livelihood will be sufficient; environmentalists are convinced that the earth will soon be an uninhabitable greenhouse, so we worry.

The disciples were worried and troubled about their future also. We see that in our scripture today: these words are post-crucifixion. The disciples were not sure what the future would hold for them. The risen Jesus appears and says, "Why are you troubled? Why do you have doubts?" Some likely feared that what happened to Jesus could happen to them, their past experience with the rulers and leaders of both the state and religious order made them uneasy. Jesus wanted to comfort them.

He showed them the holes left by the nails, which held Him to the cross. He confirmed He was alive! Their past and future had been conquered by His death and resurrection. Then He tells them to stay put until they have been given the Holy Spirit as promised by the Father. Power from on High is what we all need. On the day of Pentecost, God poured out the power of His Holy Spirit upon the disciples. Jesus made that promise and it came true (Acts 2). He also makes that promise to us. We have the power of His Spirit available for us today. All we have to do is call upon Jesus and allow the Holy Spirit to be poured into our hearts replacing all desire to control things ourselves. He will give you the power to dispel worry and doubt, to make it last you will have to go back to him again and again. He is our power, our confidence, our hope.

Lord I come to you in prayer because I have tried to do things on my own and have failed. I come overwhelmed with worry, doubt creeps in and takes away hope leaving me desolate. Send your Holy Spirit into my life and bring your hope, your healing, your peace. Empower me to turn my cares over to you. Leave me with your comfort, your peace. In the name of Jesus I pray. Amen.

"Andrew, Simon Peter's brother, said to him, "There is a boy here who has five barley loaves and two fish. But what are they among so many people?"

Do you believe in miracles? There is a great song with that title "I believe in miracles" but the most impressive thing I have ever seen on miracles has to do with the story in our scripture today – the feeding of the five thousand. A few years ago some very good friends gave us a picture of this miracle painted by Mitchell Tolle. It is a depiction of the little boy who has a basket with five loaves of bread and two fish. The artist used his grandson as model for the painting and I will have to say that it is stunning! The painting really depicts the image from the scripture perfectly.

Well, do you believe in miracles? I do. I believe miracles have happened and I believe they continue to happen. In the story of Jesus feeding the 5,000 there is one little fact I want us to focus on, the little boy. Andrew tells Jesus there is a little boy who has *"five barley loaves and two fish."* It is important for us to see and realize that Jesus took a gift given to Him and multiplied it, creating a miracle. God waits for us to put something into His hands to work with. What we must realize is that God wants us to do this so He can show us a miracle. Often, we will give God some of our material things, but decline to offer to Him our faith and trust (or lack of it).

Miracles happen when we give to God - ourselves, our time, our talents, our resources, our money, but mostly our faith and trust. If we are willing to give to God whatever we have - even when we think that we have nothing of significance to give, then that which seems impossible to us becomes possible through God because He can create a miracle. Stop trying to see this life through your own eyes. Our eyes are weak, limited and selfish. God's eyes are strong, unlimited and full of grace and truth. When we put on the eyes of Christ, we see life and everyone else in a different light. We see that all things are possible through Him who made us. Put a little something into God's hands - give Him your faith also, and then watch Him work a miracle.

Lord, forgive me for limiting the things you can do in me. In my humanness, I compare your power to the things we humans can do forgetting that you are not me; you are an all powerful; you are God. Open my eyes to see the miracles you have created around me and seeing believe in you. Use me for your purpose. Grant me your love and grace. In the name of Jesus. Amen.

"The apostles said to the Lord, "Increase our faith!" The Lord replied, "If you had faith the size of a mustard seed, you could say to this mulberry tree, 'Be uprooted and planted in the sea,' and it would obey you."

In the context of Jesus' instruction about the coming Kingdom, the disciples ask Jesus to *"Increase their faith."* Surely, a reasonable request for those who would be called on to do some rather remarkable things, don't you agree? It seems like a reasonable request even for us today. The truth was, as it is with us, Jesus told them they had enough. He told them that faith even as small as a mustard seed it would be enough. It depends upon where you direct that faith, toward God or yourself.

We all have faith! You purchase meat at the supermarket and have faith that the inspector of that meat is correct and the food is safe to eat. You drive 65 mph down the interstate having faith that the one who installed the brakes did his job well and, if need be, you can stop. You get up in the morning expecting the sun to be in its usual place and that the world will still be rotating around that sun. You have faith that the Creator of the universe set into motion things that can be trusted. We have faith in those things without much thought.

But when the Lord of the universe calls upon us to do something that we consider "beyond our faith", we question whether or not it can take place. We want our faith to be increased because we want to be the answer. We need to learn that it does not matter how much faith we have but where we direct that faith. If we have faith as big as an oak tree, but direct it towards being confident about our own efforts, we will be in despair. However, if we have faith as small as a "mustard seed" and direct it towards God, we can be confident. We must move away from the misguided idea that faith has something to do with our own efforts. Faith is a gift of God through His Holy Spirit and if He gives you faith the size of Mount Everest or the size of a mustard seed, it will always be enough if directed towards Him; if directed to yourself, no amount will be enough.

Lord, I come to you in prayer asking for forgiveness, for I know how I continue to let you down. You ask believers to have confidence in you, to trust in you, to give our cares and worries to you. Yet I continue to depend on myself; forgive me. Lead me to the place where I can finally say that I can do all things through the one who strengthens me, Jesus. In His name that I pray. Amen.

Generosity   June 19   Proverbs 11:24

"Some give freely, yet grow all the richer; others withhold what is due, and only suffer want. A generous person will be enriched, and one who gives water will get water."

Having been a minister for most of my life I have dealt with many older adults who were in their last years. There is one thing I have discovered. Some, no matter what comes their way, no matter what they have to deal with, are grateful; others can only talk about what they don't have or how life has been hard to them. Those who are grateful are also very giving, generous people while those who are ungrateful are always wanting; they drain your time and energy and give little in return. I am sure you know people who are like the ones I have described. Perhaps, you even recognize yourself.

In our scripture from Proverbs we learn that "A person who is grateful for what God has given and shares freely to those who don't have will receive more than they give." Don't misunderstand. I am not saying that if you give away 10 thousand dollars you will get 20 in return. Rather what you receive back will be worth more than you give, you will receive a grateful heart. There are two kinds of people: givers and takers. Those who give receive and have abundance in store. Those who take must continue to take in order to have anything. Takers can only see their needs, their hurts, and never see anyone else's. To move past that stage in life requires only one thing - an understanding of gratitude.

Have we treated our Lord well? Have we disappointed Him? We have, in fact, caused Jesus to hide His face in shame. Knowing this truth about us, He gave His life for us anyway. We are forgiven - NOT because we are good - NOT because of what we have done for Him - just because He loves us. Our job is to accept His love and spread it around. Dr. Scott Peck in his book, *The Road Less Traveled* described love like this: "Love is an act of the will, both an intention and an action. Will implies choice. We do not have to love - we choose to." The choice is always ours. We can choose to give generously or not. Whenever we choose to give, it will not only help others, it will help us to grow spiritually.

Lord, I come acknowledging that I have not been as generous as I could be; forgive me. You have given me more than I can even imagine and yet I still am ungrateful, wanting more. Even if I give, I do so conditionally expecting praise or gratitude, expecting what I am unwilling to give you, Lord. Open my heart that I may see your blessings as undeserved, unearned, as grace. Humble me that I may become more like Jesus. I give you my life. In His name. Amen.

"And let the peace of Christ rule in your hearts, to which indeed you were called in the one body. And be thankful. Let the word of Christ dwell in you richly; teach and admonish one another in all wisdom; and with gratitude in your hearts sing psalms, hymns, and spiritual songs to God. And whatever you do, in word or deed, do everything in the name of the Lord Jesus, giving thanks to God the Father through him."

The third chapter of Colossians tells us that when we become a Christian we now "see things from above." We begin to live our life differently. We make a complete change. We are now new creatures. It is like say when your first child is born. A child changes your whole life! Things you used to do for yourself, now you do for your child. Rather than living as you like, now you have to consider this child. Not that you resent this new responsibility, you love it – you want to make these changes, right? You are grateful to God for that child. So you make the change joyfully with no regrets.

Now that is the way it is with Christ. The old life stops and a brand new life begins; not because it must, but because you want it to. Just as having a child is a big responsibility and every decision you make not only affects you, but your child, so it is with your New Life in Christ. You must now stop and think about your actions because they will affect others, whom you now see as God's children. Now again, you are not doing this because you have too, but because you want to. Jesus now lives within your heart affecting your every decision. You have "put to death" all the things of this world, which tend too take you from your new life with Christ and you have put on the things from above.

Now everything you do, whether with your church, your work, your family, you do in such a manner as to glorify His name. Paul sums it up like this, *"Whatever you do, in word or deed, do everything in the name of the Lord Jesus, giving thanks to God the Father through him."* Once you begin to live this way you will find a joy that is beyond anything you have ever experienced. Your joy will become complete! Much like the joy one feels when giving up something for your child.

Lord God, this word speaks to the true desire of my heart that the peace of Christ rule in me. So I come giving thanks for this new life you have given me. The world tries to deny this peace is real to convince me that you, Lord, are not at work. Sometimes in weakness I fall for that lie; forgive me. Let the word dwell richly in my heart transforming my life bringing your joy. May everything I do be pleasing in your sight and bring praise to your glorious name. In the name of Jesus. Amen.

"I consider that the sufferings of this present time are not worth comparing with the glory about to be revealed to us."

I had a conversation with a relative once that went something like this: "Well, life just doesn't always go as planned." No truer statement has ever been made if we are considering our own plans. Consider your own life. How many of you "plan" to lose an irreplaceable loved one? How many plan to have serious health problems or money problems? At one time or another most of us will experience all of that. We will have problems at work, at school, at home. Some will be dissatisfied with their life, their work, or their marriage.

Paul says it well in Romans today, *"I consider that the sufferings of this present time are not worth comparing with the glory about to be revealed to us."* He then goes on to talk about the great Hope that awaits all who turn their life and troubles over to Christ. What does it mean to live in such hope? A few days before my mother died of heart failure, I was visiting her in her home. She had recently experienced a fall, but was doing fine. She had many things she wanted to tell me and talked non-stop doing so. Eunice had a talent of turning a 15 minute story into a two hour tale! We had a wonderful visit, but then just ten days later she was gone. Was I prepared for that? No! I mean it happened so suddenly. Truth is you cannot be prepared.

But we can be prepared for what is to come next. I can live in hope because I know that my mother and father, Weldon and Eunice, are joining hands and dancing in Heaven. There is a life after death and my parents are now together once again after 12 years and that makes me glad. That's what hope does for us. Paul reminds us that it is in hope that we are redeemed. Can we control the circumstances of life? Absolutely not but we can control the effect they have on us by turning over our troubles and worries to the one who gave His life for our sake. In Jesus, we can have faith and hope even in the most difficult of times.

Lord of All Hope, grace me this day with your presence. In times of great suffering I wondered if I could endure. Yet you, Father, saw me through. Many times I have wondered, why? Why should I have to endure such sorrow? Yet, you are always there to comfort, thank you. Please forgive my complaints. Give me wisdom to trust that in good times or tough times, you are with me making real my hope, making sure my faith. In the name of Jesus. Amen.

"We thank God for all of you and mention you in our prayers. For we know that God has chosen you, because our message of the gospel came to you not in word only, but also in power and in the Holy Spirit and with full conviction."

If you want to renew your life you best not mind getting your pants dirty because you will need to first drop to your knees in prayer. And I don't mean to pray to God asking Him to fulfill all that your heart desires. That's not prayer; that's begging. Too often, we want God to answer our prayers the way we want them answered. You know what I mean, don't you? Deep down, we want God to supply us with sufficient money. We want Him to give us perfect health so we never have to experience pain. We want Him to watch over our children in such a way so that we never have to worry about them. We want to be free of worry, stress, anxiety, and pain.

You probably have already discovered this, but if not, I'll let you in on a secret; it is not going to happen the way you wish. The good news is God can make you free of worry, stress, and anxiety, not by making sure you never have it, but by lifting it from you when you do. First, just go to Jesus in prayer, offer your heart to God, ask Him to purify your heart removing pain and disappointments; allow him to take away the anger inside toward those who have hurt you. You see, all of that anger blocks God's power from moving freely within you.

Remember the parable of the unforgiving servant – Matthew 18? The king forgave the servant a huge debt when he begged for mercy, but the servant refused to forgive the debt of one who owed him little. Once the king found out, he took the worthless slave - restored his debt and handed him over to be tortured until he paid the entire debt. Jesus reminded his listeners that His Father will do the same to those of us who do not *"forgive others from our heart."* You want to renew your life - you want to see things differently - you want peace inside – then get down on your knees, lift everything to God and ask Him to cleanse your heart and purify it; and don't forget to forgive those who have harmed you.

Sovereign, Most Holy Lord, I come asking you to renew my life. I have wanted to travel the easy road that does not lead to you; forgive me. I confess I have come to you many times wanting you to fulfill my plans rather than accept your will for my life. Set me free from worry and stress; take away my anxiety. Forgive me and grant me the grace to forgive those who have harmed me. I pray in the name of the one who gave his life for mine. Jesus, the Christ. Amen.

Forming Our Faith   *June 23*   *Romans 1:16f*

"The Gospel is the Power of God for salvation for all who have faith. For in it the righteousness of God is revealed thru faith for faith."

Life is much like a march to Golgotha. Most people like to sit by the roadside and view life from a distance. They don't want to take up their cross and follow Jesus down the road of humiliation and suffering unto death. But until we do, we cannot become the bearers of the Good News. How can we speak of Good News until we have experienced bad news? You had cancer; you were healed, or maybe you weren't, but Jesus gave you the strength to face the music with peace. You felt rejected or discriminated against or shunned and Jesus held you in His arms. You lost someone you dearly love, and Jesus saw you through that tragedy and gave you comfort. You wanted relief in the struggles and pains of life; you cried, "Lord, help me!" And you felt his healing touch.

It is the stories of scripture that help form our faith. As we read the stories of the Old Testament and how God reached out to help His people in need and as we see the stories in the Gospel of Jesus going around the countryside, teaching and healing and comforting people, we grow closer to God and our faith forms a solid foundation. We must be careful to not form our faith away from God's Holy Word – His living Word of Jesus. For then we may have faith, but it will not be "truth", it will not be grounded in God, but could be whatever we want it to be.

As I have said many times, "If I believe that God is with me in everything then nothing can get me down and hold me down." That is only true when I build my faith using His Holy Word. Paul said for us to "live by faith". In our scripture today he says that His Word, the Gospel, is His power for salvation and that in it we find His Righteousness and our belonging by the cross of Christ. When we seek to form our faith using His Word, it gives us a hope for today and for tomorrow. For in His Word we find His Truth, His Grace: we find God Himself!

Lord of life, you have been so wonderful to me in all my trials. You have been my guide, my sustainer, and my hope. Were it not for the bad times we might never have become so inseparable, My Great Friend; my gratitude is beyond words, a heart-truth you alone can read. Be my wisdom. Humble me for service. Experience has given me the capacity to comfort, you have given me the desire. I hunger for the chance to manifest your love and grace. For you, my Jesus, I ask this. Amen.

Three Dollars Worth of Jesus June 24 Matthew 22:17f

"Is it lawful to pay taxes to the emperor?" Jesus answered, "Why put me to the test? Show me the coin." "Whose head is this, and whose title?" They answered, "The emperor's." Jesus said, "Give therefore to the emperor the things that are the emperor's, and to God the things that are God's."

Why do people get uptight over the subject of stewardship and giving? Could it be because they feel guilty? What do you think? Well, just how much Jesus do you want, 3 dollars worth? If you want more then let's talk. The Pharisees came to Jesus with a dilemma; the Jews were paying taxes to keep up a government occupying their land. Needless to say, they were not happy giving a good portion of their livelihood to Rome, so they asked Jesus, "Is it lawful to pay the emperor." Jesus realized it was a trap and answered, *"Show me the money." "Whose head is this and whose title?"* They replied, *"The Emperor's."* Then Jesus said give to the Emperor the things that are his and to God the things that are God's.

If Jesus had sided with the despised Romans, he would offend the Jews and if he had sided with the Jews he would have risked the wrath of Rome! He did neither. And the Pharisees were stunned and amazed and walked away; their heads hanging down; their plans spoiled. Truth is taxes have been around as long as we have had a civilized world, and for good reason. You cannot have roads to pull your ox wagons or drive your car without taxes. You want to get across the river? It takes bridges built with tax dollars.

Let's take a look at Jesus' answer on this important subject of stewardship. Jesus said for us to *"give to God that which belongs to God."* So what belongs to God? Well we owe God a whole lot more than money. Do you go to God asking for only 3 dollars worth of Jesus? I doubt it! Most go to him wanting much more! Most go to Jesus to receive help with the stress and strain of everyday life, to be healed, to be made whole. So why would Jesus be worth so little to you? You want forgiveness? You want hope? You want eternal life in heaven with God and Jesus and all the angels? How much is all that worth to you?

Lord, you have given me all I have. I know this, except at stewardship time. Then, I conveniently forget. Why is this so true of so many? Is this a failure of trust or is it a failure of love? Or is it just fallen man going about his sin-fueled worst? Either way, the fact remains. My money means more to me than you do. Please, Lord, keep this between us; it's bad enough that you know. I feel such shame, yet such relief. I've named the enemy and it is I. Have mercy, Lord. Help me to become a grateful giver. In Jesus' name. Amen.

Dogs and Humans   June 25   Mark 1:27

"They were all amazed and kept asking one another, 'What is this? A new teaching? - with authority? For even the unclean spirits obey Him.'"

Let's begin with a question. Maybe you have asked this yourself. What is the difference between a human and a dog? I am sure you have an answer, but let me tell you mine. A dog usually will not bite the hand that feeds it, but often a human will. I have owned quite a few dogs and although I do not presently own one, my neighbor has several who visit. Since I love to be outside and walk in the woods, these dogs practically live with me. A few years ago this same neighbor had a black and white border collie named Smoky. He became overly aggressive one day when taking a hot dog out of my hand and accidentally bit my finger. I say accidentally because as soon as he did it, he gave me this look that said, "Oh, I'm sorry, master." That is the only time that ever happened.

Now, let's look at human beings. Often a human will bite the hand that feeds it and that does not speak well for us, does it? Humans have done atrocious things to one another for centuries! Remember the Holocaust committed on the Jews by Hitler. Remember those who were gassed by Saddam Hussein in Iraq. If we go back far enough we can recall the murder of Abel by his brother Cain (Genesis 4:8). Through out the ages, religious wars have been conducted and "good" religious people have been killing others who would not commit to their "brand" of religion. None of this speaks well for human beings. We seem to want to control the outcome of our life and the lives of everyone else around us.

The truth is life will work out only one way. That way is God's way; the way God planned it. Every other way we try will lead to destruction and "biting" the hand that feeds us. Jesus came to rid us of that destructive nature and replace it with His Spirit of love and grace. In the 1st chapter of Mark we find the story of a man possessed with "an unclean spirit". Jesus calls the spirit out of the man giving him a new life, not only a life of wellness but of wholeness. He can and will do the same for you.

Beloved Savior, I thank you for your goodness to me though I have by my actions, at the very least, taken you for granted. I have accepted your mercy, your grace. I have refused to give that mercy and grace to others. You have fed me. I have harmed you in response. I come asking you to call out of me the demon of selfishness and pride. You alone have the authority and the power. You alone love me enough to care. Forgive me; change me. In Jesus' name. Amen.

How About Frogs?　　**June 26**　　*John 14:8*

*"Lord, show us the Father and we will be satisfied." Jesus responds, "Phillip -
have I been with you all this time and you still don't know me?"*

We have a creek flowing through our property; it is fed by four medium-sized springs that begin a mile or so back in different hollows. Additionally, all along the route to our property, there are hundreds of small springs that flow year-round. One creek is next to our gravel drive. It is about 18" in diameter and flows constantly fed by an underground stream. There you will find bullfrogs, a variety of fish, crawfish, and in the summer, snakes – some poisonous. In the winter of 2001 a strange thing happened. A bullfrog left the creek and took up residence in my little spring by the drive. Now this is no small frog; stretched out, he was a good 12-14" long. Every time I would drive by, I could see those big eyes sticking above the water. If you walk that way, he will jump back into the spring and go underground. It made me question the nature of frogs. Do frogs dream? Do they have goals for their lives? Do they plan or wonder about God? Now I know that many of you will say "Of course not!" But can you say for certain? Truth is with all that we do know about bullfrogs and other animals, there is much we do not know.

Now if that is true about this simple animal, how about us? How about God? How about the universe? There is no single thing about which we have total knowledge. All of creation is surrounded by the mystery of God. Modern society's way of knowing religion is to be objective. And the way to do that is to strip away all the miraculous events, all inspiration, all the mystery, all the wonder, all the influence of other people who are spiritual and just be objective. Maybe that is what happened to the disciples in the scripture today. Phillip had stripped away all the miracles he had seen Jesus perform, all the preaching and teaching, the inspiring words he had said, all the mystery and wonder and said, *"Just show me God then I will believe."* If we try to only understand religion or even the stars in scientific terms we will miss the mystery and Jesus will have to turn to us and say, *"Have I been with you all this time and you still do not know me?"*

Lord God, have you been with me all this time and I still don't know you? Is this question meant for me too? Am I looking right at you and still asking to be shown? Do I miss your face in the eyes of loved ones or strangers? Do I discount as coincidence your acts of Divine Grace? Forgive me. Don't let the frogs instinctively see, while I, your precious child, remain blind by choice or hubris, by pride or conceit. Have mercy. In Jesus' name. Amen.

"And no one puts new wine into old wineskins; otherwise, the wine will burst the skins, and the wine is lost, and so are the skins; but one puts new wine into fresh wineskins."

The lust for newness is all around us. We want the new to improve our old life – new cars, new clothes, new spouses, new nips and tucks. As long as we don't have to change on the inside anything goes, anything money can buy. The Christian faith is all about becoming a New Creation on the inside. In Mark, Jesus talks about being a New Creation by telling us that you cannot put new wine in old wine skin. We can see throughout the Bible that God is to be trusted; that God keeps His promises; that God is always faithful. Even if it takes generations, God will fulfill His promises.

As you read these words today there may be dissatisfaction in your soul. Your life may have an emptiness that nothing on earth has been able to satisfy. You crave fulfillment, a joy that seems to have escaped you. You have searched for that which is missing in your family, your work, and in your recreation. Your search has yielded very little. I can assure you today, if you commit yourself to God, put your faith and trust in Jesus, you will not be disappointed. He will make of you a New Creation.

The desire to fulfill a restless spirit is not new to the twentieth century. In the 3rd chapter of the Gospel of John, Nicodemus, a Rabbi and leader of the Jewish Sanhedrin came to Jesus in the dark of the night telling him "I know you are from God for no one could perform the miraculous signs you have done unless God were with him." Jesus could see into the restless heart of Nicodemus; knowing what he needed he says, *"Unless a man is born again, he cannot see the Kingdom of God."* Unless you become a New Creation you cannot see the Kingdom of God. If you do not give yourself in such a way as to allow God's will to rule your heart, you will not be able to see His Kingdom. So put your faith and trust in Jesus. He can give you new direction in your marriage, new joy in your relationships, new vigor in your job; He can transform your heart from being critical and dissatisfied and fill it with joy and contentment.

Lord God, all seeing, all knowing, all powerful, you have out of your sheer wonderfulness offered me a whole new self just like Nicodemus if only I agree to accept this gift offered by Jesus. I do – this very moment. May your kingdom live in me from this time forward and forever. May the newness that I seek be found as I discard the old me and allow you to put a new me in new wine skin. In Jesus' name. Amen.

A New Standing   June 28   Romans 4:3f

"What does the scripture say? "Abraham believed God, and it was reckoned to him as righteousness." Now to one who works, wages are not reckoned as a gift but as something due. But to one who without works trusts him who justifies the ungodly, such faith is reckoned to him as righteousness."

Faith in Jesus gives us a new standing with God. In Romans, Paul is looking back at the call of Abraham and says that because Abraham believed God, it was reckoned to him as righteousness. Because of his faith, God looked at Abraham in a new way. Abraham has a new standing before God. Paul goes on to say that what was true for Abraham is also true for us today. The one who believes in the God; the one who believes and trusts in the one *"put to death for our trespasses and raised for our justification"* will be reckoned as righteous.

If your life is not centered in God through His Son Jesus, then your life is more than likely centered in yourself – your passions and your desires. If your life is not centered in God, then it is likely centered on your goals for yourself, not God's goals for you. And if that is true, Paul says there will be no hope for you. You will then live under the wrath of God. You will live with dissatisfaction in your own life, being disappointed in others because they do not live up to your standards, you will be unfulfilled because you will not be whom God intended you to be. If this is your life, you need to be set free. Free from your need to judge others and even yourself. Free from the fear of death.

Jesus can bring you into a new standing before God, one where your sins are forgiven, not because of anything you do but because of what He has already done. Faith in Christ gives us a new start where we are forgiven our debt to God and put in a new relationship with Him. Jesus made this all possible. Once you turn your will and expectations of others and yourself over to God in Jesus, you will awake each morning with a wonder and excitement that this world cannot give; nor can it take away. This feeling of completeness comes from the source of life and joy, Jesus. So today cast yourself completely on Jesus; hold nothing back.

God, father of our Lord and Savior Jesus Christ, I long to be like Abraham to believe in you so completely that all my choices and actions reflect your will and your way for my life. But Father, I am selfish and self-centered, trapped in my own insistence on having my own way, be it right or wrong. Forgive me. Free me from this trap I alone have set for myself. In Jesus' name, I earnestly pray. Amen.

The Old Piano   June 29   1 Peter 1:3

"Blessed be the God and Father of our Lord Jesus Christ! By his great mercy he has given us a new birth into a living hope through the resurrection of Jesus Christ from the dead."

When I was in high school I played in a rock and roll band. The leader of our band became a professional musician and wrote more than a few number one hits; most of us went on to do other things. While in college I played with a few bands to earn a little spending money. This one club had a beat up piano that was always out of tune. Everyone who played there complained about it. The manager tried to have it tuned, but discovered the soundboard was cracked and would not hold a tune. Know what he did? He had the piano painted! Now of course the piano looked new or different, but it sounded the same!

Let's relate this to our own life. We all want to be a good friend to Jesus, and end up with a ticket to heaven. Problem is we don't want to give up those friends or things that hold us back. A member of a church in Kentucky, the contractor that built our education building while I was there told me this story. He said that the previous Sunday he almost missed church to play golf since it was the first beautiful day of spring. As he was walking out the door, his neighbor enticed him saying, "Why don't you come play golf with me today? I need a partner." My friend said, "I can't. I've got to go to church." His neighbor said, "Church is not going to do you any good, you are just as bad as I am." My friend replied, "I know, but if I don't go to church I would be worse!"

Our inside is always in need of a tuning and church is where we can get that done. But for some reason that only God knows, if we miss our weekly tune up, we become just like that old piano, a pretty paint job but not much else! We may look good on the outside, but inside our sounding board is cracked. That is why Jesus came. Since we can never hold a tune, he holds it for us, in our stead. *"By His great mercy He has given us a new birth through his son Jesus."* That is the way Peter put it in his letter. So when you feel like you are in need of a tune up, go to the place where you can hear The Word and be lifted by the music, perhaps on an old piano not just painted but in tune.

Dear God, merciful and loving, in your wisdom, you knew that the real change needed in the human heart could only be divinely done. And in Jesus' life, death and resurrection you made that change possible. Yet, I have settled for so much less than you want to give me. Forgive me and restore me to your favor. Give me a loving hope and a new birth in Christ Jesus. Only you can do it! Only you, my Jesus, could think me worthy. In Jesus' name. Amen.

Sabbath Day — June 30 — Exodus 20:8

"Remember the Sabbath day, and keep it holy. For in six days the LORD made heaven and earth, the sea, and all that is in them, but rested the seventh day; therefore the LORD blessed the Sabbath day and consecrated it."

Sabbath is the day God set aside for rest. To be honest, Sabbath is actually Saturday. Some religions observe that day, most Christians observe Sunday, the day Jesus rose from the grave as our day of rest. Working on the Sabbath has always been controversial in religious circles. It used to be that towns and cities had what was called "Blue Laws". The Blue Law made it illegal to open a business on Sunday. Today some businesses still stay closed on Sunday. But as we can see in the twelfth chapter of Matthew, Jesus really did away with so called "Blue Laws".

Jesus and his disciples were plucking grain on the Sabbath and the Pharisees told Jesus that his disciples were doing what is not lawful on the Sabbath! Jesus reminded them that priests worked on the Sabbath (Matthew 12:8) and besides, "The Son of Man is Lord of the Sabbath", He sets the standard for the acceptable and the unacceptable. Jesus then entered the synagogue and they brought him a man with a withered hand and asked, "Is it lawful to heal on the Sabbath?" Since they could not seem to get the best of him on work, they tried healing. He answers with a question. "If you have only one sheep and it falls into a pit on the Sabbath, will you not try to save that sheep?" The obvious answer is "yes". Then he reminds them that humans are of far greater value to God than a sheep so of course it is all right to heal on the Sabbath.

The important thing is not that you mow the yard or go shopping at the local mall on the Sabbath, but whether you truly honor God in and through all the activities of life. Going to church, giving our gifts to God of our time, talents and money is done to honor God. It is true that if you go to church you should receive (if your mind is in the right frame) but going is about our devotion, our love, our gratitude to the one who created the universe and us. "Remember the Sabbath day, and keep it holy" is what God wants. For God blessed the Sabbath and in it blesses us.

Oh God, Giver of Sabbath Rest, I seek to honor you in my daily life. Thank you for reminding me that to do so I must value what and whom you value, love what/whom you love, not laws and regulations set by man. Forgive me when I choose otherwise. Revive my desire to seek Sabbath rest for my sake and for the sake of your precious son, Jesus. Remind me how important Sabbath is to my well-being, how important it is to you for me. In his name I pray.

"You have died to the law through Christ, so that you may belong to him who has been raised from the dead in order that we may bear fruit for God. While we were living in the flesh, our sinful passions, aroused by the law, were at work in our members to bear fruit for death. Now we are discharged from the law, dead to that which held us captive, so that we are slaves not under the old written code but in the new life of the Spirit."

My wife and I planted an English flower garden in our backyard. Many who visited said, "I would love to have a garden like that." Of course it doesn't just happen. One thing that gardening teaches is patience and hard work. You have to prepare the soil, purchase and plant the flowers, giving some thought to the type of flowers, the colors, when they bloom, the kind of foliage and how full they get (you don't want to hide small flowers behind tall ones). Once you plant you must spray for insects, water, fertilize, deadhead the plants so they will grow new blooms, and pull weeds.

Sounds like work, doesn't it? Actually, you can look at it two ways: resent the repetitive time it takes daily or let it become an anticipated joy, a time to spend with your flowers, meditating with God. A vital spiritual life is a lot like a garden. Giving our life to Jesus Christ also takes work. We also have a choice. We can look at that choice in two ways: resent the time He takes out of our day going to church, de-weeding our life of those things that are harmful, fertilizing our new life with His Word thru study and prayer, fellowship and worship. Or we can anticipate that new life with joy realizing how much better off we will be once we stop trying to carry the world on our shoulders. We are 'dead to the captive spirit of the law' and alive in the 'new life in the Spirit'. We can turn our worries over to Jesus, accept His forgiveness and grace, and look forward to eternal life with God. It is important that we stop and meditate, to be alone with God. As you do so, think about who Jesus is, what He has done for you and what you can do in return. It is impossible to be resentful about that.

Lord, I come to you in prayer grateful for the new life in Christ you have provided. I speak of this gratitude because my life lived may not confirm it. Forgive me, gracious Lord. I can do no better without your Spirit guiding me, controlling me. Often I have looked at the life of the Spirit as a burden. My new life in the Spirit isn't meant to be work but a privileged joy. Have mercy, Lord, and forgive. Open my heart to enjoy this new life. Knowing you, serving you, loving you, where, Lord, is the drudgery in that? In the name of Jesus. Amen.

"Are not two sparrows sold for a penny? Yet not one of them will fall to the ground apart from your Father. And even the hairs of your head are all counted"

How many of you are familiar with an insect that can inflict more damage on you than about any and yet is so small you cannot see with the naked eye? I am speaking of chiggers. Chiggers are not in the Bible as far as I know, but I am going to use them for a Biblical point. Most of us have fears that control us and hold us back from what God is calling us to be and to do. Chiggers are an example of a fear that limits us.

Let me explain. My wife and I stay out of the area with fallen leaves at our house when it is "Chigger time". Our cabin is located in a full-grown forest, so thick that there is little grass undergrowth, just a few weeds, wild flowers and native shrubs. It is a breeding ground for chiggers. When you walk in that area you can get covered with those little invisible creatures that cause you to itch making your life miserable. We always spray with everything we can find before going out and treat the bites with every medicine known to mankind, but still we itch. It can get so bad that it limits our going outside for FEAR of being bitten!

Fear has a way of causing us to hold back from God also. Many have grown up with an image of an angry, vengeful God who is always judging. Do this right, God will reward you, err and He will punish you. They don't seek God because they fear Him. For all who feel this way, you need to know that God loves you with an unconditional, unimaginable love! In Matthew Jesus reminds us that not one sparrow will fall to the ground without God taking notice. We are of more value! Jesus was telling us we are under the watchful eye of a loving Father who says to us, "Fear not, I will take care of you." We are so valuable to God that He sent His Son, Jesus to be a ransom for our sins. So whatever you fear let go of it; God is indeed watching over you.

Gracious Lord, I come before you as your sinful creature. You have called me to live in faith; I have lived in fear. You have called me to give you the reigns of my life, I have refused and continue to hold on; forgive me. Remove from me all those things that keep me from becoming the wonderful person you have created: pride, resentment, fear, and anxiety. Most of all I pray for a grateful heart, Lord. Great Love can do great things. Let me be molded by your grace that I may be your witness to others. In Jesus' name. Amen.

"For freedom Christ has set you free. Stand firm, therefore, and do not submit to a yoke of slavery."

I guess you could say that there is no such thing as absolute freedom; to exercise the freedom of one may take away the freedom of another. For example, say you are in a "rock band" and you want to exercise your right to practice in your garage but the noise is annoying to the neighbors. Your freedom has taken away their freedom to a quiet back yard.

When Paul wrote these words from Galatians about freedom he was appealing to the new Christians who had converted from Judaism. These new converts wanted to impose Jewish customs on all those who had converted to Christianity, including the Gentiles. Paul reminded them that Christ had died to free them from such requirements. So "why should we turn back and submit ourselves to the very yoke of slavery from which Christ came to deliver us?" These new Jewish converts wanted to add to Christianity the requirement to be circumcised as a qualification of faithfulness. These verses are especially relevant to us today with the surge of new churches that add "requirements" to becoming a Christian.

In Acts, chapter two, verse 21 we find these words, *"Everyone who calls on the name of the Lord shall be saved."* In the Gospel of John, chapter ten, verse 9 Jesus states, *"I am the door; if any come by me to enter, they shall be saved."* Salvation comes to all who confess Jesus as Lord and Savior. Baptism with water is the symbol that confirms we are baptized with God's Holy Spirit. It is His Holy Spirit that changes our heart and moves us to believe. Without that we cannot believe. Jesus came to set us free from all the requirements of religion; his requirement is that we accept and believe in him. All other requirements are optional and will only take away from the real thing – the freedom of grace through Jesus.

God of Freedom and Grace, in the name of Jesus I claim all that you have done for me by His life, death, and resurrection from the dead. Help me not to succumb to the ways of the world, which instill fear where you instill faith. Fears cause me to question the completeness of your redeeming grace in Christ. Let me live standing firm in the fullness of your salvation, unafraid and truly free. In Jesus' name. Amen.

"For you were called to freedom, brothers and sisters; only do not use your freedom as an opportunity for self-indulgence, but through LOVE become slaves to one another."

Freedom is something many take for granted. Having lived all my life in a country that has enjoyed freedom for over two hundred years, it is hard for me to imagine what it would be like to be enslaved. Still it is important that we not take freedom for granted. Many of our ancestors have given their lives for the freedom we enjoy today and we should honor the sacrifices they made.

Having said that, however, real freedom comes from Christ who gave His life to bring us into a right relationship with God. Paul reminds us of that in Galatians. Christ gave His life for our freedom and we are called to do the same. Not to use our freedom as a means for self-indulgence, but to give ourselves in service to those around us. That is not the normal "human" line of thinking, is it? Most people say, "What about my rights? What about my privileges? What about me!? Why should I give up my freedom so someone else can have his or hers? Never has this echoed so loudly in our society as with corporate corruption where company leaders "cooked the books" to hide declining profits and then retired taking advantage of huge stock options siphoning away all the cash.

It would be good for them to read this text of Paul's and etch it in their hearts, *"Do not use your freedom as an opportunity to take advantage of others."* But remember this text is not just for them it is also for us. We as Christians are, *"called through LOVE to become servants of one another."* It is through Love that we freely become servants of others. If we truly understand the freedom God has given us through his Son Jesus we would gladly give of ourselves so others may feel and experience that love and freedom.

All Knowing and Loving God, you know in my sinful state I would always seek to serve myself. Forgive me. You even know that I would put me first even at the expense of others, that my corruption is bone-deep. Forgive me. You also know that I long to do what is right but cannot in my own strength. Thank you for Jesus' love. Make me more like Him every day. Let me not dishonor you by any word or deed of mine. In Jesus' name. Amen.

"Let no one despise your youth, but set the believers an example in speech and conduct, in love, in faith, in purity."

How's your spiritual life? Been reading and studying the Bible more and more lately? Been going to church more - even to Sunday school? Been setting aside time to pray and meditate with God? There is a funny thing about the human race. We love to see beautiful things so we work hard to make things appear beautiful to the eye.

Back in the 1980's I served a church in Marianna, Arkansas - home of some rabid Razorback fans! It's a beautiful little town, county seat of Phillips County. One unusual feature is that the courthouse does not sit in the middle of the court square as is customary. Instead, there is a beautiful park in the court square. On the north side of the square is the courthouse and on the south side are a group of buildings that look occupied. They have painted beautiful storefronts and have things displayed in the windows just like the stores on the east and west side of the square. Only problem is those buildings were gutted by fire and never rebuilt. The faces of the buildings were fixed up to look nice disguising empty burned out shells inside.

That reminds me of many human beings. Too often we work hard to get the right hairstyle, makeup, clothes. We will spend hour upon hour trying to look good outwardly. We will work long hours to make enough money to "look" successful. But that has nothing to do with what is within us, does it? So how is your spiritual life? Do you spend the same time and effort to build your relationship with God and to grow spiritually as you do to look good on the outside? Paul says in 1st Timothy that we are to set an example before others in our speech and conduct, in love, in faith, in purity. If non-Christians are going to be impressed with the Christian faith, we who are Christians need to be who we say we are; our lives ought to speak to the world about Jesus, don't you think?

Sovereign Lord, Merciful God, today's devotion speaks especially pointedly to me. I recognize my 'false face' efforts to appear to be successful, prosperous, good. You see right through me! I bet you're not the only one. Set me straight on the path to true love, faith and purity. Only in Christ is there hope for me. Come to my rescue, Father God. How, I need you so. In Jesus' name. Amen.

The Table of the Lord   July 6   1 Corinthians 10:14

"The cup of blessing that we bless, is it not a sharing in the blood of Christ? The bread that we break, is it not a sharing in the body of Christ? Because there is one bread, we who are many are one body, for we all partake of the one bread... You cannot drink the cup of the Lord and the cup of the world. You cannot partake of the table of the Lord and the table of the world."

Remember the Road to Emmaus in Luke 24? Jesus walked the road to Emmaus with two disciples. The scripture tells us that they did not recognize the risen Christ. Why is it these disciples could not see Jesus right next to them? There has been a lot of speculation but no one knows for certain. Verse sixteen simply says, *"their eyes were kept from recognizing him."* They continued their journey to Emmaus and there they had supper together. At the table he took the bread, blessed it and broke it and gave it to them and then their eyes were opened to recognize him.

Too often we allow the things of every day life to consume us to the point that our eyes are also closed and we would not recognize Jesus if he were standing right next to us. That is why it is so important to continue to celebrate communion, the bread and the cup of the Lord's Supper. As Paul says today, we cannot partake of the table of the Lord and of the world. It is the "table" of our Lord that keeps our eyes open. Beyond that we need to develop a devotional life that keeps our eyes open so that the things of this world will not cause us to miss the most important event in our life! To see Jesus!

In developing a life of devotion, we may have to give up a few things; like people who may try to keep us in the "worldly life", hanging out at places that encourage us to do things we know are not good for us. You cannot be devoted to God and have no concern of the effect your actions have on others, even yourself. And we cannot love God and develop a life of devotion alone; Jesus came to make that clear. Communion with Jesus opens our spiritual eyes that we may see and love each other; that we may become more loving, caring, considerate, understanding, accepting and forgiving; more like Jesus.

Father God, I do so want to see Jesus in my life. Must I sacrifice to do so? Must I give up my worldly plans and pleasures? Can I not have it both ways? Soothe my conflicted heart and give me the mind of Christ, his devotion, his subservient will. Be merciful to me, a sinner. In Jesus' name I pray. Amen.

"Does the master thank the servant because he did what was commanded?"

This is a tough little parable in Luke 17. Paraphrased it says, "Will any of you who has a servant, who has been working in the field all day long and comes home say to him, 'Come at once and sit down at the table?' Will you not instead say, 'Prepare supper for me, gird yourself and serve me, and when I have finished you may eat.' Does the master thank the servant because he did what was commanded? So you also, when you have done all is commanded say, 'We are unworthy servants; we have only done what was our duty.'"

Jesus is not teaching here that God's dealings with us are based on Law and Duty; rather they are based on Grace and Faith. Jesus gives a hard and necessary lesson for all who are tempted to feel "Proud" of their "Works of Faith" for God. The Apostle Paul mentions this numerous times in his letters, warning the reader to rely on Grace (God's unmerited favor), not Works. Works are only the result of obedience, doing merely what is expected of us. So if you have the desire to boast of what you have done for the church or for God's Kingdom, resist it! It does not impress God! Remember that you are only doing what He expects of you.

The trouble with this parable is that it is so plainspoken, you cannot miss the point, unless you refuse to let it speak to your heart. It also does a number on our toes, doesn't it? We all have a tendency to say of ourselves or of others, "Look what great saints they (we) are. They work so hard for the church. They certainly deserve to go to heaven!" I wonder what God would say; not because Works are not expected of us, but doing good for God's Kingdom and His church is simply obeying and doing what is expected, nothing more, nothing less. In Ephesians 2:8f Paul states, *"We are saved through Grace; it is a gift of God not of Works so that no one may boast."* Is anything clearer than that?

Lord God, I come today in prayer asking for your forgiveness. I know that I am a sinner, I have wanted to take credit for my own goodness, for my good deeds, for being who you have created me to be, for following the commandments you have laid out for me. Forgive me and open my heart that I may truly seek to do good, not because I want others to look favorably upon me or to be recognized by this world, but because you have placed that desire within my heart. In the name of Jesus. Amen.

He Calms the Storms   *July 8*   *Mark 4:39*

"Peace, be still. And the winds ceased and there was a dead calm." Then he turned to the disciples and said, "Why are you afraid? Do you still have no faith?"

Each of us must face our own storms in this life. Often our biggest enemy is our own fear. The possibilities are endless: the fear of failure, the fear of wrong doing discovered, the fear of criticism, even the fear of success and all that brings with it. In the fourth chapter of Mark we see how the disciples responded to the storms of their life. The question is: how do we respond to the storms of our life?

The disciples were in the midst of a terrible storm and fearful for their life. They wake Jesus from a sound sleep and Jesus rebuked the wind and said to the sea, *"Peace, be still."* There was a dead calm. He then turned to the disciples asking them why they were afraid in the first place? Why they had no faith? Is that a question that comes to you from time to time? If it is, it's okay. There are times of trial when we fail miserably and we question ourselves, "Why am I afraid? Do I have no faith?" But even faith is a gift from God. Faith does not come from our strong will but is the result of reliance on the Christ within us.

Remember once the disciples asked Jesus to increase their faith and He told them that all they needed was faith as small as a mustard seed and they could move mountains. Why? Because it is not our doing - faith is God's gift. How did the disciples survive the storm in our scripture today? Did they decide everything will be okay; we will just ride this storm out? No, they went to Jesus who said to the storm, *"Peace - be still"* and it was. Our faith is not something internal that magically gives us assurance and calms the storms of life that are attempting to devour us. Faith within us gives us the courage and the wisdom to say, "Lord, I cannot take this any more. Please calm this storm." We live by the faith of the Son of God." Jesus is our faith. He is our strength. He calms our storms.

God of all creation, Sustainer of Life, Giver of Peace, I too am tossed about on the turbulent sea of life. I too try to save myself, bailing water right and left. In desperation I too call on Jesus as my last resort. Forgive me my ignorance, my tepid faith. Help me to seek Jesus from the very beginning so that together by faith we can conquer all that comes our way. Surely I could not believe you would rather sleep, Lord, than rescue me, your child. Thank you for loving me in Christ. In Jesus' name I pray. Amen.

Grace Alone   *July 9*   *Romans 1:16f*

"For I am not ashamed of the gospel; it is the power of God for salvation to all who have faith, to the Jew first and also to the Greek. For in it the righteousness of God is revealed through faith for faith; as it is written, "The one who is righteous will live by faith."

Grace alone has been the motto of the reformed church from the start. In the 16th Century, Martin Luther stood tall against the church of his day, which was selling salvation to its people through the giving of money and land. While studying Paul's letter to the Romans he was haunted by verses 16 and 17 in chapter one. In the preface to the *Latin Writings*, Luther states that when he realized that God justifies us by faith, "I felt I was altogether born again and had entered paradise itself through open gates." He said this because of the lifted burden of having to justify his own life by his doing. Luther realized that was not possible and not necessary! God has done that for us in Jesus.

Some say that if you are a Christian, others can tell because of your "good works," but that, I am afraid, is not true. Paul says in Ephesians 2:8-9, *"For by grace you have been saved through faith; it is not your own doing, it is a gift of God."* To those who say we must give physical proof that we belong to Christ, things that others can see, let me just say this. Only Christ knows our hearts. On one side, you can have a person who looks and appears saved because of the things they do. But they may be doing those things only to impress. In their heart, they still do not accept Jesus as Lord and Savior; they are greedy, envious and evil.

On the other side, you can have a person who looks and appears not to be saved because of things they do or don't do, but in their hearts they love the Lord and accept Jesus and they love and accept and forgive others. This is the visible and invisible church. The invisible one being those who only God can see and only God has the right to judge. Those who want physical proof usually want it so they can judge. The best thing for all of us is to just repent of our sins, surrender our will to Christ and witness Christ before others. Leave all the judging up to God.

God of Grace, in your wisdom, you made me seek to please you by obedience to your will; in your mercy you sent Jesus to make whole all my futile strivings, all my imperfect ways. Help me to be all you created me to be in Christ. Forgive me and strengthen me that I may repent, confess and witness your Truth. Make sufficient my immature faith. For Jesus' sake, I pray. Amen.

"Oh Lord, you have enticed me and I was enticed; you have overpowered me, and you have prevailed. I have become a laughingstock all day long; everyone mocks me."

The prophet Jeremiah withdrew and rebelled against following what God wanted him to do. He was hesitant to even be a prophet of God. He certainly was not the first man or woman nor will he be the last to fight God in that matter. To be honest, as I look at Jeremiah, I can see a lot of myself. You can probably see a lot of yourself. I can see the fight that I conducted against God. I didn't want to go into the ministry either.

I felt a call first when I was about sixteen years old and I fought against it. Mainly, I felt like I wasn't good enough. You ever felt that way? You know better than anyone else the sins that you commit and you may feel like you're not good enough to be God's person or to lead people to Christ. Not only did I see myself as a great sinner I also felt like I wasn't smart enough – my grades were O.K. but not outstanding. The truth is, I was probably like a lot of you. I could have done better. I just didn't put forth my best effort. I was concentrating more on having a good time.

This resistance went on for some fifteen years. I graduated from college, taught music for ten years; finally when I was 31 I gave in to God and began my studies. I'll bet that if you examine the motives of why you're so reluctant to answer God's call to be what he wants you to be you fight against it for the same reasons. You don't feel worthy; you don't really have the talent to teach or work with youth or whatever. Truth is we all fight for our own will and that's really what the fight is all about. Jeremiah had everything going for him. He was a man of wealth, hob-knobbed with royalty. He was an intelligent but a tormented man. God was giving the land to the King of Babylon and Jeremiah did not want to carry this message of doom to his friends and neighbors. God says to him "My Grace is sufficient." In our times of discouragement and heartache and difficulty, God says the same, "My Grace is sufficient for your needs."

Oh Lord, I see myself as Jeremiah must have, called to do or be something I'm not and cannot be nor do. Forgive me for implying that you don't know me or that my God-given talents are insufficient. Convict me of my true value to your Kingdom. Help me to gladly serve you all my days. Grant me the faith to live this marvelous truth: God's grace is sufficient for my needs. In Jesus' name I pray. Amen.

God will Supply our needs *July 11* *Jeremiah 20:8f*

"For whenever I speak, I must cry out, I must shout, 'Violence and destruction.' For the word of the Lord has become for me a reproach and a derision all day long." Verse 10, "For I hear many whisperings: Terror is all around. Denounce him. Let us denounce him. All my close friends are watching for me to stumble. "Perhaps he can be enticed and we will prevail against him, and take our revenge on him."

Why was Jeremiah hesitant in answering God's call, knowing it was God who was calling? I think part of his hesitance was because his message of impending violence and destruction was unpopular and he did not want his friends to turn against him. Clearly, they tried to denounce him and his message. They even anticipated his failure or his stumbling. His close friends even looked to entice him into silence as a defection from God's service. That happens at times, doesn't it?

Jesus went through similar injustice. Jesus rebelled against the religious order of his day and they finally maneuvered him to the cross and took his earthly life. Many did not know, however, that all of this was in God's plan from the beginning. Jeremiah confesses that the words of the Lord have become a "reproach and a derision" to him. He loved his people and it was heart breaking for him to have to denounce them and tell them about their coming destruction. So he became hesitant. As a result of all of his persecution including a stoning and being thrown into the stockade, Jeremiah forgot who was doing the calling and what the caller was capable of.

That happens at times, doesn't it? God never asks us to do for Him without also supplying us with what is needed to complete the task. Sometimes in our call from God to do some task for Him we feel the same as did Jeremiah. No one seems to listen. Many begin to criticize us and everything we do. We begin to feel isolated and alone and ask the same questions, as Jeremiah did. But there is only one person we must answer to and that is the One who created us and is calling us to carry his message. He is also the one who will supply all that is required to do so.

Oh Lord, I am both awed and afraid to be your person in this evil world. I too have questions: What if no one listens? What about my imperfect life? Have mercy on me, Lord, and forgive me. Help me to remember that the message is yours and the outcome is yours also. Give me the courage and the faith and the joy to believe and to serve. In Jesus' name I pray. Amen.

"If I say, 'I will not mention Him or speak anymore in His name,' then within me there is something like a fire burning - shut up in my bones; and I am weary with holding it in and I cannot."

For the past two days we have looked at this story from Jeremiah, chapter 20. Jeremiah was reluctant to listen to God and to do as God asked. There were many reasons, the foremost being that he was hesitant to give a word of destruction to those who were his friends and whom he loved. I asked the question, "Knowing that it was God doing the calling, why would Jeremiah be so hesitant?" So what did Jeremiah finally do? The answer can be found in verse 9. Jeremiah said that he had to speak God's words for if not there was a fire in his bones that would not let up until he did!

All of us when asked to do something difficult, like inform a friend that the road they are taking is not good for them, or to say to someone that you do not agree with their assessment of a problem, at first resist. We resist for the same reason as Jeremiah: we do not want to be at the other end of the wrath of a friend or colleague. We are then at a crossroad and we have a choice to make. We could just forget it and at least relieve ourselves of the bitter confrontation that could take place. We could just find new friends or leave the company we work for or whatever.

To the person whose life belongs to God, there is a calling and that calling will force you to speak or you will feel a fire inside all the way to your bones until you do. If something is ethically wrong the only thing that will make it right is to confront the wrong. Too many people have excused their ethics and watched as a great company, for which they work, crumble beneath them. Had they listened to that voice deep inside them and spoken, the results could have been quite different. So face your problems or flee, you decide. For Jeremiah it was to face them; he could not do otherwise. What will you do?

God of all wisdom and grace, I thank you for Jesus. I thank you for your servant Jeremiah and for the lessons of their lives. Teach me obedience in spite of my fears and reluctance. Help me to see that the power of your Word does indeed burn in my heart for a purpose – to encourage me to speak. Fulfill my purpose, Lord, in spite of my self. In Jesus' name I pray Amen.

All Flesh is like Grass   July 13   1 Peter 1:24

"For "All flesh is like grass and all its glory like the flower of grass. The grass withers, and the flower falls, but the Word of the Lord endures forever."

Here in Peter we are compared to the seasons of the year, first as spring and summer where the grass turns green and puts forth its flowers; then fall and winter where it withers, the flower falls. We are insignificant in comparison to the Word of God; we will pass away, but the Word endures forever. John in his Gospel calls the Word the "Living Word" or Jesus himself. The Living Word endures forever. Peter in the verses just before verse 24 has reminded us that we were *"purchased or "ransomed" from our futile ways, not by Gold, but by the blood of Jesus."* (Vs. 18-19) We are now sons and daughters of God through the purchasing power of Jesus.

Then Peter reminds us of our human nature. Although we are now born or reborn of imperishable seed, we are also human and perishable – we *"Wither and fade like the flower."* There is only one way that we will not fade or wither and that is through the Word of God. The Word of God can transform us into imperishable blossoms. The Word of God will transform us from the Physical - that desires and sins and fails one another and gossips and criticizes - to the Spiritual, which up lifts one another and loves and forgives and accepts. It is the Word of God that preserves us and makes us whole. Peter's call is to holiness.

For people to be in right accord with God they must keep their eyes on Jesus and their hearts open to him. It's pretty difficult for Jesus to enter our hearts if we don't. How can one who is holy enter a heart that is unholy? And how can we be holy without Jesus in our heart? By keeping our eye on the Word of God, the living Word, Jesus, we can be transformed. By keeping our mind on earthly things, our own desires, our selfishness, our greed, our desire to criticize, we remain perishable; wither like grass. Only Christ can transform our hardened hearts and melt them into loving-kindness fit for eternity.

Lord God, I thank you for your Son Jesus and for the redemption He purchased for me. Gratitude is easy to express, harder to live. In my weakness I have chosen the insignificant path. I have chosen to seek and serve that which does not last: money, status, popularity. Help me not waste a life ransomed by Jesus. Have mercy, Lord, and forgive me. Put me on the right path to remember and live by your Living Word. Jesus, be my ever-present guide. Amen.

Makes me want to Shout!   July 14   Mark 11:9

"Those who went ahead and those who followed were shouting, "Hosanna! Blessed is the one who comes in the name of the Lord! Blessed is the coming kingdom of our ancestor David! Hosanna in the highest heaven!"

Jesus rode into Jerusalem with shouts of "Hosanna" (save us – now). People spread their cloaks. This was costly as their cloak was all they had to keep them warm. They spread willing before him the most valuable thing they had. I am not sure people understood what he was doing. Many thought that he was there for a showdown with the Romans. Yet, Jesus did not ride in on a horse, to symbolize of conquering, but on the foal of a donkey, as a symbol of peace. The people wanted a mighty warrior so that is what they saw in spite of the incongruous picture Jesus must have made legs dangling over his too small a ride.

It's easy to shout: hard to serve. Throughout Jesus' ministry there were many questions about him, who he was, what he could do. Pilate said at the end of Jesus' trial, *"Are you the King of the Jews?"* (Mark 15:2) Hosanna was a sign of honor bestowed upon a king. It moved the people to faith, belief, and hope. The journey to follow Jesus is made by believing in and trusting Jesus with our very life, with all our cares and worries, with doubts and insecurities, with shortcomings, selfishness, meanness, faults, our failures, our will, our plans. Then that question mark will be answered by faith in the transforming power of Jesus.

It's so easy to shout: hard to serve. And the only way we can truly serve Him is to give our self fully to Him – let Him enter in. And that's why we shout "Hosanna!" because we know Christ is alive and leading us to serve him. Jesus did not come to make us perfect. He came to expose our sin so we can give ourselves fully to him - the good, the bad, the ugly, the nonnegotiable. On that day the people seeing Jesus were moved to forfeit the most valuable item they had, their cloak, so that the feet of the animal upon which Jesus rode would not touch the dusty road. Would you have done that? Do you spread anything costly before our Lord?

Sovereign Lord, Almighty God, in your great grace and mercy you sent your Son to save me. These have become for me tepid words that have lost their power to warm my soul and set aflame my heart. Forgive me. Forgive me fully. I cast before you now my most irreplaceable possession – a damaged and contrite heart. Don't let Jesus get dirty because of me. For his sake I pray amen.

"With my mind I am a slave to the law of God; with my flesh I am a slave to the law of sin."

I have ministered to many who speak of the battle which rages within. It is basically a battle for control. It is a battle to give God control or us. Truthfully, it is not as important that we win that battle, as it is to admit the battle is there. Without first admitting the truth, we have already lost the battle! It takes a tremendous discipline to follow God's will. You will have to know who He is, be dedicated to learn about Him, and worship Him. You cannot follow Jesus unless you seek His will everyday. God is not going to conveniently write a diary laying out what we are to do each day. We will have to go to Him in prayer every day. Not for His sake but for ours. Go and ask him to "give us this day our daily bread."

Following your own will is much easier. You just do what you want when you want. If you choose this road, it will be best to go it alone because most people don't really care for those who are selfish, self-centered, egotistical, critical, perfect, and always right. But if you want to give God control, first realize that your desire to control is a sin that tries to take you captive. Do not ignore the power sin has upon you.

Paul tells us that he realizes he is a slave to the law of sin with his flesh, but he chooses to be a slave to God with his mind! This is one of the most important passages of scripture for understanding our nature. We must understand we can choose to be a slave to the law of God with your mind, but with the flesh, you will always be a slave to the law of sin. There is nothing we can do about that, only choose to follow the will of God rather than the will of the flesh (worldly desires). There is a better self waiting to come out of you, but it is not of you, it is of God. God can change us, but He will not do so by force. He can, but He chooses not to.

God of Grace and Truth, you have in your mercy and love "made mankind a little lower than the angels, and crowned him with glory and majesty … and have put all things under his feet." (Psalm 8) I recall this truth and am awe-struck, ready to move mountains, slay dragons. But I am not humbled, I am not humbled. I am not at all like Jesus. Save me from myself and the Devil. Only you can make the surrender of my flesh a resounding victory over the Evil One. Do this for me. I cannot even if I would. In Jesus' name I pray. Amen.

"Rejoice always, pray without ceasing, give thanks in all circumstances; for this is the will of God in Christ Jesus for you!"

The Apostle Paul gives us a very helpful hint on how to live our lives in Thanksgiving. He tells the people of Thessalonica to always rejoice, to pray without ceasing and to be thankful in everything for *"this is the will of God in Christ Jesus for you."* Now our problem is fairly simple. Life has a way of stealing our joy! You know what I mean don't you? Simple things happen like our car breaks down, needs a new motor just when we are beginning to get ahead. The house needs a new roof. Or maybe more difficult things happen to us. We lose our mate to illness after only twenty years of blissful happiness, or our child is struck with an incurable disease. There are plenty of things that can happen to steal our joy!

I had an elder in a church who was joyful and a strong believer even though he had lost his only daughter. I asked him how he did it. He said, "I believe there is a God full of love and my daughter is in heaven with him right now experiencing that love. If that is not true, I would not be able to stand it." Yes, there is a God and the good news is we belong to Him. Truth is we belong to him even before we recognize it or understand it. Once we claim that truth, once we accept Jesus as God's son and our Lord and Savior, then the true Joy begins!

Paul says for us to *"be thankful in everything!"* It would be hard for us to be thankful for cancer or the loss of our mother and father, for senseless killings, and other horrible things we witness in life. But we can give God thanks for his presence and comfort in the midst of all these things. I can be thankful for the church, His Body on earth, which shows his love and comfort when we are in grief. It is that Body which helps us to get through the most difficult moments of life and be Joyful. We can rejoice and be glad for God's love and mercy – his grace.

God of all Grace, you knew that your children could not live without you to hold on to. Oh, we could exist, go through the motions, first one step followed by the next, purposeless, aimless – without you we could function, but we could not, can not LIVE! Living is what I was made for not just existing. Father God, don't let me settle for less. Bring forth the joy that lies dormant in every cell of this miraculous body. Rejoice, again I say Rejoice! Create in me a grateful heart, else I am indeed lost to you. In Jesus' name I pray. Amen.

"Jesus came into the district of Caesarea Philippi, he asked his disciples, "Who do people say that the Son of Man is?" They said, "Some say John the Baptist, others Elijah, and still others Jeremiah or one of the prophets." He said to them, "But who do you say that I am?" Simon Peter answered, "You are the Messiah, the Son of the living God."

The most important question that will ever be raised in our life is "Who do you say Jesus is?" Jesus raised this question to his disciples while discussing with them what people were saying about him. The disciples respond with various answers. *"Some say John the Baptist, but others say Elijah, and still others say Jeremiah or one of the prophets."* These possible prospects are all prophets previously sent by God to proclaim the coming of the Savior (Messiah). They are not "The One". This group of people who had been hearing Him speak was just curious to know what He might offer them. They did not know Him as did the disciples.

Even as Jesus asks this question, you sense that he is interested more in how the disciples view him than others. So He asked them, *"But who do you say that I am?"* Jesus knew that He would leave them soon and it was important that they know who He was. How can one help carry on the plan for salvation if they do not know the key ingredient of that plan? Jesus was and is the messiah. That was Peter's answer. Jesus commends him for knowing who he really is. That the disciples understood really mattered because of the mission he had for them.

It also matters to us today. It matters to Jesus who we think him to be for Salvation has been handed down from that first group of disciples to us. We are the ones called to be His disciples. We are the ones Jesus is counting on to offer up our lives in service and sacrifice to the Kingdom. Jesus is counting on us to be about the Father's business. So what we believe about Him, who we think He is, is of vital importance. It will determine the level of our loyalty to His body, the church. It will determine how committed we are. So what do you say? Who is Jesus to you?

Oh God, Creator of all that Is and Is to be, in your wisdom you knew I'd need a Savior, in your mercy you sent your Son, out of love you made him human – accessible, in your grace you made him mine for the asking – in your awesome power you fulfilled my soul's desire. Who is this Jesus to me? My all in all. Can you see it? Have I made it known? Help me, Father. I've much joy to share for His sake. Sustain me always. I pray in the name of Jesus. Amen.

"But when God, who had set me apart before I was born and called me through his grace, was pleased to reveal his Son to me, so that I might proclaim him among the Gentiles, I did not confer with any human being."

Yesterday, we talked about the greatest question we will ever answer: who we believe Jesus to be. The capacity to recognize, to see Jesus for who He is, is a gift form God. When Paul speaks to the church in the first chapter of Galatians he says, *"When God was pleased to reveal His son to me."* In other words, Paul did not learn of Jesus through the process of human effort. He had already done that as a Pharisee. God was pleased to touch Him with His Holy Spirit and reveal this truth to Him.

You see we cannot possibly receive the message that Jesus is the Son of God and our Savior through the process of human effort. Human effort gives us facts – this is what Jesus said, did. Discernment is a gift. The Holy Spirit opens our heart and we receive. Look at it like this. Do you believe in Jesus because the Bible tells you to do so? Do you believe in Him because He was a great speaker? Do you believe in Jesus because He was a great miracle worker, healer? Jesus was certainly all of these.

We believe in Jesus not because of what He did, but because of who He is! The Son of the Living God: God Incarnate: Fully human: Fully Divine. It is His very nature that attracts us and it is the Holy Spirit that reveals Him to us. Having said that, do we have any responsibility? You bet! Paul says that God revealed Himself to him for a purpose – "so that I might proclaim him among the Gentiles" (to outsiders, the unchurched). Now that we belong to Jesus, we are His disciples and He has instructed us with the miracle of Salvation - with the ministry of reconciliation - with the task to care for those who cannot care for themselves. If we belong to the Kingdom, then there is nothing more important to us than telling others who God has been to us. For that we will work tirelessly and give willingly.

Father God am I too like Paul - someone you've known forever, someone you created for a specific purpose only you can know? Is there a work you've set aside for me? Tell me, Father. I will do it. Will you help me? Will you give me a heart of love and courage? Will you rehearse in my head the scripture I've read and the stories where you have burst through in my own life or in the lives of those I know? I'll share but only if you come too. I so want not to fail you but I cannot do this alone. In Jesus' name I pray. Amen.

"Set your minds on things that are above, not on things that are on earth."

Where is your focus? It is so easy to allow our focus in life to be everywhere except where it should. Life runs us - drives us really - and before we know it, we are so out of breath we are gasping for air and yelling, "Slow down!" Our favorite phrase has become, "I'll be glad when things get back to normal." Then we discover this really is normal! What we mean is - I wish I could focus on the meaningful, rather than those things, which demand my attention. Let me give you an example. How many really want to feel tired and worn out all the time? Do we intentionally not get exercise so we can place a strain on our entire system to ensure we will have medical problems? Of course not! So what can we do? First, open our eyes to the truth and then refocus. We focus on what to do, such as a sensible diet and exercise program.

Well, what about the more important things of life, like your spiritual life? We go through life with difficulty and pain. Our job may not be to our liking, but we need the money. Our spouse may be too demanding, even controlling, but we love them. We make hard decisions that end up displeasing others or we make a poor decision and could end up displeasing even ourselves. Our children don't turn out the way we like or maybe they just try our emotions. What can we do?

We can allow our focus to be changed by the man from Galilee. As long as we keep our eyes on our circumstances, our circumstances will then control us. Paul says in Colossians 3:2, *"Set your minds on things that are above, not on things that are on earth."* Focus on Christ. Set your eyes on things that are above and watch things begin to change. We think that if we work hard enough, we can control our circumstances - not so! Focus on God and He will use whatever circumstances we are in for our good.

God of Grace, in your mercy, you sent Jesus to be the ultimate revelation of yourself. In Him I see your redeeming grace – the human life divinely lived – a life focused on God the Father. Regardless of the circumstances Jesus always demonstrated the ability to keep the main thing the main thing. Help me, Jesus. I struggle. I fail. Give me strength. In Jesus' name I pray. Amen.

Success   *July 20*   *Luke 19:15f*

"When he returned, having received royal power, he ordered these slaves, to whom he had given the money, to be summoned so that he might find out what they had gained by trading. The first came forward and said, 'Lord, your pound has made ten more pounds.' He said to him, 'Well done, good slave! Because you have been trustworthy in a very small thing, take charge of ten cities.'"

Many believe that success equals the amount of money or material possessions acquired. What is your idea of success? Could it be early retirement or the achievement of a college education? How about learning to control one's temper or raising a happy and well-adjusted child? Or, how about feeling fortunate enough to be able to pay your bills? Truth is success in worldly standards is meaningless in comparison to Christ. What I mean is, "Christ did not die so we may enjoy a boundless supply of material possessions." Now having said that, I also believe that God's will for us is to be successful (if you take the wider definition, that is). There is no scripture against people achieving prominence or becoming well to do. There are plenty warning us against allowing that success to go to our head or to allow possessions to become our god.

The point is to remember that it was God who gave us our abilities, talents, and opportunities. In the parable of the 10 pounds a ruler gave money to some of his servants while he was to be away on a long trip. When he returned, one returned the money ten fold, one five fold, and one had hidden the money in the ground and just gave it back. The first two were rewarded for the use of their talents; the third was chastised for doing nothing. The story is not one that says we are self-sufficient and can take pride in our accomplishments. Rather it is a story that tells us God gives talents to be used for His benefit and Glory. God is the source of all we have and are; we must recognize that and live accordingly. No person can truly be called successful if he or she has not learned to share what God has given.

God of all Blessings, you have blessed me beyond my deserving. You have loved me in Christ and trusted me to be a blessing to others. What wondrous love is this! Complete my joy by challenging me to use my talents sacrificially – to take a chance on the faith you have shown that I might serve you fully. May you return to find me faithful. In Jesus' name I pray. Amen.

Walking in the Light   *July 21*   *Isaiah 2:3f*

"Many peoples shall come and say, "Come, let us go up to the mountain of the LORD, to the house of the God of Jacob; that he may teach us his ways and that we may walk in his paths." For out of Zion shall go forth instruction, and the word of the LORD from Jerusalem. O house of Jacob, come, let us walk in the light of the LORD! For you have forsaken the ways of your people, O house of Jacob."

In 1995 we redid the sanctuary in the church I was serving. The sanctuary had been built in 1885 and we renewed it for our 100th celebration. It was more than spending a little money to make repairs. It was more than a new paint job and a new carpet. We were embarking upon a new phase in the life of our church. Just like buying a new outfit for your spouse or a new ring for her finger, it does more than "dress things up." It gives new life. It recharges the spirit. It lightens up your life. It says I love you, I care for you, and I want you to shine for you make my life shine.

Isaiah says in these verses "Let us walk in the light of the Lord." In the 8th chapter of John Jesus says, "I am the light of the world. Whoever follows me will never walk in darkness." The writers of the Old and New Testament sought to communicate to our somewhat logical minds that which is inexpressible. To do so, they compared the coming of Christ into the world as light coming into a world of darkness. The light shines and it illumines everything around it. It brings things to light that our eyes otherwise could not have seen. Jesus came to renew our lives; to give us a new paint job, and new carpet and to repair that which needs repairing; but more than that, He came to recharge our spirit. He did it because He loves us. As we go about living your daily life, and as you go about making the necessary changes to renew yourself, don't forget to walk in the light of the Lord.

Oh God of Light, recharge my failing spirit for the darkness has crept in to steal my light and without you it is dark in deed. Renew my life, Oh Lord. Remind me that I was made to fulfill a purpose of yours uniquely my own. Give me the grace to walk in your light all my days. In Jesus' name I pray. Amen.

"Then Jesus said to the Jews who had believed in him, "If you continue in my word, you are truly my disciples; and you will know the truth, and the truth will make you free." They answered him, "We are descendants of Abraham and have never been slaves to anyone. What do you mean by saying, 'You will be made free'?"

Jesus had told the Jews who believed in him if they continued they would finally know the truth and that truth would free them. They were confused and told Him they were descendents of Abraham and had never been in bondage to anyone! Is that true? How could these Jews have forgotten that their ancestors were in bondage in Egypt for hundreds of years? How could they have forgotten that God brought forth His servant Moses, the adopted son of Pharaoh's daughter to stand against the most powerful nation in the world and lead his real family, the Jews, to freedom? How could they forget the 40 years in the wilderness where they were given the Ten Commandments along with other laws?

Now you think about it, they could not possibly forget these things, could they? This is their heritage - this is a major part of the Pentateuch - the five books of Moses which they have read and studied all of their lives. So this could not possibly be what they meant. What they most likely meant was that they already had the truth and it was in the law. But Jesus pointed out to them that the law left them slaves to sin. The Apostle Paul would later tell them the same. In Galatians 3:23 Paul says, *"Before grace came we were imprisoned under the law."* The law only shows me how sinful I am. It does not free me but put me in bondage. That is the truth Jesus was referring to. The law enslaves. Until we understand that we cannot be set free. We often enslave ourselves. We put unrealistic expectations upon others and ourselves and then when the law is not followed perfectly, it gives reason to criticize and condemn. Then we feel and experience the full extent of the bondage of the "law". You want to be free? "Continue in my word," Jesus said, "and you will know the truth and the truth will make you free."

God of Freedom and Grace, help me to remember my own heritage of faith in the light of Jesus' words. Help me to see that in Jesus, I see, hear, and know the truth – that I am lost to you without his sacrifice on the cross – that I stand before you only by His Grace, clothed in His righteousness not my own. Forgive me when I forget this. Set me free from the bondage of self-promotion, self-congratulation. Set me free to love, to rejoice. In Jesus' name. Amen.

"When Jesus saw the crowds, he went up the mountain; and after he sat down, his disciples came to him. Then he began to speak, and taught them, saying: "Blessed are the poor in spirit, for theirs is the kingdom of heaven."

What does 'poor in spirit' mean? You could answer that question in several different ways. The answer I would give is this: the ones who are poor in spirit are those who rely totally on the grace and mercy of God for their salvation. They realize that one cannot be self-righteous and be accepted before an omnipotent and Holy God. They realize that it is fine to be proud, but pride is the number one enemy when it comes to being 'poor in spirit' and if you want to be in God's favor you must acknowledge the truth of your spiritual poverty.

Jesus says in these verses that the poor are blessed because they will receive the kingdom of heaven. He is not speaking of the virtue of poverty. Jesus is talking about the virtue of faith in a God who has provided and given you all that you have and all that you are. God the Creator and Redeemer is the ultimate source of all our security. There are times when we think, "If I just had enough money; if I just had enough land; if I just had enough possessions, then I could be in control of my life. Then I would be protected and secure." However, if you do not realize this now you will know some day, that kind of security is just an illusion.

There are times in our life when only faith in God can pull us through. Those who are poor in spirit are the ones who do not look to their own abilities or wit or wisdom or knowledge in order to find their way into God's kingdom. Instead, they rely totally upon the grace and mercy of God through His son Jesus. They maturely accept their utter dependence on God's gracious and powerful love. People who are 'poor in spirit' recognize their spiritual weakness and rely upon the righteousness of Christ to transform thought, will and life. Those who are 'poor in spirit' are those whom God has made humble and instilled with a servant's heart.

Oh Lord, my Savior, I hear you say 'poverty is a source of happiness' and I reject it as untrue; surely spiritual poverty cannot be a goal. I want to be rich in spirit! Surely you cannot mean that only when I am empty of self can I be truly full, truly blessed. O.K. - O.K., then. Pour me out and when I am empty of self-pride, self-satisfaction, and self-concern and even self-loathing then I can be God-full. I await you, Lord. Hurry! For Jesus' sake. Amen.

Beatitude: Blessed mourn   **July 24**   *Matthew 5:4*

"When Jesus saw the crowds, he went up the mountain; and after he sat down, his disciples came to him. Then he began to speak, and taught them, saying: "Blessed are those who mourn, for they will be comforted."

All of us have experienced death or the loss of someone we love. Many have expressed their loss in healthy ways; others have never expressed their loss and are trapped in the past. It is good for us to be able to express our loss. In times when we experience a loss, it is the church, Christ working through us bringing His love and healing, where we are comforted. Our mourning actually opens the door to experiencing Christ at a deeper level. Grief can even cause our faith to grow if we open our heart to His healing power.

When I was young we had to memorize a verse of scripture each week. The first one I choose was, you guessed it, "Jesus wept." (That is the shortest verse in the bible - from John 11:35) This is the story where Jesus' good friend, Lazarus is ill and Jesus reaches Him too late and he has died. The scripture tells us that Jesus was deeply moved and wept. If you mourn, you have a heart for others, a heart that feels and experiences the suffering around you as Jesus felt for his friend Lazarus.

Your loss of a loved one is not just mourning over loosing them, but also over what they have experienced and gone through. People who cannot feel the pain of others are narcissistic. They can only think about their needs; their pain, and that is truly sad. God Himself will comfort those who mourn for others. What can be more special than that? Through our mourning, we feel, experience, and grow closer to God.

Loving God of Comfort and Consolation, I too mourn many losses both within my family and my family in Christ. I must confess, Lord, I sometimes don't choose to be vulnerable to others' loss and heartbreak. I feel uncomfortable. I make unconvincingly desperate excuses not to go near. Forgive me and in your mercy have compassion. Give me the strength to focus on others' needs. When I forget me, I am available to remember you. Be my guide, Oh Lord, my grace. In Jesus' name. Amen.

Beatitude: the Meek　　**July 25**　　*Matthew 5:5*

"When Jesus saw the crowds, he went up the mountain; and after he sat down,
his disciples came to him. Then he began to speak, and taught them, saying:
"Blessed are the meek, for they will inherit the earth."

Powerful, influential, dealmaker, plan implementer, in control, strong willed. These words describe the times in which we live. Meekness is clearly absent. Most of us when we here these words of Jesus would like to say, "Meek? What do you mean meek? The meek get stepped on like ants. Why would I want to be meek? Why would anyone want to be meek?" This world operates in a different mode. You want to get ahead in life? You have to be willing to step on a few people (usually the meek).

You think of a meek person and who comes to mind? When I think of one who is meek I think of one who is kind and thoughtful and considerate of others and of me. I find that when I step on people who are meek or take advantage of them, and I must admit I have a few times n my past, I am not proud of that and it makes me feel bad about myself. It has something to do with the heart, the type of person you are. But when I am meek and kind and considerate, I find myself experiencing 'peace'. I don't know if that is the same as 'inheriting the earth', but it does make me feel good about myself. I think that it causes me to humble myself before God and rely on Him for all I have rather than stepping on others to get what I want.

The word that comes to mind is 'submit'. I submitted to God when I went into the ministry. I could have done a lot of other things; I had already been a music teacher for ten years. But God called. I submitted. It was a way of acknowledging my total dependence on Him and my complete faith and trust that he would take care of my needs. I have by God's grace never looked back.

God of Grace, Benefactor in Christ, My Inheritance, Like a strong willed child, I need to be tamed. Over and over I insist on my plans, my way, so stubborn, so hard headed – so fearful that some one might expose my fear. Gentle me with the certainly of 'inheritance' – what I gained but did not earn, what I have but do not control – the righteousness of Christ, the fellowship with a Holy Father. No child ever received more. Humble me. Gentle me. Forgive me. In Christ's name I pray. Amen.

"When Jesus saw the crowds, he went up the mountain; and after he sat down, his disciples came to him. Then he began to speak, and taught them, saying: "Blessed are those who hunger and thirst for righteousness, for they will be filled."

Don't look at this Beatitude in the wrong way. By that I mean one who works for their righteousness or seeks to be righteous by all the things they do. There are plenty of people who actually do that all the time. They seek to justify themselves by showing that they have "Never taken a drink of alcohol, never lied, never gossiped" – well maybe that is going a bit too far. I don't really know anyone who has not gossiped at least a little, do you? That is not what this Beatitude is all about.

This is about one who hungers to be made right with God. This is about wanting the fulfillment of God's creative purpose in one's life and in society. The question we must ask is "Do we really want what Christ has to offer?" What He has to offer us is Righteousness, His Righteousness. Are we humble enough to seek our righteousness from Jesus or are we arrogant enough to say we earn it on our own? I hope we choose humble because that is the only way in which we shall receive it.

God sent His Son Jesus to die for our sins and to make us righteous by His goodness not our own. "Blessed are those who hunger after righteousness from Jesus – they shall be filled with His Righteousness." We must have a strong desire to obtain this righteousness, not just so we will be saved, but so we will be filled with Christ Himself, so that we will take on the heart and mind of Christ. Through living in Him and for Him, we shall find satisfaction for our lives. Do you hunger for His Righteousness? Or for something else to satisfy your hunger?

Redeeming and Sustaining God, by your grace you have created in me a hunger and a thirst for you and for your will to come to pass in my life. But there is a danger of feeling self-satisfied and self-important. Help me not to judge others or condemn others. You know how easy that is. Remind me always that I stand only in the righteousness of Christ, as a known sinner, if only to God. Let me always seek your face. Let me never be satisfied as I am. In Jesus' name I pray. Amen.

"When Jesus saw the crowds, he went up the mountain; and after he sat down, his disciples came to him. Then he began to speak, and taught them, saying: "Blessed are the merciful, for they will receive mercy."

To obtain mercy we must show mercy. Now don't take this as the eleventh commandment or a law that must be followed, but rather as truth. In the Lord's Prayer found in Matthew 6:12 Jesus instructs us to pray, "forgive us our sins as we forgive those who sin against us." Jesus goes on to say, "If we do not forgive others, neither will our Heavenly Father forgive us." We must forgive one another.

Most people want to put a requirement on that requirement. "I will forgive others if they – come and ask – beg – tell me how wrong they were and how right I am!" That is not being merciful, that is delighting in someone else being wrong! One thing I have discovered working with marriages is that when someone is hurt because of another persons indiscretions the harmed party sets up 'conditions of forgiveness.' That might help them to somehow get back at their partner who hurt them, but forgiveness is either unconditional or it is not forgiveness.

Being merciful is not about forgiving the other person for what that will do for them alone, it is about what it does for us too. Being merciful toward others forms mercy in our very Soul. It makes us feel better about us. It puts us in charge of the situation. If we set requirements for the other person to meet, they are in charge of our forgiveness, not us. Being merciful brings us a little closer to God where we shall obtain His mercy. Isn't that what we seek?

God of All Grace and Mercy, be merciful to me a sinner. You know me – who I am, who I am not. You see the whole picture. Yet in your mercy, and knowing my repentant heart, you allow me only a glimpse of the blackness of my soul. May your gracious act of love toward me mold my response to others. Make me merciful by remembering your great mercy. For Jesus' sake. Amen.

"When Jesus saw the crowds, he went up the mountain; and after he sat down, his disciples came to him. Then he began to speak, and taught them, saying: "Blessed are the pure in heart, for they will see God."

Jesus makes an extraordinary promise here: to see God! I think this is a Beatitude that most of us really would like to have, but many for the wrong reasons. Many want others to see them as "Pure in Heart" because it would make them appear to be good in the eyes of their neighbor. Looking good on the outside is not the same as being pure in your heart. Our heart is the place where we are "meek" or "merciful".

Our heart is the place where forgiveness takes place and where we mourn and are sympathetic and empathetic. It is the very center of our soul, the seat of our will, not our emotions. When the heart is pure, the mind belongs to God. One who is 'Pure in Heart' truly will see God because their heart will be filled with God. God will be their focus. You cannot be pure unless your heart belongs to God and Him alone.

Many have told me "You have the sweetest wife I have ever met." I tell them 'thank you' but what I should say is, "She is that way because her favorite Beatitude is this one and because of that her heart is always open for God to come in and occupy a space." Those who are 'Pure in Heart' can actually see God in the hurt and pain others face, therefore their heart goes out to them and in doing so they experience God. If you are pure in heart then all the other Beatitudes will also come into play. You will also see God everywhere you look, in all things, in every face. That will be your reward!

God of my Heart, Lover of my Soul, in these words of Christ, the promise to 'see God', I stand both amazed and afraid – that it could come to pass – amazed. That it holds as qualification – purity of heart – afraid. Yet in Jesus you have made me your child and in this great gift comes a single-minded focus on your will and your presence. With open heart and hands, I come, my Savior. Do you see me? Is that you? In Jesus' name I pray. Amen.

"When Jesus saw the crowds, he went up the mountain; and after he sat down, his disciples came to him. Then he began to speak, and taught them, saying: "Blessed are the peacemakers, for they will be called children of God."

This may be one of the hardest things to actually accomplish. I cannot watch the "Miss America" pageant without thinking of 'World Peace'. It seems like when asked what they would like to see most in the world contestants have said over the years, "World Peace." At least that is what I remember. But is that what we get? No, what we get is usually 'World War'. In the twenty-fourth chapter of Matthew Jesus said that there would be "War and rumors of war." And there certainly have been!

Peace has to be worked on. Even in relationships peace does not come easy. Couples have to work to find peace in their relationships. One who is a peacemaker is one who is meek and seeks justice. Not justice for themselves only and not justice for Americans, but justice for the entire world. It does no good to say you want 'World Peace' if you only mean that you don't want a war going on. How about all those innocent people who are suffering and killed in countries under repressive regimes?

To be a peacemaker is to want justice for them also and to pray for their peace. Being a 'Peacemaker" is not to just stop war, but to strike at the very heart of the problem of war - the greed of individuals and leaders and the desire to make everyone submit to your way of thinking and being and living. Peacemakers want a better world; one in which all people are free to see God and live in peace.

Sovereign God, Christ, the Lord, you often in scripture speak the word 'Peace' or 'Shalom' as a blessing to your followers. You bring it with you; you leave it behind when you go. It is the first word of greeting; the last word of blessing as you exit. Surely significant result of an encounter with you, Lord, is peace, not just the absence of strife, turmoil, war, but the Presence of God. Settle in with me Lord. Change me and together we will change the world! Peace be unto us all. In Jesus' name I pray. Amen.

Beatitude: Persecuted   *July 30*   *Matthew 5:10*

"When Jesus saw the crowds, he went up the mountain; and after he sat down, his disciples came to him. Then he began to speak, and taught them, saying: "Blessed are those who are persecuted for righteousness' sake, for theirs is the kingdom of heaven."

It is hard for those of us who live in a free society that allows freedom of religion to understand that there are many in our world persecuted for 'Righteousness Sake'. We may have read of this in the scripture in stories like the one found in Matthew of King Herod killing all male children to get rid of the baby, Jesus. His fear was competition for this kingship. We may also have read about this in first century books or in Revelation. The early Christians were accused by Nero of burning Rome and were thrown into the arena with lions; some hung on crosses along the road. Of course history has proven that Nero himself actually set the fire so he could grab the land through 'imminent domain' and build a magnificent palace retreat for himself.

He built it but enjoyed the retreat for only a few years before his own people revolted and had him killed. Actually, Nero cut his own throat when they were in route to get him. Christians are still being persecuted for Righteousness Sake in countries all over the world. Just as John asked the people in Revelation to hold on to their faith even in the face of death, Jesus is saying here in the Beatitudes that the reward for holding on to your faith in the face of persecution is that the kingdom of heaven will be yours. Blessed are those who are persecuted because they refuse to denounce their faith, theirs will be the kingdom of heaven. We may not be persecuted in the sense of those in New Testament time or even those in other countries, but many are persecuted in the sense that others make fun of how we might worship or believe. If you happen to be one, do not worry for yours is the kingdom of heaven!

God of Grace, Sovereign Lord, I know you warned the disciples that persecution follows a commitment to you. You did that because you loved them and they you. But I, in my weakness and go-along-with-the-crowd choices, need no warning, do I? Injustice is not endangered by me. Yet you, in your strength and grace, Lord, love me still. Give my lukewarm faith, true commitment's fire that I may serve you Lord in a newness of faith. In Jesus' name. Amen.

"When Jesus saw the crowds, he went up the mountain; and after he sat down, his disciples came to him. Then he began to speak, and taught them, saying: "Blessed are you when people revile you and persecute you and utter all kinds of evil against you falsely on my account. Rejoice and be glad, for your reward is great in heaven, for in the same way they persecuted the prophets who were before you."

Some people seem to be saints no matter what happens. People can revile them, persecute them, utter all kinds of evil against them falsely and they stand firm in their faith. When Jesus addressed his disciples on the mountaintop that day He knew that the day would come when they would be persecuted for believing in Him. Jesus knew that living the kind of life that He outlined for them was going to be very difficult. In these final verses of the Beatitudes, He tried to warn the disciples that the Christian life will be filled with uphill battles and rough roads. So blessed are you when people persecute and utter evils against you falsely on my account Jesus told the disciples.

When those things happen, and they're bound to happen at one time or another, Jesus says, "*Rejoice and be glad, for your reward is great in heaven.*" Through out history saints have suffered because of their Christian faith. I mentioned a few in yesterday's meditation. There have been Christians who have taken unpopular stands and did not waver in the face of adversity, even from their so-called friends and colleagues. Such persons are examples for us. They offer us a word of hope in all that we must face in life. They endured and so can we. But in order to do so we must remember to submit our will to God. Let God mold us into the saint He is trying to make. We are not perfect people by any means, but we can be saints by trusting in Jesus, by submitting our will to God and then standing firm in this faith to which He has called us. Surrender your will to God and know that He loves you and that wherever He leads you, He will be present.

God of All Grace and Mercy, this beatitude is surely the hardest to hold near. I do not want to suffer, Lord. I already suffer for myself and those I love. Must I suffer for you too? Yet, I know even at this time you must have known the cruel death you would welcome, embrace, for my sake. But to do this standing up for you, I must have all the faith, hope, trust, joy you hold in your heart. Be with me Jesus, I'm taking the risk. I'm rejoicing, Jesus. Can you hear me? In Jesus' name I pray. Amen.

"Many live as enemies of the cross - their end is their destruction - their god is their belly - their minds are set on earthly things."

Today people live fast and hard. Some seem to want more and more pleasures in order to be happy. Others have found satisfaction in the simple pleasures of life. Which are you? I have had friends who fit into each of the above categories. One friend I will call Fast Eddie after a character from one of my favorite movies. This friend has to surround himself with all the latest "toys". Every new invention that comes on the market, he buys: the first cell phone, the first "Palm", the first four wheeler, the first laptop computer, the first Ipod, the first everything! Now, it is not wrong or bad to have these "toys". Some are important and essential. But my friend seems to need these things in order to be happy. I have never seen him "Happy", something is always wrong with everything he buys.

My other friend, I will call him John, is successful, but not in financial terms. Oh, he has enough, always says, "The Lord will provide" when he is in need. The funny thing is, the Lord always does! He always has a smile on his face and I have never heard him complain.

Paul speaks of the "Fast Eddie's" of this world when he warns of those who "set their minds on earthly things." I worry about those who cannot enjoy life unless they have the latest toys - engaged in the latest fad. Whether it is the newest sports car or the newest relaxation technique, there are many whose world is wrapped up in the pursuit of power and pleasure and possessions; there are some people who are desperately seeking happiness through sensual pleasure. There's nothing wrong with having these "things" as long as we recognize that the power and pleasure they provide us is an illusion - an escape. It is a substitute for real happiness, the happiness of experiencing Christ dwelling within us. I also am not saying that these things in themselves are sinful, just that if you have to have these things to be happy, you're in trouble. Ask yourself. Can I enjoy the simple pleasures of life? Or must I have more?

Lord God, give me the courage to examine my life and to look at what the choices I have made reveal about my priorities. Guide me in the path to true happiness in Jesus. Remind me lest I forget that true happiness comes in living out by purpose for your kingdom, being at peace with my Lord and His will for my life No earthly pleasure can ever compare. In His name's sake I pray. Amen.

Cut Out The Deadheads August 2 Matthew 7:16f

"You will know them by their fruits. Are grapes gathered from thorns, or figs from thistles? In the same way, every good tree bears good fruit, but the bad tree bears bad fruit. A good tree cannot bear bad fruit, nor can a bad tree bear good fruit. Every tree that does not bear good fruit is cut down and thrown into the fire."

Good gardeners know you must deadhead your plants. Once the flower bloom dies, you have to cut the dead off so that another bloom may come. If you do not cut off the dead heads, many types of flowers will either quit producing or produce less. A good gardener will sort out flowers and plants that no longer produce and replace them.

The Gospel of Matthew, chapters five through seven, is full of information and instructions given by Jesus in the Sermon on the Mount. In the seventh chapter, Jesus talks about 'good fruit' verses 'bad fruit'. *"Trees that do not bear good fruit will be cut down and thrown into the fire,"* he says. Paul in the eleventh chapter of Romans refers to us as branches that have been grafted into the rich root of an olive tree. Those who do not believe are broken off so that others may be grafted on. Paul is referring to Jews and Gentiles, but it can also include us. Just as one must deadhead a flower for the flower to flourish, those of us who refuse to believe are cut out of the vine in order for the vine to flourish.

Paul goes on to say in Romans eleven that we cannot boast of our fruit or our position for *"we do not support the root, the root supports us."* And if the root is Holy, and it is, for the root is Jesus; the branches that extend from it will also be Holy. What each of us must do is examine our life. Do we bear 'good fruit'? Can one whose root system is connected to Jesus actually bear bad fruit? We are connected to Jesus and we stand on our faith and bear the fruit, which comes from the Holy root.

Lord of the Vine and the Flower, I thank you that by your grace you have made possible my connection to Jesus, the Holy Vine. I want my words and my deeds to bear good fruit for your kingdom. I want to be a vigorous and vibrant part of your blessed purpose in Jesus. Prune from my soul the deadwood of my life – past hurts, past sins, past failures. Give me a new growth of spiritual fruit. Hear my prayer, O Lord. In Jesus' name. Amen.

"I have no silver or gold, but what I have I give you; in the name of Jesus Christ of Nazareth stand and walk."

In the third chapter of Acts, Peter and John were going to the temple at the hour of prayer. They saw a lame man being carried to the entry of the Temple so he could beg from the people entering. The man asked Peter and John for alms. Peter's response is today's scripture. The man not only stood, he jumped and ran around the temple praising God. The regulars were astonished for they had known this man as one who had been crippled from birth! Peter says to them, "Why are you astonished? Do you think that this man walks by our power? No, but by the power of God through Jesus." Peter took this occasion to remind them of their complicity in the crucifixion of Jesus. He reminds them that the God of their ancestors is the one who has healed this man through power in the name of his son whom they rejected and had killed even though Pilate had given them an alternative that would have spared Jesus' life. "It is by faith in this Jesus that the man you know now walks."

Most struggle much of their lives trying to understand who Jesus is. Intellectually we know, at least we have read or studied scripture, which says he is the Son of God and is at the same time human. All of that is a concept hard for us to grasp. Deep down we want to accept Jesus but we cannot quite understand. It is illogical. Either Jesus was the Son of God or he was a liar and a fake. It cannot be both.

Just as those who witnessed Peter and John that day at the temple, we too must choose. Either Jesus is the Son of God and our savior, or he is a fake. Your answer will come in the form of a commitment either to this world and its emphasis on money and material wealth or to Jesus. So what will it be? To the lame man who asked for money, Peter said, "I can give you so much more – I can give you life in Jesus." He chose Jesus. Have you? Will you? It's your choice.

Oh God, my Savior, as I read this I wonder if I have settled for the world's kind of wealth, begging at the gate of God himself yet asking for only money or today's version of silver and gold. Do you have something greater in mind for me Lord? Show me your will. Compel me to follow and I can, Lord. Make me stand in the name of Jesus. I'm standing for you, Lord! Can you see me?! Thanks be to God for His mercy, His grace. In Jesus' name. Amen.

The Mountaintop   August 4   Exodus 24:12

"The Lord said to Moses, 'Come up with me to the mountaintop and wait there and I will give you the tablets of stone - the laws and the commandments I have written for my people."

There are two experiences that go along with the Christian life: the experience on the mountaintop and the experience of service down in the valley. On the mountain-top, we encounter God in an unbelievable Holy place. We feel our souls being refreshed; we find inspiration for living the life of a Christian. Then there is the experience down in the valley where we live the Christian life in service. Through discipline and obedience; we live as the body of Christ at work in this world.

Can you imagine God speaking to you? Can you imagine the sheer awe of being in the presence of the Almighty God? Perhaps you have felt the presence of God like never before during worship, or while working in the garden, or meditating in your favorite place. The point is you will feel inspired as never before and the experience will be so powerful you will never forget it as long as you live. There is a hunger within us to live on the mountaintop; there is a hunger for to feel special, a hunger to think that God loves us so much He gives us grand experiences others, only wish for.

Even the disciples sought the same. In the tenth chapter of Mark, James and John asked Jesus to *"Grant us to sit, one at your right hand and one at your left, in your glory."* There are other places where the disciples seek to be placed above everyone else. Who can blame them!? What would you give to have such a place next to Jesus? What would you give to have an experience with the risen Christ and to sit right next to him? We all want to experience the mountaintop for those mountaintop experiences lift us, encourage us, and strengthen us to keep the faith when times are hard. Our merciful Lord intends for us to have something to hold onto when we need it or to share with another person needing encouragement during a test of faith.

Almighty God, Savior of My Soul, are you on the mountaintop now, Lord? Can I come too? Just the thought of such an experience! Joy fills my weary heart. Can I come too? Is it time? Am I empty enough to take you in? Open my eyes and ears, Oh, God, and then just a glimpse will suffice for a lifetime to hold and to share. Come, Lord Jesus. Come. Amen.

The Valley   *August 5*   *Exodus 24:16*

"And the glory of the Lord settled on Mt. Sinai and on the 7th day, the Lord called Moses out of a cloud. The appearance of the glory of the Lord was like a fire on top of the mountain in the sight of the people of Israel down below. Moses entered the cloud and went up on the mountain and was there forty days and forty nights."

Yesterday we talked about the mountaintop experience as an inspiration to faith. As a matter of fact, God calls us to such experiences. It is just as important to obey Him and follow Him up the mountain, as it is to serve into the valley. In today's text, Moses was given an incredible experience. He entered the cloud staying 40 days and 40 nights. Why did he go? What did he do because of the experience? He went in obedience to God's call. He came down ready to serve the Lord and spent the rest of his days leading God's people toward a new land and a new life. He had experienced a life-altering encounter with God.

In the seventh chapter of Matthew, Jesus took Peter, James and John up on a high mountain. There they experienced the transfiguration. Jesus changed in form. His clothes became dazzling white. His face shone like the sun. Moses and Elijah appeared with Jesus. It must have been an unbelievable experience for those three disciples who would go to the far corners of the known world preaching the Gospel and spreading the word that Jesus is God's son and our Savior. That is what usually happens if an authentic mountaintop experience with the risen Christ occurs. Our eyes are opened to see the world and others in a completely different light. Now we see the world through the eyes of Christ. We come down ready to serve Him, to minister to the poor and needy, to spread the 'Good News' that Jesus is Lord. We come down as changed persons. With the glare of the world out of our eyes, we can truly see the world as God sees it. We receive the kind of faith and courage to witness Jesus for the rest of our lives.

Almighty God, I read this devotion today and I am moved to think about my spiritual life. I do spiritual things; I read the Bible; I go to church, I even pray! Is that enough? Is that service? I know I can do more but I'm already overextended as it is. You understand, don't you, Lord? Once this time in my life is over, I'm all yours! My name! Was that my name you called from the cloud? Sure! Sure, I will! For you, Jesus, anything!! Amen and amen!

"Very truly I tell you, the hour is coming, and is now here, when the dead will hear the voice of the Son of God, and those who hear will live."

I have had the privilege to pastor thousands of people in my lifetime. Being a minister, most have been 'believers' in the sense that they believe that Jesus was and is the Son of God. Having said that, still there are some whom I feel are still dead and have not *"heard the voice of the Son of God."* I believe that when you read this verse from the fifth chapter of John it can be translated in several ways. John may be referring to those who have already died and did not have the opportunity to see and hear Jesus will have the chance and those who hear (believe) will live.

There is a verse from the fourth chapter of Ephesians that states, *"When it says he ascended what does it mean but that he had also descended into the lower part of the earth to fulfill all things."*

Another way to see this verse is the 'living dead'. Those who are alive physically yet are dead spiritually. Those are the ones of whom I am referring. There are church members who have paid their dues as one pays dues to a social club but have not placed their lives into the hands of Jesus. They are still dead. Now as I have said, I do not possess the knowledge or the authority to identify them or judge them but I have been given the privilege of witnessing for my Lord. I can say this with confidence: those who refuse to trust their lives in the hands of Jesus are still dead. Those who do not hear his voice as the voice of the Son of God and who refuse to accept him as their savior are still dead. You can believe that Jesus is God's son and still not accept him as your savior. There are plenty of the 'walking dead' who fit that statement; people who trust too much in their own 'good deeds' to save themselves; people who cannot accept that grace is a free gift for all who believe and trust in Jesus. I know it does sound too good to be true, but truly it is.

Almighty God, Sovereign Lord, am I one of these who are alive but 'dead' to you, to your voice, to your will? You know. You know the truth, Lord. Whisper it to me. I'll hear. I'll hear, Lord. Be gracious to me, Lord, for I am a sinner and I'm inclined not to believe it about myself as quickly as I do of others. Will you change that truth about me? Or else who would listen to my humble words of thankful praise? In Jesus' name. Amen.

The Son has Authority   August 7   John 5:2C

".. the Father... has granted the Son... authority to execute judgment, because he is the Son of Man....; for the hour is coming when all... will hear his voice and will come out – those who have done good, to the resurrection of life, and those who have done evil, to the resurrection of condemnation."

We will be given the opportunity to accept and believe in Jesus. The 'Good News' is we have a savior. All we have to do to be saved by Him is to accept Him! Jesus, our Savior, has been given the authority to 'execute judgment'. Most cringe at the thought. In scripture as in life judgment goes two ways. Jesus has the authority to judge us guilty or innocent. Those who believe in Him who belong to Him He will declare innocent, granting eternal life. Those who are spiritually among the 'living dead' God wants to awaken from their darkness. God refuses to give up on us. For that reason, He sent Jesus, Son of Man, to convince us that he has lived as we live, suffered the pains and agonies of life as we do and was victorious. It is not enough to experience God as Creator, we must experience Him as Savior. That is when we pass from death into life.

Christianity is less knowing about God as experiencing His transforming power in life. Most think when we experience Jesus we must change and do good to be saved. God wants transformation more than change. If it is change that is important, who is the one responsible? We are. Only God can transform us and awaken us from seeing life through the eyes of the world, trusting in our ability, in money, in material things, to seeing life through the eyes of Jesus, trusting that He is the 'one' who can save, that if we believe in Him and let Him have our will and our life, Jesus will guide us in every decision we make. Then we can live victoriously knowing that our Heavenly Father is in control and that in Jesus Christ we are truly children of the Living God both in this world and the next.

Sovereign Lord, Almighty God, in life and in death I am yours! What a wonderful, reassuring truth that is. Grant me the grace this day to live victoriously whatever may befall me or mine. Transformed by faith, may I honor you Lord in word, in deed, seeing the world through the eyes of a loving, merciful Savior. I want to do this, Jesus. Together we will do wonderful things. This is my prayer in Jesus' name. Amen.

"If you love me," says the Master, "you will keep my commandments, and I will pray the Father and He will give you another counselor."

There was a couple who had been married for years having married when they were very young. At this point in time they had a child, a grandchild, and life seemed great. However, the relationship was not as it seemed. They separated. The husband could not accept it. Depressed, he began stalking his wife. Eventually he took her life. Depression has been described as inner anger that freezes inside. Frozen inner anger! What a descriptive term for a heart meant to love, to forgive! Have you ever felt like that? Many people feel they have no one to turn to in times of trouble and therefore keep things bottled up inside.

In the fourteenth chapter of John Jesus tells the disciples that he must die but assures them He will not leave them 'comfortless' but is going to prepare a place for them and will send the Holy Spirit as a counselor for them. That promise applies to us as well. Christ has promised that if we go to him he will hear us and be with us. Where do we find comfort when our lives are desolate? In Jesus - Jesus will not leave us alone but will come at a moments notice! Just pray to Him, call on His name! The Holy Spirit is there to help you. Just pray to Him and listen.

In the first part of our text today Jesus says, "If you love me you will keep my commandments" You will act on that love by obedience. The lack of love is one of the main instigators of depression. If people do not feel loved, they feel worthless, prone to frozen inner anger. Don't wait for love to come, go out 'love one another', that way you not only keep one of Jesus' commandments, you gladden the very heart of God.

Loving and Merciful God, in Jesus you have demonstrated for all time how great is your love for your children. Help me to claim that perfect love – especially when I most need it. The world does not love like you, Jesus, and sometimes the world's voice is so loud, so loud. My fragile heart can freeze over, Lord, trapping the anger of 'unlove' inside. 'Unlove' can do terrible, cruel things. Forgive me. Give me yourself, Lord, your strength, your mercy, your comfort. Grant me grace and peace. In Jesus' name. Amen.

"He will give you another counselor, to be with you forever, even the spirit of truth, whom the world cannot receive, because it neither sees Him or knows Him; you know Him, for He dwells with you, and will be in you. I will not leave you desolate; I will come to you."

'What is Truth'? That is the question Pilate asked Jesus (John 18:38). In these verses from the fourteenth chapter of John Jesus says that 'the world cannot see or know the spirit of truth' which he describes as our counselor. It is the counselor who opens us up to hear and respond to God's truth.

Many have said that Christians live in a world of dreams; Jesus says that we live in a world of 'truth' – God's truth not the worlds'. The world says you are alone, Jesus says, *"I am with you always to the close of the age."* (Matthew 28:29) The world says that you can 'be good' Jesus says that 'no one is good but God alone.' (Luke 18:19) The world says look out for yourself! Jesus says 'love God and one another' (Matthew 22:37f). The world says to you, if you accomplish certain things you are better than those who do not. Jesus says, *"Judge not that you be not judged. For the judgment you give you will receive."* (Matthew 7:1) If we follow the world we will live by falsehoods and half-truths, but if we listen to Jesus we will live by Truth and that Truth will set us free!

There is more to life than what the world has to offer. The world offers you money and false security. Jesus offers you a 'spirit of truth'. Comfort and peace is found in love and truth. You want a life void of worry and fear? Christ came to bring you that life and it is available to us through the Holy Spirit. Truth, Love and the Presence of Christ is the key to happiness and security in our life, not money, power and worldly possessions. *"I will not leave you desolate,"* Jesus says and *"I will come to you."* (John 14:18) How will He do that? He will come in Love and in Truth and with the Presence of His Spirit. And because He lives, you also will live!

Almighty God, Sovereign Lord, I read the promises made in your Word and I am awed, humbled. You, Lord, in the Holy Spirit will be with me forever. What a glorious gift! There is a catch though; the world cannot see, know or receive it – this Spirit of Truth. The world stands as an adversary to this divine grace – an emphatic 'No' to your sovereign 'Yes'. I'm no good at spiritual battles, Lord. My heart beats too fast; my words of disclaimer don't come. You, Lord, must argue your case and fight for me. Help others see what I see. Let your Truth be victorious! In Jesus' name I pray. Amen.

"Pray then in this way: Our Father in heaven, hallowed be your name."

In our text from Luke, Jesus had just finished praying when his disciples approached him and asked him to teach them how to pray. This is a need many of us have.

We all have a tendency to pray for things that will benefit us. Most people when asked to pray out loud are either afraid to do so or they don't know what to say. They fear that others may be critical of what they say or how they say it, and with good reason. When the disciples asked Jesus that day to teach them, he left us this pattern of prayer.

Today let's look at the first component of prayer, *"Our Father in heaven, hallowed be your name."* When we pray, it is important to begin by acknowledging to whom we are praying: our Father and to acknowledge our unique relationship. We acknowledge that God is in 'heaven', an unseen celestial place and that God is 'hallowed' (Sacred or Holy). The Bible tells us that God created the 'heavens and the earth' - Heaven for His dwelling place and for those who belong to Him and Earth as a temporary place until we go to be with God. By acknowledging that God is in heaven we are acknowledging that heaven exists. By saying 'hallowed' we are acknowledging that God is Holy and to be revered, that he created us and with us, the known universe. By praying to 'our Father' we are acknowledging our need for God, our need for a power greater than ourselves to order and direct our lives. We also are acknowledging a relationship of parental authority and love as a Father to His Child. Prayer must be important to us because God is important to us. It is our way of communicating with God and allowing God to have a moment of our time to communicate with us, Father to child.

Almighty God, Father of our Lord and of me, In your mercy you left an example of prayer. We all need a guide to go by. It is so like you to acknowledge this and to provide. Thank you Lord, for the security of knowing that from the highest realms of heaven you watch over us. That those there with you whom we've loved and lost are watching too! Keep me in your sights, Lord, and in your way. I do wonder off at times. Forgive me, most Holy Father. In Jesus' name I pray. Amen.

"Your kingdom come, Your will be done, o n earth as it is in heaven."

Yesterday, we began a look at the 'Lord's Prayer' as a way of learning how to pray by first acknowledging who God is; today, we will examine the next verse in this prayer. What does it mean to pray that 'God's Kingdom come on earth as it is in Heaven'? By saying this, we are calling for God to extend His Heavenly Kingdom to earth. If we are asking for God's Kingdom to come on earth like in heaven, we might need to understand what that means.

It could be described as 'The Garden of Eden' revisited where evil is destroyed and people live in peace and joy! There are many scriptural references to God's Kingdom. It is the sphere of God's rule as seen in Luke 1:52 and Romans 13:1.In Matthew 13:44, the Kingdom of God is referred to as 'the pearl of great price' which the finder willingly goes and sells everything he has in order to purchase; 'the treasure hidden in the field' which when found, the finder in his joy goes and sells everything to buy the field; the 'net thrown into the sea' which caught fish of every kind – the good are kept, the bad were thrown out. Entering God's Kingdom can be thought of as entering by sacrifice, for we must 'take up our cross' and 'give up our life'. That all refers to the present Kingdom.

There is also a future Kingdom that is thought of as 'reward' and 'glory'! In Matthew 25, Jesus is separating the 'sheep from the goats', the sheep are asked to come and 'inherit the Kingdom' that has been prepared for them. When asked how to get into this Kingdom, Jesus tells Nicodemus *"You must be born of water and of Spirit."* (John 3:5) I guess the question we must ask ourselves is: "Do we really want God's Kingdom to come on earth as in heaven?" And do we want to be a part of that Kingdom? If so we must be 'born again', born from above. And we will then have to sell all that we have and invest our entire soul to purchase this Kingdom. But then we will want to for it is of such great value!

Almighty God, Sovereign Lord, Our Father, I know your plan for your world, your children is perfect in every respect, our Eden once more, our heaven on earth. But Father, when will it come? When? Today's world reeks with evil and unexplained tragedy. When will you come, Father, to make complete our joy and yours? When will your 'perfect will' be done on earth too? Are you waiting so that all may believe? So that not one sheep is lost? Are you waiting Lord for all sinners to relinquish the reigns of their will to you? Are you waiting for me? Come, Lord Jesus, come. Amen.

"Give us this day our daily bread."

My college roommate prayed for a date to the football game. I thought it was terrible. World hunger, world peace: these are the stuff of prayers! You don't bother the Almighty for such trivial incidentals. Clearly, I had a lot to learn about prayer and about the meaning of 'daily bread'! Prayer is something we must integrate into our daily lives as easily as eating our evening meal. It also should be just as important! *"Give us this day our daily bread."* Most of us want God to give us great knowledge, great wisdom, great power and then leave us be! That way we can have the power and attributes of God and we won't have to bother going to Him all the time showing how weak and insecure we actually are! Jesus shows us something quite different in this little verse of his prayer. We must go to Him every day for our sustenance. It is what our God wants.

Prayer is meant to be a daily exercise: part of our getting up, part of the exercise of our daily life, and part of our retiring for the evening. We are to ask for what we need, our daily bread, today, not tomorrow, but today, however incidental. Paul had this to say about prayer in 1st Thessalonians 5:16, *"Rejoice always, pray without ceasing."* To do that we must push out all the little things that try to slip into our mind and occupy space: worry, fear, resentments, despair, the little plots and schemes of daily life. Instead, we allow God to have our thoughts, our will, our very being. Turning to God only when we are desperate is not the image you get when reading these verses. God wants all of us. God wants us to come to Him about all things. Many of us don't need to ask for daily bread in the sense of the essentials. Often our spiritual need is greater! As we live life, we grow to realize our need to throw ourselves upon God's grace in order to understand our sinfulness and God's mercy. Praying to God daily comes easier once you have come to that conclusion.

Great God of Daily Life, You have been so good to me. I could never thank you enough. Yet gratitude is the greatest prayer I could offer for both our sakes or so it seems to me. When I remember your constant care in words of prayer, I am twice blessed. Is it the same for you when you hear? Oh, Father, if I cease to include you in my life, forgive me. Give to me what you want for me and it will be all I ever could ask for. In Jesus' name I pray. Amen.

Prayer 4   *August 13*   *Matthew 6:12*

"And forgive us our debts, as we also have forgiven our debtors."

Our next verse about how to pray is a real 'doozy'! The ramifications are eye opening! That phrase immediately calls forth our reasoning power and usually for the wrong reasons. We want to somehow show that it does not mean that we must forgive those who have harmed us in order for God to forgive us! Yet, that is precisely what it says, isn't it? If we expect God to forgive us, we must forgive one another.

Harboring resentment in our heart may seem like an easy way out but it really isn't. God expects us to forgive the person who harmed us as an act of obedience, but also because of what forgiveness does to us. Harboring resentment destroys our heart! It forms us into someone different from what God wishes us to be. It also robs us of our joy and happiness.

Forgiveness does not come easily. First we have to humble ourselves, which no one really aspires to do! Then we have to unconditionally let go of the harm the other person caused us (See the Parable of the Two Debtors – Matthew 18). Often we forgive as long as they have come begging on their knees for mercy. If they don't, we do not want to let them off the hook. What we must realize is that forgiveness is a gift to the other person that also lets US off the hook. We no longer have to keep that resentment bottled up inside which takes quite a bit of energy and effort. Then we must call on God to forgive us and give us the strength to forgive. We do not have within us this ability without His forgiveness and grace. This command concerning prayer is as much for us as it is for the one who harmed us.

God of Mercy and Grace, ask of me anything and I will do it willingly. Please, Father, don't ask me this! Don't make your forgiveness conditional. It's too hard. I've racked up quite a forgiveness debt, as you know. Are you teaching me a lesson for my sake? That every day I'm to forfeit my opportunity to play the martyr role, the self-righteous role? I'm to do this because you in Christ have forgiven me? How can I say no? How can I even want to? This burden was never meant for me to carry, was it? Once again your grace overwhelms. In Jesus' name. Amen.

"And do not bring us to the time of trial, but rescue us from the evil one."

This is the final command in the 'Lord's Prayer". Some translations say "lead us not into temptation" . I doubt that God would be responsible for 'leading' us into temptation. As proof, I refer to James 1:13, *"No one when tempted should say, "I am being tempted by God"; for God cannot be tempted by evil and he himself tempts no one."* Can the message be plainer? Having said that, the world is full of deceit and we are easily tricked. The important thing to remember is that we are asking God not to protect us from the evil one; not that God tempts us.

It may be difficult to ask God to protect you if you do not accept the reality of evil or the 'evil one'. The evil one has been around a long time and has far more wisdom than we do and knows every trick in the book! So if you do not believe he exists, you are subject to falling for his trickery at every corner. If you do believe he exists you are still subject to his trickery for he has had many years to perfect his assaults. How then can we prevail?

It is clear that today many need to say this petition. There are many, from politicians to the boardrooms of corporate headquarters, who are being tempted and falling to that temptation. Money and power have become the new 'gods'. There are plenty of 'good' persons being brought to a time of trial because of their own choices. They may say that God is in their lives, but clearly they have no idea of who God wishes for them to be. Rather than rescuing them, my best guess is that God has done as Jesus did to Peter in Luke 22:31, *"Turn him over to Satan to be sifted like wheat."* If you do not want that to be your fate, I suggest you get down on your knees every day and ask God to "not bring you to a time of trial and to rescue you from evil." Only God can prevail against a Spiritual foe. Not us. Never Us.

Almighty God, Lord of Heaven and Earth, I praise your most Holy Name. I willingly acknowledge my total dependence on your mercy and your sovereign power. Keep me safe from evil's snare, his cunning, his effective lies so easy to believe. Save me, Lord, or I will be lost, ensnared by my own intellectual pride, my belief in my own cleverness. Rescue me from myself. This spiritual battle is not mine to fight, not mine to win. Come Holy Spirit. In Jesus' name I pray. Amen.

"Then David blessed the LORD in the presence of the assembly; David said: "Blessed are you, O LORD, the God of our ancestor Israel, forever and ever. Yours, O LORD, are the greatness, the power, the glory, the victory, and the majesty; for all that is in the heavens and on the earth is yours; yours is the kingdom, O LORD, and you are exalted as head above all…. And now, our God, we give thanks to you and praise your glorious name."

The Lord's Prayer ends with a doxology of praise, *"For Thine is the Kingdom, and the Power, and the Glory for ever. Amen."* The 'kingdom': God has supreme rule over this world. 'The Power': God has the power to rule and sustain that kingdom. 'The Glory': God deserves our worship. Some have connected this doxology to the one David gave in Chronicles, *"Yours, O Lord, are the greatness, the power, the glory, the victory, and the majesty; for all that is in the heavens and on the earth is yours; yours is the kingdom O Lord!"* That is quite a song of praise to God.

The praise at the end of this prayer is for the same purpose to praise God for what he has done and continues to do. It is an expression of Supreme gratitude and an acknowledgement of the divine truth about our great God. These are sincere words of awe from the heart of a true child of God. Praise given from a 'human' heart can be very different. The human way is to praise someone so that you may receive, even if it is undeserved. Perhaps, they have something you want, even their good opinion of you! The best way to succeed? Praise! To keep them working hard, they need your praise so you give it. It is insincere and manipulative.

We are not giving God glory and praise because he needs it but because he deserves it! He is our Creator and Sustainer who provides all that we have and has created all that we are. He alone deserves our praise and honor. Life is difficult even for the most dedicated Christian. Prayer connects us to the source of our power and grace. We need God's daily guidance in our lives. Prayer should be a part of our daily meditation. Our Lord gave this example for a purpose. He knew that praising God cultivates a grateful heart. Grateful hearts inspire a longing to express that gratitude in humble acts of loving service. Grateful hearts best assimilate God's great love.

Great God of All There is and Ever Will Be, Yours is the name above every name and you have told it to me. Jesus! Jesus! And yet so seldom do I think of you. More seldom still do I call your name even in silence. Forgive me, Father. Give me the heart of a true child of God open to your wondrous love. Teach me to praise whole-heartedly for 'thine is the Kingdom and the Power and the Glory Forever'! Amen and Amen.

Be Like a Child   *August 16*   *Matthew 18:1f*

"At that time the disciples came to Jesus and asked, "Who is the greatest in the kingdom of heaven?" He called a child, whom he put among them, and said, "Truly I tell you, unless you change and become like children, you will never enter the kingdom of heaven. Whoever becomes humble like this child is the greatest in the kingdom of heaven. Whoever welcomes one such child in my name welcomes me."

"Who is the greatest in the kingdom of heaven?" In Matthew Jesus answers this question from his disciples by pulling a child out of the crowd and saying, *"People who are like this child."* What is Jesus teaching us here about children, about ourselves?

I suspect Jesus was demonstrating a general truth about children, whose innocence allows them to see the world differently than we do as adults. Their minds have not yet been tainted with prejudices and cynicism. Children are unburdened with doubts. We teach them those things. If you tell a child there is a pot of gold at the end of the rainbow, they will believe you; so trusting are they. Children also don't judge a book by its cover. If asked, " Should I plant flowers in an ugly pot verses one which is painted and beautiful, which one will grow the most beautiful flowers?" Children get that right away! The outside doesn't matter. What is on the outside of a person is not necessarily an indication of what is in the inside. It is the inside that counts. Because children are unburdened with the fleshly things of the world, the eyes of their hearts are open to see God.

Jesus is telling us in this scripture today to look at how a child sees Him and then open the eyes of our hearts to see Him in that same manner. Who is greatest in the Kingdom? Those who learn to love, accept, forgive, and trust, like a child. Develop a prayer life that will help you un-clutter your mind and distance you from worldly things, from prejudices and greed, from envy and worry. If you need any guidance in forming this new way of thinking, just ask a child! Jesus will guide you along the path.

Lord God, how I long for the childlike innocence that once guided my faith, not naiveté, Lord, but an unwavering trust, an uncalculated love. Oh, that I could once again be as I was then when I was young and untested, when my life had not yet been so challenging, so hard. Oh, Father, shore up my tattered faith that my life-lived has wrought. Have mercy on me, my Jesus, and rekindle the trust that once was mine. I pray in the name of Jesus. Amen.

"For the one who sanctifies and the ones who are sanctified have one Father. For this reason, Jesus is not ashamed to call them brothers and sisters."

I have seen a lot in my years as a minister. Most of it has been good, even great! Some has not. I married a couple that had children by previous marriages. They turned out to be wonderful parents to all their children, looking upon each as their own. The only problem was the neglect of a biological mother of one child who never called, never visited, and treated this child as if she never existed or mattered! I say biological because a 'real' mother would never do that! The child could never understand her mother's indifference. We need to know that God is NOT like that! Jesus is not like that!

Here in the second chapter of Hebrews the writer tells us of the actions of God in Christ on our behalf. Now what does that say about us?

It says, unlike the child forsaken by the biological mother I described above, we do matter! It says that the one who sanctifies us, Jesus, is not ashamed to call us all brothers and sisters. Christ left his place beside God in Heaven to come to earth, live as a human, experience life as we do, suffer unspeakable torture on our behalf and for our sake bearing our sins so that we can be called his brothers and sisters here and for all time.

This scripture tells us that it does not matter where you come from; it does not matter who your parents are or how they have treated you; it does not matter your economic status or your accomplishments in this worldly society; Jesus did all of this for you! We are brothers and sisters of Jesus. God is our Father too. Jesus, our brother, the very reflection of God's glory tasted death on our behalf and for our benefit. That is the outrageous truth. If you believe it and accept it, Christ becomes the focus of your life, eternity with God your destination.

God of Grace, God of Glory, in your infinite wisdom you knew that I would need a savior. Thank you for Jesus. You knew too that the brothers and sisters I long for most are the spiritual kind. Those who aren't indifferent to me or ashamed, who see the Christ in me that I in my weakness cannot, who call me to claim the abundant life Christ has made possible. Thank you for them. Someone so very blessed should just radiate joy! I am shining for you, Jesus, my brother. Do you see me? In Jesus' Holy Name I pray. Amen.

Jesus Comes to us!   *August 18*   *John 21:3f*

"Simon Peter said to them, "I am going fishing." Just after daybreak, Jesus stood on the beach; but the disciples did not know that it was Jesus. Jesus said to them, "Children, you have no fish, have you?" They answered him, "No." He said, "Cast the net to the right side of the boat, and you will find some." So they cast it; they were not able to haul it in because there were so many fish. That disciple whom Jesus loved said to Peter, "It is the Lord!"

This is a story of faith renewed. The disciples are tired and confused. They have been through a lot: the trial and crucifixion death of Jesus, surely the lowest point of their lives. At His request, these disciples had left everything to be a part of His ministry. When they saw Him nailed to the cross, they thought all was lost. The women had gone to the tomb and found the grave empty. Still they could not fully comprehend. So while they were trying to sort all of this out Peter says, *"I'm going fishing."* Since this had been their previous trade maybe it would help them clear their heads and get focused! So they fish all night. Their nets are empty. Just at daybreak, someone on the shore calls out and tells them to cast the net on the other side of the boat and they will succeed. The catch is so great they are unable to haul in the net. That is when John says to Peter, "It is the Lord!" And it is!

This scripture tells us that Jesus comes to us in our need. The disciples are confused not knowing what to do. Jesus appears to them and suddenly everything is different. Sometimes Christ comes into our lives when we are confused and down and lets us know everything will be fine. He pulls us from our doubt, insecurity, and emptiness and moves us toward our destiny. When we want to hold onto the things of this world, Jesus comes to remind us that they do not matter. To trust in the world would be to give in to every doubt and confusion, Jesus says, "I am the truth, the way, the life – your life. Trust in me."

All Knowing, All Seeing God, do you stand on the shoreline of my life? Are you watching me sweat and toil only to come away empty-handed? As with the disciples here, do you know I have not found what I seek either, despite my best efforts? Lord, how are you going to make my empty net full? No, don't tell me. Just surprise me! But Lord, please see to it that in my heart I know it's you! That is the one thing I seek most of all. In Jesus' name I pray. Amen.

Shake Rattle and Roll   *August 19*   *Acts 4:29*

"Lord, look at the threats that they are leveling against us; grant Your servants to speak Your word with all boldness, while You stretch out Your hand to heal and signs and wonders are performed through the name of Your Holy Servant, Jesus." When they had prayed, the place where they had gathered shook!"

When I was a teenager I was a part of a 'Rock and Roll' band called the 'House Rockers'. We played at local dances, even auditioned for Sam Phillips at Sun Studios in Memphis, who said "Boys, you have a unique sound and if I ever need it I'll call." He never did! It was just as well. God had other plans for me. The leader of our band went on to become a great songwriter with numerous number one hits. I myself have never looked back. Answering the call of God has always been right for me. I'm a House Rocker just in a different venue.

Wouldn't it be great if every time Christian people got together the house would 'Shake, Rattle, and Roll' and stir up people's souls for Jesus? The book of Acts contains stories about such gatherings. The most striking example comes from the fourth chapter where we find Peter proclaiming the resurrection of Jesus with such passion and enthusiasm, the house rocked. They had been arrested, jailed, and warned against continuing this ministry. Upon their release, they decide to cope with all their trouble by holding a prayer meeting. Verses 29-30 tell us they gathered, did a little singing and they prayed. Luke writes, *"When they prayed the place where they gathered shook!"* They were filled with the Holy Spirit and spoke God's Word with confidence. The place rocked.

The question we must ask is, 'How often does our response to God's presence cause the building to shake?' Don't be afraid to open your heart to God and allow him to touch you and cause you to get so excited that you will 'Shake Rattle and Roll'! We as Christians should be turning others on to the awesome power of God that can give them a new life and a new hope. That is our calling. Is that our witness?

God of all Boldness, It's me, Lord, your shy and reticent child! Oh, Father, so many times I long to be free of the constraints that the world places on me: 'What would people think!?' 'What would people say?!' rings in my ears each time I seek to step out in boldness. Yet it is your opinion that matters most, your affirming 'yes' I want to hear. Stretch out your hand, Lord and bring alive the 'wonders' you are in me. Give me the voice and heart of faith. In the name of Jesus I pray. Amen.

Joy made Complete   *August 20*   *John 17:12?*

"While I was with them, I protected them …. I guarded them. But now, I am coming to you, and I speak these things in the world so that they may have my joy made complete in them. I have given them your Holy word to make this true."

Yesterday, we talked about the release of the power of God in the faithful. The disciples felt it in such a way that they rocked the house where they were praying. Our calling is to turn other people on to this awesome power of God. Are we doing that or have we become complacent? Do we accept His gifts and keep them for ourselves, even the Good News? It is too precious, too wonderful. We must share it. Where would we be today if not for the dedication of those first Christians who rocked houses and turned the world upside down? Where would we be if they had refused to stand up for the faith, giving their life for their belief? God's Word is a living Word that can touch and heal.

Sometimes, we his followers can become lifeless. Sometimes we just go through the motions as if it means little or nothing to us. I had a professor once who, when asked by a student how he could make God's Word seem joyful and exciting to those he taught, responded, "You don't expect the Word to be exciting every time you read and study it do you?" The student said, "No." The professor responded, "Well, that is your problem. You should!" We all should. For God's Word is transforming – it is alive! Those early Christians received the 'Good News' from Jesus and it became a powerful presence in their lives. They were filled with joy and their joy was contagious. They could not hold it in.

It is a great joy to experience the presence of Christ in your life. To do so, we have to let go of much of this world, which keeps our heart divided and our joy unrealized. We must bring passion and enthusiasm into our worship of God. We need to make His house shake! You cannot experience God in that way if you hold on to the cares and worries of this world. Let go. Let the power of God be released through you that the joy of Christ may be made complete in you.

Oh Lord, My Savior, I come grounded by doubt and fear, dispassionate about the faith I claim, Your Holy Word just rote memory, not vital, not joyful! Although I claim you Lord and Savior I still trust too much in myself. No wonder I've lost the joy! Forgive me, my Father. Mend my divided heart. I long to soar on wings of a renewed joy! This I pray in the name of Jesus. Amen.

Suffering   *August 21*   *1 Peter 2:21*

"Because Christ also suffered for you, leaving you an example, so that you should follow in His footsteps."

The writer of 1st Peter was dealing with people who were getting knocked down and finding it difficult to get back up. So he advised them to "suffer with patience." He tells them that it is no credit to them to have to suffer when they have done wrong, but if they have done right and suffer for it, "You have God's approval!" Of course, most would rather not suffer at all, but truth is, suffering is a part of 'this life'. The image of the 'life to come' is one of peace and joy and no suffering (Revelation 21:4 "No more pain!") and your 'sorrow will be turned into Joy' (John 16:20).

There are some remarkable people in this world who have endured tremendous suffering and have left lasting examples for us to follow. One such person is a lady I knew while I was a band director in the Boot heel of Missouri. She and her husband were members of the church where I belonged. After going to seminary at Louisville, Kentucky, I spent one summer serving at that same church. By that time her husband had died. They had three sons; one was killed in the Korean War, a second son had been injured in that war and came back home. He suffered years of unremitting pain finally committing suicide. The older son developed cancer and also died. We sat on her back porch and talked about these things. I tried to comfort her but ended up being the one comforted! She talked about the great joy of having all these men in her life and said, "God has been so good to me. He has really blessed my life." I went away feeling truly blessed that day and humbled.

Paul speaks of his 'thorn in the flesh' in the twelfth chapter of Second Corinthians. The Lord tells him, "My grace is sufficient for you." Suffering can be used as a demonstration of God's power and grace. It certainly was in this woman. When we suffer, do we allow God's power to be demonstrated so others can see the power of the Grace of God?

God of the Glad and Suffering Heart, this devotion especially spoke to me today. I realize that like most people I see suffering as something to be avoided. Even inconvenience gives new birth to my whiny complaining self. I am so unlike the example of a suffering Christ. I am overcome with shame and regret. Yet the woman in this story, who had lost all, blessed You, Lord. Not a whine was uttered nor a complaint heard. Only the Spirit of Christ indwelling in a human heart can affect such grace and peace. Lord, please grant an undeserving sinner this great gift. In Jesus' name I pray. Amen.

Listening **August 22** *1 Corinthians 12:4*

"There are a variety of Gifts, but the same Spirit."

A few years ago I attended a seminar on 'Spiritual Gifts'. When I returned I gave the test to all my elders in the church at a winter retreat: the results were eye opening. I began by first asking each person to list what they would consider to be their 'Spiritual Gifts'. Then they all took the test. We graded the test together and many were amazed. They ended up with gifts they never knew, or thought they had! My guess is, that is a reflection of everyone.

Many people have 'Spiritual Gifts' they never considered they had. The problem could be that many look at Paul's list of 'Gifts' in First Corinthians, chapter twelve, to be all in all. This is not intended to be a complete list, there are many gifts not listed there. You may not have received the gift of 'wisdom' or 'healing' or 'speaking in tongues', but some have the gift of 'listening' or just being present with a person who is grieving. There are people who have been through much in life and need someone to just hear them out, to listen.

Many can listen in order to solve. They feel they must tell you what to do in order to solve your problem. Maybe what a person needs is for someone to just 'listen'. Our world has gotten away from listening and into the mode of offering advice and criticism. I cannot turn on T.V. any more to 'hear' the news without analysis and criticism. In such a world, it is comforting to be able to talk to someone who listens, but does not criticize or tell me how to think or feel, someone who hears and is empathetic but does not try to become my savior and solve all my problems. There is but one Savior, the same one who gives us our 'Spiritual Gifts'. Next time someone wants to talk, claim the power of God's Holy Spirit, and then, just listen. See what happens.

God of the Listening Heart, what a blessing you are to your children! In good times and bad, you are there soothing our wounded hearts, giving us the insight of your wisdom, rejoicing with us, for us. Give me, Lord, the special gift of being a good listener. Give me the grace to keep my advice to myself, my opinions silent, and my pride at bay. Remind me, Lord, it's about them not me! Remind me that, actually, it is all about you. In your name, O, Lord. Amen.

Spiritual Waste　　**August 23**　　*I Corinthians 12:18*

"But as it is, God arranged the members in the body, each one of them, as he chose. If all were a single member, where would the body be? As it is, there are many members, yet one body. The eye cannot say to the hand, "I have no need of you," nor again the head to the feet, "I have no need of you."

One of the tragedies of our day is the wasted potential of those who have chosen to escape this world and its problems by artificial means. By that I mean those who have sold themselves to addictive disease. Instead of living reality, they live in another world pumped high by artificial means. This is truly tragic. The life God intended is lost Drugs steal the soul, destroying the person in its grasp.

There is another tragedy even greater than addiction: living in a 'spiritual wasteland'. There are many people who believe in Jesus as the Son of God, as their personal Savior, but who ignore using the 'Spiritual Gifts' God has given. Paul lists some of these gifts in the twelfth chapter of First Corinthians. Paul paints the picture of a physical body that consists of arms and legs, eyes and ears, each one with a singular purpose for it alone. It would be foolish for someone to refuse to use any body part or tell that body part 'I have no use of you'. Only eyes see or ears hear.

The same truth applies to our 'Spiritual Gifts'. God has given them to be used. Each person has been gifted with different gifts. Together, we are like one complete 'body'. Separate, we are like an eye trying to function without a body. It would serve no purpose and be of no help to a body that needs sight in order to see where it is going to offer an ear. Our 'Spiritual Gifts' are given to be used for the glory of God as a revelation of His power. They are given to help others. The first thing we should all do is to pray for God to help us discover our 'gifts' and then ask Him to guide us in their use. Can you imagine what your life might be like or the world we live in different if you did?

Sovereign Lord, Giver of every Good and Perfect Gift, by your great power you have made the unique function of body a marvel of divine creative imagination, each part uniquely designed to serve a necessary function. That alone would deserve our awe, our praise. Yet in your great grace, you have honored human kind with actual gifts of yours: spiritual gifts: wisdom, knowledge, healing, faith and more. Grant me, Oh God, the awareness of my special gift and the courage to use it for the common good. Be near me Lord. I serve only you. In Jesus' name. Amen.

Good Fight of Faith   *August 24*   *1 Timothy 6:11f*

"But as for you, man of God, shun all this; pursue righteousness, godliness, faith, love, endurance, gentleness. Fight the good fight of the faith; take hold of the eternal life, to which you were called ...."

How do we run the race of life? This is a question that many have asked in various ways throughout the ages. We can gain much by paying attention to Paul's words to Timothy. Paul tells Timothy to be thankful, to train others to be thankful *"to offer prayers and supplications, intercessions, and thanksgivings are to be made for all."* (2:1) Paul tells Timothy to be careful of those who try to deceive, those who tell the truth but not the 'whole' truth; those who do not teach the 'sound words of our Lord Jesus Christ'! In verses 3-10 he lists things that can be the result of false teachings, "envy, dissention, slander, base suspicions, and wrangling". These things occur in those who do not have the Truth.

After telling Timothy what to stay away from and to keep his flock from, Paul tells him what to pursue " *righteousness, godliness, faith, love, endurance, gentleness."* The challenge is for them to 'fight the good fight of the faith' to which they have been called and have confessed to do. As disciples' of Christ we are called to a higher order. Many misunderstand that call as a call to not drink or smoke or commit specific sins. I certainly am not saying that we should not set an example to follow, but what Paul emphasizes is this: 'righteousness, godliness, faith, love, endurance, and gentleness.' Paul tells for Timothy to be a good example 'in speech, conduct, love, faith and purity.'

Our call to 'Fight the Good Fight of Faith' goes beyond giving up things; it calls us to 'do something'; love one another; be an example of faith for others to follow. Our faith must be real and must follow us into our everyday life in all that we do. Otherwise, we are but a 'noisy gong or a clanging cymbal' as Paul states in 1 Corinthians thirteen. Fight the good fight of Faith! Reach out in love even when others slander you and speak falsely about you. We answer to a higher calling.

Father God, Author and Sustainer of Life, You are so wonderful to me. I have deserved nothing. Yet you would not allow that to be the last word. You have showered me with blessings too numerous to count. Lord of All, give me the spiritual endurance to honor you in all I think, do, say. Make me righteous. Surely this grateful heart is a beginning. Surely the God-ward gaze of a grateful heart can accomplish much: by faith, in love, with gentleness. This is the prayer of a sinner graced by a merciful, forgiving God. In Jesus' name. Amen.

Keep the Commandment August 25 1 Timothy 6:13f

"In the presence of God, who gives life to all things, and of Christ Jesus, who in his testimony before Pontius Pilate made the good confession, I charge you to keep the commandment without spot or blame until the manifestation of our Lord Jesus Christ, which he will bring about at the right time – he who is the blessed and only Sovereign, the King of kings and Lord of lords.... to him be honor and eternal dominion. Amen."

Yesterday we talked of 'fighting the fight for the good faith' for the sake of being a good example and witness for others. Today's scripture tells us to do so for the sake of Jesus. We are charged to keep the 'commandment' without spot or blame until Jesus comes again. It is one thing to say, "Try and be a good example for others to follow." It is quite another to say, "Be a good example for the sake of our Lord, Jesus." That is an awesome responsibility. Many people try to be good witnesses for the sake of themselves. They want others to think well of them or to think they are 'worthy' Christians. Some will even do good deeds for others. They will try and be a good example for their spouse or children or for family to follow. Few really look at 'keeping the commandment', as Paul says, for the sake of Jesus, to bring glory and honor to His name. That is the true reason we should be examples. Does it impress you when you see an athlete score a touchdown or make a basket and pound their chest and point to themselves? Not me! It always impresses me when a running back scores a touchdown and when asked about their game says, "I cannot take credit. The team deserves credit and God deserves the glory for He gave me this talent."

What really impresses me is when someone tries by the grace of God to live a Christ-like life for the sake of bringing glory to Jesus. They keep no glory for themselves for they know that everything they have and are is because of God "who gives life to all things." When I see someone like that I know that Christ dwells within. So let us fight the fight for the good faith and give glory and honor to our Lord, Jesus.

Almighty God, once more your Holy Word challenges me to step out in faith to reach beyond my grasp and dare to be great for your sake. Lord, who gives life to all things, give renewed life to my flagging confidence, my fearful heart. Compel me by the Holy Spirit to trust that what I commit to do in prayer and act, you yourself, Lord, will accomplish by your power alone. To God be the glory for the things He has done. Forever and ever until He comes again. Amen.

The Lord arise upon you   *August 26*   *Isaiah 60: 1f*

"Arise, shine; for your light has come, and the glory of the LORD has risen upon you. For darkness shall cover the earth, and thick darkness the peoples; but the LORD will arise upon you, and his glory will appear over you."

Today, I encourage you to think victoriously! There are plenty of things going on in your life now to cause you to despair. If you are like most of us, you have been through your share of disappointments and heartaches. You may have lost someone dear to you, or possibly you are in that process now. You may just be recovering from grief. You may have just lost your job or were laid off due to company down-sizing. Your husband or wife   may have just walked out on the marriage.

I could name many possibilities of disappointment and heartache of great darkness, thick darkness, so who can be encouraged? Let me give you the best answer I know. *"Great darkness may be over the earth and thick darkness over us, God's people; but the Lord will arise upon you, and His glory will appear over you!"* Is there a better reason than that to be encouraged about what tomorrow may bring?

I am not saying that sorrow is finished with you, just that you can live victoriously. If the grief or heartache you are experiencing and will experience brings you closer to God; if it helps you value more highly the things of life that truly matter; if it causes you to stop depending on superficial things for security and throws you upon the 'grace of God', then you will have much to be thankful for and to look forward to. The Lord's light will surely have shined on you in your deep darkness. For we will know to whom we belong; we will grow spiritually because of that knowledge. We will understand that 'bad things happen' to all people. It is just a part of this human life we live. Our strength will come, not because we are untested, but because 'the Lord has risen upon us '. Through God in Christ, we will not only survive the day but, because of Him, we will prevail. We too will arise and shine.

Lord God, Light of this Darkened World, be my savior in the dark times. Dark times have a way of trapping me in despair and hopelessness, seeking explanations for faith. Confusion and evil reign there, but not you, Jesus, not you. Help me, Lord God, to seek your face, to trust that your light overcomes all darkness, that your glory indeed illuminates my life and me. Shine into my darkness and give light to my life. I pray in Jesus' name – illumine me. Make me to be light too. Amen.

"For since, in the wisdom of God, the world did not know God through wisdom, God decided, through the foolishness of our proclamation, to save those who believe. For Jews demand signs and Greeks desire wisdom, but we proclaim Christ crucified, a stumbling block to Jews and foolishness to Gentiles, but to those who are the called, both Jews and Greeks, Christ the power of God and the wisdom of God. For God's foolishness is wiser than human wisdom, and God's weakness is stronger than human strength."

Allow me to ask you this one question: What is it that thrills you? Some possibilities: seeing your spouse overjoyed as they open a special gift, seeing the joy on your children's faces, seeing a newborn baby smile for the first time, being successful in your career and making that big sale which will give you the bonus you were hoping for, or cuddling up on the couch in front of the fireplace with the one that you love?

What is it, do you think, that thrills God? How about: when we get it, when we finally realize that reason and wisdom do not proclaim God, that 'God's foolishness is wiser than all human wisdom and God's weakness is stronger than all human strength'. The Jews did not get it! The Jews could not accept that the 'Son of God' could possibly be placed on a cross between two criminals and die a shameful death! This divine contradiction became a stumbling block for those Jews who refused to believe. The Greeks did not get it! They sought 'wisdom' and wisdom would tell them that if God could strike down all the evil going on down here on earth, He would! That is not how God chose to operate.

He chose to reveal Himself not through 'wisdom' or 'power', rather through His own flesh and blood sent to die intentionally on a cross in order to bring us grace – free grace. That is His foolishness: the sacrifice of the very best for the potential to save the very worst if they choose to believe, having given them free will. In His apparent weakness God conquered evil and death through Jesus' death on the cross and resurrection to life. It makes no sense to the wise, especially if they rely on human wisdom but to the Christian who is 'called', Christ is the "power of God and the wisdom of God."

God of Paradox, God of Grace, Oh, that I could grasp the mind of God and comprehend His purposes, but you, Lord, are too great for me! I stand in awe of your 'weak' strength, your 'foolish' wisdom! Mostly, I stand in awe of your immense and forgiving love, your transforming grace. Allow me to be foolish and weak for you, Lord. Let me fly Lord, by remaining grounded – in faith, in trust, in love. In Jesus' name. Amen.

Foolishness of God August 28 1 Corinthians 1:26f

"Consider your call: not many of you were wise by human standards, not many were powerful, not many of noble birth. But God chose what is foolish in the world to shame the wise; God chose what is weak to shame the strong; so that no one might boast. God is the source of your life in Christ Jesus, who became for us wisdom and righteousness and sanctification and redemption, "Let the one who boasts, boast in the Lord."

"Not many of us are wise by human standards." Yet God chose what is weak (us) to shame the wise! Paul is telling the church in Corinth that they were not much to begin with but God turned them into something amazing! He does the same with us. We might not have been 'much' to begin with but now we are! Those who thought they were 'much' aren't! You have to look at character with the eyes of God.

I have known a few folks in my lifetime who were really smart, clever, powerful. Yet, as providence would ordain it, I sat next to some of them as they were leaving this world with the hope to reach the next on their minds and the desire to be in the same place as Jesus on their hearts. They did not think themselves smart, clever, or powerful. They were afraid, hoping God would somehow forgive their foolishness and accept them. They confessed that they had not done enough to help others and wished they had. They confessed that they had spent more time trying to gain the world than God. They thought they had the answer and could accomplish whatever they needed on their own.

That was then and this is now. Now they are in fear! Now they are praying for forgiveness! Now they are hoping against hope to be forgiven and saved and rewarded with heaven. I was there to tell them we all make mistakes, we all sin, we are all weak but Jesus became the low and despised in order to present us to God as righteous. All you have to do is accept Him, accept Jesus. *"Let the one who boasts, boast in the Lord."* He is our 'righteousness and sanctification and redemption.' We may be weak, but God has made us strong and wise in Jesus.

Almighty God, I am moved by this passage to consider the choices of my life. I have chosen your way, a few times I have, but I have chosen my way more times than I can recall, forgive me. Only the desire to claim salvation now not at the end of my life gives me the strength to pursue this confession. Oh, Lord, I am low and despised in this world, a 'thing that is not'. But you, Lord, by your grace can make me a thing that is – one 'who boasts in the Lord'. Will you do it now, Lord? I've wasted so much life already. In Jesus' name. Amen.

It Was for Love   **August 29**   *Philippians 3:12*

"I press on to make it my goal because Jesus Christ has made me His Goal.... I press on toward the goal for the prize of the heavenly call of God in Christ Jesus.15 Let those of us then who are mature be of the same mind; and if you think differently about anything, this too God will reveal to you."

Jesus died on the cross, rose from the dead, sits on the right hand of God the Father, and now intercedes for us. Have you ever wondered why? Just take a look at yourself in the mirror. Why would God send his only Son to die for you? Why for me?

In the sixteenth century a group of 600 ministers and elders got together and wrote the "Westminster Confession of Faith". In that document it states, "We are totally depraved, sinful to the core!" Why would God send His only Son to die for anyone who is sinful to the core? I can give you only one answer. Love. God did it for Love. One of the most quoted verses in the Bible, John 3:16 puts it like this, *"God so loved the world that He gave His only begotten son so that everyone who believes in him might not perish, but have everlasting life."* He did it for Love.

In our verses today, Paul says *"I press on to make it my goal (to become like Christ in His death) because Christ has made me His Goal."* Our salvation was a gift of Love from God. There is no other way to say it! There is no other reason that God would send His only Son to die, except He loved us and wanted to bring us salvation and there was no other way to make us righteous, able to stand in the sight of a Beloved yet Holy God. No greater love is there than for one to give their life for another. When we look at the cross, those are the words we hear. The cross bought us our salvation. Jesus gave his life for us. Paul says, because of that, I wish to 'live my life by giving my life to Jesus'. It is a thought worth thinking.

God of Grace, Lord of Love, by the power of God, I believe! I believe the Gospel. I believe in Jesus! I believe in the efficacy of his death as a ransom for my sinful soul. I believe that unlike other creatures, man was made for eternity! I was made to be one now and for all time with you, O God, in Christ Jesus. As astounding as that seems and is, I believe that without me there would be a minus in the great heart of God. Believing this I would do anything to respond in faith and love to the One who loves me so. May the grace of God and the mercy of God be forever praised. In Jesus' precious name. A men.

Intellectual vs. Transformational August 30 John 5:24

I have met many people who say they believe in God but what they mean is that they are committed to an idea of God which exists in their mind. Some confuse God with morality. Most people get upset over the lack of morality in people around them, for example those in 'political' office. The thought is, politicians are 'our' representatives and we want them to 'represent' what we believe! Since God is the 'Ultimate' moralist, there is the connection. Please don't misunderstand me, while being a moral person is good, it is beside the point when it comes to believing in God. If that is all there is to God, the Israelites already had in place a religion built on a relationship with God based on morality. If that is all there is to it, why would Jesus have come to show us something different?

The goal of the Christian life is 'transformation': a change in heart (attitude) that translates itself into a change in behavior (actions). Unlike morality, transformation results from a relationship with God through Jesus. Transformation allows our heart to 'belong' to Jesus, allows Jesus control of our thoughts and our will. Saying intellectually that you believe God exists, does not say you will allow Him to have your will or to control you. Your heart 'must' belong to Jesus. Such submission occurs only through transformation. There is a world of difference in saying 'I believe that you exist' and saying 'We are the dearest of friends and I trust you with my life'. An idea can be powerful but it does not have transformational power, the power to change your very nature, the condition of your heart and mind.

Only Jesus can transform our hearts to see the true immortality of our self-serving deeds. Only Jesus can transform our hearts to love the unlovable; forgive the unforgivable; pray for our enemy. Christian faith is less about knowing Jesus, as about trusting and believing and claiming Jesus with all your heart.

All Knowing, All Seeing God, to you alone I owe all of my devotion, all of my praise, for the companionship you have made possible in Christ Jesus. How can I ever thank you for the power that is mine to claim through the atonement of Christ, my Savior! By the grace of God, neither my sinful nature nor my willful heart direct my life.. These are wonders too great for me to comprehend but not too great to claim. Hold fast to me, Jesus, dearest lover of my soul. Only you will do. In Jesus' name. Amen.

Do you Love Me?   *August 31*   *John 21:17f*

"For a third time Jesus asked Simon Peter, "Simon son of John, do you love me?" Peter was hurt that Jesus had asked him a third time and he replied, "Lord, you know everything; you know that I love you!" Jesus said to him, "Feed my sheep – follow me."

"Do you love me?" Jesus asks. If your answer is 'yes', how do you show that love? Perhaps, a better question would be 'how would Jesus like for me to show that love'? At the end of the Gospel of John is a wonderful story of Jesus appearing to his disciples. He is standing on the shore. They are fishing. They do not recognize him at first, but when He tells them to cast their nets on the other side of the boat and their haul was more than they could handle, it became apparent! This was Jesus.

Jesus then asked Simon Peter three times if he loved him. After Peter answered 'yes' each time, Jesus tells him how he can show that love. "Feed my sheep". Take care of those who belong to me and 'follow me'. Follow Jesus by doing what He was doing. Continue His ministry to the poor and needy. Spread the 'Good News' that Jesus is the Son of God and has come to die for our sins: has come to bring salvation. Christ was trying to get the disciples to focus on the real mission to the world.

The disciples were easily led astray. They argued to be designated as His number one friend at the same time that Jesus was trying to get them to 'love one another', at the same time that He was saying 'the last shall be first and the first shall be last' (Matthew 20:16). They were selfish, self-centered, often not getting the point Jesus was trying to teach them. That is 'good news' to us, isn't it? For we are the same and do the same!

Jesus is calling us to love him by following in His footsteps, doing what He would be doing if He were here. When things are not going as we think they should, then 'cast the net on the other side of the boat'.

God of All Grace, Sovereign Lord, it is so good to give you thanks and praise, so good to see your power acting to fill the empty nets of my life, so good to be grateful .But gratitude alone does not complete the cycle you have set in motion. There is more. Give me the grace to act on the love I feel for you. Give me the courage to trust you fully. We could be quite a team if only I would be willing to grasp your out stretched hand! I pray this in Jesus' name. Amen.

"By faith Abel offered to God a more acceptable sacrifice than Cain's. By faith Enoch was taken so that he did not experience death; By faith Noah, warned by God about events as yet unseen, built an ark. By faith Abraham, when put to the test, offered up Isaac. By faith Isaac invoked blessings for the future on Jacob and Esau. By faith Jacob, when dying, blessed each of the sons of Joseph. By faith Joseph, at the end of his life, made mention of the exodus of the Israelites and gave instructions about his burial."

We have a tendency to look for heroes to follow, be it sports, music, or whomever. Do we know what it takes to make great heroes? Greatness has a price. Heroes don't just happen by chance. Hebrews is chocked full of heroes! The list starts here with Abel and goes on for some forty verses; some are simply called 'saints' and not mentioned by name. These heroes were created because of their faith in God.

God is still in the business of creating and revealing heroes. It is by faith that they set out on the course God had chosen for them without succumbing to the ways of this world. Those who do not walk by faith may not understand. God's calling requires that we step out on a limb and allow His grace to be sufficient for us. One who walks by faith understands that God created this world and us and everything around us. Our faith is not based on what takes place, be it what we want or not. Our faith is not based on how much money we have or how many blessings we have received. One who walks by faith bases that faith on God alone!

We are weak individuals who are made strong by trusting and believing in a risen Savior. Our courage and character come from the relationship we have with Christ. 'Heroes' acknowledge their weaknesses and lift them up to Jesus. If you choose to become a 'hero' yourself, that is where you must start. Then maintain a healthy prayer life that keeps you humble and connected to the source of our strength, Jesus. Call upon Jesus who can supply and strengthen you in your walk of faith. And if you dare to wish to be a 'hero', remember that He is our courage.

Almighty God, Sovereign Lord, As I read the list of heroes in Hebrews I am both awed and humbled by their demonstration of faith and the courage it took to act on that faith. Lord, I am also inspired. I wonder 'does a hero lie sleeping in my soul'? Could I be as one of these in the circumstances and choices of my life? Oh Father, nothing is impossible with you! I want to be an everyday hero for Jesus, grant me this extraordinary wish. In Jesus. Amen

Hope for a Dark World   September 2   John 1:1

"Darkness has become light." "In Him was life; and the life was the light for all people."

Everyone needs hope although some people live more in despair than others. Don't you just love trying something new? I say that realizing that we also love routines. There are some things which take dynamite to change, but who doesn't love trying out a new suit or a new dress? Who does not love driving a new car or a new riding lawn mower? What hunter doesn't love going to the duck blind with a new Browning 12-gage automatic? What computer whiz doesn't love exploring the Internet?

My wife and I moved to Humboldt, Tennessee in the early 1990's. The closest large town is Jackson, only a few miles away. When we first arrived there were very few major restaurants in Jackson, but soon after that the town exploded along with new restaurants. In a matter of a few years twelve major restaurants were built and twice that many fast food chains. And guess what? They were all filled to the brim! You would have to wait 30 minutes to an hour for a seat at the evening meal. People love new things!

With Christ's coming into this world things changed. The old became new - "*Darkness became light,*" John said. Despair became hope - the condemned (us) now have grace. We now have hope for a new start because the light of Christ brings the hope of light to our dark lives. He brings a hope built on more than a positive attitude or an expanding economy. It is a hope built upon a Christ who cares about us. Christ came, light entered our dark lives, and hope replaced despair. Like the flowers of spring that lift their faces to the sun and bring us beautiful color after a season of cold, gloomy, rainy weather filled with the absence of color, we have fresh hope and renewed faith; we can conquer despair because we were given that power when we became His.

Lord, just like the gloomy winter weather, life can be gloomy. I can be disappointed by my job, by friends or family. Joy is replaced with despair. Hope fades. Open my heart to the truth of your Son Jesus. Focus my thoughts on the light that He brought into this world, light that darkness cannot overpower. Remind me to claim that Power He gave, power to become your child, special because I am yours, loved for eternity. How can despair exist in the presence of such a God? In the name of Jesus I pray. Amen.

"Do not work for food that perishes, but for food that endures for eternal life, which the son of man will give you. For it is on Him that God the Father has set his seal. And then the people asked, "What must we do to perform the works of God?"

What is the first question you ask someone when meeting them for the first time? "What do you do?" Meaning what Labor pays your bills? Is that the case with you? Sometimes my kidding nature comes out and I say something like, "Oh, I'm a movie star. Haven't you seen me on the big screen?" Then of course I confess that I am a minister. I think the reason people ask is because that question breaks the 'ice' and will lead into a good conversation. Most people like to talk about their work, right?

Sometimes yes, sometimes no! Some are very unhappy with their job and may express that. Possibly they have just lost their job and talking about it helps. If you talk with a person long enough the questions may get really important. Jesus tells his listeners that they must not *"work for food that perishes, but for food that endures for eternal life!"* Most miss the point! They first work for that which will buy them what they want and for that which will put food on the table and a roof over their heads. Don't you find that to be true in your own life?

But somewhere along the way we meet the Master face to face, either in church or through a crisis in our life, and we realize there is more to life than work. At least we hope there is more. And we want to please God and so we ask, *"What must we do to perform the works of God?"* We ask because we have sought security in our labor and have not found it. The more money we make the more we feel we must have in order to survive and maintain our lifestyle! It is a trap that imprisons us. We also sought recognition through accomplishments only to realize recognition answered our need for the moment and then is gone. So what MUST we do and for whom are we working? The work we are to do is to believe and trust in Jesus. He will do the rest. We cannot serve two masters.

God of Grace, as I consider my life I realize I have focused my efforts and talents on perishable rewards not eternal ones. Will you forgive me? With pride I can relate all my accomplishments. I can talk a blue streak if asked about work. But if asked about you, Lord, what can I say? Something I've read; something someone else has experienced? To do your works, Lord, I must know you, trust and rely upon you. Be my work, my life, my story. In Jesus' name, I pray. Amen.

"The hand of the LORD came upon me, and he brought me out by the spirit of the LORD and set me down in the middle of a valley; it was full of bones. He led me all around them; there were very many lying in the valley, and they were very dry. He said to me, "Mortal, can these bones live?" I answered, "O Lord GOD, you know.""

"The toe bone connected to the foot bone, the foot bone connected to the ankle bone, the ankle bone connected to the shin bone - now hear the word of the Lord." That is a delightful little spiritual and it brings to mind the image of the valley of the dry bones, which we find in the thirty-seventh chapter of Ezekiel. Ezekiel tells us that the Lord picked him up, carried him to the valley of dry bones, and then set him down. Then the Lord asked him, *"Mortal, can these bones live?"* Ezekiel answered, *"O Lord, you know."*

This is a question we ask all the time. We look in the mirror and see the face of one who has been through much: endured disappointment, heartache, had and lost hope on more that one occasion. And so we look in the mirror and ask, "Lord, can I live again? Can I have hope for the future? Can these tired weary bones be brought back to life?" We want to know because we just can't take it anymore – people letting us down, the disappointments, people misunderstanding our thoughts and motives.

It's not that we are ready to join the Lord in heaven, we want as much time here as possible, but we want to come home, we want to feel the presence of the Lord, for we know that when we do, these 'dry bones' will be rejuvenated and brought back to life. When Ezekiel is asked by the Lord about these 'dry bones' living again he responds, "Lord, you know." Only the Lord knows and only the Lord can bring us back to life when we are spiritually dead. We find new life in God's living Word, Jesus. Our hope, our grace, our very being exists in Him alone. So if you have any thought about your 'dry bones' coming back to life and giving you hope and joy in your tomorrow, you know where to turn.

God of All Hope, You know how often we wonder 'can these dry bones live?' What we are really asking is 'can what has lost vitality find it again?' 'Can what has been lost to me in death be alive to me once more?' Lord, only you know! God of second chances, make true in my life that which is within your will to accomplish. Give me the grace to hold on and the grace to let go. May your perfect will be done. In Jesus' name. Amen.

"So I prophesied as He commanded me, and the breath came into them (the dry bones) and they lived and stood on their feet."

My grandmother on my mother's side was quite a Bible scholar. She grew up in the church and read her Bible every day. I can remember her saying many times how the Bible had given her great comfort and strength. She had crippling arthritis for the last 20 years of her life and could hardly get around. That did not extinguish the fire of the faith she had inside. She faced every hardship with great strength and courage. Her hope did not reside in herself, but in the living Word of God, Jesus.

Our hope is in the living Word of God. Holy Scripture is like the air we breathe. It brings us the necessary things to keep us alive spiritually as air sustains our physical being. God's Holy and Living Word opens our hearts to God's Son Jesus, to the Holy Spirit and to Truth. Worship nurtures that Truth and brings us closer to the One who created us and sustains us. All of this is vital to keep us out of the 'valley of the dry bones'. Worship gives us the opportunity to leave this world behind even if only for a moment; it helps clear our mind and our heart of the poison this world pumps into our being, it gives us the strength to live as God calls us to live.

Prayer is also a vital link to restoring our relationship to God and awakening our 'dry bones' from the dark valley. In our darkness we reach out in prayer and we feel and experience the presence of one who can breathe new life into us. In verse ten, Ezekiel says, "So I prophesied as the Lord commanded me, and breath came into those 'dry bones' and they lived." There is revitalizing hope for us all. We can find it in God's living Word, in worship together, and through prayer to the One who can breathe life into our spiritually dead faith and make it live again.

Almighty God, Giver of Life, Bless the Lord, O my soul. What a sight that must have been! All those dry bones joining together to reform living bodies. What a revelation of your power and your grace. Is there a revitalizing hope in the spiritually dead parts of my life and the lives of those I love who know you not? Is this the message? Forgive me, Father, for not claiming the hope you give in Christ Jesus. Incline my heart to rely on prayer and scripture to revitalize my weary heart. It's not too late, Lord. Breathe new life in my dry old bones of faith and I too will live; I too will stand! In Jesus' name. Amen.

The Lord Build the House September 6 Psalm 127:1

"Unless the Lord builds the house, those who build labor in vain."

When you accept Christ as Lord and Savior and join the church that is not the end, but the beginning of your spiritual walk. Suppose you accept Christ, but then never come to church again, never give any kind of commitment to God's church, never give a pledge of money to His Kingdom, never give God another serious thought. What kind of commitment would that be? Truth is it would be no commitment at all.

The same is true in other relationships, especially marriage. We must make a commitment and constantly work on our relationships; they don't just happen. If your house gets a leak in the roof, you had better repair it soon or the damage will continue to grow. It is the same in relationships; you must see them as a discipleship. Relationships are a two way street. You cannot have a relationship in one direction or it will be only with yourself. Paul says in Ephesians 5, *"The two shall become one."* To have any genuine relationship, there must be conversation, sharing, communication, dialogue. That is true in any kind of relationship; Husband and wife; parent and child, among siblings, between friends, or with God.

If you love someone, you have concern for their Spiritual health. You wish to build them up not tear them down. In the 4th chapter of Ephesians Paul says for us to not let evil talk come out of our mouths and to speak words that "give grace" and build up. It is easy to pick out the faults of others; heaven knows we all have plenty! We are all sinners. But we, as Christians, are called to build each other up. Often, we fail to thank the very one who helps to hold our life together and give us meaning. We also fail to nurture those who nurture us and who need our nurture. Be grace to one another but especially to your spouse, your children, your parents, and your close friends. Just remember Psalm 127:1 *"Unless the Lord builds the house, those who build labor in vain."*

God of all Grace, give me a servant's heart that seeks your guidance in every decision I face, every commitment I make, every relationship I cherish. Build the house that is my life, Lord, sturdy, stable, based on mutual love and forgiveness. Make me to be grace to all I encounter along the path you set for me. I would be more like Jesus this day and every day. Only you, Father, can make true my heartfelt prayer. In His name. Amen.

God So Loved   September 7   John 3:16

"For God so loved the world that He gave His only son, that everyone who believes in Him may not perish but may have eternal life."

Our Scripture today is one of the better-known verses of scripture, John 3:16. This verse sums up the reason Jesus came into the world. So that "we", those who believe in Him, *"May have eternal life."* Our salvation comes through Jesus Christ. God sent His Son into the world so that *"All who believe in Him"* would be given the chance to live forever in the after-life with Him. Now God did not have to do that!

I guess the question we should all ask is, "Do we deserve it?" And the answer is, "No!" We all fall short; we are all sinners. You know that if you are honest with yourself. Yet, God gave His only Son anyway. As this verse says, *"Because he loved the world so much – because he loves us so much."* Now you see? It is not because we are perfect or deserving, but because God loves us. That alone should make us feel very special. God loves us and is with us each moment of our lives. Jesus came proclaiming the good news that "we are loved by a gracious God who wants us to have eternal life."

This is more than a concept! This is more than an idea! God loves us and wants us to accept Him through His Son Jesus. God loves us and wants to save us from all our bad habits, from worry and insecurity. God wants to deliver us from the bondage of all those things, which keep us from becoming all that He created us to be, yet, being saved means more than "getting to go to heaven". It means being liberated from a life of anxiety; it means being liberated from the sorrow over the death of someone we dearly love. God in Christ has come to deliver us from our spiritual and emotional fatigue, to heal broken relationships, to help us win our freedom from bad habits, to make us loving witnesses for Jesus, the one God sent into this world because He loves us so.

Merciful and Loving God, Oh how wonderful you are! There are no words to fully express my adoration, my praise and my indebtedness to you. Forever I will proclaim the great sacrifice you made for me. Forever I will sing praises to a great and all-knowing God who loved, loves beyond reason, beyond space and time and forever. Reach down to me, Father God. I lift my waiting arms on high. Can you see me? I am loving you My Jesus, in return. Amen.

Not to Condemn but to Love! September 8, John 3:17

"Indeed, God did not send His Son into the world to condemn the world, but in order that the world might be saved through Him."

The scripture today says that God's Son did not come into the world to condemn it, but so that the world might be saved through Him. Once we believe, which is a requirement to be saved, what then? Well, believe it or not God is calling you. He called me into a full time ministry as a pastor. He may not do the same with you, but that does not mean He is not calling you into ministry. We are all ministers of God's Word. God may be calling you to quit fighting Him and to turn your will over to Him; that is harder than it sounds because we all like to control things and especially our own lives! To we will have to trust in Jesus and quit rebelling!

Maybe you trust Jesus and have been a member of His body, the church, for years. You have gone to Bible study and have been learning about Jesus all your life, now God wants you to take the next step and become an Apostle, to move from being a student to a teacher, from being a follower to being a leader. Yes, it is a risky thing to do but worth your effort. In the third chapter of John, the Pharisee Nicodemus, a leader of the Jews, comes to Jesus at night. He did so by night because of the risk of being condemned and ostracized by his fellow Jewish Pharisee's.

At the end of John's Gospel, chapter 19, we see Nicodemus bringing myrrh and aloes and linen cloths to wrap Jesus' crucified body, as was the custom of the Jews. It was a courageous thing to do. The scripture does not tell us, but chances are that decision cost him his standing with the Jews and the Pharisee's. Maybe you cannot be a teacher or a leader, officer of the church, or even sing in the choir, but you can love and pray. There is a great song that states, "What the world needs now is love, sweet love – that's the only thing that there's just too little of." So love! God is calling all of us to "love one another as He has loved us" that was Jesus' last command, so love, love, love, and forgive.

Father God, I thank you for your Holy Word, which continues to witness your great love and its power to transform and to save. You, Father, are so unlike the world and its powerful ones who seek to judge and condemn. You, Most Holy One, have every right to do just that, and yet, you seek instead our salvation. Give me the desire to know you better that, like Nicodemus, I too would be willing to risk all for a relationship with you, Most Gracious Lord, give to me a heart like his and by the Spirit's power, I'll make you proud, Father God, I'll make you smile! In Jesus' name I pray. Amen.

"Those who believe in Him are not condemned; but those who do not believe are condemned already, because they have not believed in the name of the only Son of God."

Are you a member of the "one of these days" club? Some start something and say, "I'll finish that 'one of these days.'" I had a friend who started a project to redo his son's bedroom. At the time his son was a little boy. After he graduated from high school, the room was still unfinished! Now don't get me wrong – I like this guy, we are good friends and he is a great person – just one who could not seem to get a project finished. I am sure you know people like that or maybe you are a member of the "one of these days" club yourself.

We all fit this club in one way or another. We say "one of these days I am going to quit working so hard and take it easy!" Or "one of these days I am going to take up golf or fishing." Or "one of these days I am going quit smoking and take up jogging." But that day never seems to get here. For the most part that is O. K., but not when it has to do with our spiritual life. In our scripture today Jesus tells us that those who believe in Him are not condemned – but those who do not believe are, because *"they have not believed in the name of the only Son of God."* So do you believe? This is not a question for "one of these days" but for now!

What is our purpose? To just satisfying our own wants and desires? Do we truly believe that we are saved by grace through Jesus? If so, do we dedicate our lives to him, our time and talents and money or do we say "one of these days I will do that?" The problem is "one of these days" might be too late! There are many stories in the scripture concerning this choice: the rich young man in Matthew 19, who comes to Jesus asking what he must do to inherit eternal life. Jesus tells him to sell everything and follow Him. The young man walks away for he is very wealthy. This is something too important for us to leave to "one of these days"! It is not wise to wait for we never know what tomorrow will bring and we will have missed the beauty of living a rich life now with our Lord.

Sovereign Lord, Father God, I am such a procrastinator. I always seem to delay or put off decisions until the very last moment available so afraid am I of making a mistake, of failing myself and others. This flaw in my character has cost me in my work, in my family life, but most of all it has affected me spiritually. Forgive me for my failure to trust in your promises and to act. Give me the courage and the faith to claim my inheritance in Christ. Let me not be condemned by my own procrastination or my failure to trust, to love. In Jesus' name in pray. Amen.

One in Christ   September 10   Hebrews 1: 1f

"Long ago God spoke to our ancestors in many and various ways by the prophets, but in these last days he has spoken to us by a Son, whom he appointed heir of all things, through whom he also created the worlds. He is the reflection of God's glory and the exact imprint of God's very being, and he sustains all things by his powerful word. When he had made purification for sins, he sat down at the right hand of God, having become as much superior to angels as the name he has inherited is more excellent than theirs."

We are one in Christ. We may have grown up in different areas of the world; we may have all had different earthly parents; some of us are men – some women; some young – some old; but we are all one in Christ. Our unity is unbroken. The writer of Hebrews says Jesus is the reflection of God. Now that was a far cry from how things were before that time. God had spoken to the faithful through the prophets. Now God has chosen to send His son Jesus to show people who he is.

The testimony of those who knew Jesus best was that He looked like God. When Jesus wept we saw the tears of God. When Jesus held little children in His arms, we saw the tenderness of God. When Jesus forgave the woman who was about to be stoned by the Pharisees – we saw the heart of God. The writer of Hebrews says, "Jesus is the 'reflection of God's glory and the exact imprint of God's being'".

His ministry was one of love and forgiveness and grace; his message so powerful that people followed him all over the countryside. His resurrection transformed lives and created disciples who were willing to give their life that his ministry might be carried on. We are now a part of that ministry. Through his death and resurrection he purified our sins and made a place for us along side of him with God in heaven. Our unity is unbroken. When we carry on His work His being is reflected in us and people see God's glory and image. What more can one ask for? This is the answer to everyone's dreams!

Oh God, Creator and Sustainer of All Life, can it be that you too want to be fully known? Is it possible that in all created things you reveal a piece of yourself until at last in Christ we see you face to face? Even the barrier of my great sin is removed by Jesus' sacrifice so that now I too can stand revealed cloaked in a righteousness not my own. All one with God. Glory be to God – want a moment! Want a gift! I see you Lord! Can you see me too? In Jesus' most excellent name. Amen.

Forgiving the Enemy September 11 Luke 23:33f

"They led Jesus to the place called 'The Skull' and there they hung him on a cross to die. He said on behalf of his accusers, "Father forgive them for they know not what they are doing."

On September 11, 2001 planes were used as missiles and brought down the Twin Towers in New York City. My first response on that day was much like everyone else: anger, rage, and a desire to go to war and find those responsible and do to them what they did to us. For not only did these terrorists attack our Twin Towers and Pentagon, they attacked our way of living; they attacked Christianity itself.

After I calmed down, God touched my heart and I realized that when He said, *"Forgive their debts", "Forgive one another as you have been freely forgiven", "Love your enemies"* - He *really* meant it. After all, He did forgive those who placed Him on the Cross saying, *"Father, forgive them for they know not what they do."* (Luke 23:34) Of course, forgiveness is not so bad when a person has simply hurt your feelings; it is another thing when they have caused great harm to our people, our country and our way of life. But forgiveness is not an option for a Christian; it is a requirement. Now it is impossible for me to forgive those terrorists but if I call upon Jesus, some day, somehow He may change my heart and make that possible. I also know that He has said, "Vengeance is Mine!"

The point is we must forgive others and the power to do so does not reside in us, but in Christ. If you have hurt another, or they have hurt you, at work, at home, at church, at play, be it a co-worker, a friend, a spouse or a child. Call upon the power available to you through our Lord, Jesus Christ, and then and only then can you forgive them. This event, which happened to our nation, may give us a glimpse of what those early Christians went through, being thrown into arenas and killed for their faith. And yet God gave them the strength and courage to forgive their enemy.

Sovereign Lord, Gracious God, our times, our lives are in your hands. This is a great and sustaining truth. Life-shattering events challenge our faith, our hope, and our confidence that you are indeed there and in control. Lord, I cannot unsee what I have seen; those towers will fall forever in my memory. May these sights call me to pray for those who died and for the seed of forgiveness that so needs to grow in my heart. In Jesus' name I pray. Amen.

The need of Forgiveness   September 12   Isaiah 12:2

"Surely God will save me; I will trust and not be afraid, for the Lord is my strength and my might; he has become my salvation."

September 11, 2001 was a horrible event in history. A time when the evil of mankind showed its ugly head - when devious, monstrous beings claiming to be religious and God-fearing brought down the Twin Towers and crashed into the Pentagon. It was also a day the American spirit reared its head with one plane being retaken by a group of courageous heroes who, after realizing what was going on, spoiled the hijackers' plan to crash into a probable target of the White House, Instead they crashed into a field in Pennsylvania. It was a day the worst in human nature came out and a day the very best in human nature came out.

All we can say for those who lost their lives is, "There but for the grace of God go I." Did they deserve that fate? Absolutely not! We are all imperfect, sinners; even worse when we give in to our selfishness and greed; our desires to control. We are who we are because God made us and we are who we are because of choices we allow ourselves to make. Events like 9/11 can rob us of our joy. The stock market crashes and we say, "Our security is gone." Well, only if we placed our trust in it rather than in God to begin with.

Look at it like this. Relationships do not come easily whether in a marriage or a family or just being good friends. When our relationships are going well, life is great, everything looks fine, we are joyful. Then comes the stuff of relationships; like learning how to get along with different views and being on opposite sides of politics. Dealing with conflicts and who is to do what, when. If we do not learn to handle all of this, we will stoop to fighting and name-calling. We forget that as Christians we are called to respond to one another "in love." Love is not just a feeling. It is being willing to give up things for the person you love. We do this, not because we are great people but because we have given our heart to our Lord, Jesus. We love one another because of Christ. He is our strength, he is our forgiveness, he is our salvation.

Father God, Sovereign Lord, times are sometimes such that all I can do is say 'surely God will save me' – from my circumstances, from my painted in the corner moments, from my self. God, increase my trust, my love is already great. Calm my fear; be my strength and my might. For the world is heavy on my back, my grip is slipping. Help me, Jesus, you are all I have, all I need. Amen.

Have you found Freedom?　September 13　John 8:31f

"If you continue in my Word, you are truly my disciples, and you will know the truth and the truth will make you free."

In 1996 my wife and I purchased a small cabin at Pickwick Lake located right at the Tennessee / Mississippi / Alabama state line. It quickly became a very special place for us, not just because it gave us freedom away from the telephone or freedom to get away for a day but because of the solitude and the closeness that we felt with God. The truth is we have never taken a day off there from God. He won't let us. We went at times to just rest. We walked in the woods or would get on the lake; there, God reminded us of His grace and freedom; of the wonder of His creation.

Away from the busyness of life and from the sound of television and radio and from the constant ring of the telephone, one can hear the 'still small voice of God'. That is where one finds truth; that is where one can find true freedom. Hearing God's voice does not always come easily. Just like playing the piano, it takes practice and patience. You will never be great on the piano or any instrument until you decide to spend countless hours practicing. You want to grow spiritually? You will have to spend time with God, studying, listening to God's Word, in worship, praying, being open to hear His voice.

God accepts us, as we are sinners through and through. From the mouth of Jesus himself, *"I came not to call the righteous, but sinners."* (Matthew 9:13) So if you want to hear Him you must 'continue in His Word' and confess your sins. It has been said that confession is good for the soul; it is. Confess everything for there is nothing hidden from God's watchful eyes; nothing escapes His omnipotent presence. So confess everything, God will forgive and then let the Truth set you free. Let Jesus be your Lord as well as your Savior. Turn all of your cares and worries over to Him and receive the freedom that comes through His grace.

God of All Freedom and All Grace, only when in scripture I read of who you have been to other sinners, do I dare raise my voice to a whisper of confession. Only then to I dare ask for your mercy, your forgiveness. Even in conceiving the written Word you knew, Lord, I would find through the Holy Spirit the courage to trust you there. You knew that un-forgiven sinners are never free. And we were meant to be free. To be free! Thanks be to God for this glorious truth. In Jesus' name. Amen.

Receiving More   *September 14   Luke 17:19*

"Get up and go on your way; your faith has made you well."

This scripture from Luke is about giving thanks to God. The story Jesus tells is about ten lepers who called out for Jesus to have mercy on them. My guess is that they had heard from someone that Jesus would be going that way and so they gathered to beg him for mercy and healing. According to Jewish law they should not have been there in the first place; ritually unclean people were not allowed to approach "clean" people. There was no cure for this disease and no one wanted lepers around for fear of catching that dreaded disease and ending up isolated just like they were. Yet here they are, crying out in hopes that maybe Jesus would reach out and heal them.

He told them to *"Go show yourself to the priest."* That was not unreasonable for in order to rejoin society they had to show the priest they were "clean". They did so and were healed but as the story goes, only one returned to Jesus to give thanks. This person happened to be a Samaritan; a group despised by the Jews. To him Jesus said, *"Get up and go on your way; your faith has made you well."* These lepers received much more than healing. They had been separated from loved ones and friends since coming down with this disease. Now they can go home, rejoin their families, visit again with their neighbors and friends.

So why did only one return and give thanks? Maybe the question we need to ask is: "Would we return and give thanks?" How often has God touched our life and blessed us beyond what we deserve? Did we say, "Thank you Lord?" Did we worship him and praise His name as He wishes for us to do? With most it is not a question of what God has done; it is a question of "What have you done for me lately!" Take a moment and write down all the blessings in your life. If you are honest with yourself the list will be long. Now think about all the things you have done wrong. Do you really deserve God's blessings? None of us do, but God gives them anyway because He cares about us. Now go and be thankful, realizing that you have received more than you deserve, you have haven't you?

O Lord God, Gracious Father, Loving Savior, this devotion convicts me of my ingratitude both truthfully and completely. I am not the one who came back. I am not the one. Thank you for calling me to a higher vision of living, of being, in Christ Jesus. Let me never fail to see and to respond as one who would have nothing, be nothing without you. Increase my sense of gratitude. Give me a heart like yours. Heal my selfish soul for I do love you, Lord. I love you back. Always and forever. Let me never fail you. In Jesus' name I pray. Amen.

"Today salvation has come to this house."

This is the story of a wealthy man, Zacchaeus, who worked for the hated Roman occupiers to collect taxes from his own people, the Jews. He made deals with the enemy for money. For that, he was well paid but he was also despised and isolated from his own people. But once Zacchaeus came face to face with Jesus, his whole life changed and he offered to give half of all he had to the poor and needy. Jesus confirmed the tremendous significance of what had taken place with Zacchaeus by saying, *"Today salvation has come to this house."*

We now remember the name of Zacchaeus not as a great sinner, but one whose life was completely transformed by the power of God in Jesus Christ. Unlike the rich young ruler who had been righteous and upstanding all of his life, but could not take the step to let go of his wealth, Zacchaeus will be remembered. We know his name. The rich young ruler's name is never mentioned (Luke 18). What's the point of mentioning someone who was confronted by Jesus Himself and was so self-centered he turned Him down.

Let's compare this story to ours. Like Zacchaeus we're all sinners. Maybe a few of us have even been sinners in the extreme, dramatic fashion of Zacchaeus. And few of us may have lived isolated lives like his. But the real similarity, I believe, lies at this point: our isolation from our true self and God. Like Zacchaeus, we are inclined to look for meaning in life where it's not to be found: in external things and busy activities: in important positions and wealth. Like Zacchaeus, we need to come to the point in our life where we realize that something important is missing. We need to take that decisive step to seek God, to receive Him gladly, to welcome Him into our hearts. We need to let God truly take care of us and feed our souls: submit to Him and let Him run our affairs. We need to find a way for Jesus to say, "Salvation has come into this house today!"

Lord, I am Zacchaeus; I have distanced myself from you through the things I have placed as important in life. These choices were decisions I myself made. There is no one else to blame, would that I could, forgive me. I have looked to money and work and family to bring meaning to my life. Help me, like Zacchaeus, to realize that without you, something very important and essential is missing in my life which can be found only as I come to you and give you my all. Make reconciliation with my Heavenly Father worth any humiliation such self-examination will require. In the name of your Son, Jesus, I pray. Amen.

"The Passover of the Jews was near and Jesus went up to Jerusalem. In the temple, He found people selling cattle, sheep and doves and the moneychangers seated at their tables. He drove all of them out of the temple and said, " Stop making my father's house a marketplace!"

Early in my ministry I served a church in Kentucky in a nice little town nestled in the hills of eastern Kentucky filled with some of the friendliest people you will ever meet. It is the heart of coal country. L & N Railroad has a coal-shipping yard there. If you go into the mountain areas you will find some different kinds of preaching than in the towns; one that caught my attention was the "snake handlers". They believed that if you were a true believer you could handle rattlesnakes and would not be bitten, or if bitten you would not die. One service made the newspaper because the preacher threw two rattlesnakes into the congregation. Now if he was trying to get their attention I am sure he succeeded! However there might be a better way to do so you see, two people died because of this stunt and one was the preacher!

There is no question there are times in our lives when we need someone to get our attention. I'm just not sure that's the best way to do it. Often our religious practice gets stuck in a rut and we need something to shake us up a bit. Maybe we are not growing spiritually and we look everywhere to find "the way". Jesus addressed this in our scripture today. He went into the temple and chased out those who were making God's House a marketplace. He got their attention by making whips out of cords and using it to drive out the animals, the cattle, sheep and doves; he turned over the tables used by the moneychangers. Our body is the temple of God's Holy Spirit. What does it take for God to get our attention and jolt us into reality? Spiritual growth takes place when we spend time with God. Don't wait for God to throw a couple of rattlesnakes your way, begin now spending valuable time with our Creator and Lord.

Most Holy Lord, Creator of all I behold, Merciful and Loving Savior, create again in me the desire to know you well, serve you joyously, and love you with devotion. Sometimes I just go through the motions. Present before you in body but not in soul. "Quiet time with Jesus"-check. How did I lose that spark? How did my religion once so precious, so vital, become a sleep walk? I'm in a valley of deep darkness and I cannot find my way home. Dear Jesus, I need so desperately a wake up call. You know how to reach me for your eyes have never left me. And you've always had my number! Beloved Lord, forgive and come. In Jesus' name. Amen.

"After Jesus was raised from the dead, His disciples remembered that He had said this; and they believed the scripture and the word that Jesus had spoken."

Once Jesus had driven the sellers and moneychangers out of the Temple, the Jewish leaders were not happy and asked Him to give a sign for what he had done. Jesus said, *"Destroy this Temple and in three days I will raise it up."* They misunderstood - thought he was speaking of the physical Temple, Jesus was referring to his body, the temple of God's spirit. The scripture today is very revealing and points out something we see throughout the Gospels. The disciples were also always missing the point! Verse 22 tells us that after Jesus was raised, the disciples finally got it!

But let's not be too hard on them! For although they always seemed to have trouble getting the point, Jesus never gave up on them and they finally did get the point! Now I for one like this outcome because it helps when I don't get it: I can rest assured that Jesus will not give up on me either! It is so easy for us to fill our time with busy-ness and things which satisfy us for the moment but are not lasting or even just choose religion over Jesus. You know what I mean, you go to church every time the doors are open but it doesn't seem to change the way you treat others or do much to get rid of your need to be critical and judgmental.

It is only as we give our heart and will to Jesus that he can change us. The way to spiritual growth is to admit that we are as great a sinner as anyone we might choose to criticize or judge, open our eyes to our rebellion against God (to let God fully have us), realize that they ways of the world don't work and that we must let go of our need to control. Then spend time with Jesus to build a personal relationship with Him and follow wherever He leads. If we do that, Jesus will not need to use drastic measures as he did so long ago in Jerusalem.

Gracious God, Loving Father, Merciful Lord, I know you were moved by outrage when you turned over those tables at your father's house; that you reacted to the money changers greed which sought to use church ritual shamelessly for their own financial gain, even at the expense of others. I know that you are the same yesterday, today, tomorrow. I know too that I shamelessly peddle my self-righteousness for the gain it affords me. I use your Word to bolster arguments I cannot truthfully win. I barter faith in exchange for money and worldly security. I deserve to be put out on my ear. And yet, I know your heart as you know mine. Father God, your grace is sufficient for all my needs; forgive me; restore me; come near, O Lord, I implore you in Jesus. Amen.

"Just as He chose us in Christ."

Paul begins in the first chapter of Ephesians telling us that God has "blessed us in Christ with every spiritual blessing in the heavenly places." That alone should make one feel grateful, but the blessings don't end there. He goes on to say, "Just as God chose us in Christ before the foundation of the world." Now if you don't feel special after hearing those words I am afraid there is no way to make you feel special! God has chosen us! You think about that! I am not saying that we deserve it, for the truth is, we don't! But that did not stop God from choosing us.

Now to be chosen also means "for a purpose". Paul states that purpose is to be "Holy and blameless before Him in love." Unfortunately we don't always act that way, do we? Too often we act as if we do not belong to God at all. We do just the opposite of what he wants. We treat others as if we are better than they; we are judgmental of them; we are critical of them and gossip about them behind their backs. Now does that sound like we are "Holy and blameless before God in love?" Not even close! God has made us a special people we are to do as He calls us to do, not as we want. We should be about the business of letting other people know how special they are to God.

Our challenge should be to show others the love and grace of God, given to us through His Son Jesus. Instead we end up living a life of fear and worry, not because we have to but because we have refused to give up what we desire and allow God to run our lives. To live in His love would change everything. To realize that God has chosen us and that we are special to Him should make our lives filled with joy! If that were so, others would see the Holiness of God shining through. If we don't act like God's special, chosen people, we do harm to the name of Jesus. So let us live in a way that will be "Holy and blameless before God in love!"

God of all Grace, Sovereign Holy Lord, I stand in awe of your great love for me, your child in Christ Jesus. To be chosen is the sweetest word in all of life. The world operates so differently surrounded by merit and deserving. You chose out of your own goodness, Father, and in spite of my failures. Such truth is too great for me to comprehend. Give me the grace to respond all my days and in every opportunity as your child, unbelievably blessed, chosen and irrevocably special to God in Christ Jesus. In His Name. Amen.

"I was once alive apart from the law, but when the commandment came, sin revived."

I grew up in a different denomination than the one I served as a minister for over 30 years. Let me give you one reason I changed. As a teenager, my church told me that all those attending other churches would not go to heaven, only us. Now I knew my best friends pretty well and saw myself just as sinful as they, in some cases worse! So how could I be saved and they not? Years later, I discovered my answer. I attended a different church. I remember the preacher saying "we are all sinners" and we will always be "sinners". He was preaching on a text from Romans, the seventh chapter where Paul talks about his conflict with the law and sin.

In those verses Paul states, "I do not understand myself, for I do not do what I want but I do the very thing I say I will not do." I remember this well because it changed my life! I opened my Bible and read over and over the seventh chapter of Romans. I had read and studied it before in my old church, but because it had taught that once we belong to Christ we don't sin, I guess it never struck home. The preacher , whose name I don't remember, opened up this verse for me and the truth of it changed me. It helped me to trust what I really knew from the beginning, I am myself just as sinful as everyone else.

Paul opens his inner feelings to us in these verses and tells us not to abandon the Law but to see it for what it is: a tool to let us know we are sinful. Perfection is not attainable in this life and if you think it is you will be driven mad trying! We are sinners; imperfect beings; we do not measure up; if we did, why would Christ have died for our sake? Paul concludes this inner conflict by stating that he is hopelessly trapped in sin. He asks the question, "Who will rescue me?" His answer is one that will free us forever, "Christ". Jesus is the one who takes us from the grips of sin and sets us free! We will always sin but we are free from that sin, not so we can go sin more, but so we can go live in Christ and live in joy and hope and grace.

Father God, Sovereign Lord, It takes a lot of grace to admit I am a sinner in need of your forgiveness, that I am lost without your guidance and your love, and yet here I am admitting that without you I am nothing, no one. You created me for so much more. Claim once more your wayward child; infuse in my soul the truth that you love me in spite of my faults and my complaints; that in your hands I can be all you dreamed I'd be before the world was born. In the shelter of your wings I can fly! Take my hand, Jesus, together we can do marvelous things this day. In His Name. Amen.

"In Christ Jesus, you who once were far-off have been brought near by the blood of Christ. For he is our peace - in his flesh, we have been made both groups into one and has broken down the dividing walls, that is, the hostility between us."

A few years ago I was watching a movie, a comedy-mystery, about someone trying to sabotage the Miss America contest. When they ask the contestants what they wanted, each one replied, "I wish for World Peace." It struck me because people are always connecting Peace with wishing. Paul lets us know that Jesus is our Peace. In Ephesians Paul states, *"Christ is our peace – in him, we have been brought together and the dividing walls, the hostility between us, has been broken down."* We live in a hostile, violent, divided world, don't we? Consider Iraq, Afghanistan, Northern Ireland, the Gaza Strip, the Middle East, and the former Soviet Union, even here in America.

Our nation is divided by "political party" lines, by heritage, and by of the color of our skin. Being torn by strife within is not something new. It is as old as humanity itself. Nations have been crossing one another's borders and attacking one another since the beginning of civilization. People fear different cultures and religions; some extremists want to eradicate them from the face of this earth. We may say that we want peace, but do we really? Is Peace even possible in this hostile world? Can we get beyond these barriers and truly become one people?

I don't think it is humanly possible. However, I do believe that all things are possible for God in Christ. This is the point Paul was making. He realized that he had been hostile toward this new brand of religion even to the point of stoning to death some of its leaders. Now he realized that Christ is our Peace. It is in Him that dividing walls are torn down and we are brought together. Will this ever happen in our lifetime? I don't know. I only know that we can start one person at a time; begin with ourselves!

Almighty God, Sovereign Lord, I kneel before you today pleading in earnest for your perfect will to be made real in my life. Lord, I feel so far off. Bring me near; bring me ever near. Far off I can do and be the way you never wanted, never intended: heartless, cruel, unforgiving, without remorse, always right. But near, Father, in your embrace I can only radiate the love and forgiveness I experience in you. I'd like to teach the world about living in peace but first I must learn and remember. This is my prayer in the perfect name of Jesus whom I adore. Amen.

Forgiven Little, Love Little   September 21   Luke 7:41f

"A certain creditor had two debtors - one owed 500 denarii and the other 50. He canceled them both. Now - which will love him more?" Simon, the Pharisee, said "I suppose it would be the one who had the greatest debt." Jesus said, "You have answered rightly."

Forgiveness is something most people devalue in importance in life. All you have to do is have your child make some big mistake and then see the pain and remorse in their eyes before you forgive them and then experience the relief you see once they hear the words, "I forgive you." We all carry around excess baggage in the form of mistakes made and opportunities lost. Forgiveness from another lessens our load.

Now, if that is the case with us as humans, how much more is this true in our relationship with God? To realize that we commit numerous sins of omission and commission every day and that each sin separates us even more from God makes us realize the depth of our problem. Forgiveness is the solution. God offers his forgiveness in the form of grace through His Son, Jesus. There is no way we can possibly repay God for what he has done for us. Jesus expressed this truth in a parable in Luke where he said, "A creditor had two debtors one owed 500 denarii and the other 50. He canceled them both. Which will love him more?" The obvious answer of course is the one who had the greatest debt! If you were forgiven a great debt by a creditor wouldn't you feel grateful?

I guess the question we should ask ourselves is this, "Do I feel that I owe God a great debt or a small debt?" I have found that many so-called Christians believe that they are "good", if not to the standard of Christ, certainly much better than those they see not going to church! Therefore, they feel they have little for which to be forgiven. Therein lies the problem. In response to the parable Jesus says, "The one who is forgiven little, loves little." Until we realize the depth of our sins we can never realize the depth of our forgiveness from God! The Bible tells us we are sinners –the apostle Paul called himself a "wretched sinner". Truth is we are no better than other sinners. The only difference might be that we recognize our sinfulness and fall on our knees and beg God's forgiveness!

Father God, Giver of every Good and Perfect Gift, I stand in awe of your mercy and your grace; you have been better to me than I deserve. In Christ Jesus, you have saved me from condemnation, saved me from myself. Grant me this one prayer. May I never grow cold in my love and gratitude for your mercy, in my recollection of your goodness and grace. May I love others as fully and as earnestly as you have loved me. May I in this way honor you all the days of my life. In Jesus' name. Amen.

Forgiving Others   *September 22*   *Luke 7:47*

"Therefore I tell you, her sins, which are many, are forgiven; hence she has shown great love."

Once we know and feel that our sins are forgiven by God, then and only then can we begin to forgive others. In response to Jesus' allowing this woman to touch him, the Pharisee said, *"If this man were a prophet, he would have known what sort of woman this is touching Him - she is a sinner."* I guess the obvious conclusion we can draw from this statement is that the Pharisee saw this woman as a great sinner in need of repentance but not himself. Therefore, he could only be critical and judgmental of her and of Jesus' failure to see and condemn her, as a true prophet surely would have.

These flawed insights are a clue for us to look for in trying to examine our own life. Are we forgiving and understanding of others who sin and fall short or are we critical and judgmental? Unless we wish to be mistaken as a Pharisee it might be best for us to refrain from judging. After all, what gives us the right to judge others in the first place? Unless we walk in another's shoes how can we say we would respond differently?

The real point here is centered on forgiveness. Jesus says that this woman in the story shows great love because she is forgiven and that one who is forgiven much will love much. So do we feel forgiven? Once we see the depth of our sins and the depth of forgiveness from God, then not only will we be grateful to God, we will also be more loving and forgiving of others. Let me put it like this. If you find it hard or impossible to forgive another person who has harmed you, it is because you have not realized the depth of your own sins and the depth of your own forgiveness from God. If that be the case then you are walking in the shoes of the Pharisee, Simon, not the shoes of the woman who was forgiven.

Almighty God, Father of All Creation and of me, I know I need a reality check in my busy life and scripture provides that opportunity for me. Who am I most like in this story in my interactions with others? Do I, like the Pharisee, see situations as events to test your wisdom, your godliness? If I catch you judging wrongly, as the Pharisee surmised, is my critical nature vindicated? If my God is vengeful, condemning, then my vengeful, condemning self is merely a reflection. But if my God is merciful, compassionate, loving to the most unworthy, so must I be. Don't let me fail to see you, Jesus, as the Pharisee did. Open my eyes to truth, to forgiveness, to gratitude. In Jesus' name. Amen.

Accepting God's Forgiveness   September 23 Luke 7:47f

"Therefore I tell you, her sins, which were many, have been forgiven; for she has shown great love. But the one to whom little is forgiven, loves little." Then He said to her, "Your sins are forgiven."

Today lets try to realize that the love God has for us should allow us to accept the forgiveness He gives, make sense? Jesus says that the sins of this woman were great and were forgiven because she has shown great love! But the one who is forgiven little, loves little. Have you ever wondered why some people are so loving and forgiving and others are slow to forgive and seem a little cold?

Well, let's consider this situation from another perspective. Suppose you hurt your back and you are in great pain, how would people see you act or react? Chances are your temper would be short; you would be so concerned about yourself that you could not think about those around you. I suspect your preoccupation with yourself would preclude you from being very giving or forgiving. If you have not accepted God's forgiveness, if you do not feel you deserve His forgiveness, then chances are you are still in such pain inside that you cannot show God's love no matter how hard you might try. Most likely you will show the pain that is in you until you somehow get rid of it.

How do we do that? By realizing the depth of God's love and forgiveness and accepting these acts of grace as the wonderful gifts they are. You see the one who feels loved and forgiven can reach out in love and forgiveness to others. The key is to realize that God truly loves us. He did sent His Son to die in our place! To sacrifice His life for ours! Once you realize a love that great and accept it, all your internal hurt and pain disappear to be replaced by God's love and grace. At the end of this story of the woman who kissed and anointed Jesus' feet with oil, Jesus says, "Woman, your sins are forgiven." What a blessing to have your sins forgiven; it can be a transforming experience! As it was meant to be.

Father God, Lord of my Life, Savior and Friend, I am so drawn to this picture of who you are I can barely see my own place in this story. I know that my roles in life change as my eyes are opened to the truth about myself and you. I am both the sinful woman and the hardhearted Pharisee. I have yet to become like you, Jesus, who loves fully and forgives fully. Am I the barrier to that occurring in my life? Give me a heart for you, Father God, and I can be all you imagined when first you called my name! Forgiven to be Forgiving! In your grace I stand. In Jesus' name. Amen.

"And God blessed them, and God said, 'Be fruitful and multiply and fill the earth and subdue it - and have dominion over all these things that I have just created.' "

It always amazes me the phrases some people come up with to identify who they are. News anchors have been doing it for years; "And that's the way it is." Remember who said that? Or how about, "And now for the rest of the story – good day." Or "Come on – make my day." My father- in- law had several and I used them all at his funeral. Just as you were about to leave his house he would say, "You don't have to leave do you? Thank goodness!" And "You can't say it hasn't been charming!" And truth is you couldn't because being around that old Hump Pilot from WWII was always charming!

I guess what I like about these phrases is that it tells something about the person. It identifies them. We all like to be recognized because that somehow lets us know we are special. In the first chapter of Genesis God blessed his newly created beings and tells them to, "*Be fruitful and multiply and fill the earth and subdue it - and have dominion over all these things that I have just created.*" The verse just before tells us that we were created in God's image.

Now what could be more special than that? The Bible tells us we are special and loved by the One who created us. God created the universe, billions of Galaxies, but only we are created "in his image!" Too often we grow up not feeling special and that is too bad, for God is the one who created us and God is the one who blessed us and God is the one who made us especially in his image. Human beings can be cruel. Even our parents can make us feel small and insignificant. The world hammers at us until we begin to believe it and all of a sudden we feel alone in this vast universe. When you feel that way, just turn to Genesis and read again the creation story. How can anyone not feel special after reading that God created us, made us in his image, and blessed us? We are special and loved by a gracious God. Let that form your identity.

Almighty God, Creator of All Things, Too often I accept as truth the world's assessment of my value. Forgive me. I am so much more than that. This I know. Help me to live as someone for whom the world and all of it's remarkable splendor was made. Give me the wisdom to see all things as precious in your sight, as worth my time, as worth my energy. Guide my steps. Make true my path. In Jesus' name. Amen.

"Woman, great is your faith. Let it be done for you as you wish."

Matthew tells us that a Canaanite woman comes crying to Jesus, actually shouting, *"Have mercy on me, Lord, son of David; my daughter is tormented by a demon."* Jesus has had quite a lot of successful experience dealing with demons. But, wait, Matthew tells us that Jesus doesn't even answer the woman. Here's a woman in great distress and Jesus just keeps walking, totally out of character. His whole life was directed at reaching out and helping others. So what's going on here?

Jesus tells the woman that he is called only *"to the lost sheep of Israel."* That seems clear? I could give you lots of reasoning as to why Jesus responded to this woman as he did, but none would be sufficient. Truth is I don't know and no one else does either. All we can do is guess. It could be just as he said. Or it could be that he is putting this woman to a test to reveal her faith or to see how his disciples would react. If it was for the latter, they failed once again! If it was for the woman, she passed with flying colors! Even after telling her she was not of the "right" religion, the woman persisted, "Lord, help me!"

Jesus responds with something which today would be headline news, *"It is not fair to take children's food and throw it to the dogs."* Let's just tell it like we see it. Jesus is calling the Canaanites "dogs". Her response is priceless, *"Even dogs eat the crumbs that fall from their Master's table."* This answer was evidently what Jesus was looking for and he responds, *"Woman, great is your faith. Let it be done for you as you wish."* Her daughter was healed instantly. If Jesus was testing her faith, it proved to be stronger than most he encountered. She refused to give up because she trusted that Jesus was the one who could do the impossible, who could bring her daughter back. She also trusted in a compassionate God who cared for all his own, even non-Jews. That is a great example! When the events of this life, good and bad, try to point us in another direction, we should keep our eyes focused on Jesus. He is the one who can answer our needs – no other.

God of all Grace, I too like the Canaanite woman come with nothing to offer accept the truth of my great need and you as my only hope. Oh Lord, grant me the depth of faith in your utter goodness and mercy that will move me to trust that "Even the undeserving, such as I, remain in the mind and heart of a loving God who wills my ultimate good." Let me be a witness to your truth in all I do and say. Focus the eyes of my heart on you and no other on this day and on all the days of my life. In the name of Jesus I pray. Amen.

"We walk by faith, not by sight - or feelings."

Trust. Too often we base trust on having things turn out the way we think they should, not on whether or not the other person has the best wishes of all concerned in mind. If one will trust in us only when we can prove that we deserve their trust, that person cannot be called a friend. Friends trust when there is no reason to trust. The same is true with God. Often things happen which seem to prove God does not exist or if he does, he is not paying attention to us. If I trust in God, no matter what happens to the contrary, I still believe in Him. I still belong to Him.

One can walk the path of suspicion or the path of trust, but not both. Trust is not something earned. It is our gift to God and to one another. The Christian walk is a walk of faith, not a walk of feelings. The Apostle Paul says in 2nd Corinthians that we are to walk by faith, not sight – or feelings. Being converted to Christianity means being converted from something - from a "creature of flesh" as the Apostle Paul called it, following the way of the world - to a creature of the Spirit, following the Spirit. Now that means we *"Put on Christ."*

Now don't misunderstand, this is not one of the things we must do if we are a Christian; this is Christianity. *"Put on Christ"*. Follow Him in Faith. Trust in Him. Without trust, faith is just an illusion. Any relationship we have requires a certain amount of trust. I trust my wife enough that she can go somewhere alone without suspicion. I trust my friends that they have my best interests at heart even if they are correcting me in a constructive way. If I don't trust them, I may interpret their constructive criticism as criticism designed to harm me. There is nothing someone can do to earn my trust if I chose to not to offer it. Before trust takes place in the heart, we must have an understanding of God and operate out of faith, not out of our feelings. People who don't operate out of faith are always suspicious of another's motives, even God's.

God of all Faithfulness, this reading truly hit me where I live. My feelings can and do at times run my life and color my faith. It is hard to admit, Lord. It is harder still to stop, but you know this truth already. In Christ Jesus, you lived as one of us, tempted in every way, as we are tempted, even this one, and yet did not sin. Will you help me, Jesus, to have the kind of faith you have? This world can be so cruel and I can be so easily misled. Lord I trust in you. In Jesus' name I pray. Amen.

"Do not be ashamed, then, of the testimony about our Lord or of me his prisoner, but join with me in suffering for the gospel, relying on the power of God."

Most would rather skip passages such as this. What good are they anyway? Calling for us to "join in suffering"? We had rather just consider ourselves as unworthy of suffering. Truth is, most like to see themselves as good, kind, and decent human beings. Not to say that we aren't, but if we are, why are we? The Bible tells us that we are totally depraved. It says that no one is good but God. No one. So let's not kid ourselves, without the love and grace of Jesus, we are bad to the bone.

In Paul's first letter to the Corinthians he describes the process of transformation like this. Our old body must die and a new body must be raised. The old body is built of flesh and bone but the new body will be spiritual, immortal, and imperishable. Now who would not want that "new body"? Who would want to consider themselves as good, kind and decent all on their own and bypass becoming a child of God, taking on this new body? You want the truth? All of us from time to time. You see it has to do with our old nature wanting to take credit. We want to somehow feel that we are who we are because we made ourselves. We are self-made successes. We worked hard and deserve it.

Now in order to believe that we would also have to believe that if we are good enough God will accept us as righteous. But the Bible is clear on this subject, we cannot be "good enough". In Matthew 5:20, Jesus states that if we depend on our good works, we will have to be better than the best who ever lived. Later in the nineteenth chapter Jesus says, *"It would be easier for a camel to go through the eye of a needle than for a rich man (devout person) to enter the kingdom."* When asked by the disciples then who can enter? He replied, *"With mortals it is impossible – but with God all things are possible."* So the choice is yours. Follow your own way, the way of the flesh (world) or join Paul in *"suffering for the gospel"*. It is that simple and that complex.

Father of all Righteousness, I come before your throne this day humbled by the picture of myself this scripture has revealed to me. I am the person who claims to be a Christian living under the grace of God and yet wanting credit for my "goodness" and the acts of mercy I do, wanting to be admired for the very acts you yourself are doing in me and through me that I, in my sin, lay claim to. Forgive me and grant me a fresh embrace of your wisdom and grace. Without you I am nothing. Oh, my Jesus, how true this is. I pray to you. Amen.

Justified by Faith   **September 28**   *Galatians 2:16*

"yet we know that a person is justified not by the works of the law but through faith in Jesus Christ. And we have come to believe in Christ Jesus, so that we might be justified by faith in Christ, and not by doing the works of the law, because no one will be justified by the works of the law."

We as Christians are Justified by Faith. How do I know? I take the word of Saint Paul who has written about one third of the New Testament. Also I trust Paul; he had been a Pharisee and tried to live the law perfectly; he realized that was impossible. As Paul said, "The law only showed me how sinful I was." After his encounter with Christ on the road to Damascus, (Acts 9) Paul realized that he could only be brought into right relation with God by faith in Jesus. In our scripture today from Galatians Paul says that, *"One is justified not by works of the law but through faith in Jesus Christ."*

Do you believe that? Do you believe that your own good works will not make you acceptable before God? That is a trap we all fall into. In the 20th chapter of Matthew the mother of two disciples, the sons of Zebedee, James and John, asked Jesus for a favor. She wanted her sons to be declared the greatest disciples! She wanted Jesus to allow them to sit by his side, "one on his left and one on his right in His Kingdom." My guess is that all the disciples had been jostling to be Jesus' most exalted friend. Can you blame them? They had given up everything to follow. They should have some recognition or reward for their hard work, right?

Isn't that what we want? We give of our time to God's church, His Kingdom: attend every Sunday, lead Bible Studies, sing in the choir, serve on committees, do the church books; so shouldn't we have some recognition or reward? Shouldn't we be guaranteed justification for all that hard work? Jesus let the disciples know that "if you want to be great – you must be willing to be a servant all your life." If we depend on our good words, it will be our voice we truly follow; forging our own way. But if we depend on grace, then we are justified by the righteousness of Jesus; we follow and trust his voice. That choice is ours to make.

Almighty God, Sovereign and Holy Lord, by your grace I recognize my own need to justify myself before you. Why is this so important to me? I can only look to pride, which tempts me to compare myself to weaker souls, reveling in my so-called goodness. Is it distrust of your grace? Must I compel you to accept me by good deeds, is that it? Forgive me, Lord. Grant me the gift of a servant's heart and I will, by your grace, live each day as a gift of God content and at peace in my soul and with you. In Jesus' name. Amen.

"A voice from heaven said, "This is my Son, the Beloved with whom I am well pleased."

When we enter a relationship with Christ, we have "New Life" and we become God's "beloved." Although Jesus did not need baptism, no sin to be washed away, no symbol for new life needed, no means to God's grace required, He submitted himself, humbling Himself, and when he did, God said, *"This is my Son – with whom I am well pleased."*

Think about that for a minute. What is our biggest problem in accepting and following Jesus? Most can buy into the theories and principles of the Christian faith. We can agree that we should depend upon Christ; follow the Ten Commandments; that God is our divine ruler; that we should give 10% to the church and attend church regularly. Theory is not the problem. Practice is. Its one thing to say, "We must depend on Jesus". It's quite another to surrender our all to Him and then trust His wisdom and His way. We are forever bargaining back some of what we freely gave away.

The reason for our about-face may lie in our belief that we can take care of ourselves, solve our own problems. We may even think we only need to approach God for the larger, more complex matters. The rest we can handle. That kind of rationale is another way of saying; "I can save myself if I just try hard enough." Many people truly believe that. They say, "I try to do what is right". "I try to live by God's laws." But you see Christianity is not about right and wrong or following laws. It is about following a person - Jesus. When we truly enter that relationship with Him and give to Him out all, God will look down upon us and say, *"This is my beloved and I am well pleased."* Today can be the beginning of a new life for you; even if you have been baptized; even if you've been a member of the church all your life; you can change and pledge to rededicate your life to Christ; you can start right now!

Jesus, I come to you a sinner in need of your grace. I've tried to run my own life; I have failed miserably. Today, this day, I give up this way of life. With your help, I renounce my old ways in which I depend on myself and the material things of life to give me fulfillment. I rededicate my life to you today. Strengthen me. Guide me. Save me. Make me committed to your kingdom - and to you. In Jesus' name. Amen.

"Bless those who persecute you; bless and do not curse them. Rejoice with those who rejoice, weep with those who weep."

I served a church in Humboldt, Tennessee for close to 15 years. It is a lovely town with great people. They have a festival every spring called the "The Strawberry Festival". Thousands come to the parade. Watching that parade for years made me draw this parallel to life. At times I would view the parade from a hillside in the yard of one of our church members. At other times I would watch from the sidewalk level with the street. When you are up high you can get a better perspective – from the sidewalk, you actually become part of the festivities!

Let me put it in another way. We live in a cabin in the woods with a stream running through our property. The cabin is on a hillside so I can sit on the deck and see the woods and view the stream below. I can hear the birds and the trickling of water and all of this is good for the soul. But to truly experience the woods, I have to take a walk. When I go down the hill to the creek the neighbor's dogs always come running wanting to be petted and to go along. Often I can even catch a glimpse of a deer or on a lucky day wild turkey or even be startled by a snake in the grass. It takes energy to get out into the woods and explore. From my deck, I don't sense any of that. I don't really get involved.

Ministry cannot be done if we don't get down into the middle of things. We are the bearers of the Good News of Jesus Christ. We are the people for whom *"the word became flesh."* Viewing from a high spot we can study things and tell others what we saw. You can even become judgmental and criticize the things you see. However, if you get down on ground level, you can become a part of whatever is going on. Both perspectives are needed for us to minister to God's people. To be effective disciples of Jesus, we must study and learn of God's grace and forgiveness but to rejoice with those who rejoice and weep with those who weep, we have to go down to the roadside and mingle. We are the bearers of the Living Word of God to this world and to God's people.

God of all Creation, you reveal yourself in your word and invite me to follow. What an awesome and irresistible thought; that I could indeed be the bearer of your love and grace is almost too good to be true. And yet I believe that I can. With your spirit as my guide, I can rise above my petty selfishness and serve those you've called me to serve. Together, Lord, together. I'm standing on the roadside. I'm mingling with the crowd. Can you see me, Jesus? Amen.

"He entered a certain village, where a woman named Martha welcomed him into her home. She had a sister named Mary, who sat at the Lord's feet and listened to what he was saying. But Martha was distracted by her many tasks, "Lord, do you not care that my sister has left me to do all the work by myself...? ." But the Lord answered her, "Martha, Martha, you are worried and distracted by many things; there is need of only one thing. Mary has chosen the better part, which will not be taken away from her."

Jesus' teachings stress time and again the importance of living spiritually smart. In Matthew 7:24, Jesus compared this type of living to a man building his house on a rock. There he pointed to counting the cost before we begin. In Luke 14:28, "What King would consider waging war against another without first sitting down to consider if he is able to defeat the other," (he counts the cost!). To live spiritually, we must do the same.

In order too do that first we must set our priorities. When I was young, we used to gather for a family get together in the fall and make a stew which we called, "Burgoo." The instructions went something like this: Build a fire, hang a large cauldron over the fire on a tripod, mix in water, vegetables, rabbit and squirrel and let it cook slowly all day. Years later I ran across the recipe in some of my mother's things. There was a note at the bottom of the recipe: "FIRST, catch the rabbit and squirrel." Set your priorities and meet the important ones first!

In the story from Luke 10, Mary sits at the feet of Jesus; her sister Martha does all the cooking in the kitchen. Martha complains, but Jesus teaches her about priorities. Before all else, to live spiritually means to put Jesus first. First and foremost, commit your life to Jesus. Claim Jesus as Savior. Trust Him as Lord. Do you focus on the lesser tasks (like Martha) and ignore your life in Christ? Living spiritually begins with our Lord Jesus Christ. Don't allow other things to distract you. Renew your commitment to Jesus, set priorities, count the cost, and live the life most important to you.

Lord, Please forgive me for I have allowed many things to distract me. Like Martha, I treat you as a guest, not as the only source of the life-words you have come to share, though I am too busy to hear. Like Martha, I too have hurried to offer what you have neither requested nor want. Help me to remember to ask, "Lord, what is it you want of me?" It is in Jesus' name. Amen.

"Come, now - you who say, 'Today or tomorrow we'll go to such and such a town and spend a year there doing business and making some money.' You do not even know what tomorrow will bring."

The fourth chapter of James contains a series of warnings telling us to exercise caution. James speaks of coveting something, and since we cannot have it we engage in conflicts; in trying to be a friend of this world we become an enemy of God. He warns us against judging others and then in verse 13 he warns us against boasting about tomorrow. Is that the how things occur in your life? We just venture into a city and spend time doing business and make money? Truth is most of us easily recognize ourselves in this scripture. We do make long-range plans. We have our 5-year plan, our 10-year plan, and our contingency plan. We are living deluded lives based on control we do not have. Nor are we meant to.

Life is mostly unpredictable. Just when we think that we have it all figured out or under control, the rules change. You put your money in the stock market and all the sudden it crashes and you have nothing, or at least less than you had! Do you think that's why they call such investments "speculation"? All who think they have it all figured out are misleading themselves. Suppose you are driving home this evening, a car in the opposing lane crosses over into your lane. You become another tragic statistic. Life is just unpredictable. No one knows what tomorrow will bring so don't boast about a future you don't know. Put everything into to hands of the one who does know, who will see us through no matter what. God will be with us. The life of Jesus bears witness to that truth. James is telling us to not put our hopes and trust into the things of this world but in the one who can save us from all things and who will be with us in all things – Jesus!

Gracious God, Sovereign Lord, I have been such a fool, haven't I? I have claimed you as Lord of my life but I have not consulted you on the living of it! It's true. I realize that now. Can you ever forgive me? I've caused us both a lot of heartache following my own path; stubbornly clinging to my own carefully orchestrated plans come what may. Have mercy on me, Jesus; have mercy. Let's begin anew; wipe the slate clean. You go first this time and I, by your grace, will silently, gladly follow. Not too fast! This following is a new experience for me. Here I come life! In Jesus' name. Amen.

"Yet, you do not know what tomorrow will bring. What is your life? For you are a mist that appears for a little while and then vanishes."

Yesterday we talked about the uncertainty of life. How we put our trust in ourselves rather than in God. We discussed our desire to be in control, to accomplish the plans we make. When things don't work out the way we thought they would, we are angry and afraid. James tells us that none of us *"know what tomorrow will bring."* He says that, *"we are but a mist that appears for a little while and then vanishes."* Who can argue with that? In the scheme of things we are put on this little planet for about "four score and ten" – more or less. Our time spent here is very short! James is not saying that because we are "but a mist that appears for a little while" that we should not make plans, engage in business, or even expect to make some kind of gain. Just that the uncertainty of life is real and that the future is a mystery and the only one who knows for sure is God. God alone knows what plans he has for us: the purpose for which He created us.

That should make us eager to get to know Him and His will for our lives and to do that will. It also should make us conscious of our dependence upon God. I will admit that when we look at this world that God has created, it would be easy to question some of the things which happen, certainly question why! The real choice is whether we believe that God exists at all and whether we believe He watches over us and whether we believe He cares. James is not questioning that, he is simply telling us that we have very little time here and we should spend it getting to know what God wishes for our lives. His way is the best way!

Holy One, Gracious Savior, It is I, "the mist that appears for a little while and then vanishes". Paradoxically, it is also I, "the one for whom the world was made". I am both these things by your grace and according to my need. When I lose sight of eternity, being caught up in today, will you remind me, Jesus, that I am mist?; that these things of earth are of little consequence in the great grand scheme of things? And when I am crushed beneath the weight of failed plans, and dashed dreams, will you remind me, Lord ,that I was made for eternity; that I was made for you? Amen, Jesus, Amen, Lord.

"You ought to say, 'If the Lord wishes, we will live and do this or that.'"

For the past two days we have been discussing the fourth chapter of James. James calls for us to use faith and wisdom in all decisions of life and to be doers of God's Word, not just hearers only! He says here in verse 15, our obedience to God orders our life; that we should live our life in the knowledge that all of life and the blessings of life are a gift from God; that our future is in His hands and that for us to plan our life and the "business" of life without God's input is not only foolish but also wicked!

When life gets tough, people react differently according to their faith. Some complain, moan and whine; others accept that with God's help they can get through and prevail. Our concept of God, our faith in Him, make a tremendous difference in how we see life. Some see the glass half empty no matter what happens, good or bad. Others see the glass half full even in the toughest of situations.

We should pattern our responses after our Lord, Jesus. Jesus was always praying and asking and seeking divine guidance. In one parable he praised the widow who persisted until she got what she needed from an unjust judge. He was critical of the man who was given a talent and hid it in the ground rather than taking a risk and using his talent for good. James tells us "what good is your faith if you don't use it"? Earlier at the end of chapter two he states that, *"Faith apart from works is dead."* James was concerned that people were misunderstanding faith. Some were saying that if you just believe that is all you have to do. There is no need to change your life or to help those in need, just believe and you will be saved. James was saying the same as Paul that if Jesus is in your heart, your life, your values, your priorities are God's own. Let us vow to seek God's will and let our faith manifest itself in works of His choosing.

Sovereign Lord, I do trust you with my life. Do I trust you with the life you planned for me? There's a difference. Oh, Father, these are only well meaning words if I don't live them out; just deceiving lip service before an omniscient God. Letting go is hard. Am I unwilling to accept that what I want for me isn't what you want for me and that's fine? Help me, Jesus. You know this scary struggle first hand and you were able to prevail. "Father, not my will but Thy will be done,", you said. Make it so for me, Jesus, I pray. Amen.

Battle With The Law   October 5   Mark 2:23f

"One Sabbath he was going through the grain fields; and as they made their way his disciples began to pluck heads of grain. The Pharisees said to him, "Look, why are they doing what is not lawful on the Sabbath?"

The Gospel of Mark tells us that Jesus and his disciples began to pluck heads of grain on the Sabbath when work is forbidden by law. The Pharisees, esteemed religious leaders of the day, saw them and confronted Jesus for an explanation.

The Pharisees had a valid point. The Sabbath day was declared Holy because God rested on the Sabbath from all His creation efforts (Deut. 5:12f). So they ask, "Why do you allow your disciples to break the Sabbath Law?" Jesus and his disciples' actions went against this commandment and had disturbed observers. Jesus then cited the actions of David, Israel's beloved king, saying, *"Have you not read what David did, how when he was hungry went into the house of God and ate of the bread which is not lawful to eat but for the priest?"*

Then Jesus added, *"The Sabbath was made for man not man for the Sabbath."* Jesus is not belittling our need for the Sabbath. He knew that we needed a day of rest and worship. You can't work all the time without getting at least a little rest for your tired and weary bones. The point is the Sabbath was made for us not vice versa. The law was made to help us not to imprison us. Jesus came not to destroy the Law but to help us understand that 'doing that which may look right will not change the heart.' We follow the law because we want to please God, not in order to be accepted by Him. Worship God and take your Sabbath rest.

God of Creation, Giver of the Divine Law, with all my heart I want to please you. Knowing so little and being insecure in what I do know, I sometimes listen to the critical voices of truth-tellers telling their own truth, not yours. Guide me in your way not the way of the world. Help me to commit to a daily diet of reading your Word and seeking your presence. Only then can I be truly faithful, truly your own. In Jesus' name. Amen.

God's plan for his own *October 6* *Ephesians 1:8f*

"With all wisdom and insight, He has made known to us the mystery of His will, according to the good pleasure that He set forth in Christ."

Did you know that God has a plan for your life? Most people either don't believe that statement or they spend their life in search of that truth, never finding it! It should not surprise you that God has a plan for you. Would you begin any type of project without a plan? That would be foolish wouldn't it? I purchased a cabin at about ten years before I retired. One reason I purchased it was because I needed a place for my retirement years. It was in my price range. It was a true "fixer upper" and I like to tinker around with home improvement. This cabin needed a lot of work! Over the past 12 years, we have made many improvements to this little cabin and it is now quite comfortable.

How does this example amplify our scripture for today? First of all, it took a vision for us to see that this cabin could be very special to us. Second, it took planning to make sure that whatever work we did on this cabin would turn out to our liking. We planned for several years before we finally got the design that we liked for our kitchen and then built it; it looks great! Now if we humans go to such trouble for something like a kitchen or a house, don't you think that God would go to great lengths to have a plan for us, his children? In God's plan some things are clear. We are sinners in need of His Grace. God has given us redemption through the blood of His Son Jesus. Those who accept His Son have the forgiveness of their sins and are made His adopted children. All great accomplishments begin with a dream or vision and then require a plan of action. God has given us His plan for our life. Now spend some time with Him to let Him reveal that plan to you.

Father God, Lord and Savior of my life, of me, forgive me when I behave as if I were an orphaned child wandering aimlessly, living a rootless existence, caring only about myself. Such a life is nothing even remotely similar to the dream that was yours, Father, for me. Make real for me your plans. Recreate the person you always envisioned I would be. I'll be cooperative this time. I promise. Fighting against you is so tiring, so human, and so ungrateful. Forgive me in the name of Jesus, my brother, my Lord. Amen.

Sing Us a Song   October 7   Romans 15:4

"For whatever was written in former days was written for our instruction, so that by steadfastness and by the encouragement of the scriptures we might have hope."

When I was in my younger days I had a favorite singer, Billy Joel, and my favorite song of his was "Piano Man". I loved that song so much I sang it in the shower or in the car on the way to work. (I was a teacher). Not until I became a minister did I realize the significance of that song. Listen to the words. You will discover that it is all about ministry. That is what the church should be about. The song is about people going into a bar to find comfort and relief from the struggles of life, and I don't mean in drinking, but in the fellowship of those gathered. There they have made friends with whoever will listen to their dreams. They call on the "piano man" to sing them a song because he makes them feel all right.

That is exactly what the church is called to do: to bring people before God to be confronted by his grace and so find purpose and hope. It is in the stories of scripture that we find the help to form our faith. As we hold fast to our faith though challenged by the circumstances of our lives, we obtain hope for the future. Our future would be bleak and confusing if we listened to and obeyed the urgings of our emotions and our moods. Paul says in 2 Corinthians 5:7, "Live by faith and not by what you see (with your emotions and moods)." Faith is believing in something you cannot see, believing even while your emotions try to prove otherwise. Our past experiences with our Lord form our faith. We should allow that experienced faith to control our feelings, not the other way around. If I believe that God is with me in everything, it changes my outlook even when I am going through the worst of times; it also forms my vision of the future, my hope. So call on the Lord and ask him to "Sing you a Song" – a song that will bring faith and form your vision of the future – a song that will bring hope into your life.

Holy God, Giver and Sustainer of my Faith, I thank you for Scripture. Through it I am blessed and encouraged .How intent is your focus on the ultimate welfare of your people; in scripture is told the fulfilled promise of a hope and a future. These hopes and promises are the birthright of those called and claimed by Christ Jesus, the full revelation of your divine purpose, your divine grace. So sing me a song of hope and let me never stray from the sound of your voice. My Lord and my God. Amen.

Jesus gave us freedom   October 8   Ephesians 2:15f

"He has abolished the law with its commandments and ordinances that he might create in himself one new humanity in place of the two, thus making peace, and might reconcile both groups to God in one body through the cross, thus putting to death that hostility through it. So he came to proclaim peace to you who were far off and peace to those who were near."

Do you want to be free? Belong to Jesus. For as Paul says in Ephesians 2:15 and following, *"Jesus abolished the law and formed a new humanity reconciling all to God in my body through the cross."* Now don't read into this something that is not. Paul does not mean that you no longer have to follow the law and commandments. I believe Paul is trying to help people understand that if they think they can obey the law perfectly, they had better think again! It cannot be done! We are sinners. However, we can turn our hearts over to Jesus and allow him to purify and strengthen us that we will obey the law and commandments.

Remember, Paul was very clear about the law; that we cannot possibly live up to or obey it completely. Jesus said in Matthew 5:17, *"Do not think I have come to abolish the law or the prophets teachings - I have come to fulfill them."* Jesus made it clear that we cannot fallow the Law perfectly. He said, "You have heard it said that you shall not kill, I say that if you have anger in your heart you have already killed." And who can testify that they have never had anger in their hearts? No one. Now if you are still not convinced, let me give you a short test. Look at these few laws and see how you are doing: "Have no other gods before me – you say well I don't! Well how about "you shall not make wrongful use of the name of God?" Or "remember the Sabbath and keep it holy." "Honor your father and mother." Do not murder (or even hate)." "Do not commit adultery (even look at another person with lust)." "Don't covet (ever wanted more than you have?)." Now if you passed this test let me give you some advice. You don't need church or Jesus because you are perfect! If you failed (which every one will) then give it all to Jesus and discover the freedom he will give you from the law and commandments.

God of all Grace, in great love, you made man a little less than the angels, sovereign over all creatures .It went to our collective heads. We have been trying to make it up to you, Father, ever since. Sometimes in my conceit I believe that, all in all, I'm not that hard to love; not such a failure! Then I met Jesus and I see how far I have to go. Father, please stretch your hand down as far as it takes to reach mine and save me once again from myself. Only you can. Only you think I'm worth the trouble. I pray in Jesus' name. Amen,

Lord do you not care?   October 9   Mark 4:38

"The disciples went to the stern of the boat and said, "Teacher, do you not care that we are perishing?"

I have been experiencing life on this planet earth for more than 65 years now. There is one thing I know with certainty. It is that everyone at one time or another will get to the point in life where they can totally identify with the disciples of Jesus in this story from Mark. Jesus had taken a well-deserved rest in the stern of a fishing boat. A storm has arisen and the disciples are frightened, actually terrified. They awaken Jesus saying, "Teacher do you not care that we are perishing?"

There are times in our life when we feel the same. We receive a call in the middle of the night and the voice at the other end of the line says, "Your son has been in an accident." Your first emotion is terror. So you lift up your voice to God and say, "Lord, help me! Do you not care...?" Perhaps your spouse has not been feeling well. Your regular doctor has sent you to a specialist. In the meantime, this ship that is your life bounces around in the stormy sea. You are left wondering how bad this is going to be. So you lift up your voice to God and say, "Lord, help me! Do you not care that I am perishing?" Yes, we have all experienced the kind of crisis of faith those disciples was going through. If not yet, we will, given a little time. This is the time in your life when God's Word can become a great comfort. This is the time when we recall his Word to the turbulent wind and sea, "Peace! Be still!" And they were calmed. "Why are you afraid? Have you still no faith?" The disciples were awed saying, "Who is this that even the wind and the sea obey?" Each of us must face our own personal storms. Often our biggest enemy is our own fear. We saw how the disciples responded. How will we respond? Where will we turn for help? Our Father in heaven is waiting for us to call on him so He can say once again in face of human doubt and fear, "Peace. Be still."

O Father, as I recall the many storms of my life, I can only ask mercy. Out of fear and unbelief I too accused you of not caring for me or about me. Forgive me, for I am most weak when I want to be most strong. Grant me the faith that anticipates your goodness and power even before I am shown. Allow the words "Peace! Be still!" to echo in my heart long before they are said. May I grow each day in wisdom and grace. In the name of Jesus I pray. Amen.

"Jesus took Peter, James and John upon a high mountain with him and he was transfigured before them; His face shone like the sun and his clothes became dazzling white."

I pray that sometime in your spiritual journey you have one of those life-changing experiences like the one that occurred with Peter, James and John the day Jesus took them with him upon the mountain. I can recall several. This one is the biggest. I was in my early thirties. I had a dear minister friend who went in for routine bypass surgery. Complications occurred and he died. At his funeral, I had a vision from God, which told me in no uncertain terms that I was to go into the ministry. At the time, I was a music teacher and very happy with what I was doing. However, this vision was so compelling that I quit my job, enrolled in Seminary, and began the process of becoming a minister. Truth is I was so disturbed by this vision that I did not tell anyone about it for years. I wasn't sure they would believe me. Then after studying the scripture I began to realize that the scripture calls a vision a dream of the daytime and dreams visions of the night. That one Mountain Top experience changed my life forever! I have had many such moments since, none quite so dramatic, but enough to let me know that God is alive, watching over me, over us all!

In our scripture lesson today Peter, James and John have seen the Lord transfigured, *"his face shone like the sun and his clothes became dazzling white."* They wanted to remain and continue this experience as long as possible. Who could blame them? This was a pivotal moment in their life. We would respond the same way. Instead, Jesus brought them back down and they went on with their day-to-day existence going from place to place doing God's work. I am sure that experience that day provided them with the faith to carry on even in the hardest of times. Our mountain top experiences should do the same for us.

Precious Father, It is I your loving child coming before you with a heart full of praise. I relive this extraordinary mountain top moment and I too want to pitch my tent and stay there forever. But the world needed them and the world needs me, the "me" who has met you in an illuminating experience to share what I was given. Will you grant me the courage to share my story as you intend? Will you give me the moment? Will you give me the words? It's a lot to ask of anyone but God. This is my prayer in Jesus. Amen.

"Jesus took Peter, James and John upon a high mountain and he was transfigured before them; His face shone like the sun and his clothes became dazzling white."

Today let's talk about the times we are in the valley. Being on the mountain-top can leave us with memories that last a lifetime; being in the valley can do the same. We have all been there at various times in our life and for various reasons. Your child develops some unknown disease and the doctors have trouble finding out what exactly it is and how to treat it. Your heart drops into your stomach and you don't know what to do or where to turn. You know that you can go to God, but at times it does not seem enough, surely there is something YOU can do. At times there is nothing we can do but wait and accept the outcome. The deepest valley comes. Then you truly realize that you need help from God. That is when you fall on your knees and plead with God to bring help and relief from your pain and anxiety. If I am to be honest with you I will have to admit that I have been in the valley more times than I have been on the mountaintop. If you have loved ones and children and good friends it will happen to you more often than not.

However, you can meet God in that valley just as easily as you can meet him on the mountaintop. Those mountaintop experiences can help to build our trust and faith in God, who can see us through any valley. Peter had this to say years later when retelling his mountaintop experience with Jesus, *"we ourselves heard the voice from heaven while we were with Jesus on the holy mountain."* (2nd Peter 1:18) The voice he was referring to was the voice of God saying, *"This is my beloved son."* When our feelings are tearing us apart in the bottom of the valley we must remember that this life is a walk of faith. There will be mountaintops at times; there will be valleys at others. Our faith is what will see us through. Don't let anything pull you away from that. Put on Christ. Follow him in faith. Trust in him. He may not make those valley experiences disappear, but he will see you through. May the voice of God come to you in your fear and anxiety and tell you, *"You are my beloved."*

God of All Grace, Oh, Father, when I think of the world you have made with all its joys and beauty, I am reminded that you ever willed our Good. Lord, the moments of deep darkness test my fragile faith; grant me the strength to bear witness to your love and mercy in the times of suffering and despair. Remind me that I must be still to hear the tears of Heaven. Are you crying with me, Jesus? Are you crying for me? Either way, I am comforted, Lord, as only you can do. Amen, Father. Amen, my Gracious Lord.

"Abraham believed in God, and it was reckoned to him as righteousness."

Today let's take a look at how we might center our life in God. First, we will have to look at our faith. Is your life centered in faith through Jesus Christ? Or is your life centered in yourself? If it is centered in the self, we are controlled by our passions, our desires. We measure success by accomplishments. Our financial goals control us, defining achievement and status. We turn the idols of this world into our god. Now most would say they do not believe in idols, but in God. Our behavior betrays us. Do you worry? Doesn't that mean that you do not trust fully that God will see after you? Do you depend on the stock market or your investments to secure your future? Doesn't that mean that you do not fully trust that God will take care of your future? I don't mean by this that you should not secure your future, just that it should not be something that consumes you or defines you. We are sinners. No amount of worldly success can change that truth. Only Jesus can free us giving us access to a new life.

In today's passage, Paul gives us the example of the faith of Abraham. The promises of God are realized through faith and not through the deeds. In this verse, the word "reckoned" means to charge it to someone else. Another example can be found in Philemon. Paul is pleading for a runaway slave, Onesimus, saying that if he owes you anything, "Charge it to my account". Although we have sinned greatly, our sins are charged to Jesus' account! Said another way, our belief in Jesus as Lord and Savior enables God to "reckon us as righteous". So even though we still sin, and ever will, Jesus has taken those sins upon himself. Therefore, God accepts us as righteous because we belong to His Son, Jesus. Only Jesus can make our righteousness possible! As the result of our faith in him, we are now children of God. We have been given a new life, one neither money, nor status, nor achievement, nor success can buy. How will this truth change your day? How will it change your life?

Father God, I may not be much, but I am yours. My life keeps that confession a secret most of the time. To the world I am a success, envied by some, perhaps even admired, but for all the wrong things. Take my life this day and let it be consecrated to your will not my own. Teach me to trust in Jesus. Teach me to believe and never waver. Keep me close, Lord, for the ways of the world are ever near and only you know how weak I truly am. In Jesus' name. Amen.

Under the Cross   October 13   Mark 15:39

"The centurion who had been watching over him saw the way Jesus died and said, "Truly this man was God's son.""

The year 1978 stands out in my mind because that was the year my beloved Kentucky basketball team won the National Championship. That was not the only miracle that year; it wasn't even the best! In 1978, I was pastoring a church in Kentucky. We had a Boy Scout Troop inherited from another church. These boys from a rough neighborhood had never been disciplined. Our church took on the important job of mentoring them and giving them the thrill of achieving a goal and accomplishing something. One boy, I will call him Paul, was an especially tough nut to crack! One night at the end of our meeting I had slipped into my office to pick up a few things. When I came out I noticed Paul staring up at a fifteen-foot wooden cross, which hung on the sanctuary wall. I asked him what he was doing and he said, "Is that the cross that man died on?" "No, but it represents that cross," I replied. We spent about fifteen minutes talking about that cross and the man who died on it and then I asked Paul, " Have you ever given your life to Christ?" "No," he said. "Would you like to?" and he answered, "Yes". So right there that night in 1978, beneath the cross, Paul gave his life to Jesus. He then started to cry. This tough guy crying! I asked him," What's wrong?" Then he told me that his older brother was in jail and probably on his way to prison. "I want a different life so I gave my life to Jesus".

In the scripture lesson today, when the centurion, who had been overseeing the crucifixion of Jesus, heard what Jesus said and saw the way he died, he responded; *"Truly this man was God's son!"* The cross has a way of doing that to you. How can anyone stand beneath the cross of Jesus and not be moved to confess that this was truly the Son of God. I recommend that you take a little time today to consider if you have given your life to Jesus. Go into your church, kneel before the cross of Jesus, and let God's presence touch you as you say the words that come to your mind. May God's grace pour down upon you.

Almighty God, Sovereign Lord, All my life I have settled for so much less than you wanted for me, so much less than you planned for me when first I came to mind. Give me the courage and the faith shown by that young man standing beneath that cross. I too have nothing to lose except the right to run my life my way. Such freedom is not all that I expected when first I yearned for it. I'm on my knees, Jesus! I'm on my knees with my face to the cross! It's odd how much closer you are to me from here. Be with me forever and ever. Amen.

"The man said to God, "The woman you gave to be with me, she gave me fruit from the tree and I ate."

After having done just what God told him not to do, Adam, in defense of himself, tells God that it was "that woman", whom you gave me, gave me the fruit. In other words, I would not have sinned if she had not tempted me. And besides, "You", God, were the one who gave me this woman! One could surmise from this declaration that Adam is actually placing the blame on God Himself!

Now that show of arrogance should come as no surprise to any of us. It is so hard for us to admit our wrong, so hard to admit that we are sinners, so hard for us to take blame for anything so we look for someone else to take the blame. "It wasn't me, so-in-so made me do it!" But that kind of blame assignment will not fly with God. There are sins of "omission" and sins of "commission"; sins where we omit what the law of God requires of us and we sins where we do what the law of God forbids. Sins of omission can occur when we are ignorant of God's law but that does not excuse us. All anyone has to do is read his Holy Word and we will know. But even then the law does not explain all things.

Sins of commission occur when we know God's law, such as *"thou shalt not steal"* and we do it anyway. The gist of what I am saying is that it is impossible not to sin! *"All have sinned and fall short of the glory of God,"* says Paul in Romans 3:23. That is why God made a second Covenant with us; that is why God sent his Son Jesus, to cover our sins and make us acceptable before God by His righteousness. Paul says in the verses just before this, that the "righteousness" of God is made available to us, *"all who through faith in Jesus Christ believe."* For there is no distinction or difference between the Jew and the Gentile since, *"All have sinned and fall short of the glory of God."* We are justified by faith in Jesus. There are no conditions on our part spelled out other than "Faith in Jesus". God's grace is bestowed upon us freely and without merit on our part!

Almighty God, my Creator and Lord, I stand condemned but for the righteousness of Jesus and my faith in Him. Give me the grace to live honestly, without pretense and without fear. For fear destroys the freedom to fail you and seek forgiveness knowing you cannot resist an open and contrite heart. More and more like Jesus I pray. Each day more and more like Jesus. Amen.

"Let the same mind be in you that was in Christ Jesus who, though he was in the form of God, did not regard equality with God as something to be exploited, 7 but emptied himself, taking the form of a slave…., 8 he humbled himself and became obedient to the point of death – even death on a cross. 9 Therefore God also highly exalted him and gave him the name that is above every name, 10 so that at the name of Jesus every knee should bend,… 11 and every tongue should confess that Jesus Christ is Lord….."

I remember seeing the movie 'City Slicker' when it first came out. This movie is about several close friends from the 'big city' who go to a dude ranch for a vacation, a little male bonding, a little grappling with the meaning of life. They end up in a cattle drive. One of the main characters, a ranch cowboy, told the others on a cattle drive that there is 'one main thing'. But before they found out what it was, he died. You had to watch the second movie to see what he meant. How often does that happen to us in life? We search for the 'one main thing' only to let it slip by before we truly discover what it is? The scripture tells us that 'the main thing' is to have the mind of Christ. In Romans eight, verse nine, Paul says if we are not of the 'mind of Christ' we do not belong to Christ. These verses from Philippians are an early form of confession. They tell us the essence of the mind of Christ.

First these scriptures tell us of Christ's duel nature. He was both 'Divine and Human'. He shared equally with God. Verse six says that Jesus was in the 'form of God'. In verse seven of our scripture today Paul says that Jesus 'emptied himself – taking on the form of a slave, being born human.' Now certainly we cannot be 'divine'. But we are called to Holiness through the power of the Holy Spirit. We are to let our mind and thoughts be controlled and formed by the Spirit. If we are to be 'like Jesus', we must give up our will and mind and thoughts and allow his Spirit come in and form our every thought and decide our every move. To do so we must be 'one with Jesus' just as he is 'one with the Father'.

Father God, that you could set before me the possibility of receiving through your Spirit the mind of Christ is an awesome thing. I remember how wonderful Jesus was and is – so compassionate, so certain about his calling, so centered in you. Is this the life you want for me? Is this to be mine for the asking, for the taking? Pray do give me this, Father, and day and night I will make known your greatness. You'll have to help me constantly. I can be so easily discouraged and evil knows my very name. Be one with me, Jesus. This is my plea. For your sake, in your name. Amen.

"Let the same mind be in you that was in Christ Jesus who, though he was in the form of God, did not regard equality with God as something to be exploited, but emptied himself, taking the form of a slave, being born in human likeness. And being found in human form, he humbled himself and became obedient to death on a cross. Therefore God highly exalted him and gave him the name that is above every name, so that at the name of Jesus every knee should bend, in heaven and on earth and under the earth, and every tongue should confess that Jesus Christ is Lord, to the glory of God the Father."

In these verses today we find two attributes of God: humility and omnipotence. Verse seven tells us that Jesus 'emptied himself and took on the form of a slave'. Jesus humbled himself for our sake. He did not have to, he chose to. Jesus could have remained in heaven along side of his father but instead he chose to come to this earth, live a life of a humble servant and die for our sins. Because Jesus was humble and obedient, God exalted him above everyone. Beginning in verse eight Paul says that Jesus was 'obedient even to death on the cross'. And 'therefore God exalted him and gave him the name that is above every name so that people should get down on their knees and give thanks and confess that Jesus is Lord of Lord'.

We cannot be divine – we also cannot be all humble and all powerful. But we are called to be of the mind of Christ. As we know him and we study about him, we realize how he was and how we should be. It is just that humility is not our strong suit – yielding power, yes! Trying to prove we are better than those around us, yes! Being humble – no! But that is precisely who Jesus was and if we are to be of the same mind, so must we. We have the template against which we can measure ourselves. We are called to 'empty' ourselves, to be other-directed, not self-centered. We are called to not judge, to forgive and even pray for those who harm us. We are called to love and have faith and hope and to reach out to those less fortunate. Knowing the mind of Christ is so much easier than 'being of the mind of Christ'.

God of All Power and All Humility, You have set before us all the example of Christ Jesus, the humble life divinely lived. You have said "This! This is what I desire from you, for you." You have even defined the way – 'he emptied himself', humbled himself and became obedient even unto death. Oh, Father God, you ask so much of me. I am afraid and just a little bit stubborn and willful. But you, Father, can make true your requests. Give me a mind like Jesus and I will soar on eagle's wings for you. Empty of self. Humble of heart. Obedient unto death. I am free – so free! In Jesus' name. Amen.

"Now concerning spiritual gifts, brothers and sisters, I do not want you to be uninformed. Now there are varieties of gifts, but the same Spirit; and there are varieties of services, but the same Lord; and there are varieties of activities, but it is the same God who activates all of them in everyone."

Paul begins his chapter on spiritual gifts telling his audience that he does not want them to be "uninformed" or ignorant of gifts given by God. There had clearly been some problems in the church concerning gifts and Paul wants them to know that he understands spiritual gifts better than anyone. There were some in the church who were saying their gifts were "from the Spirit". The one gift they were speaking of was the one Paul spends a lot of time explaining, the gift of "tongues". The practice of "utterances" was common in cults of pagan worship in Corinth.

Paul reminded his readers that there are a variety of gifts, but the same Spirit who distributes them; a varieties of services, but the same Lord; and a varieties of activities, but it is the same God who activates them all in everyone. This is not to indicate that there are three categories of gift, but that they are all related to God the Father, Son, and Holy Spirit – the Trinity. These gifts are given by the Holy Spirit; used in services of our Lord; but it is God who activates them all! God has his hand in the giving of gifts to each one of us, is that not amazing?

Where believers use their gifts outside of grace, they are also outside the favor of God. Gifts are given by God to be used for God. Anyone using a gift to benefit them or to make them "look better" in the eyes of those around them are misusing their gifts. Spiritual gifts are given for the purpose of helping bring people to God and to teach them about God. Any other reason would be to misunderstand their purpose. We all have spiritual gifts, let us use them wisely and to uplift those around us.

Lord God, Maker of heaven and of earth and of me, in your wisdom you gave me my place in this world and talents with which to make my way. That is all anyone could ask. Yet you wanted to give more. By your grace and through your great and generous heart, you gifted me with a gift of your very own, a spiritual gift, part of the very being of God. Will you open my eyes so that I might recognize my gift and begin to use it for your Kingdom? And will you give me courage, stamina and self-control? I'll need all those things too. But mostly I'll need a heart for you alone, Lord. Without love, I'm nothing. This is my prayer, Lord. Make it sufficient. In Jesus' name. Amen.

Different Gifts   October 18   1 Corinthians 12:27f

"You are the body of Christ and God has appointed in the church first apostles, second prophets, third teachers; then deeds of power, gifts of healing, forms of assistance, forms of leadership, various tongues. Are all apostles? Prophets? Teachers? Do all work miracles or possess gifts of healing? Do all speak in tongues or interpret? Strive for the greater gifts. And I will show you a more excellent way."

Paul gives a list of spiritual gifts in these verses today. What are those gifts and what gift is really important to have? He begins with apostles and then asks the question, "Are all apostles? Or prophets? Or teachers? No. But strive for the greater gifts and I will show you a still more excellent way." We all have different gifts, which are to be used to help us in relationships and in our work, but mainly to spread God's Word and to glorify Him.

The first question we should ask is, "What are my Spiritual Gifts and am I using them for the glory of God?" Now don't worry too much if you do not possess any of the gifts listed above for I doubt seriously that Paul meant for this list to be complete. When studying Spiritual Gifts early in my ministry I was overwhelmed with the thought of God going to all the trouble to make sure that we are unique and blessed with different gifts. God in His wisdom designed within His plan for the world that each of us would have different gifts and talents and abilities. When we use those God given gifts as God intended, the world and all those around us are blessed and our lives are enriched.

The second question these verses bring up in my mind is what is 'the greater gifts' Paul mentions for which we are to strive? I believe he is referring to the gift of Love as the motive behind the use of our spiritual gifts. Surely with divine love as the driving force, the exercise of all these gifts is the still more excellent way – the way of Christ himself. In the next chapter Paul says, "If I have not love, I am nothing." He ends that thought by saying, "Faith, Hope and Love abide. But the greatest of these three is Love." I think he is right, how about you?

Creator and Redeeming God, Sovereign Lord, I stand in awe of the completeness of your plan for this wondrous world and for us your creatures. That you should consider me worthy or capable of serving you in the fulfillment of your Divine Will is an awesome and humbling thought. Grant me, Lord, your heart of love that all I do, say, or intend may achieve your divine purpose. Oh for the gift of the heart of Jesus, to share and for his sake – truly this is the more excellent way. This is my prayer. In Jesus' name. Amen.

Our Will - Our Downfall   October 19   Matt 10:24

"A disciple is not above the teacher."

This is probably the downfall of many a good Christian. We believe that our hope is in the Lord, but somehow we try to place our will - our decision-making above the teacher – Jesus our Lord. Let me give you an example. I have counseled many older people who want to go on to the 'life after'. God does have a purpose in mind about how we will make our departure from this earth and when. Some will not hear of it. They want their exit to be now and to be the way they want to go. Most believers wish to just go to sleep one night and wake up in heaven.

It is not that God wants us to suffer; it is just that the physical body does not quit working without some good reason. The workings of the human body are pretty remarkable and complicated. In order for it to stop doing what it is programmed to do takes more than a 'wish'. Our only hope is in Jesus, our Lord. We may not get our wish as to 'how and when' to die, but our Lord is there with us every moment of every day whenever we call. It is by His strength and His will that we can make it from day to day. And anytime we decide we want it our way and give up His, we end up being sorry. Jesus alone is Lord of all and the way to salvation, but even more, He is the way to happiness and contentment even when we can no longer do the things we used to do.

We are called to give up our will and to allow His to take over. That is the hardest thing in life to do and this is where we, the disciple, try to put ourselves above Jesus, our teacher. When you find yourself in that situation, just get down on your knees – humble yourself – confess that you have tried your way and failed and ask Jesus to come in and save you from yourself. True gratitude is being thankful for getting what God wants for us in our circumstances even if His will is contrary to our own.

Gracious God, Sovereign Lord, Matters of life and death are so difficult for believers. We want what we want! We are not in a compromise mood. We know your love is great, your knowledge complete, yet we presume to question what you do or fail to do. Forgive me, such hubris and pride deserves to be ignored. And yet you are still beside me, loving me, willing my good, in spite of myself. Thank you Father. Give me the gift of a trusting and grateful heart. In Jesus' precious name. Amen.

The Gift   *October 20*   *1 Corinthians 6: 19*

"Or do you not know that your body is a temple of the Holy Spirit within you, which you have from God, and that you are not your own? For you were bought with a price; therefore glorify God in your body."

Psalms twenty-four tells us *"the earth is the Lord's and everything within it."* The Bible reminds us over and over of that fact. We are told to give of our 'First Fruits'. Since everything is the Lord's, created by Him, we are to return a portion for the upkeep of His Kingdom on earth, the church, and to help care for the needy. All of that is expected. It is not something to brag about. That is just the beginning. We are to remember that 'everything' we have belongs to God; we ourselves were 'purchased with a price.' Our body is a temple of God's Spirit. We are not our own.

That not only means we should watch what kind of food we place in our body and to keep our bodies 'fit', we should also watch what kind of thoughts we allow to go on in our mind for that to is the dwelling place of God. I have seen people who will eat only 'healthy' food and exercise religiously because they believe these words of Paul, "our body is a temple of the Holy Spirit". However, they forget the more important matters of the law: 'justice, mercy and faith'. They are very judgmental and unforgiving. In the fifteenth chapter of Matthew Jesus reminds us, 'it is what comes out of the mouth that defiles' because what comes out of the mouth comes from the heart.

Jesus calls us to honor God in all that we do and say. You want a measure to determine how close you are to God? Listen to your heart. What comes out of your mouth? How do you treat others? Do you treat them with justice and mercy – with love, understanding, and compassion? Or do you find yourself being critical and judgmental? Our body, our mind, our soul is a dwelling place of the Holy Spirit. Allow God's Spirit to abide there; you will see a transformation of your heart. With a change in your heart, you will notice a change in what you think; what you say.

Oh, God, Giver of Every Good and Perfect Gift, I acknowledge before you that all I have is a gift from you. Talents, abilities, money, time, children, even our very being – all gifts, all undeserved but provided by a loving and gracious God. Oh, Father, I have many times given you the leftover parts of my many blessings: some of my talent, abilities, money, time, some small part of myself. Forgive me. Draw me near. I've a distance to go in learning to trust, to let go. Father God, have mercy on me a sinner in your sight. Yours is the only opinion that counts. In Jesus' name. Amen.

Look At Jesus　　　*October 21*　　　*John 8: 1f*

"Now in the law Moses commanded us to stone such women. What do you say?" "Let anyone among you who is without sin be the first to throw a stone at her."

In Matthew 16 Jesus asked the disciples, "Who do people say that I am?" They responded. Then Jesus asked, "But you - who do you say that I am?" That is a very important question still because who Jesus is tells us about who God is; what His nature is like and it tells us about ourselves. Who are we as Christians? What is required of us? How are we to act toward one another? Well, (says the Bible) look at Jesus. The God Jesus taught us about loves all people equally. This God also sees all sins as Sin. No sin is greater than another. Also, God plays no favorites - whether by race or color - whether you are male or female - whether you were born in the United States or some third world nation matters not, God loves all.

So if we take on the task of living the life of a Christian seriously, we need to know how. The Jews live by the law, Christians look to a person, Jesus. The reason there is so much chaos in our society today is because there are too many people choosing different reference points by which to live. Some live by the law; some live by the heart of Christ. When the Pharisees bring a woman caught in adultery to Jesus and tell him the law says stone her, what do you say? Jesus said, "The one WITHOUT SIN cast the first stone." They all walked away. Jesus then says to the woman, "Neither do I condemn you - go and sin no more."

Jesus could easily have condemned her, he met the qualification of sinlessness He set and yet He did not. Why? What did Jesus intend to teach her and us? By refusing to condemn he affirms the potential blessings of the life of a forgiven sinner who gets another chance. Now it is not that Jesus does away with the law, he made it clear that he did not come to abolish the law but to fulfill it. (Matthew 5:17) Follow the law, but temper justice with mercy, compassion, and forgiveness. To accept Jesus is to turn from your life of sin as quickly as you can: not that you can avoid being selfish or a gossip but once you start, allow the Holy Spirit to convict you of the wrong and change - right then! To accept Jesus is to look to Him for the answers to every problem and every situation of life.

Gracious and merciful Lord, God of second chances, guide me in your way of living; make me humble, loving, and compassionate. I have a weakness for vengeance, to see people pay for their actions, their misdeeds. But I am blind to my own sin, dismissive of my own faults. Give me a heart of wisdom, a heart for Jesus. Lead me, Father, in your way. Oh, Lord, be merciful to me, a sinner. In Jesus' name. Amen.

"The Kingdom of God is as if someone would scatter seed and the seed would sprout and grow, he does not know how. But when the grain is ripe the harvest has come."

Jesus used parables to explain the kingdom of God. He uses two in particular in the fourth chapter of Mark. The first is about planting seeds. Once in the ground the seed will grow producing *"first the stalk, then the head, then the full grain in the head. And once it is ripe out comes the sickle and the harvest."* This parable points out that our job as Christians is to sow God's love, mercy, kindness, and forgiveness. Not to make it grow, for we truly don't know which seeds will grow and which will not. We are to just scatter God's seeds.

The second parable is one about the mustard seed, "When sown is the smallest of all seeds, but grows into the greatest of all shrubs." The point being, even the smallest thing we do can sometimes result in a great outcome. We must be careful what seeds we are scattering for there are many, both children and peers who may be young in the faith, watching and picking up on what we do.

Before answering the call to ministry, I was a school teacher. I worked with the youth in churches in several different communities. I recall a couple of kids who had very different family experiences. One was a boy from a well to do family who was sadly mistreated. Although he was very popular and a straight A student, he ended up a drug addict and dealer. The other boy was from a poor family. All his family had to give was love and character. He ended up becoming a teacher. The point Jesus made in the parables above is clear. Whatever seed you plant will grow into a large shrub so be careful what you sow. Make sure the seeds you scatter are the ones you want to plant and are helpful and beneficial to God's Kingdom and especially to those you love.

Oh God, Sovereign Lord of the harvest, give me the faith to sow the seeds you entrust to me and the grace to wait as you, Lord, call them forth to life in your time. Help me to appreciate the potential harvest of even the smallest seed. Keep me in your good care, patient, and humble, ever hopeful, ever trusting in all times. In Jesus' name. Amen.

"This saying is sure and worthy of full acceptance, that Christ Jesus came into the world to save sinners – of whom I am the foremost."

I think one of the chief human temptations is to think of ourselves as better than those around us. Not that we see ourselves as perfect but our "sins" are not as bad as someone else's "sins". Jesus warned us of that human fault in the 18th chapter of Luke. There a Pharisee who built his life around following and obeying the law thought of himself as better than a sinful tax collector. The Pharisee even said so in his prayer, *"God, I thank you that I am not like others - robbers, evildoers, adulterers - or even like this tax collector. I fast twice a week and give 10% to the church."*

Don't come down too hard on him without first looking in the mirror. We need to think we are better. We even go out of our way to try and prove we are better. Why do we do that? I think it is because we fear that if we are not "good enough" God will not allow us into heaven. So we pretend that we are. The thing we can learn from this story is this - It was the tax collector – the "known sinner" who was justified before God, not because he deserved to be justified, but because he did not deserve it and he knew it! So he prayed for "mercy".

There is always a danger in judging yourself to be better than others because in doing so you are tempted to believe you are justified by being better. And if that is so, Christ did not come and die for your sins – you don't need him. You see the danger? Jesus told this Parable so we might see that God wants us to look at ourselves honestly. We are sinners; no matter what we do or how good we are, we cannot justify ourselves before a Holy God. It would be far better for us to beat our breast and say, *"God be merciful to me, a sinner."*

Oh Holy and Merciful God, let me release to you the burden of the "perfection" pretense, which weighs heavily on my shoulders. Give me the assurance to come before you as did the tax collector with my defenses down and my excuses left unsaid, unneeded. Enable me to have the courage to trust your Word completely, sinner that I am. Every day make me a little more like Jesus. In His name. Amen.

Greatest Commandment *October 24* *Matthew 22:34*

"A lawyer asked, "Teacher, which commandment in the law is the greatest?" Jesus said to him, "You shall love the Lord your God with all your heart, and with all your soul, and with all your mind. This is the greatest and first commandment."

This time of the year is considered Stewardship Season. Most churches begin before Thanksgiving and Christmas to set goals for the following year. This is a time for each person to sit down and examine your giving to the Lord of your time, talents and gifts. But even more than that, Stewardship Season is a time to examine your priorities. It is so easy to become deceived in this world as to what is truly important. You know the old saying, "The squeaky wheel gets the grease."

Often, when we sit and examine priorities, we discover that life is running us rather than the other way around. The world is manipulative, controlling, power-hungry and in the long run - destructive. The world uses lies and trickery to get us to do things we normally would not do. Let me put it this way: When a lawyer, one of the Pharisees, came to Jesus and ask Him what was really the top priority, Jesus responded, "You shall love the Lord, your God, with all your heart and with all your soul and with all your mind." And, "You shall love your neighbor as yourself."

The world constantly tries to turn this around so we will put other priorities first. Take a close look at your life, how your time is managed and see if you are placing God first. What are the things that pull us away? Often, they are things that at first glance look good. Your children want to be in little league. You want them to take dancing or karate, piano or voice. It all sounds harmless enough. But then, because your time is limited, you begin to choose a minor priority for them and begin skipping the top priority. It's so easy to do, isn't it? We've all done it. Or, you find yourself wrapped up in the demands of helping the community and serving on this board or that, then wanting to spend your spare time in rest and with family, again, nothing at all wrong with that - except - except, maybe God gets left the leftovers. This is a good time to reexamine your priorities and pray that God will help you to set first priorities first.

God of Grace, Sovereign Lord, when I consider the blessings of my life I am moved to express my gratitude to you Lord, over and over. But my life is busy and gratitude takes a back seat. Forgive me Lord, and accept my full heart as silent testimony. Help me live as though no one is more important to me than you. In Jesus' name I pray. Amen.

Angels Will Come   October 25   1 Kings 19:4

"Elijah then went a day's journey into the wilderness and came and sat under a solitary broom tree. He asked that he might die... then he laid under a broom tree and fell asleep. An angel touched him and said, "Get up and eat."

This is a wonderful story for us because it shows the doubt and fear of a faithful servant of God. That is important for we too have doubt and fear. This story illustrates that in our distress God will send his angels to come and minister to us. This story is a story of success followed by unqualified doubt. Elijah has just defeated 450 prophets of Baal in a contest to determine whose God is not only real but powerful. The contest was to have each side call upon their god to send fire to burn a sacrifice placed on an altar of wood. The prophets of Baal call upon their god all day to no avail. Elijah then had four jars of water poured on his sacrifice, not once but three times, thus upping the stakes. Then he calls upon God to send fire. The fire consumes the entire altar. The people rose up at Elijah's command and killed all 450 prophets. This outraged Queen Jezebel, wife of King Ahab, and she sent word that she would kill Elijah.

After this success over the prophets of Baal, after having God answer his prayer and send fire from heaven, Elijah on hearing of the word of Jezebel ran for his life like a scared jackrabbit! Now doesn't that sound like us? God does some wonderful or miraculous deed for us and at the first hint of danger we forget everything He has done. The police have picked up your son driving while intoxicated. Or your daughter was called back for a suspicious mammography test. All of a sudden, fear takes over. Where fear exists, doubt lies close at hand. When God calls upon us to take the leap of faith, to do what seems impossible, we look to ourselves for strength and thus lose confidence in our Lord. However, when we trust, when we don't give in to our fears, when we hold on to our confidence in God, when we turn to the Lord, like Elijah, we find ourselves ministered to by angels. God sends his angels to minister to us because He understands what we must face. He knows what life will be like and he knows it will be hard. He knows that we will question and wonder and doubt, so, he sends his angels to minister to us.

Father God, in my moments of distress I am tempted to be afraid and to doubt both your promises and You. Forgive me. Give me the faith to believe, to trust, and to endure with grace and joy. The outcome? Well, I leave that up to the One who only wills my good. Precious Lord, take my out-stretched hand. Lead me Home. In Jesus' name. Amen.

"Since we are surrounded by so great a cloud of witnesses, let us lay aside every weight and the sin that slings so closely, and let us run with perseverance the race that is set before us, looking to Jesus the pioneer and perfecter of our faith, who endured the cross."

Most of us carry more weight than we need. Have you ever noticed that? And many wait around hoping some pill will be invented to make losing that weight "a piece of cake" (no pun intended). But it seems like everything that comes on the market has side effects that make it too dangerous to fool with. So we keep waiting. Nutrition experts and doctors all agree that the best way to loose weight is to eat right and exercise.

These verses today give us advice much like that to get ourselves in Spiritual shape for the race of life. It tells us to lay aside the weight and sin that drags us down and run with perseverance – seeing Jesus as the pioneer and perfecter of our faith. You see, besides carrying around more weight in pounds than we need, we humans also have the habit of carrying around other kinds of weight. They are the ones that more than likely cause the pounds to start with. So do yourself a favor and take the advice Hebrews offers. Lay aside the weight of fear and anxiety and worry. Lay aside those sins like selfishness and pride and arrogance and gossip and being judgmental of others or of yourself.

Don't fret over every little sin you commit; don't worry over every little mistake you make. Instead keep your eyes fixed on the race ahead and look to Jesus to perfect you. Look to Jesus as the pioneer of your faith. Don't get bogged down in unfinished business or regrets, hurt feelings, things that drain your emotional and spiritual energy. Every time they come to grab a piece of your time and energy, look to Jesus. Trust in Him. So, get in shape. Shake off those parasites that are slowing you down and get focused. There is nothing in this life that can defeat us if we look to and depend on Jesus. Nothing.

Jesus, my Lord and my Savior, help me look to you as my guide and my stay. Help me to rely on your strength, your courage to follow the path you set for my life. Help me run my race and not falter, remembering all you endured to make my relationship with you possible. Take from me the weight of my sin. Unburdened, I can anything! Do you see me Lord, I'm running the race! In Jesus' name I pray. Amen.

Slave to Sin   **October 27**   *John 8:34f*

"Jesus answered them, "Very truly, I tell you, everyone who commits sin is a slave to sin. The slave does not have a permanent place in the household; the son has a place there forever. So if the Son makes you free, you will be free."

In these verses Jesus tells the Jews that if they listen to Him and follow His Word, that Truth will set them free. They responded by telling Jesus they were descendants of Abraham and did not need Him or His advice. He tried to help them understand that 'anyone who commits sin is a slave to sin'. You may not kill but your actions toward another and your hatred for them has killed them in your heart. There is no one who does not commit sin and everyone who does is a slave to sin and can never be whom God created. What Jesus was saying is that as long as one refused to admit to the anger or hatred inside, the heart could not belong to God and the Spirit could not occupy the central and important place there. Instead the heart would belong to anger or hatred.

I have known people who have drawn a conclusion about someone and disliked them because of the conclusion drawn, even when they were totally wrong in their assessment. As long as we harbor hate or contempt in our heart about anyone we will never be able to see that person as God created them to be. It is only as we ask God to cleanse our hearts and ask Jesus to come dwell in our hearts and control our will that can we change. It is only as 'the slave turns to the master for a place to live does the master make him or her a part of the permanent household.' It is the Master who sets us free from sin. Until then we are all 'slaves to sin.' And once we are set free from sin we can now view others in the same way. If we refuse to see ourselves as sinful and imperfect, we will never be able to see that those we dislike or call our enemy are no different. To have your eyes opened to that Truth is to be set free!

Almighty God, I too want to be free to have a place in your household as a true child of God through Christ. But, Father, I am not free. I am still a slave to ambition, pride, to my selfish, self-filled heart. This slavery is my choice. You have done all you can to free me in Christ but I must want to be free; I must desire freedom more than life itself. Only you can do this. Forgiveness in Christ Jesus is your greatest gift, repentance a tiny price. Set me free, Lord, and I will me free indeed. In Jesus'. Amen.

"The LORD said to Joshua, "You shall march around the city, all the warriors circling the city once. Do this for six days, with seven priests bearing seven trumpets of rams' horns before the ark. On the seventh day you shall march around the city seven times, the priests blowing the trumpets. When they make a long blast with the ram's horn, as soon as you hear the sound of the trumpet, then all the people shall shout with a great shout; and the wall of the city will fall down flat, and all the people shall charge straight ahead."

Too often in life we will pray to the Lord and ask him to give us guidance and direction only to continue to follow our own direction rather than His. God reveals to us a path through His Holy Word, through His servants, or through the Body of his Son, the Church, and we obey but only to a point. Then when things don't go our way, we decide that we know what is best and we take it on ourselves to do what we think God should have done.

This story from Joshua gives us a glimpse of what will happen if we follow to the letter what the Lord says. God told Joshua that we would hand Jericho over to him. This was a city with a large wall around it and next to impossible to penetrate. God told him to have all his warriors march around the wall circling the city once; to do this six days in a row. On the seventh day Joshua was told to march around the city seven times and to have the priests blowing trumpets. At the end of that march the priests are to make a long blast with the ram's horn and the people are to shout a great shout and the wall will come down.

Joshua did what the Lord commanded down to the letter of the law and when he did here is what happened; the walls fell down flat and the people charged into the city and captured it. (verse 20) The purpose of this story in God's Holy Word is to let us know that we cannot follow the Lord by doing only a part of what He asks, we must be willing to put all of our faith and trust in Him, and when we do, the results can be amazing! Just give it a try; what do you have to lose?

Almighty God, Sovereign Lord, So often in my life, I have prayed for a miracle and then questioned how you went about it. Forgive me. This scripture reminds me that the ways of God and man are and must ever be different or else what is faith for? Thank you Lord, for this portrait of obedient faith and abiding trust. I needed to be reminded what an awesome God I serve! Keep me grounded in the name of Jesus, my savior and my friend. Amen.

Trust in the Lord   *October 29*   *Proverbs 3:5f*

"Trust in the Lord with all of your heart, and do not rely on your own wisdom. In all that you do, put God first and He will make straight your paths."

In midsummer of 1996, we bought a cabin on the Tennessee River near the historic Civil War battlefield of Shiloh. It was then and remains still a gift from God Himself. This little cabin provides for us a sanctuary from the intensity of ministry and the stress of living in today's fast -paced world. We saw the cabin late one Friday evening but had to spend the night in order to accommodate the realtor who had the listing and the key. That night at the state park I quickly fell asleep. My wife wasn't so fortunate. Picking up a Bible left by the Gideons, she began searching for a "word" from the Lord. Not wanting to disturb me, she retreated to the only other room with a light she could find, the "necessary" room, and began her search.

After some time, she turned to the front of the Bible where scriptures are listed according to need. When she got to the word "guidance", she knew she was home. The Proverbs verse above drew her attention. There was an immediate awareness that her plea had been received. The question that haunted her, "Lord is this where you want us to be" and "How will we know?" These verses: the answer. "Trust (ME) with all your heart. Quit trying to figure it out alone. Put ME first and I will lead you without error or backtracking where you are meant to go."

Having read these verses brought some comfort and she was at least able to get some sleep. It was not until the next day that she realized the extent that God would go to ease her mind and her worry. That morning the lady who had shown us around the day before ushered us into another realtor's office where we made an offer. On his desk, a gift form his grandchildren, was a plaque with a scripture that began, *"Trust in the Lord with all your heart...."* The rest, as they say, is history.

Heavenly Father, Almighty God, I stand in awe of your goodness and grace to the least of these your children and a sinner of great renown. Such proof of the intimacy with which you behold your children calls for a like response. So I come to you, Father, humbled and forever grateful. I kneel before you a loving and forgiven soul with a life-changing story to claim and to tell. Thank you, Jesus, my Lord and my Savior. Thank you, Jesus. How I love you so! Amen.

"But I say to you that listen, Love your enemies, do good to those who hate you, bless those who curse you, pray for those who abuse you. If anyone strikes you on the cheek, offer the other also; and from anyone who takes away your coat do not withhold even your shirt. Give to everyone who begs from you; and if anyone takes away your goods, do not ask for them again. Do to others as you would have them do to you."

Too many people have the false idea that Christians are 'perfect' people and the church is a 'perfect' place. Those people will have a rude awakening. Although they may attend church for a while, they will soon drop out because of the hypocrisy they see and encounter. That being the case, who and what should the church be?

The church should be filled with ordinary people trying to be extraordinary saints! Jesus gives us a few guide lines to follow: 'to be a good listener, love our enemies, do good to those who hate and hurt us; to not strike back (with a blow of the fist or with harsh words of criticism); to give until it hurts you and to do unto others as you would have them do to you.' Now if ordinary people in ordinary churches do their dead level best to fulfill that commandment, what a difference that would make!

Whenever Paul wrote letters to different churches all over the area he served, he always addressed them as 'Saints' in the church. We also know that most of these letters were responses to letters he received asking his advice in solving 'problems' within those churches. The picture the New Testament gives of the church is certainly not one of perfection! It is rather a picture of ordinary people striving to faithfully serve an extraordinary God; it still is. Sometimes the selfless deeds referenced in Luke above occur not just outside the church, but also within it! We are reminded that those who give their hearts to Christ belong to Him and their sins are now covered. No longer a slave to sin, we now become slaves to God in Christ; ordinary people becoming extraordinary saints.

Father God, Thank you for all you have done for me in Jesus, for all your goodness and grace, abundant and free. Give me a grateful and merciful heart that I may serve you joyfully and well. Help me to listen to your voice, The chatter of the world is ever near whispering evil, negative words, robbing me of my confidence, my joy. This standard you set for me is high, Lord, but I stand on the footstool of faith and together nothing is beyond our reach! In Jesus' name. Amen.

Listen, hear and do   *October 31*   *James 1:22*

"Be doers of the Word, not hearers only."

Most of us have some type of hobby. My hobbies consist of golf, fishing, and refereeing college basketball from my armchair. I used to love gardening. Maybe some day I will get back into that. The point I am trying to make is this: whatever your hobby, it takes a certain amount of knowledge to make it successful and enjoyable. Take golf for instance. I began by taking lessons from a pro to develop the proper swing. I then would go to the practice range and practice at least once or twice a week. After a few years of practicing and playing I developed a pretty decent game of golf. I would never have been any good if I had not tried to develop knowledge of the game.

The same is true concerning God's Word. James tells us to *"be doers of the Word, not hearers only."* How can one be a doer of God's Holy Word if in fact you do not know His Word? Knowledge of God's Word is imperative if we intend to obey God's commands. Even so, knowledge does not automatically translate into action. Even if I know the proper way to swing a golf club, doing so every time without making some error is virtually impossible!

The same is true of living according to God's Word. Knowledge does not give me the ability or the desire to obey. If it did then Jesus came for naught. If I can do on my own what God wants me to do, why would I need Jesus? In the seventh chapter of Romans Paul tells of his struggle with doing what he knows is right and concludes that he continues to fail. He then asks *"Who can save me from myself?* His answer? God through Jesus! Christ is the one who saves. To be a doer of God's Word, I must first know His Word; I must let go of my own selfish nature, and let Jesus guide me and cover my many sins!

Almighty God, Sovereign Lord, I come as a sinner. I know that this state of sin is ever my companion until I am finally Home with you. This truth weighs heavy on me - so much so that I hide my sin by being a prodigious "hearer" of the Word. As soon as I hear enough then I can be a 'doer.' It's a time-worn excuse, Even my motives aren't new. Yet, I come before you, Father, as one whom Jesus loves, knowing for His sake and in His name you can make even me of some small use to your Kingdom. It would be a miracle of sorts. So whenever you're ready, Lord, so am I. In the name of Jesus, whom I love. Amen.

Imitate Me   *November 1*   *Philippians 3:17*

"Join in imitating me - honor those who live as examples for others to follow."

Let me ask you a question. Are you seeking, by the grace of God, to live a Christ-like life? If you answer "yes" there are some things to consider. Your life should be an example for others. Don't misunderstand; you cannot live a perfect life for that is impossible. The scripture is clear "We are all sinners." However, you can be a wonderful example even if you are a sinner; for a good example look to the Old Testament at David. He was considered a "man after God's own heart." Also don't think that by living your life as an example for others means you cannot enjoy life. There is no use talking about eternal life or enjoying life on the other side of the grave if we do not enjoy living for Jesus on this side of the grave.

Let me give you a couple of examples we should or should not imitate. First a cult leader named Jim Jones who started his ministry in California and dreamed of helping his followers escape the problems of this world. That was his first mistake. God never said that we as Christians could or should escape the problems of this world, rather that we are to live in this world with our eyes fixed on the next. Jones convinced his followers to sell all they had and purchase land in Guiana to establish "his" earthly kingdom. His life ended along with most of his followers after he took the life of the U. S. Congressman who was there to investigate him. They drank poisoned cool-aid and died in mass. Whatever potential they each had to imitate God in selfless living died with them.

The other person is Steve Brown. I first heard of Steve while serving a church in Arkansas in the early 1980's. One member gave me a tape of his. I was hooked from the beginning. Not only because of his "great" voice for preaching, but because of the great content of his sermons. His sermons on grace are the best I have ever heard and I have heard a bunch! Steve dedicated his life to preaching God's Word through his radio ministry, tape ministry, book ministry, and seminars. I have heard him several times at Lake Barkley Fellowship in Western Kentucky. These two men had similar gifts and opportunities. One kept his eye on heaven; the other set his eyes on his own earthly ministry. One we should imitate, you choose.

Lord, I want to be faithful to your call; I want to become more like Jesus with every new day you provide, every new opportunity you create. Give me the grace and courage to trust you completely, to be one others can imitate, sinner though I may be. In Jesus' name. Amen.

Self-Discipline   *November 2*   *John 18:37f*

"Pilate asked, "So you are a king?" Jesus answered, "You say that I am. For this I was born, and came into the world, to testify to the truth. Everyone who belongs to the truth listens to my voice." Pilate asked, "What is truth?"

As Christians, we are called to live a spiritual life - to be in this world, but not of this world. The difficulty comes in the fact that the world continues to try and pull us into its power. To resist takes more than courage, it takes more strength and will power than we possess, it takes the power of God. We are saved by Grace. God sent His Son Jesus to purchase our salvation and the only way to grow spiritually is to submit our life to God and to a different lifestyle.

For instants, let's say God gave you a talent for playing a musical instrument and you wish to be great at that talent. Can you accomplish that by spending your time watching TV and playing video games? No, you accomplish it by practicing your scales, learning about chords, reading music and eventually you will become what you love to do. To grow in one area, you must give up some things in another. We only have so many hours in a day. Paul calls it the gift of "self-discipline." You want to grow spiritually? Then you must give up the freedom of lying in bed on Sunday morning and doing as you wish; you will have to give yourself to God's Kingdom and to his church - the living body of Jesus Christ.

How can one think that it requires discipline to play the piano or a guitar and yet think they can enjoy the fruits of God's grace without sacrifice or dedication? Jesus says, *"If you follow in My words, you shall know the truth and the truth shall set you free."* Pilate asked Jesus before he had Him nailed to the cross, *"What is truth?"* Well, Jesus is truth. God loves us deeply. He wants us to return that love. We do so by giving our life, our will, our time, and our talents to Him and to His Kingdom.

Sovereign Lord, Merciful God, The temptation to be seduced by worldly affirmations is too great for me. I want to choose what you would choose for my life but I need your guidance. Help me to seek you where you may be found – in your Word, in prayer, and in the community of faith. Give me discipline and dedication to this effort that I may not seek you in vain. In Jesus' name. Amen.

Stewardship   *November 3*   *2 Corinthians 9:5f*

"I thought it necessary to urge the brothers to go ahead and arrange in advance for this bountiful gift you have promised, so that it may be ready as a voluntary gift and not as an extortion. Each of you must give as you have made up your mind, not reluctantly or under compulsion, for God loves a cheerful giver."

Although I haven't hunted in a long time, I was an avid hunter growing up, purchased my first shotgun when about fourteen. I found it in a second-hand store. It was in terrible shape, rusty and needed bluing and sanding and to be stained. I spent hour upon hour on that old gun and hunted with it until I was about 27 and then received a new shotgun for Christmas one year. My father did not have a gun so I loaned it to him. Told him it was his until I wanted it back – to use it as often as he wanted. He loaned it to a relative who lost it, so he says! And you know what, I was very disappointed. I had put blood, sweet and tears into that old gun.

Thinking over that experience one day it dawned on me. This is what we do to God! God has given us all that we have, made us all that we are. He has allowed us to use and enjoy everything around us but it does not truly belong to us. We can say that we worked hard and earned the land we live on or the house we built, but God made it all possible. He gave us life and all that we have. I am sure that he too is disappointed when we take the gift that is His and not return it.

The gift that we have received is an indescribable gift of love – it is grace. Paul calls on those in Corinth to take up an offering as a gift to other Christians in need. He reminds them of their offer of an extraordinary gift and tells them he is sending someone ahead to arrange for the gift so that *"it may be ready as a voluntary gift and not as an extortion."* For as Paul tells them, *"God loves a cheerful giver."* Remember as you think about the stewardship of your time, talents, and money that you would have none of it without God first giving to you.

God of All Grace, You have been merciful to me. You have blessed me beyond enumeration. Yet I have credited myself. I have felt entitled. I have not been generous. I have given expecting something in return. But you have withheld nothing – correct my selfish heart that I may give in this same spirit. Thanks be to God for His indescribable gift – Jesus. In His most precious name. Amen.

Called　　　　*November 4*　　　　*John 21:15f*

"Jesus said to Peter, "Simon son of John do you Love me?" Peter responded, "Yes Lord, you know that I love you." "Feed my sheep." "Follow me."

At the beginning of the Gospel of John Jesus called his disciples and said "Follow me." Here at the end of the Gospel he says the same, "Follow me." This was his final instruction before he left them. They were at the Sea of Tiberias fishing, had caught nothing. A man on the shore tells them to cast the net to the right side of the boat and "You will find some fish." They did and there were so many they could not haul the net into the boat. That is when Peter recognized the man on the shore as Jesus. They came ashore and Jesus fed them breakfast.

Jesus asked Peter *"Do you love me?"* As a mater of fact he asked three times, the exact number of times that Peter had denied him in the courtyard on the night of Jesus' arrest. Each time Peter said, *"Yes Lord, you know I love you."* And each time Jesus asked him to *"feed his sheep."* Then before he ascended into Heaven Jesus says, *"Follow me."* Too often we look at the call to follow and wonder if we can. But you see Jesus is not saying "go do" on your own, he Is saying "come follow me." Wherever you are, whatever you will do, I will be there with you carrying the load. All we have to do is decide if we want to follow or not.

In the early 1980's I served a church in Eastern Kentucky. We needed to build an education building and many were afraid that we could not pay for it. Our oldest member, at 85, stood and said, "We built this sanctuary when we had no money only the faith that God wanted us to do so. We can do this." Then one of our youngest members walked down front and laid a check on the communion table and said, "I have just written a check for $10,000 and somehow I'm going to make that check good. I challenge all of you to do something by faith." We built the building and it was paid for. The call Jesus gives us is not always an easy challenge. To follow Him takes faith, more faith than I have, more faith than you have. We are not called to lead, but to follow!

God of Grace, You stand on the shore of my life and call to me to cast my net again. Give me the courage to obey and to follow wherever you lead. Ask of me the same question you asked Peter and let me say again an again, "I love you, Lord – lead me where you will. I will follow. I will follow." In Jesus' name. Amen.

"But we see Jesus, who for a little while was made lower than the angels, now crowned with glory and honor because of the suffering of death, so that by the grace of God He might taste death for everyone."

This scripture from Hebrews tells the outrageous truth about Jesus. Jesus was sitting at the right hand of his father in heaven, but was made lower than the angels so that "by the grace of God He might taste death for each and every one of us!" Now think that over. Jesus tasted death for us – for you and me. Jesus tasted death on our behalf and now we do not have to "earn" our salvation. The problem is not that this is not so, but rather many have a problem accepting this outrageous truth!

Why do people become critical of one another? Because they have this false notion that we are supposed to be "good" and "perfect" and if you do not measure up, then you become the butt of their criticism. Only problem with that is they too are not perfect, no one is except God and if we can be perfect why would Jesus come to save perfect people? Jesus says, "I came not to save the righteous, but sinners." But people continue to think "If only I could be perfect – if only I could have enough faith – if only I could do the right thing and avoid sin – I could ride my way into heaven!" But the New Testament is clear, salvation is not earned, it is a gift called grace and was purchased for us by a man named Jesus.

Jesus, who was the very reflection of God's glory, emptied himself and became a part of our family. He suffered death so that he might by the grace of God, taste death on our behalf. He could have called a league of angels to His rescue, instead he submitted himself to death on the cross, the purpose for which he was sent. Have we heard the Gospel message so often that we don't hear the radical nature of it or the life-changing importance of it? It is a claim that is so outrageous that it leaves no room for one to sit on the fence - it's either true or it's not. You must make the choice. Jesus came to suffer a lowly death so that we might receive grace, given as a gift from one who loved us so.

God of Grace, Sovereign Lord, In Jesus Christ you have offered the ultimate sacrifice for my life that I might be reconciled to you. Let the truth of this great gift be the controlling factor in all I do and say. May the sacrifice of Christ bear fruit in my life to the honor and glory of your name. In Jesus' name. Amen.

Law or Grace?   November 6   Ephesians 2:15f

"Jesus has abolished the law with its commandments and ordinances. . ."
"Jesus reconciles us into one body through the cross."

In the letter to the Ephesians, Paul tells us that Jesus frees us from the law, that he has *"abolished the law with its commandments and ordinances. . ."* Now, don't let this statement confuse you. Paul does not mean we no longer must follow the Ten Commandments or any of God's other laws. In the fifth chapter of Matthew, verse 17, Jesus says, *"Do not think I have come to abolish the law or the prophet's teachings - I have come to fulfill them."* In other words, He will stand in their place.

In the fifth chapter of Matthew, Jesus is trying to get the Jews and Pharisees to understand that if they think they can follow the law perfectly and become righteous, they have another thing coming. The 6th commandment says, "Thou shalt not murder." Most can acknowledge that they do not murder, but here is what Jesus has to say in the follow up, *"If you are ever angry with your brother/sister, you have committed murder in your heart!"* Now who can say they have never done that?

The point being: one cannot live this life perfectly by following the laws of God - not that we are to abandon the law, just don't depend on the law to measure who you are as a Christian or who anyone else is for that matter. Jesus came to bring us freedom from the law. He has led us into a new kingdom where He forgives us our sins and calls on us to forgive one another. He abolished the law and brought us freedom with His blood. Ephesians 2:16, *"Jesus reconciles us into one body through the cross."* It was the cross that changed forever how we look at the law. The law binds us; Jesus sets us free. The law says, "Do this - don't do that." Jesus says, "Follow me, let your heart obey me out of love, for I gave my life for you – stand on My righteousness not your own."

Lord of Love and Forgiveness, please overlook my arrogance. At times I have believed that I can somehow save myself by following the Law perfectly. It is only by trying to do so that I realize the absurdity of all that. Save me from myself. Grant me your Grace and cover my sins with your righteousness. I pray in the name of the one who came and set me free from the bondage of sin and of the Law, Jesus. Amen.

"The Good!"　　November 7　　Romans 3:23f

"All have sinned and fall short of the glory of God. They are justified by His Grace as a gift, through the redemption which is in Jesus Christ."

Salvation is by faith alone. Most every church where I have served as minister there have been at least a few people who somehow believe that they are 'good', at least better than others. I have always felt sorry for them for they seem to be desperately trying to prove how perfect they are by finding others who are not so perfect, and by focusing on their flaws they think it somehow makes them look 'good'. Do you know people like that? Sure you do! Maybe you are one of them, but I hope not – I pray not, for the Gospel is not about our desperately reaching out to prove our virtue to God.

The Gospel is about a God who reaches down to us in love and mercy and forgiveness. It is about a God who reaches down to pull us out of sin and self-destruction. It is about a God who knows that we *"sin and fall short of His glory"* and calls us his children nonetheless. Being a part of God's Kingdom – being recipients of His Grace is not an accomplishment, which we are somehow smart enough to pull off. Saying our prayers giving our tithe going to church will not save us. Becoming an officer or teacher or choir member or treasurer will not save us. Now those things are all well and good. The church needs that kind of devotion from us. God's Kingdom needs our work.

But the point is, as meaningful as these things are, they do not contain the power to save us. Only one power can save us and that is the Love and Grace of Jesus. *"We are justified by His Grace as a gift, through the redemptive power of Jesus Christ."* God has provided a way for us to know that our sins are forgiven and to experience the joy of His presence in our lives and it is through believing and accepting His Son Jesus; by accepting the gift which God gives and letting his love mold our lives to live as we were created to live. That is why it is called 'Good News' and not 'good works'.

God of Mercy and Grace, In Christ Jesus you have claimed me. Let me never forget that my right relationship with you, God, comes only through Jesus' sacrifice. You know, Lord, how tempting it is to trust in my own goodness, to compare my devotion to others at their expense. Such behavior reflects so poorly on you. Forgive me. Give me the faith to live by grace alone. In Jesus' name. Amen.

Legalism   November 8   James 2:10

"Whosoever shall keep the whole law, and yet offend in one point, is guilty of all points."

Due to inclement weather and only a tentative promise of rising temperatures, church services were cancelled for a snowy, icy Sunday morning. Most of the church members were in agreement, especially the elderly most at risk of getting out and getting hurt. Some were horrified. 'What will people think?' 'What will people say?' We stuck by our original judgment and the 'concern talk' soon abated. What we had unwittingly unearthed was a case of legalism. The definition of legalism is as follows: a strict, literal adherence to the law. Legalism has been a problem for centuries as the faithful have attempted to live faithfully.

Paul's argues in Romans 3:20, "through the law comes the knowledge of sin." Then in chapter seven he gets into the conflicts caused by the Legalism of the law. Beginning with verse fifteen Paul states that he does not understand his own actions, *"For I do not do what I want but the very thing I hate!"* He goes on to say that he does not have the power to do what he wants. *"I can will what is right, but I cannot do it."* Paul found that one can actually see what is good and right and even desire to do it, but that is about as far as we can get. We do not have the power to always be good or do good. As hard as we try sin has a way of spoiling our 'good'.

So the law holds us captive and we become slaves trying to obey it. The law can show us right from wrong but it is powerless to make or help us to do it. James throws in another clinker. *"If you try and keep the law and fail on one point, you fail at all points."* It doesn't sound fair but it is true. That is the problem with legalism. It is impossible to live perfectly. So who can rescue us from this? Paul states in Romans 7:25, *"Only Jesus can rescue me."* Those who live in Jesus live by his perfection and his righteousness. God has done what the law could not do – made us righteous in His sight by Jesus' sacrifice on the cross. Jesus freed us from the curse of the law and we now receive the promise of the Holy Spirit through faith.

God of Grace, Host Holy and Righteous Lord, Thank you for the Law. Without it I would not be forced to admit my need for a Savior. It is only by trying to be 'good' that I realize my goodness is not good enough. Thank you for your servants Paul and James who's honest words so resonate with my life. Thank you most of all for Jesus - my savior. Let my humility grow, my pride diminish, my faith increase. In Jesus' name. Amen.

"Give to Caesar that which belongs to Caesar; to God the things that are God's."

Stewardship is when we consider what we give to God and His church and why. One thing that is probably hard for most to comprehend is that God does not need our money; it is we that need to give. If the images of heaven are correct, as we see in the 21st chapter of Revelation's, the Holy City is made up of "*gold, jasper, sapphire, agate, emerald, onyx, and every precious jewel known to mankind; the gates are made of pearl; the streets are of pure gold.*"

So why in the world would God need our precious money? There is nothing that we have that God needs, you see. Our gold is asphalt - Our pearls are used for gates - God doesn't need our money - it's easy for us to have this misconception that God MUST have our resources to fulfill his plan. Nothing could be further from the truth. When we give our gift to God, it is not because God needs anything - it is we who need to give. Now why do we need to give? Well scripture does tell us that God has commanded us to Give. But also we need to give in order to combat the power of materialism in our lives. There's no more deceptive and deadly power on the face of this earth. Jesus did not say that money is evil, but that money is the root of evil. It can become very addictive and here's how that works.

The more material things we have, the more we feel we need. Luxuries become a necessity - what was once considered extravagant becomes essential. And even worse, the more we have, the more we feel we deserve - until all of a sudden, the power of materialism separates us from each other and ultimately from God. We begin to look at those who don't have and blame them for their misfortunes - we forget that sometimes we are born with a silver spoon in our mouths or we are given a gift by God - like a professional athlete or actor - or God just puts us in the right place at the right time. Giving to God helps break the hold that materialism can have on us. Our gift to God is not because God has a need - but because we need to give. We need to show that God is essential in our life - we need to show that Jesus is Lord of our life.

Lord, you have given me so much that it is difficult to measure. Yet I continue to pretend that all I have comes because of my efforts, not because of your gifts and your grace. Forgive me and fill my heart with gratitude and a spirit of giving. Please don't let the greedy hands of materialism posses my soul. In the name of Jesus I pray, Amen.

Being Thankful   November 10   Luke 17:15f

"Then one of them, when he saw that he was healed, turned back, praising God with a loud voice. He prostrated himself at Jesus' feet and thanked him. And he was a Samaritan. Then Jesus asked, "Were not 10 made clean? But the other nine, where are they? Was none of them found to return and give praise to God except this foreigner?"

How do you react when you are thankful? It is clear that people react in different ways; the question is, "How do you react?" In the scripture story today, nine lepers are cured of a dread disease for which there was no known cure and which caused them to be outcasts from society. Only one returned to give thanks and praise to God. This one was actually a foreigner, a Samaritan, not of the established accepted religious order. Ever find that to be true? The "non" Christian reacts in a way a Christian should and does not?

So how do you react? Maybe Jesus has not cured you of leprosy, but he has cured you of something! Perhaps He has healed a broken heart, a dependency on drugs, or a life of greed and self-absorption. Perhaps He has rescued you from meaninglessness and into a life of hope and faith and love. Not only has Jesus given you a new life, he has given you eternal life! Once we all realize the depth of that gift and the price paid, how do we react? We could spend the rest of our life saying, "Thank you, thank you, thank you, Jesus!"

If that is your response, where does it take you? Our "Thank You" should move us beyond the words to giving of ourselves. We can express our thanks in many ways – just ask God to direct you in the way He wants you to express yours: giving of yourself in some way to the building of God's Kingdom – the church, visiting shut-ins, reaching out to the needy. One thing is for sure, God has given us far more than we deserve or could ever pay back! The question is, "Are we thankful?" Is there thanksgiving in our heart? Then let it show and let it work to advance the Kingdom.

Father God, Savior, Benefactor, and Most Holy Friend, I'd like to see myself in this story as the one who returns. I pray that I am the one but I know I'm probably not. I am the one who has missed many, many opportunities to be grateful out loud and with great joy. I too as these lepers was in such a great a hurry to resume my life I forgot you. Forgive me, Father. Give me a grateful heart, O God, and I will to declare over and over again your praise. Just another chance, Jesus. I'll not fail you. This is my earnest prayer in Jesus' name. Amen.

Live by Faith　　*November 11*　　*Galatians 2:20*

"And the life I now live in the flesh, I live by faith in the son of God, who loved me and gave himself for me."

Paul was a converted Pharisee who had a lot of experience living in the flesh. He had spent the better part of his life judging others by the "Law". His phrase "living in the flesh" is a reference to the earthly part of a person, representing our desires, weakness and sinful nature. In his letters Paul compares and contrasts a life of the flesh as opposed to a life lived by the Spirit. When we are "in the flesh" we cannot please God only when we are empowered by the Spirit and so live can God be made glad.

After his conversion experience on the road to Damascus, Paul changed from a life of flesh, depending on his own works or the ways of the world, to living by faith in Christ. Here in Galatians 2:20 he puts it like this, *"The life I now live in the flesh, I live by faith in the son of God, who loved me and gave himself for me."* These words can be found in a wonderful Lenten Anthem called "Why Should He Love Me So." Paul still lived a life in the flesh, after all, that is something none of us can avoid, but now he no longer depended on that life to justify him before God. He now lived by faith that Jesus will save him from his life of flesh.

People who live a life of the flesh – depending on good works to save them, also live a life of fear; always worrying whether or not they measure up. In that life, we must be guarded, measuring everything we do and say, because those things will determine whether or not God accepts us. When one lives by the spirit, by "faith in the Son of God", then everything we do we lift up to Christ and ask for his guidance. Then our life will be a reflection of Him – Jesus came to be a servant – he came to show compassion and forgiveness – love and grace. Our calling is great but our greatness is found in Christ as we attempt to live our life in the flesh "by faith in the Son of God who loved (us) and gave his life for (us)."

Almighty God, Author and Perfecter of my Faith, I am once more made aware of how far I fall short of the life you purchased for me by your death on the cross. Though I have the power to choose a life of faith, too often I choose my own worldly way, striving for recognition and acclaim. Forgive me, Father. Remind me often that, the life I live, I live by faith in the Son of God, who loved me, who loved ME, and gave himself for ME. What a powerful truth to remember, to embrace. I love you, Jesus; I love you back. May my life be a true reflection of your great grace and my great joy. Forever amen and amen. Come, Lord Jesus!

Change in Attitude   November 12   James 1:18

"In fulfillment of His own purpose, God gave us birth by the Word of Truth."

My wife is a wonderful teacher and has a saying in her Bible study: "The scripture opens our hearts so we can have a change in attitude. A change in attitude then translates itself in a change in behavior." After graduating from Seminary and being in the ministry for about six months, I realized that I could not handle all of the pressures of God's work alone. I decided that I had to get away from the church for a while and sort things out. Louisville Seminary was having a seminar on preaching and teaching led by a guy I had never heard of, Walter Wink.

After about 8 seminars with Walter, I now know him well. However, I'll never forget that first session. We did a study on the scripture concerning Zacchaeus. Afterwards, a minister in the group said, "That was really profound. It has changed the way I see things. I wish all Bible study could be just like that." To which Walter Wink said, "You don't believe that one should be transformed every time one hears and studies the Word, do you?" The minister said, "Well, no I really don't." To which Walter said, "That's your problem. You don't believe or expect transformation."

Do you believe that reading and studying scripture will transform your life? Of course we must make ourselves available for transformation. It would be hard to be transformed if we refuse to open our heart and mind to God's Holy Spirit. James states that God in fulfillment of His own purpose gave us birth "By the Word of Truth." Jesus is the Word of Truth. He tells us to be like him "humble in heart" and that if we will *"Understand with our hearts and turn (trust in him) then he will heal us."* It is only as we give our hearts to Jesus that we can truly be transformed. Otherwise we will continue to be slaves to sin and to our own wishes and desires. When you read and study the scripture open your heart so you may experience a change in attitude resulting in a change behavior.

God of Grace, Holy Lord, I come before you with a glad and thankful heart for I know that every good and perfect gift comes undeservedly to me from you, Lord, as an act of love and grace. Such extravagant generosity threatens to turn my head, tempting me to think too highly of myself, too critically of others; so I ask you to give me a humble heart, a heart for Jesus, a heart open to Truth. Make real in me the Spirit of Truth, which urges me to seek you wherever you may be found. Transform me, Lord, into the person who lived in your imagination even before I was born. Be near me, Jesus. Be very near. Amen.

Satan is after us!   *November 13*   *Mark 1:9*

"Jesus was baptized by John in the Jordan. When he came up out of the water, he saw the heavens immediately open and the Spirit descending like a dove; and a voice came from heaven, "Thou art my beloved son; with thee I am well pleased. The Spirit immediately drove him into the wilderness and he was there for forty days, tempted by Satan."

Sadly most people do not know much about Satan. Although there has always been a curiosity about Satan, most people do not know much about him. Many get their information about him from unreliable sources such as poorly researched books, television, or movies. Believe it or not, these sources don't always give accurate portrayals of the subject matter. Now don't get me wrong, I have seen a few movies, which I think, depict accurately who Satan is, but most don't.

This story from the 1st chapter of Mark, also found in Matthew 4 and Luke 4, gives a pretty good picture of Satan and how he operates. Satan confronted Jesus in this story as he confronts us even today. You will find him attacking you through both your strengths and weaknesses. There is a wonderful movie, which shows how Satan attacks us through our vainly and pride. You could also add your own favorite form of these two vices, you know what they are, stubbornness, a desire to be self-sufficient, to run our life the way we wish; our need to be accepted by others, or admired, looked up to and made over; our desire to be rich and famous, knowledgeable, smart and witty, or powerful, even our worry!

There are as many ways for Satan to enter us, as there are people available to be entered! The apostle Paul says in Romans 7:21, *"I find it to be a law - whenever I do good, evil lies close at hand."* I think that if you will examine your life you will discover that every time you have tried to do good evil tried to somehow tear down your well-meaning efforts. You volunteer to serve your church and immediately are beset with conflicts in your schedule or nagging doubts about your abilities or fitness for service. We can see evil all around us every day in a multitude of ways. We as Christians need to learn to follow Jesus' example in the wilderness – Jesus resisted Satan and so must we through the power of the Holy Spirit.

Father God, I come before your presence asking for your protection and guidance, for evil does indeed lie all around and I am out maneuvered; out done at every turn. Will you remind me as often as needed that, for the believer, all battles are spiritual battles? That I alone can never out wit evil nor was I meant to? Remind me that I have an advocate seasoned in battle who stands ever ready to come to my aid - Jesus! Let me not be too proud or foolish. In Jesus. Amen.

Satan is too strong for us **November 14** *Mark 1:13*

"Jesus was in the wilderness 40 days, tempted by Satan; the angels waited on Him."

Yesterday I mentioned that many people do not know much about Satan and the image that most have comes from Hollywood. Not only that, others don't even believe Satan exists! In learning how to deal with Satan we must realize that "Satan is too strong for us alone!" Now what I mean is that Satan has been around since the beginning; who knows for sure how long - that fact alone should tell us that he has perfected his ability to trick us with his deceit. So don't underestimate his power over you, but also don't underestimate the power of God!

Mark tells us that, *"Jesus was in the wilderness 40 days, tempted by Satan;* (then comes the important part) *and the angels waited on Him."* As we read the temptation story found in the first chapter of Mark or Matthew and Luke 4 we clearly understand that God allowed Jesus to be tempted by Satan. As a mater of fact, verse12 states, *"The Spirit drove Jesus into the wilderness."* After all, Jesus was not only divine, He was human and thank God for that! For if Jesus had lived his whole life and never been tempted, how could he have known what it was like to be us? The part of the story I like best comes at the end of verse 13, *"And the Angels waited on Him."*

In the end we discover that God may have allowed the Spirit to drive Jesus into the wilderness and Jesus may have allowed himself to be tempted but he was never alone, God was watching and had His Angels come minister to Jesus. After the Last Supper Jesus predicts Peter's denial. Peter argued but Jesus said, *"Simon, Simon, Satan has demanded to have you to sift you like wheat."* And then comes the key, *"But I have prayed for you that your faith may not fail."* The point of the story is not that Satan tempts us, but that God is more powerful and will watch over us just as he watched over Jesus. Jesus will pray for our faith as he did for Simon's. We are not in this battle with Satan alone; we have Jesus.

Father God, so often I am tempted to believe that I am all alone in the most difficult moments of my life. Forgive me for believing that you would leave me thus. Such indifference is impossible for you, Father God. I know. Keep me ever in your watchful gaze for I am weak and the Adversary knows just what lies are meant for me to hear, to take to heart. Guard me and guide me for I am easily swayed but I am still yours. In your care I can do anything, even this. In Jesus' Name. Amen.

"And the Spirit drove Jesus out into the wilderness to be tempted by Satan."

The last two days we have been looking at the temptation story of Jesus. We have mentioned that Satan does exist so we best learn how to deal with him; we also mentioned that Satan has been around a long time and is smarter than those of us who have been on this earth God created a few decades. One more point I think we all need to be aware of when it comes to temptation: there is nothing wrong with temptation!

Temptation is simply a reality of life that we cannot avoid. You go on vacation to Florida and are anxious to spend a little time on the beach and come face to face with someone who is nude, or close to it. There is a temptation to lust, however we can decide to resist; when we do we are strengthened. There is a Biblical principle here: The more we give into temptation the easier it gets and the weaker we become – but the more we resist temptation the easier that gets and the stronger we become.

I mentioned yesterday about the dispute the disciples were having about who will be considered the greatest in the kingdom. That is our temptation also. We want to be considered greater than someone else, why else would we gossip and criticize those around us if we are not saying; "The things they do are more sinful than the things I do!" As I said, there is nothing wrong with temptation but there is plenty wrong with the way we might deal with it. Greatness does not come from being honored and recognized but through humility. "The one who is a servant of all" is the one considered great in the Kingdom. Temptation was used on the disciples – it was used on Jesus – and you can bet it will be used on us! Our concern should not be "will we be tempted" but how do we handle it? Can we resist the devil? Alone we stand no chance, with God, With Jesus, With the Holy Spirit we can resist!

Sovereign Lord, in your wisdom you made the world to operate as it does. For this I am grateful. I know that temptation is a part of being human and that even what can undo me in your hands can teach me wonderful and lasting lessons about myself and thankfully about you. Watch over me for I am weaker than I know and evil is vastly more clever, more deceitful. Believing what is bad about me is so much easier than believing what is good. Protect me from unworthy thoughts and deeds. Remind me I was, at least in your estimation, once worth your life. In Jesus' name. Amen.

Everything Good   November 16   Geneses 1:31

"God saw everything He made and everything He made was good."

Do you know what confuses many new Christians, even old ones? The misconception that being Christian means to become religious. What I mean is that many see it as doing something or accomplishing something or changing their whole being so that they are now sinless! Nothing could be further from the truth! We are sinful and that is that! But we are creatures created by God and once our God created us and everything else he looked at it and said it was Good! (Genesis 1:31) Now that means "Warts and all".

Hears my take: if you see that being a Christian means changing your whole being you will fail and fail miserably! You see, we are not experts on human change, but God is so if you want to be changed you best call on Jesus otherwise you will just be wasting your time. Now the other thing I see is that if you believe you must develop a life of sinlessness, you will end up becoming just what God does not want you to be! People who strive for perfection usually end up measuring their accomplishments against others who have not accomplished as much. They end up being critical and judgmental of the other person.

Can we talk? – Jesus do not judge. Well, what he really said was, "Don't judge unless you wish for God to judge you on the final day in the same manner!" Now one reason for us to not judge is because if you look for fault in another, you will find it – remember we are sinners! I have lived my whole life trying to be what God has called me to be. But I guarantee you that you will not have to look very far to find fault with me. Now truth is, I am better that I used to be, but I still have far to go. The important thing about being a Christian is not "do we sin or not" but whom do we serve? Who is our savior? Who do we go to for answers to life? If we say "Christ" then we are Christians. No one will ever be perfect and no one will ever do anything perfectly. But we can belong to Christ where we will be counted as righteous by God's grace through Him.

God of all things, I stand in awe of your mighty power and benevolent grace. Give me a heart for you. We are competitive creatures, we human beings you've made in your likeness. We are ever like little children competing for your attention, your approval. I too am guilty of showing off to impress you or hiding when I've done wrong. When I most need you my sin requires I avoid you and I turn away ashamed. Remind me that you Father never turn from me your good creation, your hapless child. I want to come home. In Jesus' name. Amen.

"Through Jesus we have access to one Spirit - the Father - you're no longer strangers and aliens, but citizens with the saints and members of the household of God, built upon the foundation of the Apostles and prophets, with Jesus, himself as the cornerstone. In Him, the whole structure is joined together and grows into a Holy Temple in the Lord: in Him you are built together spiritually into a dwelling place for God."

Here in Ephesians we find some of the most extraordinary words in all of scripture, *"In Jesus, we will grow into a Holy Temple – a dwelling place for God!"* Is there anything more wonderful? In Jesus we become a dwelling place for God himself in the Temple of ourselves! But the problem is most want to build their own temples designed they way they want! And end up building temples with walls of our own weaknesses: prejudice and hate, fear and doubt, worry and anxiety, selfishness and pride! God cannot live in such a place. When we attempt to build our own temples apart from God we are opening ourselves to the naked truth. We want to build walls to keep people out! We want to exclude all those who do not think like we do, look like we do, and value what we value!

Certainly we cannot attach the name of Jesus to a place like that. It is in Jesus that we have access to God's Spirit. It is in Jesus that we are no longer strangers and aliens, but citizens with the rest of the saints. It is in Jesus that we all come together and grow into a Holy Temple. Don't wall yourself away from Jesus with your hate and fear. Christ came to destroy the walls that separate us from one another. He came to tear down the walls we build locking God in and aliens and strangers out! He died to bring all his children back into the household of God. Walls of prejudice and stubbornness and hate, walls of self-righteousness and un-forgiveness and fear: in the strong name of Jesus, we say, "Come down you barriers to God's will for our lives!" Open your life to him and allow him to build your life into a Holy Temple, a spiritual dwelling place.

Almighty God, Sovereign Lord, as I consider your invitation to live in my house with me, I am overwhelmed, not just with awe and excitement, but with anxiety and dread. This place is a mess; good intentions lie everywhere undone, hurtful words and thoughts still linger in the air, I'm not exactly sure where my Bible is. Truth is I'm not ready, Father God. I'll never be worthy to be your housemate. There it is; I've said it. I don't deserve the blessing you've been to me not in the past nor in the future. Oh, my Jesus, I took and took and never gave back. Can you ever forgive me? You have! Already! Is that a knock on my door? Is that really you? Hold on to your hat, Lord, I'm opening the door! Welcome Home to me, Jesus. Amen, Most Gracious Father, Amen.

Faith vs. Fear   November 18   Matthew 14:31

Jesus says to Peter, "You of little faith, why did you doubt?"

This story from the Bible occurs after Jesus has fed 5,000 and has sent the disciples to the other side of the lake. He then goes up on the mountainside to pray and be alone with God, His Father. When morning comes, Jesus walks out onto the lake to meet the disciples as they ply their nets. They are frightened thinking they have seen a ghost. Jesus reassures them that it is he and to not fear. Peter then asks Jesus to command him to come to him on the water. Jesus does and Peter begins walking on water! However, a big wind comes up distracting Peter and he begins to sink. Jesus responds, "You of little faith, why did you doubt?"

This story illustrates that fear is the opposite of faith. Fear caused Peter to take his eyes off Jesus. Remember the acronym for FAITH? (Forgetting All I Trust Him!) Belief can change everything! It is a powerful word. We can say that the world is round and rotates around the sun and science can prove that. Believing is different. There is another side to belief: trusting when we don't have proof. An example where believing can affect outcomes is in sports. The national polls' rankings predict, "This team is much better than that team." We assume that the outcome will be that the better team will win. But not always! Sometimes the lesser team will have such a strong belief in itself that it will win in spite of the polls! I have seen it happen many times. I am sure that you have also.

There is genuine power in believing! In the 9th chapter of Mark, Jesus says, *"All things are possible for the one who believes."* It is truly amazing what belief in God can accomplish. There have been times in our lives that we have stood in Simon Peter's shoes and cried out, *"Lord, save me!"* Like Peter, we have felt His loving hand reach out to catch us. When will we learn? When will we stop being afraid? How many times has Jesus said of us, *"Oh ye of little faith."* Real faith holds onto beliefs even when our feelings tell us otherwise. Real faith believes in spite of our moods. Real faith dispels our fear, our distractions by the storms of life.

God of All Grace, in your great providence you made me; in your great mercy you saved me by faith in Jesus who loved me and gave his life for me. By your grace I live as one who believes in Jesus as Lord and Savior. Then my workday commences and thus distracted I forget whose I am; I forget why I am here. I become a creature made in the world's image, directed by the world's demands. Lord, save me for I've lost sight of you once again. Oh Lord, increase my faith. By your power, sweet Jesus, may I live, as I believe. In Jesus, Amen.

"A great windstorm arose on the sea, so great that the boat was being swamped by the waves."

Peace. How would you define that word? It can mean a lot of things to a lot of people according to the situation. If you have a colicky baby who has been crying for 5 or 6 hours then you might define peace as silence! If you work for a super critical boss who is constantly putting you down you might define peace as having a boss who listens and appreciates you. If you are a young parent with children involved in activities like soccer, dance lessons, piano lessons, and the like you might define peace as having thirty minutes with no interruptions! If your life has been filled with busyness you might define peace as finally being retired. If you are in a nursing home staring at four walls twenty-four seven you might define peace as a visit from someone you love.

No matter how young or old you are, no matter where you are in the stages of life, there comes a time when we want peace; we crave peace even just one moment of it! Peace is a precious commodity and most of the time it is too hard to come by, isn't it? There is so much in life that tries to rob us of our peace. In the eight chapter of Matthew we find the story of the storm which Jesus "Stilled." This storm robbed the disciples of their "peace" and they were frightened. Stress has a way of doing that, doesn't it?

I have been on the lake in my boat when a storm suddenly arose and can vouch for those disciples, it can be very frightening. You become so tense that the peace that one feels by being on the lake quickly disappears! I found myself praying harder than usual for the Lord to get me safely to shore. It is in moments like these, that we discover the true meaning of peace. There is no peace apart from Jesus and with Jesus you can have peace even in the worst of life's storms. He is there for you anytime you call on his name, waiting to bring you His peace.

Father God, Creator/Redeemer, Oh, Lord, I kneel before you knowing that the peace that eludes me comes only from you as a gift of fellowship with the Holy Spirit. Give me the grace to seek your face every day of my life. Help me to cultivate my own spiritual rest. Remind me of this truth: if I wait until my work is done to seek you I will never stop for my work is never finished. I need you to remind me, my Great Friend, how my value is much greater than what I do; that I was made for a greater world than this, I was made for Eternity. May the Peace that passes understanding grace my life. In Jesus. Amen.

Lack Nothing!   *November 20*   *Deuteronomy 8:7f*

*"For the LORD your God is bringing you into a good land, a land with flowing streams,
with springs and underground waters welling up in valleys and hills, a land of wheat
and barley, of vines and fig trees and pomegranates, a land of olive trees and honey, a
land where you may eat bread without scarcity, where you will lack nothing, a land
whose stones are iron and from whose hills you may mine copper. You shall eat your fill
and bless the LORD your God for the good land that he has given you."*

These words tell of God bringing the Israelites into a land that lacks nothing! A beautiful land filled with beautiful things of nature. The question that arises out of that might be - why? Did these people deserve this? Well let's take a look. When Moses led the Israelites out of Egypt and brought them to the Red Sea, did they trust God for their deliverance from Pharaoh? No, they feared they would all die. When they crossed the Sea and camped out at the foot of Mount Sinai and Moses ascended to receive the Ten Commandments, did they trust God?

No, they began to question God and ask if they had been brought out to this desert to die. Once they reached the Promised Land and found it inhabited by "giants" so the report says, did they trust God? No, they feared they would all die in battle against these giants. So, why did God do this for them? Because they were His chosen ones, not because of anything they did, but because He chose them and loved them and was faithful to them.

In that sense, we are just like those Israelites, aren't we? We continue to sin and are unfaithful to God even as He is faithful to us. We continue to refuse to trust in a God who has already brought more miracles into our lives and blessed us with more than we deserve. And although we fail Him, He remains faithful to us. Not because of what we do - but because of who God is. He gave us the land we live in - He made us who we are. He created our life, our brain and our will and He continues to choose us and watch over us. As you think about your life you might want to recall your blessings, that because of God you lack nothing!

*Faithful and Loving God, Thank you for the evidence of your Word
which reveals to me the utter truth of your gracious steadfastness to those whom
you chose out of your great grace as your people – even when they failed over
and again to put their trust in you. I too am yours in Christ and I too fail to
trust you utterly. Forgive me and enable me to be a blessing once more. In
Jesus' name. Amen.*

Called to be Saints   *November 21*   *Romans 1:7*

"To all God's beloved in Rome who are called to be saints."

One Sunday a year is set-aside on the Christian calendar to honor the saints of the church. Most people understand saints to be those ordained by the church to be saints because of the wonderful work they have done in their lifetime - like Saint Paul or Saint Teresa. However, the Apostle Paul himself speaks of saints in terms of being a Christian - belonging to Christ. He opens most every one of his letters to "the saints" of that community. Believers are called saints. In other words - all those in the church - those who have given their life to Christ, who trust in Him as Lord and Savior are saints.

Saint means one who is holy or sacred, set apart. How are we saints? Jesus said in the Beatitudes, Matthew 5, verses 3 and following, "Blessed are the poor in spirit, the meek; those who hunger for righteousness, those who are merciful, those who are peacemakers, blessed are you who stand firm when people persecute you for my sake." A saint is any person who trusts in Jesus, anyone who submits his or her will to God. When life comes at you and hits you hard, instead of blaming God, a saint gives thanks for they know that in those moments God is present, giving the strength to carry on.

That is what it means to trust. A saint does not put their trust in money or worldly things, but in God. It does no good to say you trust and then surrender to the fears and anxieties of life. A saint stands firm in the faith, going beyond trusting in God to surrendering the will to God and allowing God to substitute it with His. The world wants us to design our faith to follow it; as saints we do not follow anyone or anything but Jesus. He is our truth. He is our life. He is our salvation. A saint stands firm on the foundation of faith that God has given through Jesus no matter how difficult that may be. It is Jesus who makes us holy and set apart.

Oh, God, All I ever wanted to be, holy and sacred, set apart for you, beloved, if only in your eyes, you have made possible in Christ Jesus. Washed in the blood of the Lamb; reconciled to my Holy Father! How do I say thanks? Are there words enough, deeds enough, prayers enough to ever express my gratitude? I am willingly in your debt, Father. Speak the word; I have ears only for you, my precious Jesus, my incomparable Friend. Thanks be to God. Amen.

Who is this Jesus?   November 22   John 1:14

"The Word became flesh and lived among us, and we have seen His glory, the glory as of a Father's only Son, full of grace and truth."

Who is this Christ whom we worship? One of the difficulties we all face as Christians is discovering who Christ is. We all want to make Christ be who we want Him to be and we want the church to exist for us. A few scriptures should give us a Biblical image that is helpful. John 1:14 states, *"the Word became flesh . . . full of grace, and truth."* In the Old Testament, we see hundreds of references of God as the "Good Shepherd." That theme is prevalent in the New Testament as well and attached to Christ. Jesus is the "Good Shepherd" who knows and loves His sheep. At the end of John's gospel, Jesus calls on His disciples to love and tend to His sheep - His little children. Jesus was willing to lay down His life for His sheep.

But then in Matthew 25:31 and following, we find a disturbing passage concerning sheep. There we read that at the end of time, Jesus will separate the sheep from the goats. *"On the right he will place the sheep, and on the left the goats. The sheep will inherit the Kingdom of Heaven."* Now I say disturbing because we all want a meek Jesus, who overlooks all our faults, is blind to our shortcomings, ignores our meanness. We don't like to think of Him as judge, but judge He will be!

He will judge us according to how we have cared for others. *"I was hungry, you fed me; a stranger, you welcomed me; naked, you gave me clothes; sick, you cared for me."* At times we all fail and must fall upon His mercy. But His mercy does not give us an excuse. His Kingdom will finally come in its fullness. And although at the present time we live in two kingdoms, this world and the Kingdom of God, we are called to give up the ways of the world. There is no place in God's Kingdom for pettiness, selfishness, or pride. Don't give yourself to your feelings of selfishness, anger, loneliness, want, need, and desire. Instead, give yourself to Jesus and live a life of love and forgiveness for that is who He has been to you.

Oh, God, Shepherd of My Soul, I want to know you better, serve you better, trust you more. Yet, I am still a sheep prone to wander, prone to get lost following my own way or the lead of others as lost as I am. Come to me as in Christ full of grace and truth for I am trapped in a quagmire of my own sin and home in Jesus' keeping is far, far away. Come, my Jesus, how I need you so. Come my Good Shepherd. Amen.

"So have no fear of them; for nothing is covered up that will not be uncovered, and nothing secret that will not become known. What I say to you in the dark, tell in the light; and what you hear whispered, proclaim from the housetops."

How many of you like practical jokes? Well, while many people like practical jokes - not many like to be the brunt of these jokes. When I turned fifty, my wife and some members of our church threw me a party. People brought gag gifts. One gift was a fake leg that you close up in the trunk of a car, which gives the appearance that someone is trapped in the trunk. My son took the foot, let it stick out of his trunk and parked the car on the property next to the street. An older couple called the police! The police actually got a kick out of it but the couple did not.

There is a sharp contrast between illusion and truth isn't there? There is a sharp contrast between the illusion of self-control and the realization that our hope lies in Jesus. Many think that they have control of their life and future only to find themselves on their deathbed frightened about what is to come, frightened because of what they did or did not do in their lifetime. In this scripture from Matthew, Jesus brings into the light of day the sharp contrasts between those who value the things of this world and those who value faith.

Christians should live by a different set of rules! On the one hand, we believe in a changing world - but on the other, we believe some things stay the same. The prisons are full of people who would never do anything wrong if they knew others would find out about it. However, under the cover of darkness and in secret, they have robbed and stolen. Many of these thieves were members in good standing of churches and religions, at least on the surface. In other words, they appear to be good, upstanding citizens but secretly they are totally different. Why did they rob and steal? They did it because they placed their value and faith in the things of this world. And if the truth be known, many of us fall for that. Many have placed their faith in the things of this world falling for the illusion that worldly wealth can take care of us only to realize *"nothing can be kept secret from God - ever!"*

All Knowing, All Powerful God, I live my life out loud in believed silence, Father, but you hear, you hear. I live my full-lit life in believed darkness, but you see Father, you see. Forgive me and open my ears and eyes to the truth about myself. Let me hear whispered the truth about Jesus and let me Lord have the grace to shout it from the housetops. In Jesus' name. Amen.

Faith Vs Law   *November 24*   *Galatians 2:16*

"We have come to believe in Christ Jesus, so that we might be justified by faith in Christ and not by doing the works of the law, because no one will be justified by the works of the law."

In reading Paul's letters you come away with the overwhelming message that Paul felt we are justified by faith in Jesus and no other way! Paul makes that clear here; in the seventh chapter of Romans he states that all the law does is to point out our shortcomings! That it is impossible for anyone to live perfectly before a Holy and Almighty God. But he was thankful for the law for without it he would not have known "what it was to covet" had the law not pointed that out for him. Paul then pointed to Jesus as the one who saves us from sin and ourselves.

We want God to see how "good" we have been and all the hard work we have put in to accomplish "good deeds" for His kingdom. We want at least for the church to notice and give us some appreciation! To be noticed and honored for our "good works" by those who hold in their hands the task of overseeing God's kingdom on earth. Some even say of those who have diligently served God's church, "I know that they will go to heaven because of all the good they have done!" But Paul says "No"; you will not earn heaven on "good works" because no one will be justified by works of the law. Instead, you will be justified through faith in Jesus.

You see if we depend on our good works, it is our voice we follow for we are making our own way. But if we depend on "being justified" by grace through faith in Christ, it is his voice we follow and trust. So what will it be? Will we continue to do good works to be justified, or will we do works because we love the Lord and wish to continue his work on earth showing his compassion and forgiveness, his love and grace? When we live by faith in the Son of God, it is to no longer ourselves that people see, but Christ who lives in us! It is no longer our deeds, but the deeds of Jesus who dwells in our hearts.

Most Gracious and Merciful Father, I am so sorry that Jesus' life has made so little impact on my need for attention, for affirmation. You would think I am a nobody - so intent am I to prove otherwise with my well-publicized good deeds. The disciples' competitive spirit is alive and well in me. Would that it were not so! But it is. How can the Divine Yes from Calvary's Hill be too small a Word, too small an act of Divine Love to fill to the utmost my unworthy heart? Perhaps I am too busy earning my way to take hold of the greatest gift of all. Face down in shame; I now look, at long last, UP! Thank you, Jesus. Amen.

Christian Seasons   November 25   Matthew 1:23

"A virgin shall conceive and bear a son, and they shall call his name Emmanuel," which means, "God is with us."

People, as long as recorded history can tells us, have observed seasons of fasting and festivals of worshiping God. They felt that God had appointed and created these times in order to worship and praise Him better. Jesus observed festivals in His day. The New Testament church transformed these festivals from the Old Testament and gave them new meaning and purpose - pointing to Jesus: His birth, life, death, resurrection, ascension, and promised return. This is the order, which we use and proclaim in the life of the church.

The first is Advent - a season to recall the hope of the coming of Jesus and to look to His coming again. Next is Christmas, the celebration of the birth of Christ: a time to remember His coming into the world and the visit of the shepherds at the stable. Then comes Epiphany, the day for celebrating God's manifestation to all people shown in the story of the Wise Men from the East. The season of LENT follows: the season of Spiritual discipline and preparation for the coming of the death and resurrection of Jesus. Lent begins with Ash Wednesday and lasts for 40 days (not counting Sundays). It represents the 40 days Jesus spent in the wilderness.

Holy Week follows which is the week before Easter. Holy Week begins with Palm Sunday, the day Jesus rode into Jerusalem on a donkey. Then Maundy Thursday, the night Jesus was flogged and tried; Good Friday - the day he was put on the Cross; and his burial. Holy Week is a time of remembering and proclaiming the suffering and death of Jesus who atoned us. Easter follows and is the day we celebrated and rejoice in Jesus' resurrection. This season lasts until Pentecost, the day we celebrate the gift of the Holy Spirit to the church. We observe other days also such as the Baptism of our Lord, the Holy Trinity and so forth. But these seven point out the major Seasons of the Christian Year. The purpose for these seasons is to help us focus on the Proclamation of the Gospel and to dedicate and rededicate our lives to the one who gave His life for us.

Lord God, as I begin this the first season of the Christian year help me to recall what God has done for me in His Son Jesus. Thank you for sending your Son, born of a virgin, Emmanuel with us: for He truly came to save us from our sins. Forgive me when I do not recognize or celebrate the significance of Jesus coming into the world or His gift to me. Help me to recall and celebrate each season of the Christian year. I pray in the name of Jesus. Amen.

Thanksgiving: Talents   November 26   Matthew 25:24f

"Then the one who had received the one talent said, 'Master, I knew that you were a harsh man, reaping where you did not sow; so I was afraid, and I hid your talent in the ground. Here is what's yours.' The master replied, 'You wicked and lazy slave! You knew that I reap where I did not sow, and gather where I did not scatter?"

This is the season of thanksgiving - a time we celebrate along with those first pilgrims the blessings God has bestowed upon us. A day and time in which we offer up to God our thanks for all the times that He has seen us through when life delivered us a difficult blow. In the twenty-fifth chapter of Matthew we find the text about the master who was going on a trip. He gave to three of his servants a certain amount of money. To one, he gave 10 talents, to another 5 and to a third one. When he returned, the servants with 10 and 5 talents had invested the money wisely and gave the master twice as much back.

He commended them for their work. The servant who had been entrusted with one bag - had hidden it in the ground and returned it to the master saying He knew the master was a harsh man so he hid the talents and returned it to him. The master was irate and calls him a wicked, lazy servant! He then took away that which he had and threw him into utter darkness saying, *"To those who have much will be given. To those who have not even that which they have will be taken away."*

The lesson from this parable is: life is not to be hoarded - it is to be lived. Blessings are not to be thrown away but shared. Talents are not given to be kept for our use only, but to be used for God's Kingdom. We all need a way to say thank you for all that God has done and given us - using what He has given to glorify His kingdom and His people is what He wants. The world measures success in terms of what one accumulates - God measures success by what we do with all that we have - because everything we have is a gift from Him - we cannot take credit for the mind we were given or our blessings in life. God has truly blessed us. Let us be thankful and share all that God has given.

Oh, God of All Good an Perfect Gifts, You have blessed me in so many ways but I, so like the unfaithful servant, have hidden my blessings away, burying them in the ground until your return. Thinking I would please you, I have only revealed my ignorance. Forgive me. For another chance I would even give my life. Let me not have you come only to find me failing you once more. For Jesus' sake I pray. Amen.

"You are the salt of the earth. But what happens when salt has lost its taste?"

Here in Matthew, Jesus compares us, His disciples, to salt. He says this right after his teaching on the Beatitudes. I guess it would be good for us to first examine what salt is used for if in fact we are to be compared to salt! I grew up on a farm and we had a little shed which housed most of our tools and in that barn was a salt trough made of wood. We would lay a ham in the trough and rub salt on the ham every so often until it was considered "cured". At that time we would hang it from the rafters until we were ready to cut it for breakfast ham and serve. Salt preserved the ham and kept it from spoiling.

Now of course salt is also used most especially for flavor. Have you ever tasted food that had no salt whatsoever? Salt gives flavor to food. Jesus said that we are like that in relationship to him. We give flavor to God's kingdom. But what if we are like the salt that has lost its taste? The main reason salt lost its taste in Jesus' day was because since it was so valuable and expensive to purchase, some vendors tried to stretch what they had to make a little more money. They would do so by adding to the salt something that looked like salt, possibly sand. Such actions would cause the salt to lose its taste and become useless.

What if we were to add something to God's Holy Word that is not there in order for his Word to become more agreeable to what we think? Jesus said then we would no longer be of use. We cannot mix the views of this world with the Laws of God and remain pure. We cannot mix any other ingredient to what God has already given. Not that we must be pure and sinless, that we cannot do and He does not expect us to be. If that were the case then we would not need His Righteousness. We are not to pollute God's Word, but allow it to remain pure and Holy. So be salt and be pure!

Father God, Savior and Lord, I am guilty of succumbing to fear and doubt. Sometimes my emotions rule over me and I cave in under the pressure of worldly priorities and goals. Forgive me for the times I have allowed my desire to be accepted and loved by others to override who I am in Christ Jesus. I have diluted your Word. I have remained silent when I needed to speak a word of caution or guidance or truth. Forgive me and strengthen me by your Spirit. Let me be salt for you! I can if you help me. Otherwise I am undone and no use to anyone least of all to you. In the name of Jesus I pray. Amen.

Light   *November 28*   *Matthew 5:14*

"You are the light of the world. A city built on a hill cannot be hid."

In this verse from Matthew Jesus compares us to light calling us "the light of the world." After I graduated from college I taught school in Southeast Missouri. We lived in Malden, which is located at the top of the boot hill close to the New Madrid earthquake fault. If you are driving from the east to town you find some rich soil, but the stickiest I have ever encountered when wet; we called it "gumbo". You get it on your shoes and for the most part they are ruined! Just as you drive into the city limits of Malden you come up a small hill and all the sudden the land is sand. The small hill is actually one of the faults caused by the earthquake many years ago.

Anyway back to my point! From my house in Malden I could clearly see a ridge about 15-20 miles away. The land around town is very flat and the ridge is called Crowley's Ridge, which was formed by the glaciers back during the Ice Age. Any little light on that ridge can be seen for miles and miles away. Dexter, Missouri is about 18 miles to the north. I can remember driving there at night and it looked like a beacon of light in the dark night sky.

Jesus was reminding his followers that we are to be a beacon of light for all the world to see. We are to be let others see our devotion to our Lord; we are to let others know Jesus has made a difference in our lives; we are to let our faces shine bright that others may see the joy in our hearts – a witness to the presence of Jesus, our Lord and Savior. So don't play it safe and hide your devotion, venture out into the real world and *"Let your light shine before others, so that they may see your works and give glory to your Father in Heaven."* After all, that is who we are. Jesus' "light to the world".

Almighty God, Giver of every good and perfect Gift, Source of all Light and Love, I your servant come before your presence with a glad and joyful heart knowing you desire for your children only what is good. Help me to see the potential blessing in all circumstances, in all people whose paths I cross or who cross mine. Let me see Jesus in every face. I am asking for the floodgates to be opened I know! But this world so needs a loving Savior to save it and a willing soul to spread your grace. Empowered by your Light to be Light I can do anything for you, my beloved Lord. ANYTHING! In Jesus, I pray. Amen.

"When Israel was a child, I loved him, and out of Egypt I called my son. The more I called the more they went from me… Yet it was I who taught Ephraim to walk, I took them up in my arms; but they did not know that I healed them. I led them with cords of kindness, with bands of love. I was to them like those who lift infants to their cheeks. I bent down to them and fed them…. How can I give you up, Ephraim? How can I hand you over, O Israel? My heart recoils within me; my compassion grows warm and tender. I will not execute my fierce anger; I will not again destroy Ephraim; for I am God, the Holy One in your midst. Go after the LORD… and I will return you to your homes, says the LORD."

Have you ever wondered about God's compassion? Wondered how much he cares about you or if he cares at all? Well just read these verses from Hosea. There you will not only see God's compassion, you will feel his despair over the waywardness of his people, us! This scripture uses the love of a parent for their child as a metaphor for God and his people. It recalls the time when God, the parent, taught the child to walk and how he fed his child and took care of them. But even as God was caring for the child, the child was bent on turning away from God and molding his life in the image of this world.

The scripture from Hosea recalls the many times that Israel and it's people turned from God and how he continued to take them up into his arms and heal them and give them his love. The real picture of God's compassion comes in verse eight after the scripture sites all of the waywardness of God's people, "How can I give you up, Ephraim? How can I hand you over, O Israel? My heart recoils within me; my compassion grows warm and tender. I will not execute my anger." This reminds me of a passage from Paul's letter to the Romans, 5:8, "But God proves his love for us in that while we were still sinners he gave up His Son, Jesus to die for us." With love and compassion like that how can we possibly not come to God and give our life to Him? Knowing that God has that much love and compassion should give us comfort through all the trials and difficulties of life. Will you think about this truth in your own life?

Almighty God, Merciful Lord, Daddy (Abba) in Heaven, I hear in these verses the anguished heart of a loving parent stricken by the thoughtless acts of a beloved child. I hear the conflicted heart of a long-suffering parent who wishes mightily to let go but cannot lest he die. I easily see myself as fellow sufferer. But I must first see myself as rebellious child in the captive gaze of an omniscient Father, who loves me beyond all things. From such humility I can be the instrument of healing grace; I can give what I have received. Be with me, Father, always. Amen.

"I want all of you to be free from worry. An unmarried man worries about how to please the Lord. But a married man has more worries."

Christians are to live in this world but are not to become a part of this world; be in the world but not of the world. This can be misunderstood to mean that we are to back away from the world with an attitude of "do not touch"! In order to live in this world we have to be a part of it, just not become a part of it. Not allow the ways of this world to rub off on us and follow the teachings of the world. Instead follow the lead of God.

Paul appears to be telling us in the above verses to not marry for fear of having too many worries, which will take away our ability to please the Lord. He is just being realistic in observing that when one is married one has more distractions that lure them away from pleasing God: more things, which call for their attention. Like trying to appease a spouse or help raise a child. Trying to provide for a family and make enough money to clothe and feed and keep a roof over their heads; whereas the unmarried man does not have as many worries to distract.

Paul is just making it clear that we are to keep focused on the real thing, God; that it is important to keep God first, even in a marriage, especially in a marriage. It does not matter how talented you are or how organized you have become, if God is not first in your life, your marriage, your family, your life will not be ideal. The important thing is to put God first and all else will fall into place.

Almighty God, Sovereign Lord, I come before you with a heavy heart for I know that I have honored you with my lips, nor my life. I have not asked your input in matters of great concern. I have sought to run my life as though I was orphaned with no one's counsel to seek or to consider in my decisions but my own. Forgive my arrogance and pride. Restore my ancient and dust covered faith. Give me a heart for Jesus for without You I am lost and my relationships are built on sand. Have mercy on me and set me right. In Jesus. Amen.

Advent 1: Hope   *December 1*   *Luke 1:26f*

"In the sixth month the angel Gabriel was sent by God to a town in Galilee called Nazareth, to a virgin engaged to a man whose name was Joseph, of the house of David. The virgin's name was Mary… and you will conceive and bear a son and call him Jesus and he will be the son of the most high God."

Today we celebrate the first Sunday of Advent. Churches around the world light the candle of HOPE reminding us of the Hope that came that first Christmas in the form of a child, wrapped in cloths, lying in a manger. People for generations have turned to scripture to discover God. Others have been turned off by the evil they see in the world and claim there is no God. They see the destruction of hurricanes and storms and question how God could allow that to happen. There are terrorists using the name of God as the reason for their acts of terror. Is that what God is like? I not only hope not, I believe not! So how can we know God?

Well, take a look again at Luke 1:26-28. How can we know Almighty God? These verses tell us. Can the tiny human brain that has trouble understanding computers ever hope to comprehend the wonders of the Most High God? No, but fortunately, we don't have to. As scripture said, *"God sent his son to us."* God came to a humble young girl and her husband in a village named Nazareth. He didn't come to the family of some philosopher or to Caesar or to mighty rulers; he came to a humble young couple, Joseph and Mary of Nazareth.

I find that extraordinary! No wonder the pagans of this world reject such nonsense. Who among us can resist talk of angels and humble maidens and divine revelations!!! Then a phone call interrupts our peaceful reverie. The news comes of the tragic illness of someone that we love. The world ever intrudes even in moments of sheer Presence. Yet, it is on such a foundation that our faith rests. God will remain a mystery to us, but hope is found in the birth of his son in that stable. How very much the Almighty and Everlasting God must care for us to come in such a way.

Lord God, I come asking forgiveness for I know how I have failed you. I peeked. Just a glimpse of my sinful self moves me to tears. Have mercy, O Lord. For you came in human form to bring me hope yet I have tried to produce hope on my own. You came that I might know you and yet I have preferred to know other things; forgive me. Come into my life this Advent season in the way you know is best with thundering voice or the smallest whisper and bring me your Hope. I pray in the name of Jesus. Amen.

God has Plans for us   *December 2*   *Ephesians 2:19f*

"We are fellow citizens with the saints and members of the household of God, built upon the foundation of the apostles and prophets, Christ Jesus being the cornerstone, in whom the whole structure is joined together and grows into a holy temple; in whom you also are built for a dwelling place of God in the Spirit."

In the second chapter of Ephesians we find Paul speaking of the plans God has for us. God has designed our lives and his plans will come to fulfillment unless we step in the way. He wants us to see ourselves as he sees us, as members of the very household of God. He desires for us to become a dwelling place of God in the Spirit. What an extraordinary destiny! How will we respond? There are obstacles all along the way.

Our own emotions and feelings, our own plans and willfulness, derail our decision. We put them before the fulfillment of God's kingdom. In other words, we put our own desires, wants, and wishes before God's. In this way we become blind to his plans for us. It isn't that we can't see; we choose not to see. However, when we focus on God, on his desire for us, when we entrust our feelings to him, then his Spirit can take us and mold us into the Holy Temple God wishes us to be. Once that occurs we realize that we are not the ones doing "good deeds" for God or anyone else. Rather, it is from his Spirit, which dwells within, that any good can come.

What then is our role? It is to prepare ourselves by relinquishing our wishes, wants, and desires. It is by taking control of our emotions and feelings and turning them over to God who will mold us into a dwelling place. Then, we are open to experience God in wonderful ways. When we gather in His name we feel His presence, in worship, in fellowship, in Bible Study, and in the Sacraments. Many say that they feel God's presence the most during special services such as Christmas Eve or Holy Week services. However, the goal is not a one-time experience, but a giving of ourselves to Him in such a complete way that we in fact belong to Him. Fulfillment occurs. Destiny comes.

Lord God, I come in prayer knowing how foolish it is for me to assume that I can somehow control my own emotions or my own actions. I know that I was made a part of the household of God when I gave of my life to you. Help me to release my feelings and emotions so that I can become the Dwelling Place you designed me to be. I know that you have plans for me. Give me the wisdom to embrace those plans, the grace to be content. In his name. Amen.

Advent: Jesus is coming   *December 3*   *Malachi 3: 1f*

"I'm sending my messenger to prepare the way before me, and the Lord whom you seek will suddenly come to His temple. The messenger of the Covenant in whom you delight - indeed, He is coming, says the Lord of Hosts. But who can endure the day of His coming, and who can stand when He appears?"

Can you imagine a life without Christ? The scripture from *Malachi* is a prophecy of the coming of Jesus. It is used often during the season of Advent when we look forward to the birth of the Christ Child. *"He is coming, says the Lord of Hosts. Who can endure the day of His coming?"* But what if He had not come? Some in this world truly believe Jesus never came! If that is true, not only is there no Christmas, there is no Easter. There is no "peace on earth, good will to all." There is no forgiveness for your sins. There is no grace. There is no promise of salvation and no eternal life. So *"Who can endure the day of his coming?"*

Those who believe Jesus did come and who surrender their life to him, they can endure the day of his return. What I mean is this. Don't live this life as if Christ never came. Don't live for this world and the things in it or you will surely die spiritually. Live for Christ now. Give him your life before you die. There is no chance after that. Die to the things of this world and be reborn in Christ. Die to fear and worry and anxiety and wants and desires. Die to the "What about me?" way of living. Be reborn in Christ.

It is in Christ and in Christ alone that we are capable of really caring about others, that we are capable of love. It is in Christ and in Christ alone that we can place the needs and desires of others above our own. It is in Christ and Christ alone that we can look past this thing called death and truly live. *"Who can endure His coming?"* Those who accept Jesus, those who believe in His name, those who give Him their life, they (we) shall look forward to that day – "the day of His coming."

Lord God, I thank you for the coming of your precious Son, Jesus. Were it not for his coming, cloaking me in his righteousness, I would be a sinner lost, my birthright as a child of God denied. Help me to focus on His coming during this holy season of Advent. Let me remember all that the Christ Child brought to me; the gift of his life that gave me eternal life; the gift of his birth that gave me hope, the gift of his Spirit that gave me joy everlasting. May I await his coming with joy and praise. In Jesus' name I pray. Amen.

When is God Coming   December 4   Isaiah 64:1

"O that you would tear open the heavens and come down."

Advent is the season when we remember the first coming of our Lord and look forward to his coming again. Every once in a while you hear someone predicting when Jesus is coming again. Back in the 1980's, one group even sold everything they had and went up on a mountaintop to wait. It did not happen. Somehow they explained away their mistake. In the Gospel of Mark we find these words, *"No one knows when God is coming, not even the angels."* But that does not stop people from trying to predict and for good reason. We all want to know, don't we? So we continue to ask, "God, are you coming? And if so, when?"

Isaiah's cry was something like that. He cried out to God in today's text, *"O that you would tear open the heavens and come down."* Isaiah had been yearning for some sign from God because it seemed that God had turned his back on his wayward people. Isaiah wanted them to return to God and he wanted God to somehow help him out. He felt forsaken by God. Have you ever felt that way? Ever blamed God for your misfortunes? I think every believer at one time or another has felt that way. Struggle may very well be a natural part of our spiritual growth.

Truthfully, God never forsakes us but there are times we feel that way. Usually it is because we have fallen into hardships or circumstances, which we can neither predict nor control. Our car quits on the way to work. The Service Manager calls with the bad news. The repairs will cost of hundreds of dollars when we don't have two pennies to rub together. Just when we begin to feel comfortable with our new job, we get laid off. Our spiritual mate in life is called home to God, leaving us to live alone. There are dark moments in our life when we struggle and ask, "God, where are you?" Yet, even if we don't feel it at times, God is with us. When you have moments like that just remember, it is in those times that God comes to heal our wounds. God does not and will not forsake us. Advent reminds us of that truth.

Lord God, there are times when I feel abandoned; even though I know in my heart you would never forsake me. Forgive me. There are times when life takes its terrible toll and I feel so all alone; it is then that I pray, "Oh, that you will tear open the heavens and come down", bringing me your hope, your joy, your very self. Beloved Jesus, draw ever near. Amen.

We are but Clay   December 5   Isaiah 64:8

"Yet, O Lord, you are our Father; we are the clay, and you are our potter; we are all the work of your hand."

One of the hardest realities of life is that bad things happen to everyone, good and bad alike. There are no guarantees that justice in this life will be fair or swift. Sometimes justice will set things straight quickly or it may not be set straight for a long time. Others things will have to wait until God's final judgment. We have to trust that God is in control and continue to be faithful to God's promises.

God promised that he would come and he did, in the form of that little child in a manger. God has promised that he will come again to make all things right and he will. God's job is to work; ours is to trust. Isaiah states that clearly. Though most know that to be true, we find life can color our vision. People misunderstand us. We feel that all our life we have worked to have a good reputation; now it is compromised by gossip or innuendo. Or we have been laid off from our job after working with the same firm most of our life and we don't know where to turn. We know God will take care of us, but we are not as trusting as we would like, the rug has just been pulled out from under us. We hear Isaiah say, *"We are but clay in the Potters hand."* God has come.

That is what Advent is all about; remembering that God came down in the child of Bethlehem and God will come again. For those who are living a life of desperation, for those who feel like they cannot hold on much longer, you need to know, God has not forsaken you! God will come and you shall see his salvation. Just place yourself in his hands and let him mold you into the vessel he has always intended for you to be. You can trust the master potter. Even though we do not know what the future holds, he does. Trust in him with all your might. Just call on Him. He will come into your heart today. He cannot resist even one look of love.

Lord God, you have made plans for my life, but I am weak. I lack the trust I need. Forgive me. Life comes at such a fast pace. I do not know how to deal effectively with all that bombards me. I struggle on forgetting that clay is what I am and clay is meant to be molded. Clay cannot mold itself. Never could, never was meant to. I have lived as though the Master Potter was my nemesis instead of my savior. Come into my heart. Comfort me. I am indeed the work of your loving hands. Sear my soul with this wonderful truth   In the name of Jesus I pray. Amen.

"Do not be afraid, Mary, for you have found favor with God. You will bear a son, and name him Jesus." "He will be great, and will be called the Son of the Most High, and the Lord God will give to him the throne of his ancestor David. And he will reign over the house of Jacob forever, and of his kingdom there will be no end."

The angel announced that God would not be content to communicate with his creation by E-mail or cell phone. He would actually become one of us. This truth is mind-boggling when you think about it. Have we heard the story so many times that we've forgotten what it is saying? God chose to reveal Himself in human flesh! We believe that the God of all creation came to a young girl in a little village called Nazareth and told her she was going to bear a child and that child is to be son of God and the hope of the entire world. That is the message of Christmas.

Many who put their hope in power and possessions soon discover that they are all illusions. There is no guarantee that your possessions will be worth anything tomorrow and power can be stripped as quickly as one company can purchase another. Our pride tries to lead us away from God by telling us that we can do everything on our own. Finally we come to the conclusion that only one thing matters, only one thing is eternal: our relationship with God. Do you know Him?

God came to a humble young girl in the little village of Nazareth and told her she would bear a child and that this child would be His. This child would be the hope of the world. Is he your hope? That's the real question. Jesus can be alive in us today if we open our hearts and surrender our will to Him. Let God come alive in you. We cannot possess God by doing good deeds, but as soon as we open our hearts to Him, God, our Father, will possess us! He will come to us. There is our hope.

Lord God, this Advent season brings me the hope of your Son Jesus. Open my heart to receive him. Give me wisdom to let go of my pride or what ever it is that causes me to depend on myself. Give me the faith to believe that in this child, this Jesus, you sent your hope into the world and that through this hope alone, I have life everlasting. Now and forevermore. In His name. Amen.

"There will be signs in the sun, moon and stars. And on the earth distress among nations confused by the roaring of the sea and the waves."

Advent is a time of getting ready. The word comes from the Latin meaning "coming to". It is a time for preparing our hearts for the Lord who came into our world at Christmas and who is coming again on the last day. Jesus points out signs to come in today's scripture, "there will be signs in the sun, moon and stars; people will fear so greatly that they will faint!" Then *"they will see the Son of Man coming in a cloud with power and great glory."* Quite vivid, isn't it? In a way, it is even scary.

So what should we say about this? Let's acknowledge that some day the Day of Judgment will come. The Bible is very clear about that. I realize that many have tried to make predictions as to when. I pointed out a few days ago one group in Arkansas sold all their possessions and went to a mountaintop to wait the time, which never came. Other groups have made predictions only to see the time come and go without the end occurring. People have short memories, particularly for predictions of when the world will end. History tells us that these predictions have been going on for over 2,000 years. But, no matter how many times people set dates that are never realized, there will those who take them seriously.

It matters not that Christ said that not even he knew the day or the hour. Even the disciples asked this question. And people will continue to ask "when" until the end does come. This is not to take away from Biblical prophecy. There will be an end to this world, as we know it. Science is just as adamant on that point as the Bible. No one knows, though, when that's going to be. Another 2,000 years before Christ fulfills his promises or even tomorrow, who knows? The only thing we do know for sure is this. Jesus said, *"About that day and hour no one knows... So keep alert."* That is our answer; just live your life as if tomorrow is the day that Jesus comes as he promised.

Lord God, forgive me when I spend time trying to predict when you will come again and this world will cease. Such behavior is a waste of time, a waste of energy. There are mysteries that are yours alone, not mine to know or to decide. This is the way of things; this is the way of faith. Keep my mind on the things that are truly important. Help me to keep alert and to focus my time and energy on spreading your love so that others may experience the wonder of your grace. In the name of Jesus I pray. Amen.

Advent 2: Peace *December 8* *Isaiah 11:6*

"The wolf shall live with the lamb. The leopard shall lie down with the kid. The calf and the lion and the fatling together, and a little child shall lead them."

Today we celebrate the second Sunday of Advent as churches across the world light the candle of peace, the Shepherd's candle. It symbolizes the peace to which we are called and the peace that comes to those who surrender their will and life to Jesus. It is both a challenge and a task, this peace of God to which we aspire. God's Peace does not make sense in a world filled with hate and anger. Isaiah writes that when God's Kingdom comes even natural enemies will look on each other differently, no longer as predator and prey but as companions on the journey. It seems like conflict and war has been around forever, doesn't it? One war ends; another begins.

Let's acknowledge a few things. War is terrible. War is not what we want, nor what God intends. Terrible prices have been paid. The Christ child brought peace into this world from a cross on Calvary with blood staining His arms and legs from nails driven into his body, as he was left there in the baking sun to die that we might live in peace with a righteous God. As you read the pages of the Old Testament, they are stained with the blood of God's children. We somehow have the mistaken idea that war is horrific now because of all of our weapons of mass destruction but, the truth is, war has always been that way. We expect peace to be the outcome of war; we want the wolf to live with the lamb; the leopard to lie down with the kid; the calf and lion to exist peacefully together. We want all nations to live in harmony. Do we ask for the impossible?

The Scripture says, *"A little child shall lead them."* Peace does not come naturally, for sin and hatred and war are deeply rooted in the human soul. But peace can happen. It can happen if we acknowledge that all people of the world have a right to be here. All the world's people are created in the image of God and by working together with God's help the world can become more of a place of peace.

Lord God, I come today with thanksgiving in my heart for all that you have given me. I come wanting peace: peace in our nation, peace in the world, peace in my life, peace in my soul. I come, Father, with the condemning truth that I have not always contributed to the peace I desire. Have mercy on me and forgive me. I pray in the name of Jesus. Amen.

Wanting for Christmas *December 9* *Isaiah 40:5*

"And the glory of the Lord shall be revealed, and all people shall see it together, for the mouth of the Lord has spoken."

I can remember as a youngster growing up in western Tennessee that Christmas was always special. You never knew what Santa was bringing you for Christmas. I remember one Christmas in particular. I wanted a tricycle. That Christmas morning I woke early, ran from my room to the Christmas tree. There was no tricycle. I was very disappointed. My grandmother, who was a devout member of the Church of Christ, said something like this, "You know the Lord has really blessed you, Herbert. You've got to remember that. Look around you. Most people don't have a home like this one and a family who loves them like we love you." I looked at her with a look of "What do know - I don't feel blessed at all!"

We all feel that way at times, don't we? We get caught up in wanting what we want and completely miss all the blessings God has given us. Now, I can agree that the things listed by my grandmother are things to be thankful for, but sometimes, it isn't enough, is it? We want more! Too often we look in the wrong places for that "more". We feel that our spouse should somehow make us happy, or our family, our children, or our job. Truth is, they can add to our happiness but they cannot give it to us. Many people have all the possessions, friends, and loved ones they could ask for, but still have a deep emptiness within their hearts.

Christmas comes as an eternal reminder to us of what Isaiah said, *"People will rejoice because the glory of the Lord will be revealed."* We hunger to see that glory and experience that peace. Peace does not come from any other source; happiness neither; they come as we follow the light which came into the world, the Christ Child, the fulfillment of all our prayers. (P. S. The tricycle was out in the garage.)

Lord God, I confess that too often I define joy as having my prayers answered precisely as I want. Have mercy on me and forgive my arrogance. The last impression I intended to leave is that I know more about my happiness than you, my dearest Lord, my Great Friend. Help me to find contentment in the simple gifts of life: your gift of peace that passes all understanding, the joy that is your calling card, sustaining hope, and the gift of unconditional love, which came in that child in a manger. May I look at all that you have given me and see what a wonderful life I have! Give me a grateful heart, Oh Lord; give me a heart for Jesus; in his name. Amen.

"A shoot shall come out from the stump of Jesse - the spirit of God shall rest on him - he shall judge by righteousness - and all shall live in harmony."

Isaiah paints a picture of what heaven on earth would be like. In these words, God's plan is for all his creatures to live in harmony and righteousness. War is a byproduct of sin and the sinful nature of mankind. War is a part of the sickness that has fallen upon our world. Of course we all believe God's presence is with us, not to bring conflict, but to bring peace to all. Unfortunately, fighting is a byproduct of preserving peace when others want war. This planet and its people are very important to God. Although, there are other planets, God visited this one. He spoke to us through his prophets and he visited us in the form of a baby in a stable. The angels sang at his birth, *"Peace on earth; good will to men."*

Christmas serves as an eternal reminder that Peace is what God wants for us all. You and I are called to be peacemakers. This scripture of Isaiah certainly alludes to that. Letting us know that God's plan is for us to live in harmony with all life. In 2nd Corinthians 5:18, Paul tells us that, *"God was in Christ, reconciling the world to Himself, and giving to us the ministry of reconciliation."* Jesus said in the Sermon on the Mount, *"Blessed are the peacemakers, for they shall be called children of God."* That is our calling. That is our task to be peacemakers serving God as ministers of his reconciling grace; what an awesome responsibility God has entrusted to us through his son Jesus upon whom the spirit of God fully rests.

Some people have a tendency to say, "Well, this person is more important because . . .," and then name some criteria which they have set. But that is not so with God. We are all very important to Him. We may be called to do different things but no one is more important than another. That truth applies to everyone in this world. If we can all begin by believing that all people are important to God, then we have the makings of real peace.

Lord God, I come in prayer acknowledging that I am a wretched sinner in need of your forgiveness and your mercy. I have not tried to accept all people as yours; preferring to see some as more valuable than others. In this way I have limited those people whom I must love as God in Christ has loved me. This season of Advent open my heart to your Peace so that I can live in harmony with all people and in this small way glorify God to whom I owe my life. I pray in the name of Jesus. Amen.

Second Coming   *December 11*   *Luke 21:27*

"You will see the Son of Man coming with power and great glory."

A few days ago we talked about the "end time". We do not know when that will be, nor will we ever know, so it is best to just keep alert and be ready. We don't know what kind of opportunity may present itself tomorrow. We certainly don't know what tragedies we may have to face. So it is best to simply live each day prepared. Today's scripture gives us the reason why. We will see the return of our savior in all his power and glory so "be alert" so we can stand before the Son of Man.

Some preachers build in fear when talking about the prophecies of the end time. As if to say that when the Lord returns it is something that we, God's children, should dread; that standing before the Lord will be something to fear. Let's look at His first coming. What did Jesus do when he came the first time? He traveled from town to town, place to place preaching the Gospel, healing the sick, gathering little children into his arms, comforting those who needed to be comforted, and teaching about God. Even as he was dying, he was forgiving those who placed him up on that cross, forgiving a criminal who was on a cross next to him; giving his life for his friends, for his enemies, saving our sinful souls.

Is this the one whose coming we are supposed to dread? I think not. We should look forward to his second coming with great hope and expectation. Our future is in the hands of a loving God and we shall not be disappointed. Our salvation is assured by faith in Jesus to whom we belong in life and death. What began in a little out of the way manger will come full circle and we shall be surrounded with wonder and majesty: with love and joy and grace. Even if we do not know the day of his return, we should stay ready. Ready for the most beautiful and wonderful experience that God's children will ever have: to be in the wonderful presence of God forever!

Lord God, I have lived in fear all my life. Have mercy on me, a sinner. Remove all fear from my life and give me peace. I cannot do it for myself; I am overwhelmed. I fear what might happen tomorrow; I fear what others will think of me; I fear failure, especially failing you, my Savior. Remove from me any fear of meeting you face to face. I believe, I trust in Christ alone for my salvation. Unbind my faith from the constraints of fear that I might long for your coming, and anticipate your coming as I would that of a Beloved Friend. In the name of Jesus. Amen.

"From now on, therefore, we regard no one from a human point of view; once we knew Christ from a human point of view, but no longer."

For nine months, give or take a few days, we are surrounded in our mother's womb with the waters of life. Once we enter the new physical world, our life starts with a smack on the rear end. You might say the welcome of a harsh and cruel world. That world will remain harsh and cruel until and unless we have a second birth, one that can open our eyes to summoning the birth of the Spirit within us! Scripture speaks of the impact of this rebirth on the way we see. There is the human way of seeing this world and others through limited physical sight.

The world can look as if it is under the control of evil, rather than God. Listen to the evening news or any 24-hour news station and you will get a picture of how worldly eyes see our world. Faith sees differently. Faith tells us that God is in control no matter how things look on the news. We can choose to see through the eyes of faith or eyes of no faith. Many judge people without walking in their shoes diminishing their worth until eventually they live down to "our" expectations.

I have a relative who raises hogs. I remember going into the "pig parlor" for the first time asking, "How do you stand the smell?" He laughed and said, "What smell?" He had worked in it so long, he had gotten used to it. So it is with us. When we engage continually in lying, stealing, and cheating; or in gossiping, judging and condemning; we become numb to the damage we either sustain or inflict. The more we follow the ways of the world, the more we think we are right and everyone else is wrong. However, when our eyes are opened to God's "new world" we accept God's ways; we become a "New Creation." The more we follow God's way instead of the way of the world, the more we will see through the eyes of faith and the more we will see that we are as big a sinner as the one we used to criticize. This is what it means to be born again.

Lord God, I come today as your child in need, a great sinner in need of your mercy and grace. I see others though my eyes judging them as unfit and unworthy of my concern. I live as though I have done no wrong and I have wronged you most of all, forgive me. Open the eyes of my heart that I may see this world and others through the eyes of Jesus– as sinners, forgiven by a loving and gracious God, just as I am. I pray in the name of Jesus. Amen.

Justice   *December 13*   *Jeremiah 33:15*

"In those days and at that time I will cause a righteous Branch to spring up
for David; and he shall execute justice."

We find these words in Jeremiah, "*The day is coming.*" There is something inevitable about those words: you can put your money on it. That's what Advent is about. The day is coming when God will "execute justice" and this world needs justice, doesn't it? That's the first promise Jeremiah tells us of the coming of the Messiah. When you watch some of the proceedings of those charged with a serious crime, it appears that justice can be bought with a wad of cash. Those who are well known only have to serve a short period of time in comparison to "common" folk who sometimes serve the maximum! It's just insane!

That's how many feel when we hear of some miscarriage of justice. It is repulsive to us that some people get away with murder, literally. There is something built down deep within us that yearns for justice! Life is not always fair; the innocent are convicted and the guilty get off scot-free. There are times when we are driving down the interstate highway following a line of speeding cars. We are pulled over and they fly on by. It's just not fair! We buy a new car; our neighbor buys one just like it. Our car spends half its time in the garage being worked on; he puts 200 thousand miles on his with no problems. Life is not always fair.

Nevertheless, the day is coming, says the Lord, when that will all change. The day is coming when that which is unfair will be set right. When the Bible speaks of justice, it is not merely talking about individual justice. God's call is for social justice. God calls for fairness and equality for all. God calls for a new kind of society; where all people will respect one another and the rights of each. That's what justice is all about. During Advent, we need to ask ourselves whether we are contributing to a just society or not. The day is coming; does your life honor a just God?

Holy Lord, have mercy me when I allow injustice to go on around me without lifting a finger or saying a word. I was afraid, Father, of the reactions of others, of being condemned, or shunned. Friendship and acceptance was more important to me than you, Jesus, or so my actions reveal. Oh, Father God, forgive me when I am a part of injustice toward any of your children. Open my heart, Lord, that I may not only feel the injustice directed to me, but to be empathetic with others who experience injustice in this world. Give me strength to stand and to make right that which I can. In the name of Jesus. Amen.

Righteousness   *December 14*   *Jeremiah 33: 14f*

"The days are coming says the Lord, when I will do a good thing which I have promised to the house of Israel and the house of Judah. "I will cause a righteous Branch to spring up for David; and he shall execute justice and righteousness."

Yesterday we discussed God's justice, which refers to how we treat one another in our society and the world. Today let's look at God's righteousness. Righteousness refers to how we treat the individual soul. I have heard different ministers argue about what the Gospel is all about. Some saying it is about civil rights and others arguing that it is about personal piety, prayer and high moral conduct. Isn't it really about both? In these passages from Jeremiah, we are reminded that God will execute both justice and righteousness. As Christians we need to expect both.

When we look at justice in our society, life is not always fair. The same can be said of righteousness. I am an avid football fan and in 2006 there was a college football kicker who attacked and stabbed a kicker on his team who was ahead of him on the chart. He did so in order to gain the starting position on his team. That painted a disturbing picture of how highly trained athletes can become so engrossed in starting that morality and sportsmanship, which is what the sport is all about, got lost.

You can see the same happening in some of our pro sports. There is a disturbing "Me First" attitude, a morality that is anti-ethical to the teachings of Jesus. This describes an attitude that assumes there is no interest by the Almighty God in the personal behavior of those he has created. Nothing could be further from the truth. What we do really matters do God. It's not enough during Advent to decorate our churches and yards – to put up the Advent Wreath and give gifts. We need to think about the very heart of the Advent message - and that is *"the Messiah is coming to bring justice and righteousness."* Does His justice and righteousness, burn within you, within us?

Lord God, forgive me when I live my life with no thought to righteousness, with no desire to be virtuous, giving no indication that you and I, Lord, have ever even met. Forgive me when I think of myself first, oblivious to anyone else even those I love. In these ways I refuse to become your servant, a disciple of Jesus. Bring into my heart your message of Advent that you are coming and with you justice and righteousness; may I be a part of that "coming". In the name of Jesus I pray. Amen.

Advent 3: Joy   *December 15*   *Luke 2: 10*

"But the angel said to them, "Do not be afraid; for see – I am bringing you good news of great joy for all the people: to you is born this day in the city of David a Savior, who is the Messiah, the Lord."

The angels said to the shepherds, "*I bring you glad tidings of great Joy.*" Christmas is only days away. For some that means not only has the time already been hectic, but this week it's going to be even more so, trying to get last minute gifts purchased and wrapped, and everything ready for Christmas. It may be good to take a few moments to collect yourself and center on the majesty of the Christmas message. Church is the place to be at this time of the year. This is the third Sunday of Advent and candle everyone lights is the Angels candle, the "rose" colored one, to represent joy. We say that Christmas is just for children, but that's really not true is it? For us to see a child open a toy from Santa with all the excitement on their face brings excitement to us as we watch.

There's one child that brought more joy into people's lives than any other and he is the one we will talk about today. He is that child born to the Virgin Mary, the Christ child of Bethlehem. He reminds us that there is some one beyond watching over us who loves us deeply. What are you thankful for this Christmas? Most would say for family, for the love that we share, for health and home and the blessings this world has brought, yet, it's not enough, is it? Many people possess these things but still have an empty heart. Deep down we yearn to believe that there is still something more, something beyond calling us, claiming us, and there is no escape.

I believe that's why even though some may ignore going to church at other times, they love to come at Christmas. Christmas reminds us that there is something beyond, a spiritual dimension of life. And although our health can desert us, we lose loved ones to death, even lose our home, our job, yet there is still reason for us to go on because the true meaning of our life is measured by God. God has sent his own son into this world just for you and me. That I believe is the truth of the angel's message and it is truly good news of Great Joy to us.

Lord God, this world with all its trials and challenges threatens to rob me of my joy; give me a faith that you, Lord, are greater than the world. By your power, convict me that your joy is forever and nothing can take it away. Fill me with your joy as I go about my daily life that in faithful living I may glorify your name. In the name of Jesus. Amen.

Glory Revealed   December 16   Isaiah 40:5

"Then the glory of the LORD shall be revealed, and all people shall see it together, for the mouth of the LORD has spoken."

In the 1980's I was serving a church in eastern Kentucky. There was a young family who joined the church and the father had never been a churchgoer. He appeared one Sunday morning just before Christmas and lo and behold he hardly ever missed church after that. I talked to him later and here is what he told me. "My little girl was saying her prayers the other night and prayed for God to help me start going to church. She was afraid that I would not accompany her and her mother into heaven and she would really miss her daddy up there. So I finally realized that if it was that important to her, it needed to be that important to me."

This little girl wanted God to give her daddy eternal life. From time to time, we also need to be reminded of that in our own lives, don't we? We need someone to wake us up and remind us that there is more to life than property and houses and taxes and cars and work and physical bodies. Christmas is that reminder. Isaiah said, *"People will rejoice because the glory of the Lord would be revealed."* The world hungers to see that glory. For a moment let us concentrate on the beauty of this time of the year, the carols that are sung, the beauty of Christmas trees and yards decorated with colored lights and Christmas scenes, the brightness of the stars at night reminding us of that one star the Wise Men followed, all the love that is expressed through the buying and giving of gifts, through all this we can catch a glimpse of the joy that is revealed.

If we are not careful, we can go through this whole busy season of Christmas and miss the meaning of it. It makes little difference that Mary and Joseph could find no room in an inn 2000 years ago, but if Jesus can find no room in our hearts today, that makes an enormous difference. The glory of the Lord is being revealed. Are we missing the comfort and assurance that eternal life is waiting for us? It's not too late.

Lord, I tend to clutter my life with so much busyness at this time of the year that it is easy to miss the things that are really important. Forgive me. Help me to see your handiwork in the simple things of life: the beauty of Christmas, the joy in the eyes of little children, the love that is shared, Jesus' birth, the joy of knowing I belong to you and I was made for eternity. May I become an effective witness so that even one person may feel the comfort of your eternity because I lived, because I loved Jesus. In His name I pray. Amen.

We are Special   December 17   Luke 1:30

"The angel Gabriel came to Mary and said to her, "Do not be afraid, Mary, for you have found favor with God."

One Christmas while pasturing a church Tennessee I overheard one of our children tell her mother that she was to be an animal in the Christmas play. Her mother said, "That's wonderful, dear." The little girl cried and said, "But I want to be an angel!" Now I'm not sure but I think this little girl wanted to be an Angel because she thought that was more special than being one of the animals. Angels in scripture were the bearers of "Good News"; special messengers of God sent to bring his word; "glad tidings of great Joy." This little girl wanted to be an angel because she thought angels were special and she wanted to be special.

Isn't that what we all want, to be special? Truth is everyone is special to God, even those who do not know the "Good news of great Joy" of which the angels sang. This Joy came for all. The coming of this Christ Child is for all who are special in God's eyes, those who know they haven't been all that they should have been, for those of who have regrets over time misspent, and for those who have let down the ones they love. God sent His Son for all of us anyway; the Christ child came for all. God cares for everyone.

Sin is a part of human nature, but just because it is a part of my nature does not allow me to disclaim responsibility for my actions. I do not get off that easily. Still, sometimes we need to be reminded that God loves us, naughty or nice; He loves us with a love that abounds even sin. But even more importantly, God's acceptance is not something that we must earn. God sent Christ into the world as a helpless infant and that is also how we come to God. Not one of us can measure up to the absolute perfection of a Holy God. But, the good news is we don't have to. Jesus is God's free gift to all who would receive Him.

Lord God, I come to you today with prayers of a grateful heart, for I know how special I am to you. You do love me despite my sin. This I know. You love me even when I have failed you and have taken your commands lightly. But to love me in my sin costs you dearly, costs you all. Forgive me when I doubt you, forgive me when I want to be an angel instead of accepting the role you have selected for me to play. Lord, I will do as you ask. Just let me know, Lord. I am listening. Give me another chance to love you in return. In the name of Jesus. Amen.

Lord please Intervene **December 18** *Isaiah 64:5f*

"You meet those who gladly do right, those who remember you in your ways. But you were angry and we sinned; because you hid yourself, we transgressed. We have all become like one who is unclean, and all our righteous deeds are like a filthy cloth."

Many folks make jokes about sin. People laugh about it. Some make light of the darkness of a person's heart. But think about this; what would society be like if sin were the "in thing" to do? We would have a society where husbands and wives couldn't count on each other's faithfulness. We would have a place where little children could not count on a home with parents who love them and nurture them. We would have a place where people live for pleasure and never accept responsibility for their own actions.

Sins of the flesh are bad enough but they are not the worse sins you know. The worse ones I believe are the sins of the spirit. Let me give you a few examples. When one takes pleasure in putting other people down, when one delights in gossip and backstabbing, or when one attends church regularly but cheats and steals from those around them, or when one hates another and wishes they would go to that place – you know, where it is hot and desolate. Let's call them – sins of love and sins of hate. Sins of love have to do with mistakes in love. Sins of hate have to do with taking delight in harming someone else. There is nothing that will destroy the joy in your life like a steady diet of spiritual decay.

That is why as Christians we should think seriously about our society. Once you see the effects of sin you realize that there has to be a better way. Isaiah saw this; he saw the unhappiness; He saw the tragedy; He saw the sinful ways of the people. So he stated the deplorable circumstances of godlessness in Today's text. Any one who has tried to shake off sin knows how difficult it is. You can understand Isaiah's frustration. It's very hard: difficult to change. Sin can swallow you whole. Isaiah saw that and concluded that there would be no hope unless God would come down. Call on the Lord to come down and make Himself known that we may change the way we treat one another and God.

Lord God, I confess that I have become like one who is unclean. Even my righteous deeds are tainted with selfishness; forgive me. This world is lost without you and I have added to its sinfulness by not remembering your ways. My sins have indeed swallowed me whole. Come down, Lord Jesus, and once again become known in my waiting heart. In Jesus I pray. Amen.

Joy, Joy, Joy!   *December 19*   *Psalms 16:11*

"Thou dost show me the path of life; in thy presence there is fullness of joy."

Are you filled with Joy? As Christians we should be, for every sin we have committed and every sin we shall commit has been forgiven and covered by the grace and righteousness of Jesus! Let me tell you a true story of a fellow who was a member of a church I served in Kentucky. I'll call his name Fred. He was one of the most joyous people I have ever known. Fred had a daughter who lived out of state. She had a chronic debilitating disease.

One Christmas she was not doing so well and I asked him what his plans were for Christmas? He said that he was not going to his daughter's this year because of her health and did not want to burden her. I said, "Fred, I don't want you to spend Christmas alone, come to my house." He responded, "Preacher, thanks, but there are some needy kids on my street and I've bought presents for them and I'm going to have a little party." You just could not get old Fred down: no way to steal his joy!

The 16th Psalm states why. In the presence of God we have fullness of joy. When you look through the Old Testament, the Hebrew Bible is a book full of joy. And what do we call the New Testament? "The Good News." Now, don't get the idea that we have the capacity to "make" our own joy, we don't, but we do have the capacity to decide that we will not allow the troubles and misfortunes of life to rob us of joy.

Joy is never within our power. It is not something we can possess. We can long for it, but to receive it we must go to God. He is the source of all joy. Jesus is our joy. Christmas joy is something we can find as we give of ourselves to others, as we visit shut-ins, make gifts for needy children on your street, give food to make sure no one goes hungry, share yourself with your own children and let them know how special they are to you. As we do these things, joy comes into our hearts.

Dear Lord, merciful Father, I must confess as I read this story of sacrificial love, I see myself as I want to be, not as I am. I would be thinking of my own needs, my own unmet expectations. Oh, I would hide it well but inside where the real me runs rampant, I would be sullen and pouting, not joyful, not joyful. Forgive me and teach me that true joy comes only in your presence and in obedience to your perfect will. Forgive me for making the easy way so hard. In Jesus' Name, Amen.

Announcing His Coming December 20 Malachi 3: 1f

"I'm sending my messenger to prepare the way before me, and the Lord whom you seek will suddenly come to His temple, indeed, He is coming. But who can endure the day of His coming, and who can stand when He appears?"

Here in the third chapter of Malachi we have what has been called the "Prophecy of the coming of John the Baptist" foretold by Isaiah in chapter 40, verse 3. John the Baptist we know as the one who came to "prepare the way for the Lord." Malachi tells us that the nation was not ready for his coming, *"Who can stand when He appears?"* The same can be said of today, "Who can stand when Jesus appears again?" Advent is a time for us to look forward to the next coming of Jesus. Will we be prepared? Will we be able to "endure that day"?

I believe that some who will not be able to endure his coming are those who don't believe in God or his Son Jesus. Wouldn't it be difficult to be prepared for someone you are not expecting? If you are like my family, when someone is coming over you quickly clean the house, sweep the floor, dust the furniture, pick up the old newspapers and other things that you normally leave lying around. You get prepared and then you can "endure" or enjoy their coming, but how about if one just drops by?

How about if you are trying to save yourself? Some say they believe in Jesus, but then live their life trusting in the good deeds they do instead of trusting in the saving grace of Jesus. Preparing for the second coming means that we not only believe in Jesus, but we trust that he is the way to salvation. God sent his Son into this world to bring us His grace and love and forgiveness. Jesus died for our sins, those committed, and those yet to be committed. To trust in him means that we trust our life to him. We trust our future salvation and we trust our every day. What ever your problem, and we all have plenty of them, go to Jesus and ask for his advice and direction so you will be prepared for his coming.

Father God, Savior And Lord, in Christ Jesus, you have become the fulfillment of my every wish, my every dream. By your grace, I seek to begin each day with the desire to love you more and to serve you better and fully. Freed from the need to save myself, I can focus on you, Jesus, and on those you bring into my life to love in your name and for your sake. What a privilege, Lord and what a gift. Don't let my fragile enthusiasm wane before your return. I want you to find me faithful and prepared for your coming. This is my prayer, Jesus. This is my prayer.

Comfort Ye, My People   December 21   Isaiah 40:1

"Comfort, comfort ye my people says your God. Speak tenderly to Jerusalem and cry to her that she has served her term, that her sins have been paid."

Have you ever noticed how funny some people are? Take for instance this story. Last year our favorite store was burned to the ground. It happened because a couple of guys were trying to steal drugs from the pharmacy. The building was one of those metal buildings so they brought a cutting torch one night and tried to cut their way into the building. Two things went wrong. The first was that the torch accidentally caught the insulation on fire. The second got them nailed. Once the building went up in flames, they took off leaving their cell phone behind!

Now there is a lesson here for us all. The reason they were doing this in the first place was they wanted "comfort" – that's right, why do people do drugs anyway? Because drugs somehow help them escape the pains of this life for a moment and bringing them comfort, not lasting comfort, but comfort nonetheless. Life is hard, at least it can be, and everyone wants relief from the harshness of life. Some turn to drugs in order to find relief. Others turn to something more lasting – God.

We all have to live through unspeakable tragedies in life and sometimes we wonder if God is there at all; the death of a loved one, sometimes expected, after all no one lives forever. But then there are those others. The five year old succumbing to incurable cancer, the eighteen-year-old basketball player collapsing on the court from a heart attack, loosing your job, or going through a divorce. There are many tragedies waiting to happen, we all want comfort, and we begin to wonder if peace is even possible. Then the Word comes to us from Isaiah, *"Comfort, comfort ye my people says your God"* and all seems well. Our God cares, loves, forgives His people and He will send comfort.

Almighty God, Author and Sustainer of My Faith, My Comfort and My Joy, I read about the careless thieves and their failed attempt to steal their way to "comfort" and I laugh at their ineptness. But their effort to secure comfort for themselves makes me pause and consider my own choices. To whom do I look, Lord, other than to you? Will you give me just a peak? The full truth would lay me low, but a peak I could bear. Is it worldly success, position, power, money, acclaim? You know, Father. Whisper it to me and I won't argue or make excuses. I'll just nod and say," How could I have ever settled for less than you? Forgive me, your wayward child." Amen.

Advent 4: Love   *December 22*   *Isaiah 7:14*

"Therefore the Lord Himself will give you a sign: Behold, the virgin shall conceive and bear a Son, and shall call His name Immanuel."

We know that the Messiah for which Isaiah spoke was born to Mary and Joseph in the little town of Bethlehem. It occurred in a stable, a strange place for the birth of a King: plain, shabby surroundings. They placed the baby Jesus in a trough used to feed the animals! Who would have thought to look there for the fulfillment of this prophecy of Isaiah? Only a few shepherds and those astrologers from the east, but they knew only because someone let them know. That someone was God. The angels brought the message to the shepherds and the stars shone above and guided these astrologers to the place where the child was born.

As for everyone else? As far as we know, from stories found in scripture, no one else heard the angels and no one else saw the star. The rest of the world only saw a baby born much like many others in the world. But what they did not know was that in that manger contained the Advent of love to the entire world. I recall a wonderful song that our choir sang on Christmas Eve, "There has Never Been Such a Night." *"There has never been such a night that the shepherds saw and the wise men - this child who came to bring us salvation. God came down to earth as a mortal and the star sent its light to reveal the holy sight, there has never been such a night. There has never been such a child."* Isn't that a wonderful song?

This song tells about the LOVE that came down that night. It was God's way of telling us how much we mean to him. Christmas is that time of year when we try to express to others how much they mean to us. A gift may not be the best way to say that, but we do need those opportunities to say, "I love you, how glad I am you are in my life." That is what God has told us. You might just ask yourself, "Who am I that God should love me so?" Should rejoice in my presence?

Lord, you were born in a stable, but nonetheless a King! Yet, I have neglected to trust you as my Savior, my Lord. I have given you my heart yet kept a part for myself. I have resisted your will for my life, as if my plans are better. Overwhelm me with your Love and Grace, Father. It was never my circumstances that gave me true happiness. With you, Jesus, even in poverty I can be rich; even living in a stable I could feel like a king. In Jesus. For Jesus. Amen.

Love Freely Given December 23 *Matthew 1:20*

"Joseph, son of David, do not fear to take Mary your wife, for that which is conceived in her is of the Holy Spirit; she will bear a son and you shall call His name Jesus, for He will save His people from their sins."

I'm sure when people hear the Christmas story for the first time they probably think how in the world can a little baby save the world? That is what the scripture says. That is what took place! The angel appeared to Joseph in a dream with an astounding prophecy, a divine plan to forever impact his life and that of Mary, his betrothed. Joseph realized this was a divine act of love and grace for him, for her, for all. The most important thing in this world for us at Christmas is to realize that this baby came to save us from our sins in a divine act of love and grace.

I had a retired elder in a church I served whose father and brother had been a minister. He chose another field. He loved kids and saw it as his responsibility to single handedly provide Santa stockings for them all. He purchased the toys, fruit, and trinkets, filling each stocking with love and care. He put names on tags on each one except the extras for those he knew might come. Come Santa night, he would put on a Santa suit and play Santa for the kids of the church and for those who were visiting that night. It was always a special night for all, full of shining smiles and shouts of glee. It was a divine act of love and grace. He's gone home now to Jesus but Santa night will always recall him to our minds and hearts. He served God wonderfully and simply.

That's what we all need to do, give from the heart to all who are in need, preparing extras so none is left out. That's the kind of love we received from God, the kind we should be willing to share. Truth is you don't have to have wealth to give a gift: only a desire to give. This elder certainly was not wealthy in a material sense, but in a spiritual sense I have never met anyone wealthier. So give the best that you can; give a gift that comes from heart of God. Christmas usually causes us to be truer to our faith. So lets offer our best this Christmas season, to God and well as to others. After all, what else can we offer Him?

Lord God, I come begging on bended knee for I know how I have failed you. By Divine Plan, you came offering salvation for the forgiveness of sins, yet what I have received, your love and grace, I have been unwilling to offer others. Forgive me, Lord. Open my heart this day so that I may experience afresh the joy that is Christmas I pray in the name of Jesus. Amen.

Christmas Eve   *December 24*   *Luke 2: 1f*

"In those days a decree went out from Emperor Augustus that all the world should be registered... Joseph went from the town of Nazareth in Galilee to the city of David called Bethlehem, because he was descended from the house of David. He went with Mary, to whom he was engaged. While they were there, the time came for her to deliver and she gave birth to her firstborn son and wrapped him in bands of cloth, and laid him in a manger, because there was no place for them in the inn."

Advent is the season for believing, a time of looking forward to the coming of Jesus. It is the season to believe that Jesus is the Son of God, conceived by the Holy Spirit, born of the Virgin Mary. Christmas Eve is a time for us to remember the birth of Jesus and to recall His birth in our hearts. It is a time to believe that Jesus is Emmanuel, God with us, the one who came to save us from our sins, it is a time to believe that in everything we do and see we, the presence of Jesus exists and can be felt.

Now, to believe in something is quite different than believing something. For instance, to believe in God is an intellectual position and it takes no more effort than saying, "Well, I believe in the Grand Canyon." But to believe God is quite something else. To believe God is a journey, something that stirs inside you and gives meaning to your life; something that affects who you are and what you do and how you do it. Believing God can change the way you feel; cause you to give up worrying and change your focus from problems and troubles to the needs of others. Believing in something doesn't do that, but believing God, can and does!

Scripture tells us that Jesus was born in Bethlehem in a stable; shepherds and wise men recognized the significance of this birth. The importance of this story is not how they responded but how we do. Do we accept that this is the birth of the "Son of God" and if we do, have we accepted him Savior and Lord of our life? To believe "him" is to accept him and to accept him is to obey his commandments. This night, which changed the course of history, can change our life forever if we believe

Father God, I come believing. I come with an open mind and an open heart. I want to believe as surely as those whose experience is captured in this wondrous event. To them the promise was made, the journey taken, and the fulfillment seen. Jesus was born in their lives and hearts because they believed. Father, with an open heart, I once more make a manger bed for Jesus. Won't you come, Lord Jesus? The world is still cold, and believing, trusting hearts your only true home. In the name of Jesus. Amen.

Christmas: God's Promise to us December 25 Luke 2:9

"While they were there, the time came for her to deliver her child. She gave birth to her firstborn son and wrapped him in bands of cloth, and laid him in a manger, because there was no place for them in the inn."

I always enjoy seeing the Christmas Pageant with all the little children playing Mary and Joseph, angels, shepherds, wise men, even the stable animals. I know there are some wonderful Christmas plays around that can be very entertaining and professional. But for me it is the Christmas Pageant that brings a smile to my face and my heart. Maybe it is because the story means so much. This is the most important story ever told, that ever happened, if you are a Christian.

God had made promises throughout the Old Testament through his prophets, but the greatest was the one that promised "a child would be born of a virgin and we shall call his name Immanuel (God with us)." We find that verse in Isaiah 7:14 and again in Matthew 1:23. We know that promise came true in the birth of His Son Jesus and we celebrate that birth on Christmas day, December 25th. The shepherds were told of this event by the angels of God who said, "I bring you tidings of great joy for all people! For unto you is born this day in the city of David, a savior, who is the Messiah." The Wise Men from a country far away were told of this birth and followed a star until "it came to rest over the place where the child was."

So when I see Mary and Joseph standing on that stage and placing the little baby, "wrapped in swaddling clothes", into the little manger, it always brings tears to my eyes. And when I see all those precious little children on stage with their bright eyes and beaming faces, it always brings a smile to my face and in my heart, great joy. There is no promise bigger or more important than this: A child to be born who will come to save us all from our sins! A child to be born portrayed by children born of God!

Father God, in your grace you created us as your own, and in your mercy you came to earth as a child. Immanuel: "God with us." Never again can I live my life as if unheeded or unloved: "God with us." Never again can I live my life as if I have no purpose or direction: "God with us." The great promise given life: "I will never leave you, nor forsake you." Immanuel. At Christmas time and forever. Thanks be to God for his indescribable Gift. Amen.

"There was a prophet, Anna who was of a great age, having lived with her husband seven years, then as a widow to the age of eighty-four. She never left the temple but worshiped there with fasting and prayer. She came, and began to praise God and to speak about the child who all were looking for the redemption of Jerusalem."

Not only is the Christmas Story the greatest story ever told, it is one that should be shared. After Joseph and Mary brought the baby Jesus to the temple to present him to the Lord (according to Jewish law) there was a prophet, Anna, who had lived at the temple for most of her eighty four years, patiently waiting for her prayer to be answered. Anna knew in an instant that this child was the one she had spent all of her life seeking.

Once she met this child face to face, she just could not keep it to herself! Why should we keep to ourselves something as wonderful and as important as the gift of God's Son? The Promises of God are not to be kept; they are to be shared. The Apostle Paul also stated that we are the "guardians" of this promise and it is not ours just to receive but to share. That is the truth of the Christmas story. The message to the shepherds in Luke 2:10 was that *"I bring you good news of great joy for all the people!"* This "good news" is not for some of the people, but for all the people!

The ways to share are many. If you have been touched with the redemptive promise of God through His Son, Jesus, then you should feel overwhelmed with great joy. The promise is that God will forgive all your sins and shortcomings. To be able to live the rest of our life forgiven for all the wrong we have done, all the people we have hurt, all the mistakes we have made, should make us overcome with joy at God's limitless Grace. You will have to pass that joy on to all looking for the redemption of God. As you gather with friends, families, and neighbors, share the forgiveness, the good news of grace you have been given and the great joy.

Almighty God, I am so very impatient, ready for life before life is ready for me. I could never equal the kind of patience that the prophet Anna displayed in waiting for your arrival even as decades of living passed her by. Is this kind of faith, hope and purpose available for the asking, for the wanting? I could wait with such patience and such joy if you were at the end of it. Waiting in confidence and joy is one of the great promises fulfilled at Christmas. Give me the words and the chance to share. In Jesus' name, Amen.

The Price of God's Promise — December 27 — Luke 2:33f

"And the child's father and mother were amazed at what was being said about him. Then Simeon blessed them and said to Mary, "This child is destined for the falling and the rising of many in Israel, and to be a sign that will be opposed so that the inner thoughts of many will be revealed - and a sword will pierce your own soul."

The last few days we have been talking of God's promise of his Son who came that first Christmas to bring us forgiveness and grace and salvation. It is a wonderful gift to undeserving people, like us! It is also a gift we are called to share. Today let's talk about the price of God's Promise. There is no question that Jesus paid a price for our salvation, but what about us? Do we pay a price, should we pay a price?

In scripture before the story of Anna, there is the story of Simeon who had been promised by God that he would see the Messiah before his death. He too was at the temple when Mary and Joseph took their son there to *"present him to the Lord."* Simeon praised God and said to Mary that this child was destined for the falling and rising of many in Israel and that *"a sword will pierce your own soul."* Can you imagine what must have gone through Mary's mind? I am sure that she thought of this moment often, especially at the end of Jesus' life and at the cross. God kept his promise, but there was a price that came with that promise.

The Christian life is not exempt from problems. It is a life lived in the midst of problems, but with new eyes. For our eyes have seen our salvation in Jesus; God is in control. Things we used to "see" as problems, by faith we now see work for Good! Things we used to question, "Why does this always happen to me?" we now see will work for Good! Will we experience disappointment? Will we be let down by those we thought were friends? "Yes!" There is a price to pay and that price is to give our self fully to God knowing that He is in control; His promises will be fulfilled!

Almighty God, Sovereign Lord, I stand in awe of your great purpose for my little life. How can it be that the sovereignty of an Almighty Father applies to the likes of me? "All things work together for good for those who love God." And I do love you, Lord. Can you find a use for one so insignificant and so small? That question was certainly answered in the birth of your only begotten son in a stable. Give me the sense of purpose that Jesus made possible and I will serve you in and through all of the circumstances of my life. Call my name and I will ever say, "YES". In Jesus' name. Amen.

"In those days a decree went out from Emperor Augustus that all the world should be registered. This was the first registration and was taken while Quirinius was governor of Syria. All went to their own towns to be registered. Joseph also went from the town of Nazareth in Galilee to Judea, to the city of David called Bethlehem."

When the Emperor sends out a decree, an official command; all people must register in their home of record. Obedience was not optional. God also issued decrees, universal laws to which all of us are subject and that God expects everyone to follow. God's laws were written so that we might live together in harmony and peace. The Emperor sent out a decree because he wanted to collect money and conscript soldiers for the occupying army. In most cases such people do not want to follow the laws and decrees of the Emperor but they do.

Can the same be true with God's laws? Most people believe in the Ten Commandments and the Golden Rule, but how many truly follow? Many consider they apply to everyone else but not to them. Since people did not follow his laws, often to their own harm, God decided to have his laws sent in a different way- in a person, the baby Jesus. God is aware of our problem with authority. Our rebellious nature is legendary. We often resent being told what to do, to be ordered to do something really gets our goat! God wanted things to be different so he sent his Son Jesus. Now we do not live by rules and laws, but by grace and love.

Don't misunderstand, we still are under the law, it is just that we follow our Lord Jesus, that Baby born in the stable. In doing so he will touch our hearts so that we follow the law not from necessity but out of love. Even when we do not live the law perfectly, which is impossible anyway, we fall upon the grace and righteousness of Jesus who is our Lord and Savior. Obedient as an act of love for the one who gave us forgiveness, grace, and a divine relationship with one who knows us better than we know ourselves!

Merciful and Loving Savior, I recognize myself in this. I would rather I hadn't. I would rather I had recognized my neighbor or my enemy. But you care too much for me to leave me unchallenged and unchanged. You always want the best for your children even in our rebellion and pride. Change me, Lord, for only you can heal the hardness of my heart and make me whole. Can you hurry, Lord? The day is at hand and I don't' want to be the way I am another moment. This is my earnest plea, the prayer of my soul. In Jesus' name. Amen.

The Community of Faith   December 29   Luke 2:8

"In that region there were shepherds in the fields, keeping watch over their flock. An angel of the Lord stood before them, the glory of the Lord shone around them - The angel said, "Do not be afraid; for bring you good news of great joy for all people."

Many have declared, "I don't need to go to church. I believe in God. That's enough. Besides, the church is full of hypocrites!" In one way they are correct. The church is full of people who say they believe in God, trust in his Son, but their lives don't always show that to be true. There is a reason for that contradiction: we are all sinners through and through! There is no way around that fact. But where better for a sinner to be?

The Bible is the only written "Word of God" we have and that Word is clear on this subject. God works through the Church, the community of believers. God comes to us through revelation, through the hearing of His Holy Word preached, and through His sacraments of Baptism and The Lord's Supper. This is His way and it is not for us to decide how God should come: just accept how He has chosen. The angel comes to the shepherds in the fields revealing the coming birth of Jesus *"I am bringing you "good news" of great joy for all the people."* These were people who cared, who watched over their sheep and loved them and did everything they could to protect them.

Living in Community says that we care about one another. As Christians we know that none of us is perfect but we accept and encourage one another anyway. We are brothers and sisters in Christ working together in an imperfect world spreading the "good news" that Jesus is Lord – telling others of the message the angels brought long ago. It is in the church that we learn this, live this and share this truth. Without the church we would be left alone with our ideas of who God is and how he comes to us. That could cause one to be the greatest hypocrite of all, don't you think?

Almighty God, in your mercy you gave me freedom to think and to question. In your wisdom you created the church for me to live in community with others, knowing I have much to learn about you, Lord. In the church you can test my faith, my pride, my capacity to give and receive mercy, my willingness to forgive others, knowing that you, Father, would be with me every step of the way. You could have left me on my own, but you know, Lord, that I am much too fragile, much too easily misled. Guide me Lord and may I not fail you. In Jesus' name. Amen.

"Then an angel of the Lord stood before them and the glory of the Lord shone around them and they were terrified. But the angel said to them, 'do not be afraid; for see - I am bringing you good news of great joy for all the people: to you is born this day in the City of David a Savior, who is the Messiah, the Lord.'"

Yesterday we talked about the community of faith: the Spiritual body of Christ on earth and the importance of us worshipping together to hear God. Why is so important? What do we receive worshipping together? We worship together because God has asked us to do so both in the Old Testament and in the New. We do so not because we are perfect but just the opposite, because we are not! We need to hear God's Word so that God can enter our lives and change can occur.

That is the real reason for worship isn't it? To praise God for who He is and for what He has done for us; to know that God sent his Son, a son who died in order to reconcile us to God giving us access to his grace and forgiveness that we can forgive one another and ourselves? Is that the only reason? Don't we also gather together for ourselves? Don't we want to hear God's voice and receive hope for our lives? If the truth be known, that is the real reason we come; the desire to praise God comes once we have felt his presence.

Don't feel bad if your reasons for coming to church are selfish, after all we are human and imperfect! So let's just admit the truth. We want to hear God's voice and the word we want most is "hope". Hope tells us that we are living for a reason. There is purpose in our lives. Hope can be contagious especially if shared. Hope is the truth of the message brought to the shepherds by the angel. We want to hear that God has brought us good news and that good news is "Hope" for every day of our lives. Hope means there is another chance for us, that we are loved and forgiven and accepted and cherished and have an eternal relationship with the one who created us. Is there any greater "good news" than that?

Father God, I stand in awe of your continual and providential care for your people and your Church. Such love and steadfast faithfulness to me a sinner humbles me and inspires me to want to know you and to believe that you long to know me too. Do you speak to me, Lord, and in my busyness I fail to hear? Embrace my longing heart and open my mind to your message of hope and life. In Jesus' name. Amen.

Religion vs. Relationship December 31 Malachi 3:3f

"He will purify the descendants of Levi - until they present right offerings to the Lord in righteousness."

We are in the middle of the season of Christmas – the twelve-day period of time from Christmas day when we celebrate the birth of Jesus to the Epiphany, January 6, when we celebrate the visit of the Wise Men. This is a time for us all to remember the birth of Jesus and examine how that coming has affected our lives, if at all. I have to be honest. There have been some who have attended churches whose sincerity of faith one would have to question; those who seem to live by the Law rather than by the Grace of God. They are the ones always judging and condemning the actions of others without having "walked in their shoes."

So when I see them I am reminded of these words from Malachi prophesying the coming of one who would prepare the way for the Lord. Malachi says the one who is to come *"Will purify the descendants of Levi – until they present right offerings to the Lord in righteousness."* God attempts to communicate to us in various ways: his prophets, His Holy Word, His Sacraments, through those who love Him – but still we don't get the message! He has said, *"Don't judge"* but we do. He has said, *"Forgive as I have forgiven you"* but we don't. What happens is this. We end up following a religion rather than building a relationship with God.

To follow a religion would be to follow rules and regulations. To build a relationship would be to get to know the one whom we claim to be following. We all need to be "purified" to some extent. We need to let go of our need to have others consider us "worthy" and fall on our knees before the risen Lord, asking for his forgiveness and his grace. Religion will not save us, depending on the grace and righteousness of Jesus will. More evil has been done in the name of religion than one can count. Build a relationship with God and receive his love, grace, and forgiveness.

Almighty God, Sovereign Lord, I see myself in this reading. I know I keep the Law to avoid judgment as much as to please you. Father, forgive me. I know that I obey your Word to parade my "goodness" before others. Oh, Lord, my beloved savior, forgive me for your sake, I do not deserve it. Give me new life, Lord. My old life glorifies only myself, serves only me. Help me, Lord Jesus. I know you are merciful or else you would have given me a full glimpse of my wretchedness. But you knew, didn't you, that I could not bear it and live. Receive my plea and come to me, a sinner. In Jesus' name. Amen.

Quotes:

Feb 14th   Bonhoeffer "The Cost of Discipleship"

April 12th   Billy Joel "A matter of trust"

May 2nd   Frederick Buechner says, "Doubts are the ants in the pants of faith."

May 11th   C. S. Lewis, "Christ did not come to torment your natural self, he came to kill it."

May 28th   Steve Brown – "When being Good is not good enough" "If Jesus has Come"

June 11th   Steve Brown "New Phariseeism"

July 9th   Martin Luther – "Latin Writings" – preface

October 7th   Billy Joel "The Piano Man."

Topical Index

Scripture | Index

Reference	Date	Reference	Date
Matthew 6:14f	May 19	Mark 11:2f	March 30
Matthew 6:33	March 19	Mark 11:9f	July 14
Matthew 6:34	January 2	Mark 14:32f	June 14
Matthew 7:16f	August 2	Mark 15:34	April 6
Matthew 7:24f	March 20	Mark 15:39	October 13
Matthew 8:24	November 19	Luke 1:26-32	December 1
Matthew 9:13	January 17	Luke 1:30	December 17
Matthew 10:24	October 19	Luke 1:30-33	December 6
Matthew 10:26f	November 23	Luke 2:1-5	December 28
Matthew 10:29f	July 2	Luke 2:1-7	December 24
Matthew 10:40f	March 24	Luke 2:6f	December 25
Matthew 14:31	November 18	Luke 2:8f	December 29
Matthew 15:28	September 25	Luke 2:9f	December 30
Matthew 16:13	July 17	Luke 2:10f	December 15
Matthew 16:18	January 12	Luke 2:19	January 1
Matthew 16:18f	March 26	Luke 2:33f	December 27
Matthew 16:21	April 1	Luke 2:36f	December 26
Matthew 17:1	October 11	Luke 2:48	January 19
Matthew 17:1f	October 10	Luke 2:52	January 3
Matthew 18:1f	August 16	Luke 6:27	January 21
Matthew 18:26f	May 26	Luke 6:27-28	February 3
Matthew 19:26	February 24	Luke 6:27f	October 30
Matthew 20:26f	March 23	Luke 6:37	February 1
Matthew 22:17f	June 24	Luke 7:41f	September 21
Matthew 22:21	November 9	Luke 7:47	September 22
Matthew 22:34f	October 24	Luke 7:47f	September 23
Matthew 25:24f	November 26	Luke 9:23	April 16
Matthew 26:20f	April 4	Luke 9:28-36	February 4
Matthew 26:72f	April 2	Luke 9:62	April 30
Matthew 28:6	April 9	Luke 10:25f	May 14
Matthew 28:10	April 8	Luke 10:38f	October 1
Matthew 28:19-20	June 1	Luke 12:39f	March 18
Mark 1:9	November 13	Luke 13:2	March 3
Mark 1:12	November 15	Luke 13:24	February 16
Mark 1:12	March 8	Luke 14:12	May 18
Mark 1:13	November 14	Luke 14:26-28	February 14
Mark 1:27	June 25	Luke 16:1f	May 6
Mark 2:22	June 27	Luke 17:5f	June 18
Mark 2:23f	October 5	Luke 17:9	July 7
Mark 3:20f	January 23	Luke 17:15f	November 10
Mark 3:22	January 22	Luke 17:19	September 14
Mark 4:26f	October 22	Luke 17:33f	January 8
Mark 4:38	October 9	Luke 18:1	February 23
Mark 4:39f	July 8	Luke 18:7	May 2
Mark 4:40	February 5	Luke 18:11	May 3
Mark 6:31	June 10	Luke 18:13	May 4
Mark 8:4	April 12	Luke 19:5	February 28
Mark 8:34	February 15	Luke 19:9	September 15
Mark 10:45	May 13	Luke 19:15f	July 20
Mark 10:48f	June 12	Luke 21:7f	April 15

1 Corinthians 12:18f	August 23	1 Timothy 6:13f	August 25
1 Corinthians 12:27f	October 18	2 Timothy 1:8	September 27
2 Corinthians 5:7	September 26	Hebrews 1:1f	September 10
2 Corinthians 5:16	March 17	Hebrews 2: 9	November 5
2 Corinthians 5:16	December 12	Hebrews 2:11	August 17
2 Corinthians 5:17f	May 8	Hebrews 11:17f	September 1
2 Corinthians 9:5f	November 3	Hebrews 11:1f	May 20
2 Corinthians 12:7	March 16	Hebrews 12:1f	October 26
Galatians 1:15f	July 18	Hebrews 13:8	April 21
Galatians 2:16	November 24	James 1:18	November 12
Galatians 2:16	September 28	James 1:19	January 31
Galatians 2:20	November 11	James 1:22	October 31
Galatians 5:1	July 3	James 2:10	November 8
Galatians 5:13	July 4	James 4:13	October 2
Ephesians 1:4	September 18	James 4:14	October 3
Ephesians 1:5	January 29	James 4:15	October 4
Ephesians 1:8f	October 6	1 Peter 1:3	June 29
Ephesians 1:11	February 22	1 Peter 1:3	February 11
Ephesians 2:13f	September 20	1 Peter 1:6f	March 7
Ephesians 2:15f	November 6	1 Peter 1:24	July 13
Ephesians 2:15f	October 8	1 Peter 2:9	January 15
Ephesians 2:18f	November 17	1 Peter 2:21	August 21
Ephesians 2:19f	December 2	1 Peter 5:6	May 28
Ephesians 2:8f	April 18	1 Peter 5:8	May 27
Ephesians 4:12	June 5	1 Peter 5:7f	May 29
Ephesians 4:29	February 27	1 Peter 5:10	May 30
Ephesians 5:15-17	March 1	2 Peter 1:21	February 20
Ephesians 5:19f	May 7	1 John 4:10	May 1
Ephesians 5:21	March 2	Revelation 3:20	January 16
Ephesians 6:4	June 7	Revelation 7:13f	May 31
Ephesians 6:11	February 2	Revelation 21:1f	April 20
Philippians 2:5f	October 15		
Philippians 2:5f	October 16		
Philippians 3:12f	August 29		
Philippians 3:17	November 1		
Philippians 3:17f	May 16		
Philippians 3:18-19	August 1		
Philippians 4:6f	January 25		
Philippians 4:11	March 9		
Philippians 4:11f	April 19		
Colossians 3:1f	April 17		
Colossians 3:2	July 19		
Colossians 3:15	June 20		
1 Thessalonians 1:5	June 22		
1 Thessalonians 5:15f	May 17		
1 Thessalonians 5:16	July 16		
2 Thessalonians 1:3f	February 21		
1 Timothy 1:15	October 23		
1 Timothy 4:12	July 5		
1 Timothy 6:11f	August 24		